[redacted]



# Learning Ext JS 3.2

Build dynamic, desktop-style user interfaces for your data-driven web applications using Ext JS

**Shea Frederick**

**Colin Ramsay**

**Steve 'Cutter' Blades**

**Nigel White**

[PACKT] open source
PUBLISHING
community experience distilled

BIRMINGHAM - MUMBAI

[redacted]

# Learning Ext JS 3.2



First published: October 2010

Production Reference: 1061010

Published by Packt Publishing Ltd.
32 Lincoln Road
Olton
Birmingham, B27 6PA, UK.

ISBN 978-1-849511-20-9

`www.packtpub.com`

Cover Image by John M. Quick (`john.m.quick@gmail.com`)

# Credits

**Authors**
Shea Frederick
Colin Ramsay
Steve 'Cutter' Blades
Nigel White

**Reviewers**
Jonathan Julian
Jorge Ramon

**Acquisition Editor**
Usha Iyer

**Development Editor**
Wilson D'Souza

**Technical Editor**
Pallavi Kachare

**Copy Editor**
Laxmi Subramanian

**Indexer**
Tejal Daruwale

**Editorial Team Leader**
Aanchal Kumar

**Project Team Leader**
Ashwin Shetty

**Project Coordinator**
Poorvi Nair

**Proofreader**
Aaron Nash

**Graphics**
Nilesh Mohite

**Production Coordinator**
Kruthika Bangera

**Cover Work**
Kruthika Bangera

# About the Authors

**Shea Frederick** began his career in web development before the term 'Web Application' was commonplace. By the late 1990s, he was developing web applications for Tower Records that combined the call center interface with inventory and fulfillment. Since then, Shea has worked as a developer for several companies—building and implementing various commerce solutions, content management systems, and lead tracking programs.

Integrating new technologies to make a better application has been a driving point for Shea's work. He strives to use open source libraries as they are often the launching pad for the most creative technological advances. After stumbling upon a young user interface library called YUI-ext several years ago, Shea contributed to its growth by writing documentation, tutorials, and example code. He has remained an active community member for the modern YUI-ext library—Ext JS. Shea's expertise is drawn from community forum participation, work with the core development team, and his own experience as the architect of several large, Ext JS-based web applications. He currently lives in Baltimore, Maryland with his wife and two dogs and spends time skiing, biking, and watching the Steelers.

Shea is the primary author of the first book published on Ext JS, a book which helps to ease beginners into the Ext JS library. He is also a core developer on the Ext JS project along with writing columns for JSMag and running the local Baltimore/DC JavaScript Meetup. His ramblings can be found on his blog, `http://www.vinylfox.com` and open source code contributions on Github at `http://www.github.com/VinylFox/`.

**Colin Ramsay** began his career building PHP and ASP websites as a part-time developer while at university. Since then, he's been involved with a range of web technologies in his work with a range of companies in the North East of England—everything from flash-in-the-pan web frameworks to legacy applications. After forming his first company in 2007, putting his past experience into action, he went on be a partner at Go Tripod Ltd, a design and development company with clients across the UK. From writing articles and blog posts across the web, Colin has made the leap to book authoring with the patience and kind assistance of his friends and family.

**Steve Blades** (who goes by the name of 'Cutter'), a Virginia native, raised in Georgia, began his computing career when he started learning BASIC at age 12, hammering out small programs on a Timex Sinclair 1000. As a linguist and Intelligence Analyst for the US Army, Cutter began learning HTML while stationed at the National Security Agency. On leaving the service, Cutter became part-owner of a growing Advertising Specialty company, developing business automation processes for the company by writing MS Office-based applications. From there, Cutter went on to become a Customer Support Technician with a local Internet Service Provider. Upon showing programming aptitude, he was later moved into their Corporate Support department, providing maintenance and rewrites to existing websites and applications. It was here that Cutter began to really dive into web application programming, teaching himself JavaScript, CSS, and ColdFusion programming. Cutter then took the position of IT Director for Seacrets, a large resort destination in Ocean City, Maryland, while also holding the same position for one of its owner's other companies, Irie Radio. Now, Cutter is the Development Manager for Dealerskins, a company that develops and hosts websites for the automobile dealership industry. He lives and works in Nashville, Tennessee with his wife Teresa and daughter Savannah.

Apart from work, side projects, and maintaining his blog (`http://blog.cutterscrossing.com`), Cutter also enjoys spending time with his family, is an avid reader and videophile, and likes to relive his band days with a mike in hand.

---

I would like to thank a few people for their support while I have been working on this project. First, thanks to Abe, Aaron, and the Ext JS crew at Sencha for giving us such a great topic to keep writing about. Thanks to everyone at Dealerskins and Dominion Enterprises for all of their support. Special thanks to my parents and my Grandma for giving me their guidance and advice all of these years. But, most of all, thanks to my beautiful wife, Teresa, and daddy's Little Girl, Savannah, for their continued patience, love, and encouragement. I never could have done it without them.

In memory of William "Pop Pop" Blades, who always believed in me and taught me that I could do anything I set my mind to do, and be anything that I chose to be.

---

**Nigel White** has 20 years of experience in the IT industry. He has seen computer systems evolve from batch processing, back room behemoths which dictated user behavior into distributed, user-centered enablers of everyday tasks.

Nigel has been working with rich Internet applications, and dynamic browser updating techniques since before the term "Ajax" was coined.

Recently he collaborated with Jack Slocum in the germination of the ExtJS project, and has contributed code, documentation, and design input to the ExtJS development team.

Nigel works as a software architect at Forward Computers where he oversees development of both the Java server tier and the browser interface of the company's evolving web UI.

He also runs Animal Software, a one man consultancy specializing in ExtJS UI development, consulting, and training.

Work displacement activities include rock climbing and bicycling!

# About the Reviewers

**Jonathan Julian** is an application developer living in Baltimore, MD. He builds amazing web applications using Ruby on Rails and occasionally has the pleasure of creating web interfaces using Ext JS. You can find out more information about Jonathan on his website, `http://jonathanjulian.com`.

**Jorge Ramon** is currently the Vice President of Development for Taladro Systems LLC, where he has led the design and development of a number of software products for the law industry. He is also a mobile software development instructor and coach.

Jorge has over 16 years of experience as a software developer and has also worked on creating web applications, search engines, and automatic-control software. He actively contributes to the software development community through his blog `MiamiCoder.com`.

Jorge Ramon is also the author of *Ext JS 3.0 Cookbook*, with more than a hundred step-by-step recipes for building rich Internet applications using the Ext JS JavaScript library.

---

To my parents. They showed me the way.

---

# Table of Contents

# Preface

Ext JS is a JavaScript library that makes it (relatively) easy to create desktop-style user interfaces in a web application, including multiple windows, toolbars, drop-down menus, dialog boxes, and much more.

This book covers all of the major features of the Ext framework using interactive code and clear explanation coupled with loads of screenshots. Learning Ext JS will help you create rich, dynamic, and AJAX-enabled web applications that look good and perform beyond the expectations of your users.

## What this book covers

*Chapter 1, Getting Started,* covers the basics of Ext JS and what it can do for us. Unlike other JavaScript libraries, Ext JS handles the messy foundation work for you, so with only a few lines of code, you can have a fully functional user interface. The main goal of this chapter was to get Ext JS installed and working, so we can start creating some really sweet widgets and web applications.

*Chapter 2, The Staples of Ext JS,* shows how to create more functional widgets, and how to configure them to behave exactly as we require. We will start to use and interact with Ext JS widgets for the first time, by creating a series of dialogs that interact with each other, the user, and the web page.

*Chapter 3, Forms,* shows how to create Ext JS forms, which are similar to the HTML forms that we use, but with a greater level of flexibility, error checking, styling, and automated layout. The form created in this chapter can validate user input, load data from a database, and send that data back to the server.

*Chapter 4, Menus, Toolbars, and Buttons,* covers how to use menus, both as components in their own right—either static or floating as popups—and as dependent menus of buttons. We will have the chance to play with a couple of different ways to create toolbar items, including using a config object or its shortcut.

*Chapter 5, Displaying Data with Grids,* covers how to define the rows and columns, but more importantly, we will learn how to make the grid a very useful part of our application.

*Chapter 6, Editor Grids,* shows how the data support provided by the grid offers an approach to data manipulating that will be familiar to many developers. It also shows how standard Ext JS form fields such as the ComboBox can be integrated to provide a user interface on top of this functionality.

*Chapter 7, Layouts,* demonstrates how components such as the grid can be integrated with other parts of an application screen by using the extensive layout functionality provided by the Ext JS framework.

*Chapter 8, Ext JS Does Grow on Trees,* demonstrated that the strength of the TreePanel is not simply in its ease of use, but in the way we can use its wealth of configuration options to deliver application-specific functionality.

*Chapter 9, Windows and Dialogs,* covers the difference between `Ext.Window` and `Ext.MessageBox`, built-in Ext JS methods to show familiar popups, and tweaks the configuration of a window for advanced usage.

*Chapter 10, Charting New Territory,* starts off with a basic pie chart, and moves on to more complicated charts from there. It also shows how easy it can be to get a basic chart working, and switching between the different chart types can also be quite easy depending on the type of chart.

*Chapter 11, Effects,* discusses the range of built-in Ext JS options for animation and effects, creating custom animations and tweaking the existing ones, using multiple animations together, and other Ext JS visual effects such as masking and tooltips.

*Chapter 12, Drag-and-drop,* takes a look at one of the most typical examples of Web 2.0 glitz: drag-and-drop. In a typical Ext JS manner, we're going to see how it's not only simple to use, but also powerful in its functionality.

*Chapter 13, Code for Reuse: Extending Ext JS,* discusses how we can create our own custom components by extending the Ext JS library. It talks about how we can create our own namespaces, differentiating our custom components from others. It also discusses some other core object-oriented concepts and the concept of Event-driven application architecture.

*Chapter 14, Plugging In,* discusses how to write and use plugins, and how a plugin differs from a component.

*Chapter 15, It's All About the Data,* covers the many different ways in which you can retrieve from and post data to your Ext JS based applications.

*Chapter 16, Marshalling Data Services with Ext.Direct,* discusses how a developer can write his/her own Ext.Direct server-side stacks for marshalling data services under a single configuration.

*Chapter 17, The Power of Ext JS: What Else Can You Do?,* shows you a few hidden gems of the Ext JS framework, and talks about some community resources for further information.

# Who this book is for

This book is written for Web Application Developers who are familiar with HTML but may have little to no experience with JavaScript application development. If you are starting to build a new web application, or are re-vamping an existing web application, then this book is for you.

# Conventions

In this book, you will find a number of styles of text that distinguish between different kinds of information. Here are some examples of these styles, and an explanation of their meaning.

Code words in text are shown as follows: "If you pass a function to `Ext.onReady` when the document is already fully initialized, it will be called immediately."

A block of code is set as follows:

```
var myVariable = "A string literal";
alert(myVariable);
myVariable = function() {
  alert("Executing the function");
};
```

When we wish to draw your attention to a particular part of a code block, the relevant lines or items are set in bold:

```
{
   xtype: 'datefield',
   fieldLabel: 'Released',
   name: 'released',
   disabledDays: [1,2,3,4,5]
}
```

**New terms** and **important words** are shown in bold. Words that you see on the screen, in menus or dialog boxes for example, appear in the text like this: "One of the most striking examples is the **Feed Viewer**".

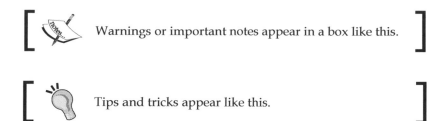

[ Warnings or important notes appear in a box like this. ]

[ Tips and tricks appear like this. ]

# Reader feedback

Feedback from our readers is always welcome. Let us know what you think about this book—what you liked or may have disliked. Reader feedback is important for us to develop titles that you really get the most out of.

To send us general feedback, simply send an e-mail to `feedback@packtpub.com`, and mention the book title via the subject of your message.

If there is a book that you need and would like to see us publish, please send us a note in the **SUGGEST A TITLE** form on `www.packtpub.com` or e-mail `suggest@packtpub.com`.

If there is a topic that you have expertise in and you are interested in either writing or contributing to a book, see our author guide on `www.packtpub.com/authors`.

# Customer support

Now that you are the proud owner of a Packt book, we have a number of things to help you to get the most from your purchase.

[ **Downloading the example code for this book**

You can download the example code files for all Packt books you have purchased from your account at `http://www.PacktPub.com`. If you purchased this book elsewhere, you can visit `http://www.PacktPub.com/support` and register to have the files e-mailed directly to you. ]

## Errata

Although we have taken every care to ensure the accuracy of our content, mistakes do happen. If you find a mistake in one of our books—maybe a mistake in the text or the code—we would be grateful if you would report this to us. By doing so, you can save other readers from frustration and help us improve subsequent versions of this book. If you find any errata, please report them by visiting `http://www.packtpub.com/support`, selecting your book, clicking on the **errata submission form** link, and entering the details of your errata. Once your errata are verified, your submission will be accepted and the errata will be uploaded on our website, or added to any list of existing errata, under the Errata section of that title. Any existing errata can be viewed by selecting your title from `http://www.packtpub.com/support`.

## Piracy

Piracy of copyright material on the Internet is an ongoing problem across all media. At Packt, we take the protection of our copyright and licenses very seriously. If you come across any illegal copies of our works, in any form, on the Internet, please provide us with the location address or website name immediately so that we can pursue a remedy.

Please contact us at `copyright@packtpub.com` with a link to the suspected pirated material.

We appreciate your help in protecting our authors, and our ability to bring you valuable content.

## Questions

You can contact us at `questions@packtpub.com` if you are having a problem with any aspect of the book, and we will do our best to address it.

# 1
# Getting Started

In this chapter, we will cover the basics of **Ext JS** and what it can do for us. If you're accustomed to the standard Web development, then you'll be excited when you learn about the elegance in the architecture of Ext JS, just as I was. Unlike other JavaScript libraries, Ext JS handles the messy foundation work for you, so with only a few lines of code, we can have a fully functional user interface.

In this chapter, we will cover:

- Some JavaScript fundamentals which are key to understanding Ext JS code
- What Ext JS does and why you'll love using it
- How to get Ext JS and start using it in your Web applications
- Creating a simple "hello world" example
- Using "adapters" to allow Ext JS to co-exist with other JavaScript libraries
- Taking advantage of AJAX technology
- Displaying Ext JS Components in your own language

## A word about JavaScript

JavaScript is an object-based language. Every data item is an object. Numbers, strings, dates, and Booleans (true or false values) are all objects.

JavaScript variables reference the objects we assign to them. Think of a variable as a "pointer" to the object, not a "box" into which a value is placed. A variable assignment statement does not move any data. It simply changes where the variable is pointing to.

In JavaScript, functions are also objects, and may be assigned to variables and passed as parameters just the same as other objects. A function declaration is a literal in just the same way that a quoted string is a literal.

Consider the following example. A variable is assigned to a string and then a function.

```
var myVariable = "A string literal";
alert(myVariable);
myVariable = function() {
  alert("Executing the function");
};
myVariable();
```

The variable `myVariable` is set to reference (point to) a string literal which is then alerted to the user.

Then the variable is set to reference a function literal. That variable is then used to call that function. Appending the `()` causes the referenced function to be called.

This concept is central to your understanding of much of what follows. Functions will be passed as parameters into Ext JS methods to be called by Ext JS to handle user interface events or network communication (AJAX) events.

Ext JS also provides its API in an Object Oriented manner. This means that it does not simply provide a mass of utility functions; instead, mnemonically named classes are provided which encapsulate discrete areas of functionality. Functions are called as member methods of a class. All Ext JS widgets: grids, trees, forms, and so on are objects. For more information on this concept, see `http://en.wikipedia.org/wiki/Object-oriented_programming`.

It is important to remember that when a function reference is passed, it's only a pointer to a function object. If that function was a member method of an object, then this information is not included. If the function is to be executed as a member method of an object, then that information must be included when passing the function. This is the concept of **scope**, which will be very important in later chapters.

If that went a bit over your head, don't worry. Put a bookmark in this page, and refer to it later. It will be important!

# I'm asynchronous!

The Web 1.0 way of doing things has all of our code happening in succession—waiting for each line of the code to complete before moving on to the next. Much like building a house, the foundation must be complete before the walls can be built and then the walls must be complete before the roof is built.

With Ext JS, we can easily start working on the roof of our house before the foundation has even been thought about. Imagine the roof of our house is being built in a factory, while at the same time we are building the foundation, then the walls, and we come in when all of this is done and set the roof that has already been built on top of it all.

To visualize this, look at the following diagram. Contrast the linear assembly of the house on the left with the assembly on the right in which manufacture of the roof happens concurrently with the walls and foundation:

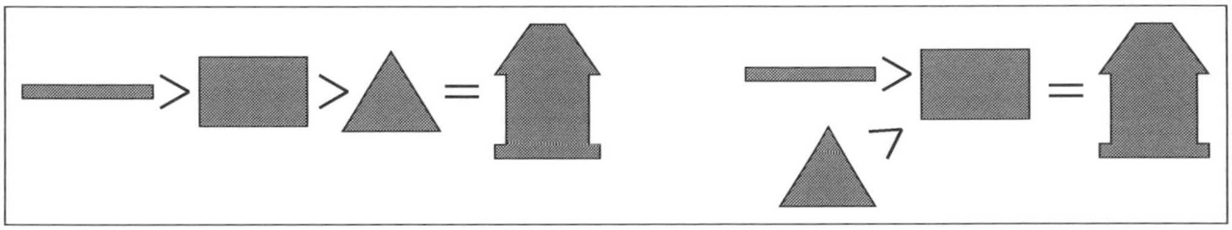

This introduces some things we're not used to having to cope with, such as the roof being complete before the walls are done. No longer are we forced to take a line-by-line approach to Web development.

Ext JS helps us out by giving us events and handlers to which we can attach our functionality. As described above, we can specify a function to be called later, when the walls of the house are built, which then sets the roof on top once this has happened.

This method of thinking about Web pages is hard for most people who have grown up in Web development. We must be aware of not only what our function does, but also when it does it. We might embed a function literal inside our code which does not run immediately, but just sits dormant until an event fires at some time in the future.

# About Ext JS

We will be working with the most recent release version of Ext JS which, at the time of writing, is the 3.x branch. However, the examples used in this book will be compatible with the 2.x branch unless specifically noted. The change from 1.x to 2.x was a major refactoring that included taking full advantage of the newly-created Component model, along with renaming many of the components to provide better organization. These changes have made the 1.x code mostly incompatible with 2.x, 3.x, and vice versa. An upgrade guide that explains in more detail what has changed is available on the Ext JS website:

`http://www.extjs.com/learn/w/index.php?title=Ext_1_to_2_Migration_Guide`

The 3.x branch is backwards-compatible with 2.x, so many of the examples in this book will work with both versions. The Ext JS development team is dedicated to making future releases backwards-compatible.

The Ext JS library started out as an extension to the moderately popular, yet very powerful Yahoo User Interface library, providing what the YUI library lacked: an easy-to-use **API** (**Application Programming Interface**), and real world widgets. Even though the YUI Library tried to focus on the 'User Interface', it didn't contain much that was useful right out-of-the-box.

It wasn't long before Ext JS had developers and open-source contributors chipping in their knowledge to turn the basic YUI extension into one of the most powerful client-side application development libraries around.

Ext JS provides an easy-to-use, rich user interface, much like you would find in a desktop application. This lets Web developers concentrate on the functionality of Web applications instead of the technical caveats. The examples given on the Ext JS website speak the loudest about how amazing this library is:

`http://www.extjs.com/deploy/dev/examples/`

One of the most striking examples is the **Feed Viewer**. This demonstrates the many aspects of Ext JS. However, it is a bit too complex to be used as a learning example. So for now, we can just revel in its brilliance. The following screenshot illustrates the familiar border layout with user-resizable regions, which you may notice being used in programs like email readers:

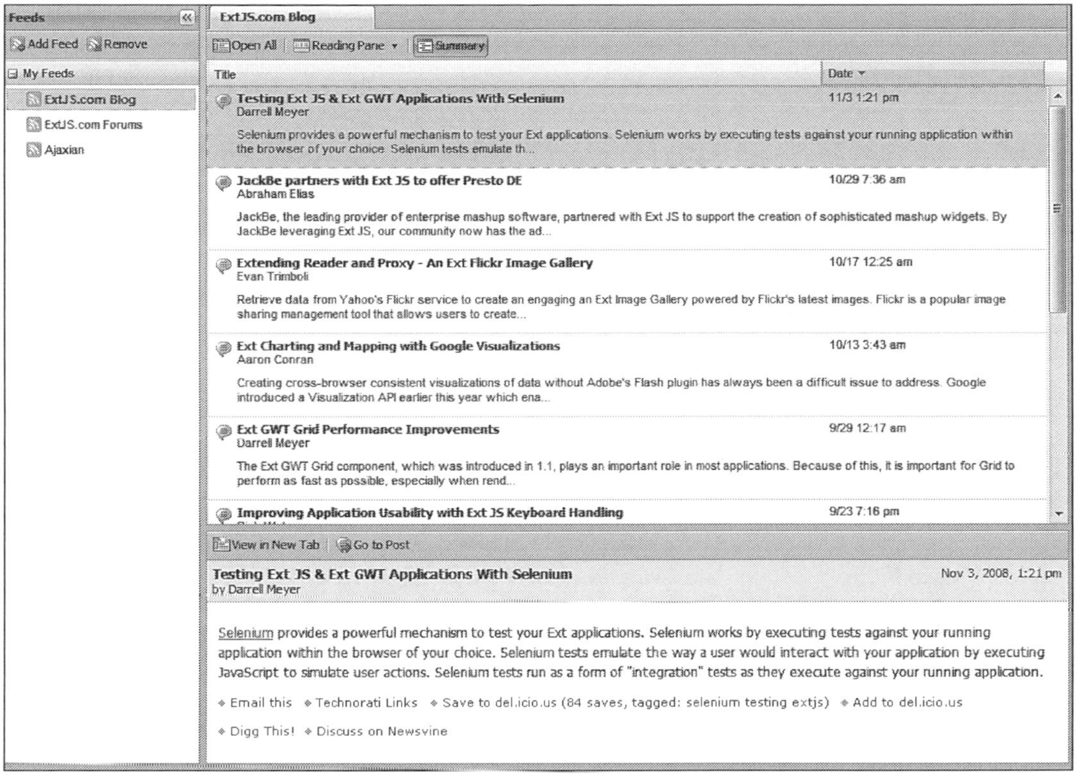


Another excellent example is the **Simple Tasks** task-tracking program, which utilizes a Google Gears database.

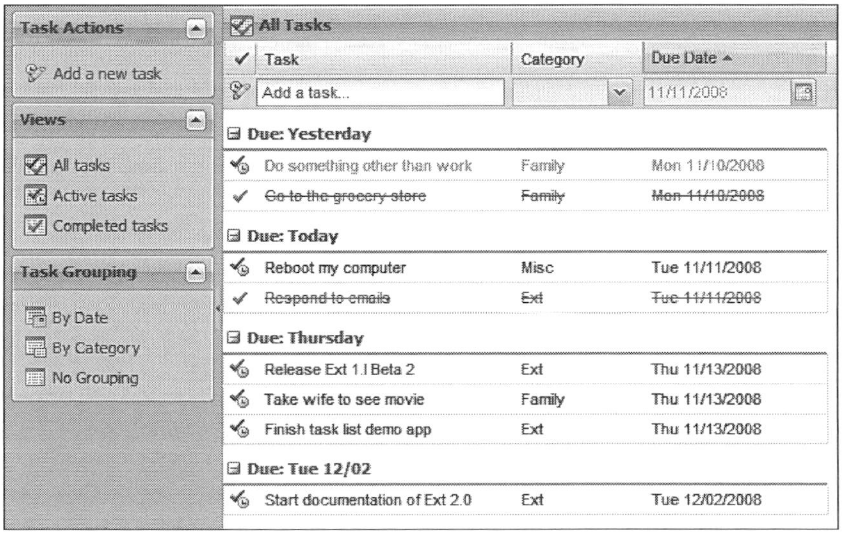

Over the course of this book, we will learn how to build Web interfaces as impressive as these.

# Ext JS: not just another JavaScript library

Ext JS is not just another JavaScript library. It is a fully featured client UI library capable of creating dynamic, fluidly laid out user interfaces which are bound to structured data which itself is linked to server-side data sources. Ext JS can, however, work alongside other JavaScript libraries by using adapters. We'll see how to work with adapters later in this chapter.

Typically, we would use Ext in a website that requires a high level of user interaction—something more complex than your typical website, most commonly found in intranet applications. A website that requires processes and a work flow would be a perfect example, or Ext JS could just be used to make your boss gasp with excitement.

Ext JS makes Web application development simple by:

- Providing easy-to-use cross-browser compatible widgets such as windows, grids, and forms. The widgets are already fine-tuned to handle the intricacies of each web browser on the market, without us needing to change a thing.
- Interacting with the user and browser via the EventManager, responding to the user's keystrokes, mouse clicks, and monitoring events in a browser such as a window resize, or font size changes.
- Communicating with the server in the background without the need to refresh the page. This allows us to request or post data to or from our web server using AJAX and process the feedback in real time.

# Cross-browser DOM (Document Object Model)

I am sure I don't need to explain the pitfalls of browser compatibility. From the first time we create a DIV element and apply a style to it, it becomes apparent that it's not going to look the same in every browser unless we are very diligent. When we use Ext JS widgets, the browser compatibility is taken care of by the Ext JS library, so that each widget looks exactly the same in all supported browsers, which are:

- Internet Explorer 6+
- Firefox 1.5 + (PC, Mac)
- Safari 2+

- Opera 9 + (PC, Mac)
- Chrome 1+

## Event-driven interfaces

Events describe when certain actions happen. An event could be a user action such as a click on an element, or it could be a response to an AJAX call. When a user interacts with a button, there is a reaction, with not just one but many events happening. There is an event for the cursor hovering over the button, and an event for the cursor clicking on the button, and an event for the cursor leaving the button. We can add an event listener to execute some function when any or all of these events take place.

Listening for events is not strictly related to the user interface. There are also system events happening all the time. When we make AJAX calls, there are events attached to the status of that AJAX call to listen for the start, the completion, and possible failure.

## Ext JS and AJAX

The term **AJAX** (**Asynchronous JavaScript** and **XML**) is an overly-complicated acronym for saying that processes can take place in the background, talking to the server while the user is performing other tasks. A user could be filling out a form while a grid of data is loading—both can happen at the same time, with no waiting around for the page to reload.

# Getting Ext JS

Everything we will need can be downloaded from the Ext website, at `http://www.extjs.com/products/js/download.php`. Grab the Ext JS SDK (Software Development Kit), which contains a ton of useful examples and the API reference. Most importantly, it contains the resources that Ext JS needs to run properly.

## Where to put Ext JS

Once you get the SDK file, uncompress it onto your hard drive, preferably in its own folder. My approach to folder naming conventions is based on the standard Linux structure where all libraries go into a `lib` folder. So for the sake of the examples in this book, uncompress all of the files in the SDK into a folder named `lib`.

After extracting everything from the SDK download file, your directory tree should look like this:

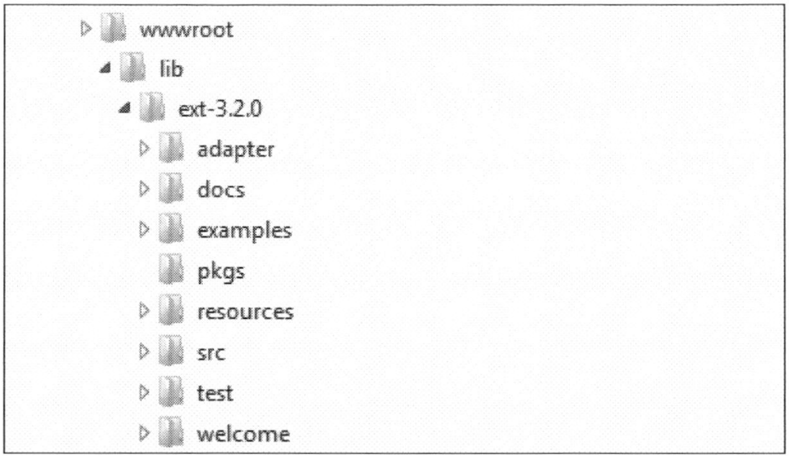


To make it easier when we upgrade our Ext library to the most recently-released version, let's rename the `ext-3.2.0` folder to `extjs`.

If your company is using source control, along with quality assurance testing, then sticking with a folder name based on the library version number might be more appropriate.

The SDK contains a version of Ext JS that has everything we need included in it, commonly called `ext-all`. It also contains a version used for development referred to as the `debug` version, which is what we will primarily use. The debug version makes it easier to locate errors in our code because it's uncompressed and will report back relevant line numbers for errors. When it's time to release our creation to the general public, we can switch our application to use the standard `ext-all`, and everything will continue to work as it was.

Included in the SDK file are a specification of dependencies, documentation, example code, and more. The `adapter` and `resources` folders shown in **bold** are required for Ext to work properly; everything else is just for development purposes:

- `adapter`: Files that allow you to use other libraries alongside Ext JS
- `docs`: The documentation center (this will only work when run from a web server)
- `examples`: Plenty of amazing and insightful examples, plugins, and extensions
- `pkgs`: Packaged up Ext JS modules used when building Ext JS

- `resources`: Dependencies of the Ext JS library, such as CSS and images
- `src`: The complete source code for Ext JS
- `test`: The test suite for Ext JS
- `welcome`: Miscellaneous image files

When you're ready to host your page on a web server, the `adapter` and `resources` folders will need to be uploaded to the server in addition to the `ext-all.js` and `ext-all-debug.js` files.

# Including Ext JS in our pages

Before we can use Ext JS in our pages, we need to reference the Ext JS library files. To do this, we need to include a few of the files provided in the SDK download in the `HEAD` portion of our HTML page. In our simple pages, we will not use a doctype. Ext JS supports running with no doctype (quirks mode), across all browsers.

```
<html>
<head>
   <title>Getting Started Example</title>
   <link rel="stylesheet" type="text/css"
      href="lib/extjs/resources/css/ext-all.css" />
   <script src="lib/extjs/adapter/ext/ext-base.js"></script>
   <script src="lib/extjs/ext-all-debug.js"></script>
</head>
<body>
   <!-- Nothing in the body -->
</body>
</html>
```

The path to the Ext JS files must be correct and is relative to the location of our HTML file. These files must be included in the order shown. A theme CSS file may be included after the `ext-all.css` file to customize the look of the UI.

# What do those files do?

We have included the following three files, which Ext JS requires to run in our page:

- `ext-all.css`: A stylesheet file that controls the look and feel of Ext JS widgets. This file must always be included as-is, with no modifications. Any changes to the CSS in this file would break future upgrades. If we decide that the look and feel of Ext JS needs to be adjusted, another stylesheet containing the overrides should be included after the `ext-all.css` file.
- `ext-base.js`: This file provides the core functionality of Ext JS. It's the foundation upon which Ext JS builds its capabilities, and provides the interface to the browser environment. This is the file that we would change if we wanted to use another library, such as jQuery, along with Ext JS.
- `ext-all-debug.js/ext-all.js`: All of the widgets live in this file. The debug version should always be used during development, and then swapped out for the non-debug version for production.

Once these files are in place, we can start to actually use the Ext JS library and have some fun.

[ If you are working with a server-side language such as PHP or ASP.NET, you might choose to "include" these lines in the header dynamically. For most of the examples in this book, we will assume that you are working with a static HTML page. ]

# Spacer image

Ext JS needs to use a spacer image, a 1 pixel by 1 pixel, transparent, GIF image to stretch in different ways, giving a fixed width to its widgets. When run on modern browsers, Ext JS uses an image encoded as a data URL—the URL begins with **data:** not **http:**. But on legacy browsers, the default URL references a GIF at the extjs.com website. This may not always be accessible or desirable. We can change this to reference the image on the local server using the following code:

```
if (Ext.BLANK_IMAGE_URL.substr(0, 5) != 'data:') {
    Ext.BLANK_IMAGE_URL = ' lib/extjs/ resources/images/default/s.gif';
}
Ext.onReady(function(){
    // do other stuff here
});
```

You're probably wondering why we need a spacer image at all. The user interface of Ext JS is created using CSS, but the CSS needs underlying HTML elements to style so that it can create the look and feel of the Ext JS components. The one HTML element that lays out inline, and is sizeable in both dimensions across all browsers is an image. So an image is used to size portions of the Ext JS Components. This is a part of how Ext JS maintains its cross-browser compatibility.

# Using the Ext JS library

Now that we've added the Ext JS library to our page, we can start writing the code that uses it. In the first example, we will use Ext JS to display a message dialog. This might not sound like much, but we need to start somewhere.

# Time for action

We can play with some Ext JS code by adding a script element in the head of our document, right after where the Ext JS library has been included. Our example will bring up an Ext JS style alert dialog:

```
<html>
<head>
   <title>Getting Started Example</title>
   <link rel="stylesheet" type="text/css"
      href="lib/extjs/resources/css/ext-all.css" />
   <script src="lib/extjs/adapter/ext/ext-base.js"></script>
   <script src="lib/extjs/ext-all-debug.js"></script>
   <script>
if (Ext.BLANK_IMAGE_URL.substr(0, 5) != 'data:') {
   Ext.BLANK_IMAGE_URL = 'lib/extjs/resources/images/default/s.gif';
}
      Ext.onReady(function(){
         Ext.Msg.alert('Hi', 'Hello World Example');
      });
   </script>
</head>
<body>
   <!-- Nothing in the body -->
</body>
</html>
```

We're not going to cover exactly what our example script is doing yet. First, let's make sure that the Ext JS library is set up properly by running this basic example. If we open up our page in a web browser, we should be able to see an alert message like the one shown as follows:

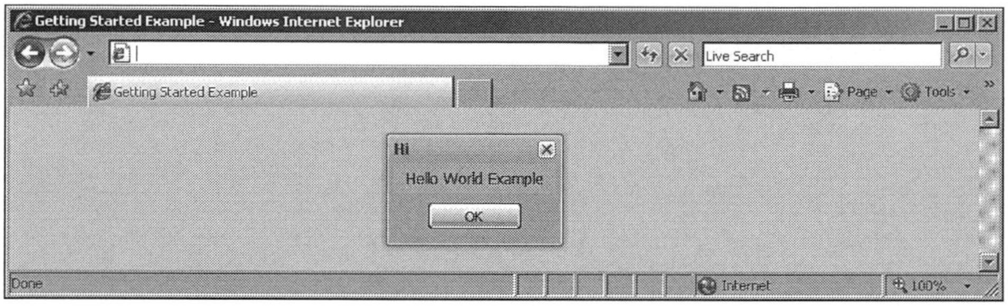


Just like a "real" dialog, we can drag it around, but only within the constraints of the page. This is because this isn't a real dialog; it's a collection of DIV tags and images put together to imitate a dialog. We can also see that the **Close** and **OK** buttons get highlighted when we move the cursor over them—not bad for one line of code! Ext JS is taking care of a lot of the work for us here, and throughout this book, we'll see how to get it to do much more for us.

> In this example, we start with an empty document which contains no HTML. Ext JS does not require any pre-existing markup, and will create it as needed. However Ext JS also has the ability to **import** pre-existing markup, and use it as the basis for new widgets. This will be discussed in Chapter 2.

# The example

Let's take a look at the example code, which we just ran:

```
Ext.onReady(function(){
   Ext.Msg.alert('Hi', 'Hello World Example');
});
```

After referring back to our discussion of JavaScript objects earlier in this chapter, you can see that this code fragment passes a function literal as a parameter to Ext.onReady.

The Ext.onReady function accepts a function as its first parameter. It will call that function when the page has fully loaded, and the HTML document is ready to be manipulated. If you pass a function to `Ext.onReady` when the document is already fully initialized, it will be called immediately.

That passed function calls a method upon the Ext.Msg object which is a pre-initialized object which Ext JS provides to show simple dialogs.

The Ext.Msg.alert function displays a dialog with the first parameter as the title and the second parameter as the message in the body.

# Using the Ext.onReady function

Ext JS can only render widgets when the HTML document has been fully initialized by the browser. All Ext JS pages must only begin accessing the document within an Ext.onReady call.

We could have written the code like this:

```
var mainFunction = function(){
    Ext.Msg.alert('Hi', 'Hello World Example');
};
 Ext.onReady(mainFunction);
```

In this version, we can see more easily that it is a function reference which is passed to `Ext.onReady`. It's slightly more longwinded this way, but while still a beginner, this may be a useful style for us to use.

# Not working?

If the library is not set up correctly, we might receive an **'Ext' is undefined** error.

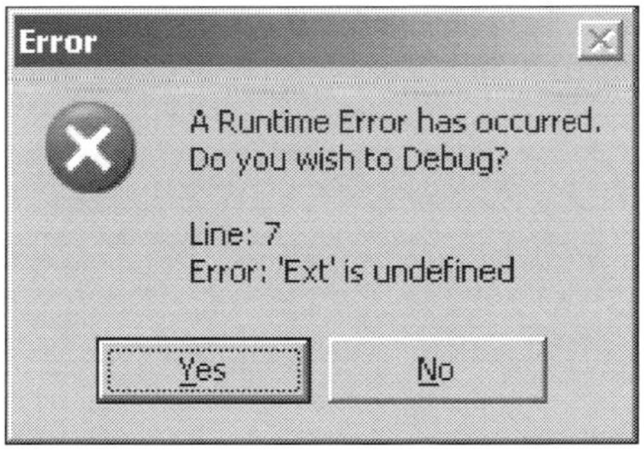


This message means the Ext JS library was not loaded. Usually, this is caused by having an incorrect path to one or more of the Ext JS library files that are included in our document. Double-check the paths to the included library files, and make sure they are pointing to the right folders and that the files exist. If everything is in its correct place, we should see an `adapter` folder along with the files `ext-all.js` and `ext-all-debug.js` in our `lib/extjs` folder.

Another common problem is that the CSS file is either missing or is not referenced correctly, which will result in a page that looks awkward, as shown in the following example:

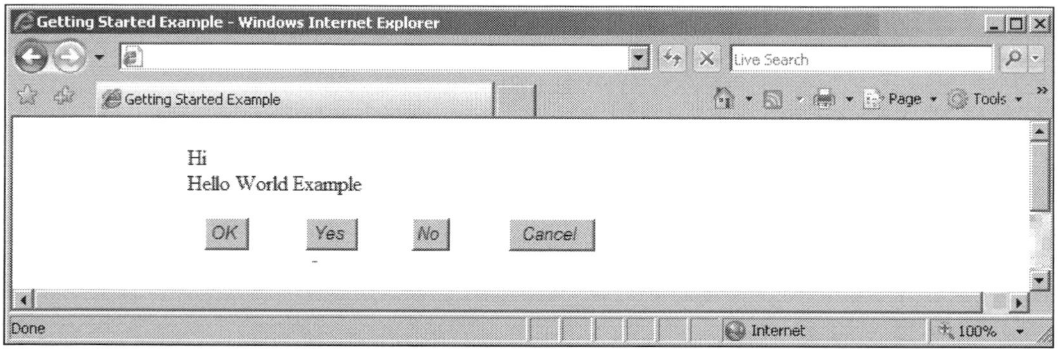


If this happens, check to make sure that you have extracted the `resources` folder from the SDK file, and that your paths are correct. The `resources` folder should reside under the `lib/extjs` folder.

The best way to debug failures like this is to use the Firefox browser with the Firebug debugging add-on. This provides a display of the status of all network requests. If any fail, then they will be highlighted in red, as follows:

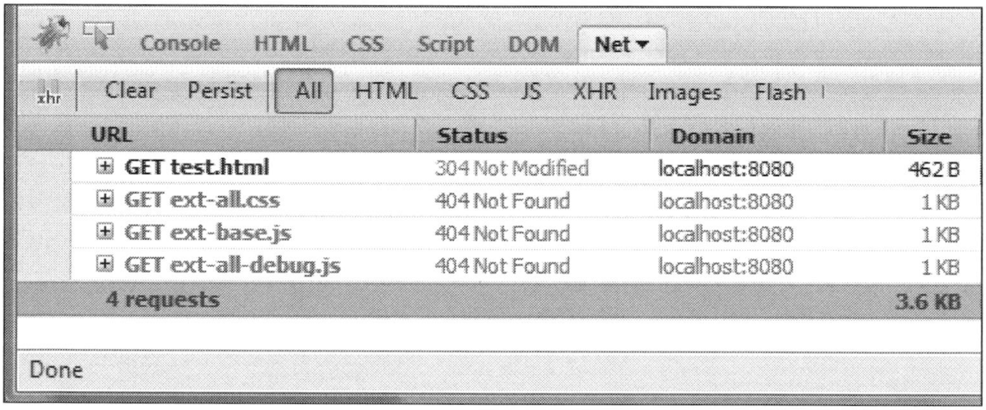


# Adapters

When Ext JS was first being developed (initially called "yui-ext"), it required the YUI library to be in place to do the behind-the-scenes work. Later on, Ext was given the option of using two other frameworks—jQuery or Prototype with Scriptaculous (Protaculous).

This means that if we were previously using other libraries or if we felt some other base library was somehow superior or better suited our needs, we could continue using that library in conjunction with Ext JS by using the appropriate adapter. Either way, Ext JS functions the same, and all of the components will work identically, no matter which adapter we choose.

Ext JS also has its own adapter which interfaces directly to the environment. If you have no preference for another library or framework, then go with the Ext JS built-in the adapter.

# Using adapters

To use an adapter, we must first include the external library that we want to use, and then include the related adapter file that is located in the adapter's folder of the Ext JS SDK. Our example code uses the Ext JS adapter. To use any of the other libraries, just replace the default Ext JS adapter script include line with the lines for the specific libraries, as shown below:

Default Ext JS adapter:

```
<script src="lib/extjs/adapter/ext/ext-base.js"></script>
```

For jQuery, include the jQuery library file in the head of the document, along with any plugins you might use:

```
<script src="lib/jquery.js"></script>
<script src="lib/jquery-plugins.js"></script>
<script src="lib/extjs/adapter/jquery/ext-jquery-adapter.js">
                                                    </script>
```

For YUI 2, include these files in the head. The `utilities` file is located in the `build/utilities` folder of the YUI 2 library download:

```
<script src="lib/utilities.js"></script>
<script src="lib/extjs/adapter/yui/ext-yui-adapter.js"></script>
```

For "Prototype + Scriptaculous", include the Prototype library, along with the Scriptaculous effects in the head:

```
<script src="lib/prototype.js"></script>
<script src="lib/scriptaculous.js?load=effects"></script>
<script src="lib/extjs/adapter/prototype/ext-prototype-adapter.js"></
script>
```

After the adapter and base libraries have been included, we just need to include the `ext-all.js` or `ext-all-debug.js` file.

# Localization

Ext JS Components can be displayed in our specific language, and currently there are over 40 translations (unfortunately, Klingon is not yet available). All of these translations are created by the community—users like you and I who have the need to use Ext JS Components in their own native language. The included language files are to be used as a starting point. So we should take the language file we want to use and copy it to our `lib` folder. By copying the language file to our `lib` folder, we can edit it and add translated text for our custom components without it being overwritten when we upgrade the Ext JS library files.

There are three scenarios for localization that require three separate approaches:

- English only
- A single language other than English
- Multiple languages

# English only

This requires no modifications to the standard setup, and there are no extra files to include because the English translation is already included in the `ext-all.js` file.

# A language other than English

The second option requires that we include one of the language files from the `build/locale` folder. These language files are named to comply with the two letter ISO 639-1 codes, for example: `ext-lang-XX.js`. Some regional dialects are also available, such as a Canadian version of French and British version of English. This option works by overwriting the English text strings present in the `ext-all.js` file, so it should be included after all of the other library files, as shown below:

```
<link rel="stylesheet" type="text/css"
   href="lib/extjs/resources/css/ext-all.css" />
<script src="lib/extjs/adapter/ext/ext-base.js"></script>
<script src="lib/extjs/ext-all-debug.js"></script>
<script src="lib/extjs/build/locale/ext-lang-es.js"></script>
```

I have included the Spanish translations for this example. Let's see what our test page looks like now:

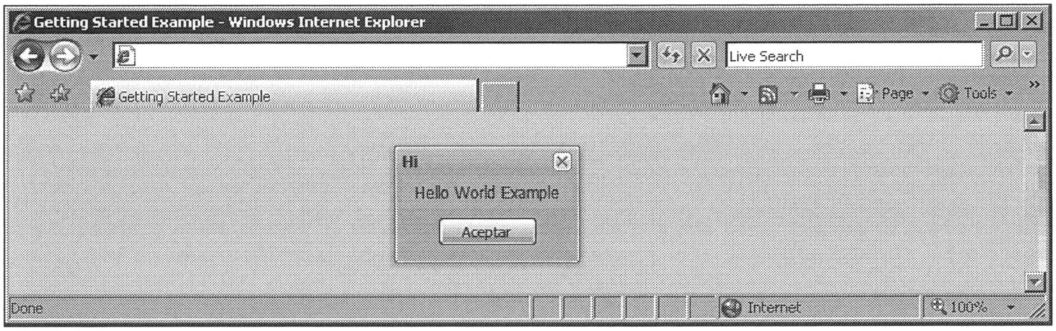


Elements that are part of the UI have been localized—these generally include calendar text, date formats, error messages, tool tip info messages, paging info, and loading indicators. Messages that are specific to your application, such as the **Hi** title and **Hello World Example** text, will need to be translated and added to our copy of the `ext-lang-XX.js` file (where 'XX' is your two letter language code) or added to a new language file of your own. Another method is to create a language file of our own with just the additions and changes we need; this leaves us prepared for upgrades and fixes in the primary language file.

## Multiple languages

The third method of switching between different languages is basically the same as the second. We would just need to add some server-side scripting to our page to enable the switching between language files. Unfortunately, switching between languages cannot be done entirely dynamically; any component that has already been created must be re-created to switch languages. In other words, we can't do it entirely in real time and watch it happen on the screen.

# Ext JS online help

If you have a problem which cannot be solved by reading this book, then there are several sources of help available at the Ext JS website.

## Online API docs

The API documentation contains information about every class and every method in the library. This is not the regular API documentation we have become used to with many JavaScript libraries which simply informs you that a class exists, and that a method exists.

Classes are fully described, and all configuration options, properties, methods, and events are listed with each one being expandable and having a full description of its purpose and usage. It is also a great example of a rich Ext JS application:

`http://www.extjs.com/deploy/dev/docs/`

# The FAQ

The FAQ contains solutions for hundreds of issues which real-world Ext JS users have encountered in the past. This is the second line of help:

`http://www.extjs.com/learn/Ext_FAQ`

# Ext JS forum

The online community for Ext JS is full of very knowledgeable people, and often, the Ext core developers are answering questions on the forum. The forum is the place to go to pose your question for assistance if the answer cannot be found in this book, in the API docs, or in the FAQ. The API docs and the FAQ are actively maintained by volunteers, and are updated in response to frequent forum questions.

`http://www.extjs.com/forum/`

If you run into problems, or run up against a wall, a search of the forum is likely to yield what you are looking for. I would suggest using the Google forum search tool that is available in the **Learn** section of the Ext JS website.

`http://www.extjs.com/learn/`

> When asking questions in the forum, be sure to include as much detail about the error(s) as possible.
>
> - Post in the **Help** section
> - Use a meaningful thread title
> - Ensure that you are using `ext-all-debug.js`, and position the exact text of an error message and only the relevant portions of your code

# Summary

In this chapter, we have covered the basics of what we need to do to get Ext JS up and running, and what a simple script looks like. It's easy to miss a minor detail and get stuck with an error message that makes no sense. But now, you should be prepared to conquer any initial errors that you might come across.

The example we created showcases what Ext JS excels at: providing the user interface. We only used dialogs, but, as you now know, a few lines of code are all that are needed to display an Ext JS widget. The main goal of this chapter was to get Ext JS installed and working, so we can start creating some really sweet widgets and web applications. In the following chapter we will learn how to create more functional widgets, and how to configure them to behave exactly as we require.

# 2

# The Staples of Ext JS

In this chapter, we will start to use and interact with Ext JS widgets for the first time, by creating a series of dialogs that interact with each other, the user, and the web page. We will be using the `onReady`, `MessageBox`, and `get` functions to learn how to create different types of dialogs and modify HTML and styles on our page. Furthermore, in this chapter, we will be:

- Finding out how to configure Ext JS widgets easily
- Using dialogs to figure out what the user wants to do
- Dynamically changing the HTML and CSS on our page in response to the user's inputs

We will start by covering some of the core functions of Ext JS. We will take a look at how the example given in the Chapter 1 worked, and will expand upon it. The following core functions of Ext JS will be used on every project that we work on during the course of this book:

- `Ext.Msg`: This function creates application-style message boxes for us
- `configuration objects`: These define how Ext widgets will act
- `Ext.get`: This function accesses and manipulates elements in the DOM

## Meet the config object

In the examples of this chapter, we will be configuring our widgets using what's called a `config` object. This is the primary way to get Ext JS Components to look and act the way we need. The `config` objects provide the specification of the different options that are available for the class that is being used.

# The old way

We used to call functions with a pre-determined set of arguments. This means that we had to remember the order of the arguments every time the function was used.

```
var test = new TestFunction(
    'three',
    'fixed',
    'arguments'
);
```

This old way of using functions can create many problems:

- It requires us to remember the order of the arguments
- It does not describe what the arguments represent
- It provides less flexibility in dealing with optional arguments

# The new way—config objects

In JavaScript, an object is simply a collection of names and values. An object literal may be coded into a JavaScript statement just as a string literal may be:

```
var myObject = {
    propertyName: 'String value',
    otherPropertyName: 3.14159
};
```

This is an assignment statement which creates on-the-fly a new object which contains two properties. It sets the variable `myObject` to reference this new object (Remember our discussion of JavaScript assignments in *Chapter 1*).

By using objects to configure classes, we are able to have a greater level of flexibility, and can tell how the class is being configured because configuration property names are mnemonics where possible, and convey their meaning. The order of our arguments no longer matters—`firstWord` could be the last item, and `thirdWord` could be the first, or they could be in any random order. With the `config` object method of passing arguments to our functions, the arguments no longer needs to be tied down to a specific place.

```
var test = new TestFunction({
    firstWord: 'three',
    secondWord: 'fixed',
    thirdWord: 'arguments'
});
```

This method also allows for unlimited expansion of our function's arguments. Using fewer arguments or adding new arguments is simple. Another great result that comes by using a `config` object is that the prior usage of our functions will not be harmed by the addition or subtraction of arguments at a later point.

```
var test = new TestFunction({
   secondWord: 'three'
});
var test = new TestFunction({
   secondWord: 'three',
   fourthWord: 'wow'
});
```

Here are some key things to remember when working with an object literal:

- A matched pair of curly brackets encloses the literal. Within the brackets there may be zero or more property definitions.
- Each property definition consists of a name/value pair, with the name and value separated by a colon. As with regular variables, a property references the value assigned to it which may be any type of object.
- Multiple properties are separated by commas.
- The property values can reference any type of data, including Boolean, array, function, or even another object:

  ```
  {
      name0: true,
      name1: {
          name2: value2
      }
  }
  ```

- Square brackets identify an array, and simply contain a comma separated list of objects, each of which may be of any type:

  ```
  {
      name: [ 'one', true, 3 ]
  }
  ```

  It is important to think of an array as an array of references. Setting an array item does not move data. It sets the reference at that index to point to the specified object.

# What is a config object?

If you are familiar with CSS, JSON, or the JavaScript object literal, you'll notice that a `config` object looks similar to these, mostly because they are all the same type of thing. In fact, an Ext JS config object is simply a JavaScript object literal. The point is to give us a way to structure data so that it can easily be read by a programming language—in our case, JavaScript.

For an example, let's take a look at the `config` portion of our example code:

```
{
   title: 'Milton',
   msg: 'Have you seen my stapler?',
   buttons: {
      yes: true,
      no: true,
      cancel: true
   },
   icon: 'milton-icon',
   fn: function(btn) {
      Ext.Msg.alert('You Clicked', btn);
   }
}
```

# Widgets and classes

Ext JS has many "widgets". As mentioned in Chapter 1, these are implemented as classes. These include components such as a message box, grid, window, tree, form, and pretty much everything else that serves a particular user interface function. These will mostly be referred to as 'Components'. There are also data, utility, and other base classes to aid with development. Methods like `onReady` are part of the core functions. We only refer to classes that provide a specific user interface role as "widgets"—like the grid that is used to present tabular data to the user.

# Time for action

Let's create a new page (or just modify the 'getting started' example page) and add the code to display a dialog when the page is ready.

In this example we will use a slightly more complex `config` object to describe how we want the dialog to look and behave:

```
Ext.onReady(function(){
```

```
        Ext.Msg.show({
            title: 'Milton',
            msg: 'Have you seen my stapler?',
            buttons: {
                yes: true,
                no: true,
                cancel: true
            }
        });
    });
```

As we did in the previous chapter, we have passed a function which performs our desired actions into the `onReady` function. We configure a dialog using a `config` object. The `config` object used for this dialog has three elements, the last of which is a nested object which configures the three buttons we want to be shown.

Here is how our example now looks in a browser:

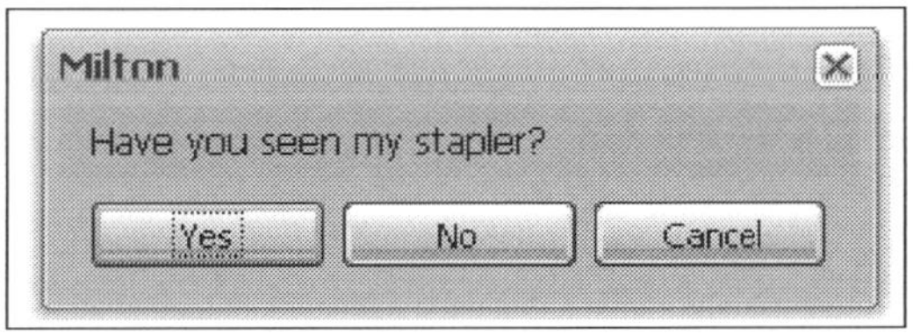


This displays what appears to be a very minimal dialog, but if we start clicking on things, the built-in functionality of Ext JS becomes apparent. The dialog can be dragged around the screen by grabbing the title bar, just like the dialog in a typical desktop application. There is a close button built-in, and pressing the *Escape* key when the dialog has focus, or clicking on the **Cancel** button will close the dialog.

# What just happened?

Let's take a closer look at the core Ext JS functions and Components we have just used:

- `Ext.onReady`: This was covered in the previous chapter. This function calls a passed-in function only when DOM is ready for use.
- `Ext.Msg.show`: This is the method used for showing a dialog in various different ways. In this case the `Ext.Msg` class is a singleton that shares one single dialog instance. It takes care of everything needed to have a simple working dialog. There are other methods that can be used for common dialog types, such as `prompt`, `alert`, and `wait` which will help us save time. We will cover these in just a minute.

It's time to examine the code we just used to display our dialog.

```
Ext.onReady(function(){
   Ext.Msg.show({
      title: 'Milton',
      msg: 'Have you seen my stapler?',
      buttons: {
         yes: true,
         no: true,
         cancel: true
      }
   });
});
```

Again, we have passed an anonymous function into `Ext.onReady`.

If we were executing a function that will be used again, then we could define and call it like this:

```
var stapler = function(){
   Ext.Msg.show({
      title: 'Milton',
      msg: 'Have you seen my stapler?',
      buttons: {
         yes: true,
         no: true,
         cancel: true
         }
   });
}

Ext.onReady(stapler);
```

When we start to make our application bigger, we are not likely to use many anonymous functions and will probably opt for creating re-usable functions like the one above, or even larger classes made up of many functions.

> The `buttons` config can also specify the text to display on the button. Instead of passing a Boolean value, just pass it the text you want, for example, `{yes: 'Maybe'}`, or use the constants provided by Ext JS, such as `Ext.Msg.YESNO`.

# More widget wonders

Let's get back to making our little application as annoying as possible by adding an icon and buttons! This can be done by adding a style for the icon, and modifying the `config` object to have an `icon` property, and an fn property which references a button handler function.

First, let's discuss the CSS we need. Add the following code into the head of the document, within a style tag:

```
milton-icon {
   background: url(milton-head-icon.png) no-repeat;
}
```

Also, we will make some changes to our widgets configuration. The `icon` property just needs our style name as the value, `milton-icon`. We have also included a function to be executed when the user clicks on any of the buttons in the dialog. This function is created as an anonymous function, but the property could also reference a function that was defined elsewhere, possibly as part of a class. In this case, the function is merely used to alert the user which button was pressed, so we will keep it as an anonymous function:

```
Ext.Msg.show({
   title: 'Milton',
   msg: 'Have you seen my stapler?',
   buttons: {
      yes: true,
      no: true,
      cancel: true
   },
   icon: 'milton-icon',
   fn: function(btn) {
      Ext.Msg.alert('You Clicked', btn);
   }
});
```

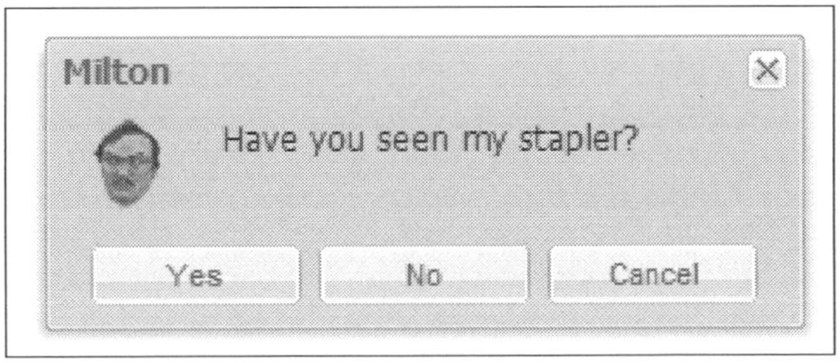

In our case, the function has only one argument, which is the name of the button that was clicked. So if our user was to click the **Yes** button, the `btn` variable would contain a value of `Yes`. Using the example code, we are taking the name of the button clicked, and passing it to alert, as the message.

> The built-in functionality takes care of making sure the **Cancel** button, the **close** icon in the upper right corner, and the *Esc* key are all tied together to perform the cancel action. This is one of the many ways in which Ext JS makes the coding of web applications easier for us.

# Time for (further) action

Ok! So now we've seen how to get our Ext JS party started and ask the user a question. Now let's see what we can do with their answers. Let's add to our dialog's function so that we can decide what to do in response to each of the button-clicks. A `switch` statement can take care of deciding what to do in each case:

```
fn: function(btn) {
   switch(btn){
      case 'yes':
         Ext.Msg.prompt('Milton', 'Where is it?');
      break;
      case 'no':
         Ext.Msg.alert('Milton',
                       'I\'m going to burn the building down!');
      break;
      case 'cancel':
         Ext.Msg.wait('Saving tables to disk...','File Copy');
      break;
   }
}
```

> Note how an apostrophe may be inserted into an apostrophe-delimited string by prefixing the character with a backslash. The same principle applies to inserting a "double" quote into a quote-delimited string.

Remember those built in dialog types I mentioned earlier? Well we just used some of them. They offer us pre-configured dialogs which let us accomplish some common tasks without spending time writing the `config` needed for each standard scenario.

Click **OK** and we get a prompt. A **prompt** is the common name for a small window that allows you to enter a single value, and is a standard element in almost every user interface.

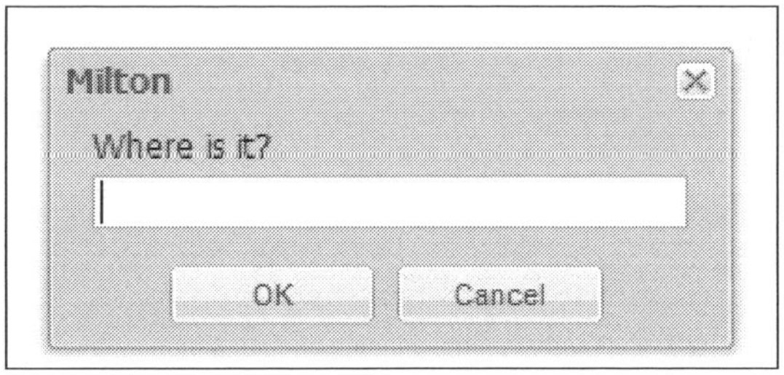


Click **No** and we get an alert. I'm sure you are familiar with the standard **alert** dialog in JavaScript. I remember the first time I used an alert dialog in JavaScript; I was so excited to have an alert message on my home page that I made it pop up and say "**Click OK if you are a moron**". Sometimes it's the little things that make us the happiest.

Click the **Cancel** button (or click the close button or press the *Escape* key) and we will get a wait message that's using a progress dialog.

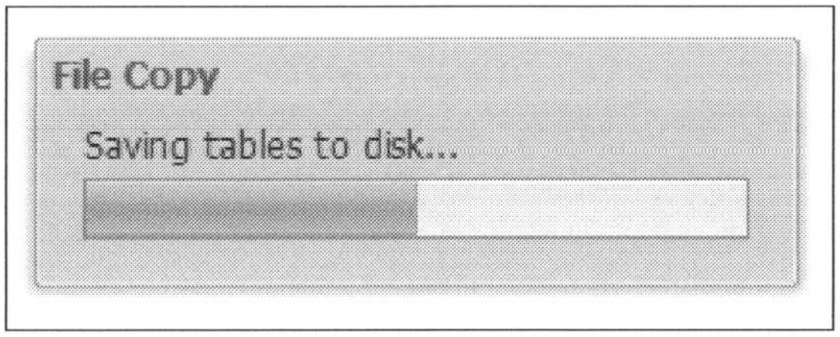


The progress dialog we are using can be controlled by Ext JS and be notified when it should disappear. But for the sake of simplicity, in this example, we are letting it run forever.

> Button focus and tab orders are built into Ext JS. Typically the **OK** or **Yes** button will be the default action. So pressing *Enter* on our keyboard will trigger that button, and pressing *Tab* will move us through the buttons and other items in the dialog.

# Lighting the fire

Now, we can start causing some reactions in our page, based on the users' responses to the dialogs. We are going to add to our `switch` statement, which takes care of a **Yes** button click. The `prompt` function can handle a third argument, which is the function to be executed after the **Yes** button has been clicked. We are defining this so that the function will check to see if the value entered into our prompt dialog is equal to `the office` and then write this text to a DIV in our page if it is, and a default text of **Dull Work** if it is not. The code also applies a style to the same DIV, which uses a "Swingline" stapler background image.

```
case 'yes':
   Ext.Msg.prompt('Milton', 'Where is it?', function(btn,txt)
{
       if (txt.toLowerCase() == 'the office') {
          Ext.get('my_id').dom.innerHTML = 'Dull Work';
       }else{
          Ext.get('my_id').dom.innerHTML = txt;
       }
       Ext.DomHelper.applyStyles('my_id',{
         background: 'transparent
            url(images/stapler.png) 50% 50% no-repeat'
      });
    });
break;
```

If the user types `'the office'` into the prompt box, the result will be as shown below:

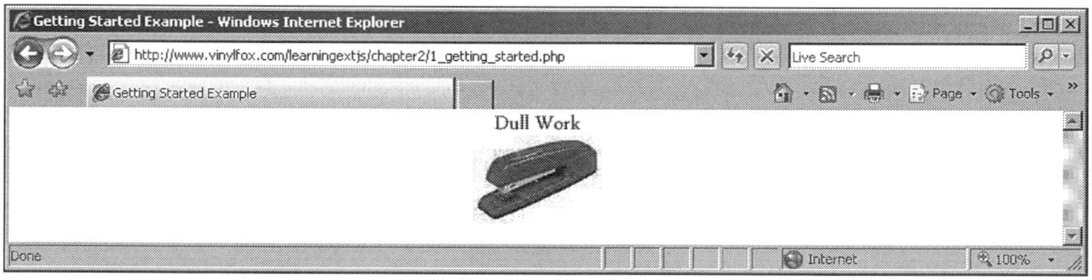


The `no` case will display an alert message, which also styles the document when the **No** button is clicked.

```
case 'no':
   Ext.Msg.alert('Milton',
     'Im going to burn the building down!',
     function() {
```

```
            Ext.DomHelper.applyStyles('my_id',{
              'background': 'transparent
                url(images/fire.png) 0 100% repeat-x'
           });
            Ext.DomHelper.applyStyles(Ext.getBody(),{
              'background-color': '#FF0000'
           });
            Ext.getBody().highlight('FFCC00',{
              endColor:'FF0000',
              duration: 6
           });
       });
   break;
```

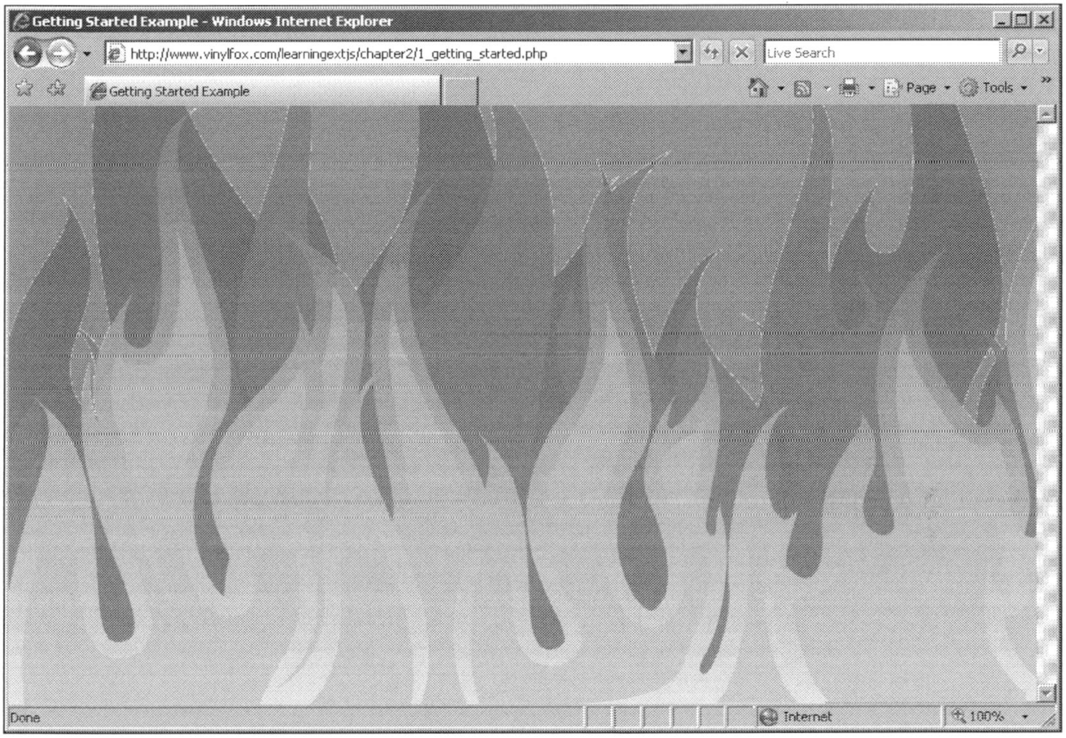

# The workhorse—Ext.get

Ext JS is able to work so well, because it has a foundation that provides access to the DOM, and to many functions that allow manipulation of the DOM. These are part of the Ext Core library. Of these functions, `get` is one of the most used.

```
Var myDiv = Ext.get('my_id');
```

This gives us access to an element in the document with the ID, `my_id` by wrapping it in an `Ext.Element` object which provides cross-browser methods to work with DOM elements. If we take a look at the first example, it is using `getBody`, which retrieves the body element and applies our effect to that. Let's switch that around to use `my_id` instead. But first, we will need to create a `my_id` element in our document:

```
<div id='my_id'
  style='width:200px;height:200px;'>test</div>
```

If we add this to the body section of our document, and change our effect to reference this instead of the body, then our effect will happen only to the `my_id` div we created:

```
Ext.get('my_id').highlight('FF0000',{
   endColor:'0000FF', duration: 3
});
```

If we now look at our document in a browser, we would see a 200-pixel square box changing color, instead of the entire body of the document changing color.

Bear in mind that DOM element IDs must be unique. So once we have used `my_id`, we cannot use this ID again in our document. If duplicate IDs exist in our document, then our results will be unpredictable. When creating the DOM structure of widgets, Ext JS creates and tracks its own IDs. It is hardly ever necessary to create them on our own. One exception is when using HTML **scaffolding**—pre-existing HTML elements which are to be imported into Ext Components.

> Having duplicate IDs in our document can lead to strange behavior, such as a widgets always showing up in the upper-left corner of the browser, and must therefore be avoided.

# Minimizing memory usage

If an element is not going to be repeatedly used, then we can avoid the caching mechanism which `Ext.get` uses to optimize element lookups. We can use something called a "flyweight" to perform simple tasks, which results in higher speed by not clogging up the browser's memory with cached elements which will not be needed again.

The same highlight effect we just used could be written using a flyweight instead:

```
Ext.fly('my_id').highlight('FF0000',{
   endColor:'0000FF', duration: 3
});
```

This is used when we want to perform an action on an element in a single line of code, and we do not need to reference that element again. The flyweight re-uses the same memory over and over each time it is called.

A flyweight should never be stored in a variable and used again. Here is an example of using a flyweight incorrectly:

```
var my_id = Ext.fly('my_id');
Ext.fly('another_id');
my_id.highlight('FF0000',{
   endColor:'0000FF', duration: 3
});
```

Because the flyweight re-uses the same memory each time it is called, by the time we run the highlight function on our `my_id` reference, the memory has changed to actually contain a reference to `another_id`.

# Can we use our own HTML?

As mentioned earlier, pre-existing HTML elements may be "imported" into Ext JS widgets.

The easiest way is to configure an Ext Panel with a `contentEl`.

The following page creates a Panel which uses a pre-existing HTML element as its content by specifying the element's ID as the `contentEl`:

```
<html>
<head>
<link type="text/css" rel="stylesheet" href="../lib/extjs/
resources/css/ext-all.css"/>
<style type="text/css">
.my-panel-class {
    font-family: tahoma,sans-serif;
}
</style>
<script type="text/javascript" src="../lib/extjs/adapter/ext/
ext-base.js"></script>
<script type="text/javascript" src="../lib/extjs/ext-all.js"
></script>
```

```
<script type="text/javascript">
Ext.onReady(function(){
    new Ext.Panel({
        renderTo: Ext.getBody(),
        title: 'Panel with pre-existing content',
        height: 400,
        width: 600,
        cls: 'my-panel-class',
        contentEl: 'main-content'
    });
});
</script>
</head>
<body>
    <div id="main-content">
        <h1>This is some pre-existing content.</h1>
        This element is "imported" and used as the body of a Panel
    </div>
</body>
</html>
```

Another way to do this is to use the `Ext.BoxComponent` class to encapsulate an existing element of a page. The `BoxComponent` class is a very lightweight widget which simply manages an HTML DIV as an Ext widget. As mentioned, it will create its own HTML structure if required, but we can configure it to use an existing element as its main element. In the following example we use a Panel to contain the `BoxComponent`:

```
<html>
<head>
<link type="text/css" rel="stylesheet" href="../lib/extjs/resources/
css/ext-all.css"/>
<style type="text/css">
.my-panel-class {
    font-family: tahoma,sans-serif;
}
</style>
<script type="text/javascript" src="../lib/extjs/adapter/ext/ext-base.
js"></script>
<script type="text/javascript" src="../lib/extjs/ext-all.js"></script>
<script type="text/javascript">
Ext.onReady(function(){
    new Ext.Panel({
        renderTo: Ext.getBody(),
        title: 'Panel with pre-existing content',
```

```
            height: 400,
            width: 600,
            cls: 'my-panel-class',
            layout: 'fit',
            items: new Ext.BoxComponent({
                el: 'main-content'
            })
        });
    });
    </script>
    </head>
    <body>
        <div id="main-content">
            <h1>This is some pre-existing content.</h1>
            This element is "imported" and used as the body of a Panel
        </div>
    </body>
    </html>
```

Both the previous examples will produce the following output:

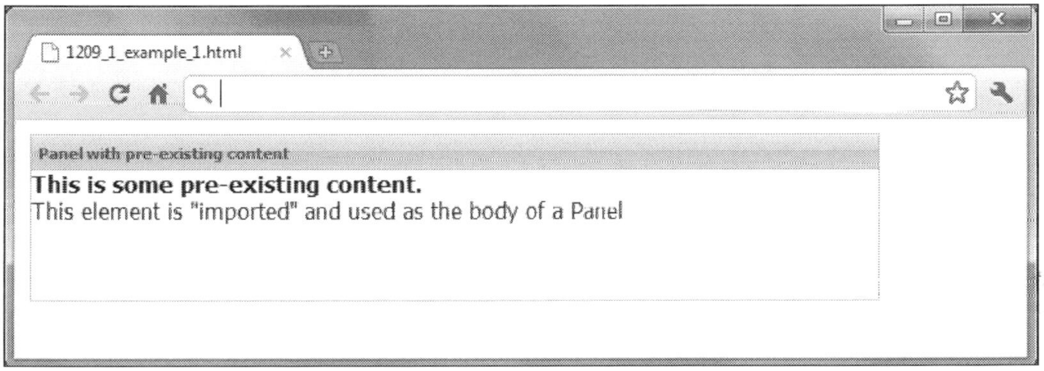

# Summary

Using only a few lines of code, we have created a fun program that will keep us entertained for hours! Well, maybe not for hours, but for at least a few minutes. Nonetheless, we have the beginnings of the basic functionality and user interface of a typical desktop application.

We have learned the basics of using configuration objects, and I'm sure this will make even more sense after we have had the chance to play with more of the Ext JS widgets. But the real point here is that the configuration object is something that is very fundamental when using Ext JS. So the quicker we can wrap your heads around it, the better off we will be.

Don't worry if you are not entirely comfortable with the configuration object yet. We have plenty of time to figure it out. For now, let's move on to one of my favorite things—forms.

# 3
# Forms

In this chapter, we will learn how to create Ext JS forms, which are similar to the HTML forms that we use, but with a greater level of flexibility, error checking, styling, and automated layout.

This functionality is encapsulated in the `FormPanel` class. This class is a panel because it extends the `Panel` class, and so it can do everything a panel can do. It also adds the ability to manage a set of input fields that make up the form.

We will use some different form field types to create a form that validates and submits form data asynchronously. Then we will create a database-driven, drop-down Combo Box, and add some more complex field validation and masking. We will then finish it off with a few advanced topics that will give our forms some serious 'wow' factor.

The goals of this chapter include:

- Creating a form that uses AJAX submission
- Validating field data and creating custom validation
- Loading form data from a database

## The core components of a form

A form has two main pieces, the functionality that performs form like actions, such as loading values and submitting form data, and the layout portion which controls how the fields are displayed. The `FormPanel` that we will be using combines these two things together into one easy-to-use Component, though we could use the form layout by itself if needed, which we will take a closer look at in *Chapter 7*.

The possibilities are endless with Ext JS form fields. Key listeners, validation, error messages, and value restrictions are all built-in with simple config options. Customizing a form for our own specific needs can be done easily, which is something we will cover later on in this chapter. To start with, we will be adding fields to a standard form. Here are some of the core form components that we will become familiar with:

- `Ext.form.FormPanel`: A specialized Panel subclass which renders a `FORM` element as part of its structure, and uses a form-specific layout to arrange its child Components.
- `Ext.form.BasicForm`: The class which the `FormPanel` uses to perform field management, and which performs the AJAX submission and loading capabilities.
- `Ext.form.Field`: A base class which implements the core capabilities that all form fields need. This base class is extended to create other form field types.

> Extending is a major part of the Ext JS architecture, and just means that common functionality is created in a single place and built upon (extended) to make more specific and complex components.

# Our first form

To start with, let's create a form with multiple field types, a date field, validation, error messages, and AJAX submission—just a simple one for our first try.

For this example, our fields will be created using an array of `config` objects instead of an array of instantiated `Ext.form.Field` components. This method will work just the same as an instantiated component, but will take less time to code. Another benefit which may come in handy is that a `config` object used to create items in this way may be stored and reused. A basic HTML page like the one we used in the previous example will be used as a starting point. The standard Ext JS library files need to be included and, as with everything we create in Ext JS, our code will need to be wrapped in the `onReady` function:

```
Ext.onReady(function(){
   var movie_form = new Ext.FormPanel({
      url: 'movie-form-submit.php',
      renderTo: Ext.getBody(),
      frame: true,
      title: 'Movie Information Form',
      width: 250,
      items: [{
```

```
            xtype: 'textfield',
            fieldLabel: 'Title',
            name: 'title'
          },{
            xtype: 'textfield',
            fieldLabel: 'Director',
            name: 'director'
          },{
            xtype: 'datefield',
            fieldLabel: 'Released',
            name: 'released'
          }]
      });
  });
```

When we run this code in a browser, we end up with a form panel that looks like this:

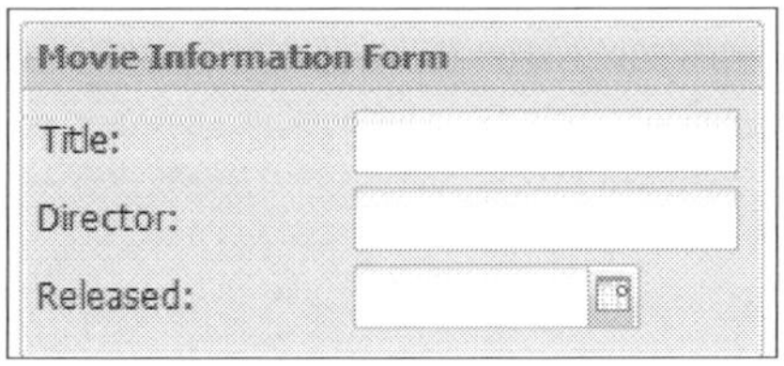


# Nice form—how does it work?

The `FormPanel` is very similar to an HTML form. It acts as the container for our form fields. Our form has a `url` config so the form knows where to send the data when it is submitted. As it is a Component (inherits from the Component base class), it also has a `renderTo` config, which defines into which existing element the form is appended upon creation. As we start to explore layouts in *Chapter 7*, the `renderTo` config will be used much less often.

# Child items

The `items` config option is an important one as it specifies all of our child Components—in this case they are all input fields. The ability to house child Components is inherited from the `Container` level of the Component family tree—our FormPanel in this case. The items config is an array which may reference either component config objects, or fully created Components. In our example, each array element is a config object which has an `xtype` property that defines which type of Ext JS component will be used: text, date, number, or any of the many others. This could even be a grid or some other type of Ext JS component.

Be aware that the default `xtype` is a panel. Any {...} structure with no `xtype` property, as an element in an items config, results in a panel at that position.

But where do `xtypes` come from, and how many of them are there? An `xtype` is just a string key relating to a particular Ext JS Component class, so a 'textfield' `xtype` refers to its `Ext.form.TextField` counterpart. Here are examples of some of the form field `xtypes` that are available to us:

- `textfield`
- `timefield`
- `numberfield`
- `datefield`
- `combo`
- `textarea`

The key point to remember is that child items may be any class within the Component class hierarchy. We could easily be using a grid, toolbar, or button—pretty much anything! (Though getting and setting their values is a different story.)

This is an illustration of the power of the Component class hierarchy mentioned in Chapter 2. All Ext JS component classes, because they share the same inheritance, can be used as child items, and be managed by a Container object—in this case a form.

Our basic field config is set up like this:

```
{
   xtype: 'textfield',
   fieldLabel: 'Title',
   name: 'title'
}
```

Of course, we have the `xtype` that defines what type of a field it is—in our case it is a `textfield`. The `fieldLabel` is the text label that is displayed to the left of the field, although this can also be configured to display above the field. The `name` config is just the same as its HTML counterpart and will be used as the parameter name when sending form data to the server.

> The names of most of the config options for Ext components match their counterparts in HTML. This is because Ext was created by web developers, for web developers.

Creating the subsequent date field isn't much different from the text field we just made. Change the `xtype` from `textfield` to `datefield`, update the label and name, and we're done.

```
{
    xtype: 'datefield',
    fieldLabel: 'Released',
    name: 'released'
}
```

# Validation

A few of our sample fields could have validations that present the users with error indicators if the user does something wrong, such as leaving a field blank. Let's add some validation to our first form. One of the most commonly-used types of validation is checking to see if the user has entered any value at all. We will use this for our movie `title` field. In other words, let's make this field a required one:

```
{
    xtype: 'textfield',
    fieldLabel: 'Title',
    name: 'title',
    allowBlank: false
}
```

Setting up an `allowBlank` config option and setting it to `false` (the default is `true`) is easy enough. Most forms we build will have a bunch of required fields just like this.

Each type of Ext JS field also has its own set of specialized configurations that are specific to the data type of that field. The following are some examples of the options available:

| **Field Type** | **Option** | **Value type** | **Description** |
|---|---|---|---|
| `numberfield` | decimalPrecision | Integer | How many decimal places to allow |
| `datefield` | disabledDates | Array | An array of date strings that cannot be selected |
| `timefield` | increment | Integer | How many minutes between each time option |

For instance, a date field has ways to disable certain days of the week, or to use a regular expression to disable specific dates. The following code disables every day except Saturday and Sunday:

```
{
    xtype: 'datefield',
    fieldLabel: 'Released',
    name: 'released',
    disabledDays: [1,2,3,4,5]
}
```

In this example, every day except Saturday and Sunday is disabled. Keep in mind that the week starts on 0 for Sunday, and ends on 6 for Saturday.

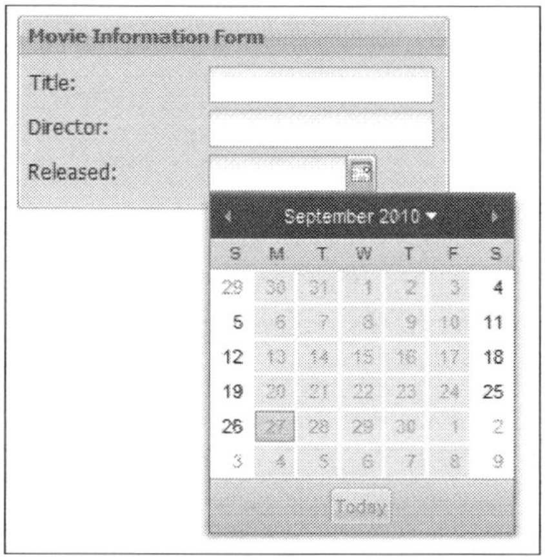


When we use other types of fields, we have different validations, like number fields that can restrict the size of a number or how many decimal places the number can have. The standard configuration options for each field type can be found in the API reference.

> There are many more configuration options, specific to each specialized Ext JS Component class.
>
> To easily find what options are available in the online documentation, use the **Hide inherited members** button at the top right. This will hide config options from the base classes of the Component's heritage, and only show you options from the Component you are interested in:

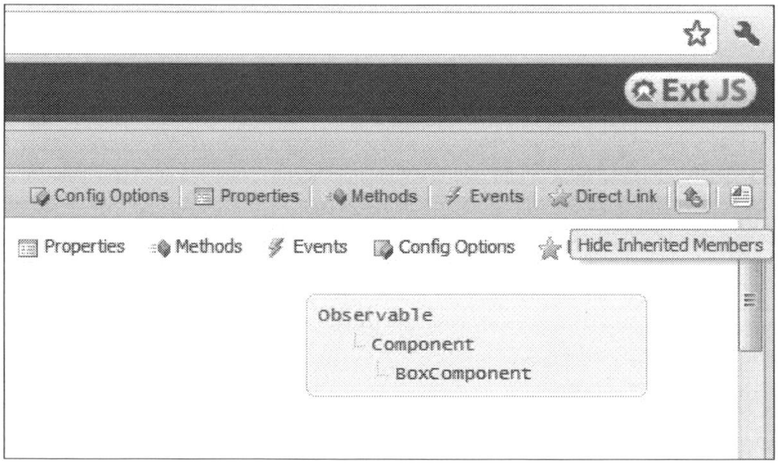

# Built-in validation—vtypes

Another more flexible type of validation is the `vtype`. This can be used to validate and restrict user input, along with reporting back error messages. It will work in just about any scenario you can imagine because it uses a function and regular expressions to do the grunt work.

Here are some built-in `vTypes` that can come in handy:

- email
- url
- alpha
- alphanum

These built-in `vtypes` come included by default, and we can use them as a starting point for creating our own `vtypes`, which we will cover in the next section.

The following is an example of an `alpha` `vtype` being used on a text field:

```
Ext.onReady(function(){
  var movie_form = new Ext.FormPanel({
    url: 'movie-form-submit.php',
    renderTo: document.body,
    frame: true,
    title: 'Movie Information Form',
    width: 250,
    items: [{
      xtype: 'textfield',
      fieldLabel: 'Title',
      name: 'title',
      allowBlank: false
     },{
      xtype: 'textfield',
      fieldLabel: 'Director',
      name: 'director',
      vtype: 'alpha'
     },{
      xtype: 'datefield',
      fieldLabel: 'Released',
      name: 'released',
      disabledDays: [1,2,3,4,5]
     }]
  });
});
```

All we did was add a `vtype` to the director field. This will validate that the value entered is composed of only alphabet characters.

Now we're starting to see that the built-in `vtypes` are very basic. The built-in `alpha vtype` restricts our fields to alphabet characters only. In our case, we want the user to enter a director's name, which would usually contain only alphabetic characters, with just one space between the first and last names. Capitalizing the first characters in the names could possibly make them look pretty. We will create our own custom vtype soon enough, but first let's take a look at displaying error messages.

> A search of the Ext JS forum is likely to come back with a `vType` that someone else has created that is either exactly what you need, or close enough to use as a starting point for your own requirements.

# Styles for displaying errors

Forms are set up by default with a very bland error display which shows any type of error with a squiggly red line under the form field. This error display closely mimics the errors shown in programs like Microsoft Word when you spell a word incorrectly. We do have other options for displaying our error messages, but we will need to tell Ext JS to use them instead of the default.

One built-in option is to display the error message in a balloon using an Ext JS object called `QuickTips`. This utilizes the standard squiggly line, but also adds a balloon message that pops up when we mouse over the field, displaying error text within.

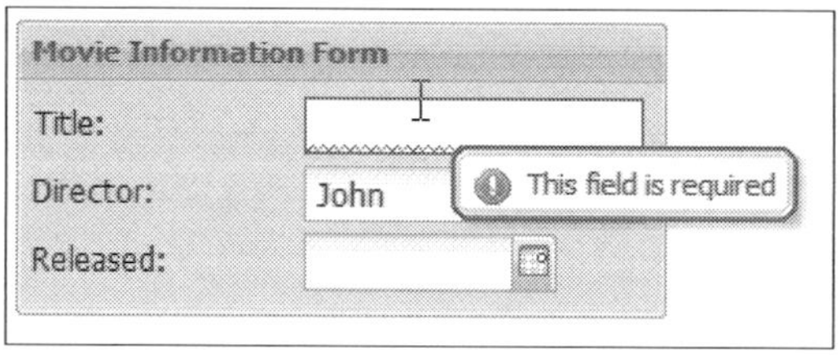

We just need to add one line of code before our form is created that will initialize the QuickTips object. Once the QuickTips object is initialized, the form fields will automatically use it. This is just one simple statement at the beginning of the script:

```
Ext.QuickTips.init();
```

This is all that needs to happen for our form fields to start displaying error messages in a fancy balloon.

The `QuickTips` object can also be used to display informational tool tips. Add a `qtip` attribute which contains a message to any DOM node in the document, and when we hover the mouse over that element, a floating message balloon is displayed. Without the red "error" styling shown above.

# Custom validation—creating our own vtype

In this section we will create a custom `vtype` to perform validation based upon matching the input field's value against a regular expression. Don't be afraid to experiment with regular expressions. They simply match characters in a string against a series of patterns which represent classes of characters, or sequences thereof.

Our `vtype` will check that the input consists of two words, each of which begins with a capital letter, and is followed by one or more letters.

> A hint for working with regular expressions: use the browser's JavaScript debugging console to test regular expressions against strings until you come up with one that works.

To create our own `vtype`, we need to add it to the `vtype` definitions. Each definition has a value, mask, error text, and a function used for testing:

- `xxxVal`: This is the regular expression to match against
- `xxxMask`: This is the masking to restrict user input
- `xxxText`: This is the error message that is displayed

As soon as we figure out the regular expressions we need to use, it's fairly straightforward to create our own `vType`—so let's try one out. Here is a validation for our director's name field. The regular expression matches a pair of alpha strings, separated by a space, and each starting with a capital letter. Sounds like a good way to validate a name—right? The `Ext.apply` function is just a simple way of copying properties from one object into another—in this case from an object literal which we create, into the `Ext.form.VTypes` object.

```
Ext.apply(Ext.form.VTypes, {
  nameVal: /^[A-Z][A-Za-z]+\s[A-Z][A-Za-z]+$/,
  nameMask: /[A-Za-z ]/,
  nameText: 'Invalid Director Name.',
  name:  function(v) {
    return this.nameVal.test(v);
  }
});
```

It's hard to look at this all at once, so let's break it down into its main parts. We first start with the regular expression that validates the value entered into our form field. In this case it's a regular expression used to test the value:

```
nameVal: /^[A-Z][A-Za-z]+\s[A-Z][A-Za-z]+$/,
```

Next, we add the masking, which defines what characters can be typed into our form field. This is also in the form of a regular expression:

```
nameMask: /[A-Za-z ]/,
```

Then, we have the text to be displayed in a balloon message if there is an error:

```
nameText: 'Invalid Director Name.',
```

And finally, the part that pulls it all together—the actual function used to test our field value:

```
name:  function(v) {
  return this.nameVal.test(v);
}
```

Put all this together and we have our own custom `vtype` without much effort —one that can be used over and over again. We use it in just the same way as the 'alpha' `vtype`:

```
vtype: 'name'
```

The result should look like this:

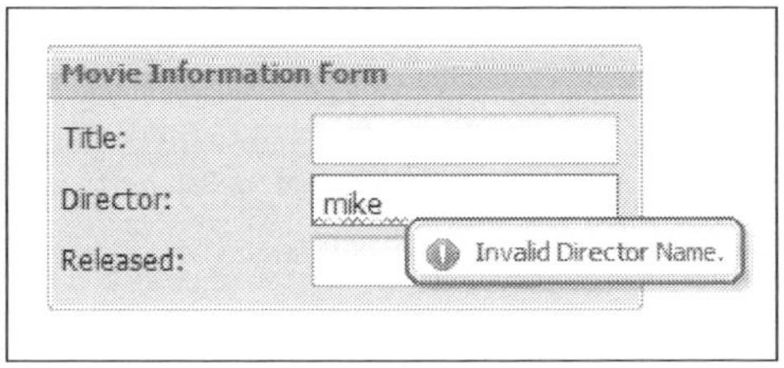


Even though our example used a regular expression to test the value, this is not the only way `vTypes` can work. The function used can perform any type of comparison we need, and simply return true or false.

# Masking—don't press that key!

**Masking** is used when a particular field is forced to accept only certain keystrokes, such as numbers only, or letters, or just capital letters. The possibilities are limitless, because regular expressions are used to decide what keys to filter out.

This mask example would allow an unlimited string of only capital letters:

```
{
  xtype: 'textfield',
...
  maskRe: /[A-Z]/,
...
}
```

Instead of using the masking config, consider creating a `vType` to accomplish your masking. If the formatting requirements should happen to change, it will be centrally-located for easy updating.

So when the day arrives where your boss comes to you freaking out and tells you, "Remember those product codes that I said would always be ten numbers, well it turns out they will be eight letters instead", you can make the change to your `vType`, and go play Guitar Hero for the rest of the day!

# Radio buttons and check boxes

Radio buttons and check boxes can be clumsy and hard to work with in plain HTML. However, creating a set of radio buttons to submit one of a limited set of options is easy in Ext JS. Let's add a RadioGroup component to the form which submits the film type of the movie being edited.

# It's not a button, it's a radio button

The code below adds a set of radio buttons to our form by using the `'radiogroup'` `xtype`. We configure this RadioGroup to arrange the buttons in a single column. The default `xtype` of items in a RadioGroup is 'radio' so we do not need to specify it:

```
{
  xtype: 'radiogroup',
  columns: 1,
  fieldLabel: 'Filmed In',
  name: 'filmed_in',
  items: [{
    name: 'filmed_in',
    boxLabel: 'Color',
    inputValue: 'color'
  },{
    name: 'filmed_in',
    boxLabel: 'Black & White',
    inputValue: 'B&W'
  }]
}
```

The RadioGroup's `name` allows the form to be loaded using a single property value. The `name` in the individual button configs allows submission of the selected `inputValue` under the correct name. These radio buttons work much like their HTML counterparts. Give them all the same name, and they will work together for you. The additional config for `boxLabel` is needed to show the informative label to the right of the input.

# X marks the checkbox

Sometimes, we need to use checkboxes for Boolean values—sort of an `on`/`off` switch. By using the `checkbox` `xtype`, we can create a checkbox.

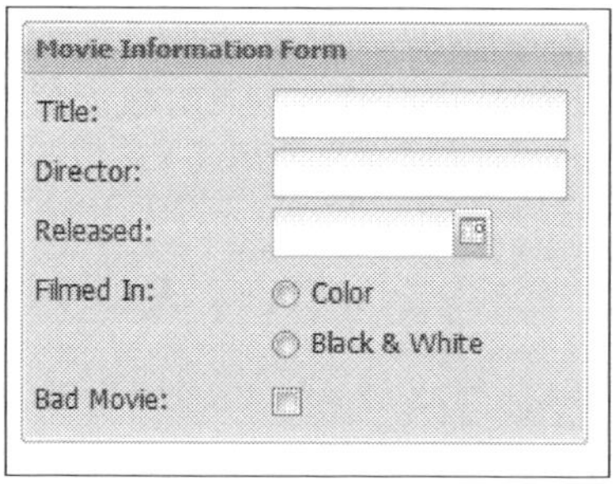

```
{
   xtype: 'checkbox',
   fieldLabel: 'Bad Movie',
   name: 'bad_movie'
}
```

Both the radio and checkbox have a 'checked' config that can be set to `true` or `false` to check the box upon creation.

```
{
   xtype: 'checkbox',
   fieldLabel: 'Bad Movie',
   name: 'bad_movie',
   checked: true
}
```

Sets of checkboxes can be arranged in columns by containing them in a CheckboxGroup. This is configured in exactly the same way that a RadioGroup is, but the default `xtype` of its child items is 'checkbox'.

# The ComboBox

The `ComboBox` class emulates the functionality of the HTML `SELECT` element. It provides a dropdown box containing a list from which one value can be selected. It goes further than simply imitating a `SELECT` box though. It has the ability to either provide its list from a loaded data store, or, it can dynamically query the server during typing to load the data store or demand to produce autosuggest functionality.

First, let's make a combo using local data from a loaded data store. To do this, the first step is to create a data store.

A data store is a client-side analogue of a database table. It encapsulates a set of records, each of which contains a defined set of fields. Full details about data stores are contained in Chapter 15. There are a few different types of data stores, each of which can be used for different situations. However, for this one, we are going to use an Array store, which is one of the shortcut data classes we will cover in more detail in both the Grids and Data chapters. The `ArrayStore` class is configured with the field names which its records are to contain and a two-dimensional array which specifies the data:

```
var genres = new Ext.data.ArrayStore({
   fields: ['id', 'genre_name'],
   data : [['1','Comedy'],['2','Drama'],['3','Action']]
});
```

A few new config options are needed when we are setting up a combo box.

- `store`: This is the obvious one. The store provides the data which backs up the combo. The fields of its records provide the descriptive text for each dropdown item, and the value which each item represents.
- `mode`: This option specifies whether the combo expects the data store to be pre-loaded with all available items ('local'), or whether it needs to dynamically load the store, querying the server based upon the typed characters ('remote').
- `displayField`: This option specifies the field name which provides the descriptive text for each dropdown item.
- `valueField`: This option specifies the field name which provides the value associated with the descriptive text. This is optional. If used, the `hiddenName` option must be specified.
- `hiddenName`: This is the name of a hidden HTML input field which is used to store and submit the separate value of the combo if the descriptive text is not what is to be submitted. The visible field will contain the `displayField`.

Just like the other fields in our form, we add the combo to our `items` config:

```
{
    xtype: 'combo',
    hiddenName: 'genre',
    fieldLabel: 'Genre',
    mode: 'local',
    store: genres,
    displayField:'genre_name',
    valueField:'id',
    width: 120
}
```

This gives us a combo box that uses local, pre-loaded data, which is good for small lists, or lists that don't change often. What happens when our list needs to be pulled up from a database?

> A quick way to specify a few static options for a ComboBox is to pass an array to the store config. So if we wanted a ComboBox that had 'Yes' and 'No' as options, we would provide ['Yes','No'] as the store config value.

# A database-driven ComboBox

The biggest change that needs to happen is on the server side—getting our data and formatting it into a JSON string that the combo box can use. Whatever server-side language is used, we will need a JSON library to 'encode' the data. If we're using PHP 5.1 or higher, this is built in.

> To check our version of PHP, we can either execute a command in a terminal window or run a single line of PHP code. If we have access to this command line we can run `php -v` to check our version, otherwise, running a script that just has the single line `<?php phpinfo(); ?>` will do the job.

This is what we would use to generate our JSON data using PHP 5.1 or higher:

```
<?php
// connection to database goes here
$result = mysql_query('SELECT id, genre_name FROM genres');
If (mysql_num_rows($result) > 0) {
   while ($obj = mysql_fetch_object($result)) {
      $arr[] = $obj;
   }
}
Echo '{rows:'.json_encode($arr).'}';
?>
```

When we use remote data, there are a few more things that need to happen back on the JavaScript side. First, the data store needs to know what format the data is in. When we use shortcut store classes like `ArrayStore`, this is implicit (It's an array). In this example, we specify the format of the data being read by using a data reader—in our case, it's the JSON Reader.

```
var genres = new Ext.data.Store({
    reader: new Ext.data.JsonReader({
        fields: ['id', 'genre_name'],
        root: 'rows'
    }),
    proxy: new Ext.data.HttpProxy({
        url: 'data/genres.php'
    })
});
```

The data reader is configured using two config options:

- fields: This is an array of the field names which the records in the store will contain. For a JSON Reader, these names are also the property names within each row data object from which to pull the field values.
- root: This specifies the property name within the raw, loaded data object which references the array of data rows. Each row is an object.

We can see the root and field properties specified in the configuration in this example of the returned JSON data:

```
{rows:[
    {
        "id":"1",
        "genre_name":"Comedy",
        "sort_order":"0"
    },{
        "id":"2",
        "genre_name":"Drama",
        "sort_order":"1"
    },{
        // snip...//
    }]
}
```

We have also set up the proxy, a class which takes responsibility for retrieving raw data objects. Typically this will be an `HttpProxy` that retrieves data from a URL at the same domain as the web page. This is the most common method, but there is also a `ScriptTagProxy` that can be used to retrieve data from a different domain. All we need to provide for our proxy is the URL to fetch our data from.

> Whenever we specify a `HttpProxy` we are actually using Ajax. This requires that we have a web server running; otherwise Ajax will not work. Simply running our code from the file system in a web browser will not work.

Let's throw in a call to the `load` function at the end, so the data is loaded into our combo box before the user starts to interact with it.

```
genres.load();
```

This gives us a combo box that's populated from our database, and should look like this:

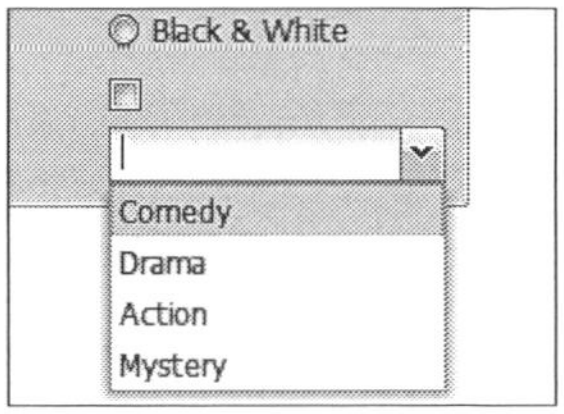


Another way to pre-load the data store is to set the `autoLoad` option to `true` in our data store configuration:

```
var genres = new Ext.data.Store({
    reader: new Ext.data.JsonReader({
        fields: ['id', 'genre_name'],
        root: 'rows'
    }),
    proxy: new Ext.data.HttpProxy({
        url: 'data/genres.php'
    }),
    autoLoad: true
});
```

# TextArea and HTMLEditor

We are going to add a multiline text area to our movie information form, and Ext JS has a couple of options for this. We can either use the standard `textarea` that we are familiar with from using HTML, or we can use the `HTMLEditor` field, which provides simplistic rich text editing:

- `textarea`: Similar to a typical HTML `textarea` field
- `htmleditor`: A rich text editor with a button bar for common formatting tasks

We will use a couple of new config options for this input:

- `hideLabel`: This causes the form to not display a label to the left of the input field, thus allowing more horizontal space for the field.
- `anchor`: This config is not a direct config option of the Field class. It is a "hint" to the Container (in this case a FormPanel) that houses the field. It anchors the child item to the right or bottom borders of the container. A single value of `'100%'` anchors to the right border, resulting in a full-width child component.

```
{
    xtype: 'textarea',
    name: 'description',
    hideLabel: true,
    height: 100,
    anchor: '100%'
}
```

By changing just the `xtype`, as shown below, we now have a fairly simple HTML editor with built-in options for font face, size, color, italics, bold, and so on:

```
{
    xtype: 'htmleditor',
    name: 'description',
    hideLabel: true,
    height: 100,
    anchor: '100%'
}
```

The `HtmlEditor` can now be seen occupying the full panel width at the bottom of the panel:

# Listening for form field events

Ext JS makes it extremely simple to listen for particular events in a Component's lifecycle. These may include user-initiated events such as pressing a particular key, changing a field's value, and so on. Or they may be events initiated by code, such as the Component being rendered or destroyed.

To add event handling functions (which we call "listeners") to be called at these points, we use the `listeners` config option. This option takes the form of an object with properties which associate functions with event names.

> The events available to the `listeners` config option of a Component are not the same as the standard native DOM events which HTML offers. Some Components *do* offer events of the same name (for example a click event), but that is usually because they "add value" to the native DOM event. An example would be the click event offered by the Ext JS tree control. This passes to the listener the tree node that was clicked on.
>
> Adding our own listeners to DOM events of the constituent element of a Component is explained later in this chapter.

A common task would be listening for the *Enter* key to be pressed, and then submitting the form. So let's see how this is accomplished:

```
{
   xtype: 'textfield',
   fieldLabel: 'Title',
   name: 'title',
   allowBlank: false,
   listeners: {
      specialkey: function(field, eventObj){
         if (eventObj.getKey() == Ext.EventObject.ENTER) {
           movie_form.getForm().submit();
         }
      }
   }
}
```

The `specialkey` event is fired whenever a key related to navigation or editing is pressed. This includes arrow keys, *Tab*, *Esc*, and *Enter*. When an event is fired, the listener function associated with that event name is called.

We want to check to see if it was the *Enter* key that was pressed before we take action, so we're using the event object—represented as the variable 'eventObj' in this example—to find out what key was pressed. The `getKey` method tells us which key was pressed, and the `Ext.EventObject .ENTER` is a constant that represents this key. With this simple listener and if statement, the form will be submitted when we press the *Enter* key.

# ComboBox events

Combo boxes commonly need to have events attached to them. Let's take our `genre` combo box and attach a listener to it that will run when an item in the list is selected.

First let's add a dummy item to our data as the first item in the list and call it `New Genre`:

```
var genres = new Ext.data.SimpleStore({
   fields: ['id', 'genre_name'],
   data : [
      ['0','New Genre'],
      ['1','Comedy'],
      ['2','Drama'],
      ['3','Action']
   ]
});
```

Then, we add the listener to our combo:

```
{
   xtype: 'combo',
   name: 'genre',
   fieldLabel: 'Genre',
   mode: 'local',
   store: genres,
   displayField:'genre_name',
   width: 130,
   listeners: {
      select: function(field, rec, selIndex){
         if (selIndex == 0){
            Ext.Msg.prompt('New Genre', 'Name', Ext.emptyFn);
         }
      }
   }
}
```

The `listeners` object in the code above specifies a function which is to be called when a combo item is selected. Each event type has its own set of parameters which are passed to listener functions. These can be looked up in the API reference.

For the `select` event, our function is passed three things:

- The form field
- The data record of the selected combo item
- The index number of the item that was clicked on

Inside our listener function, we can see which item in the list was selected. The third argument in our listener function is the index of the item that was clicked. If that has an index of zero (the first item in the list), then we will prompt the user to enter a new genre using the prompt dialog we learned about in the previous chapter. The result should look like this:

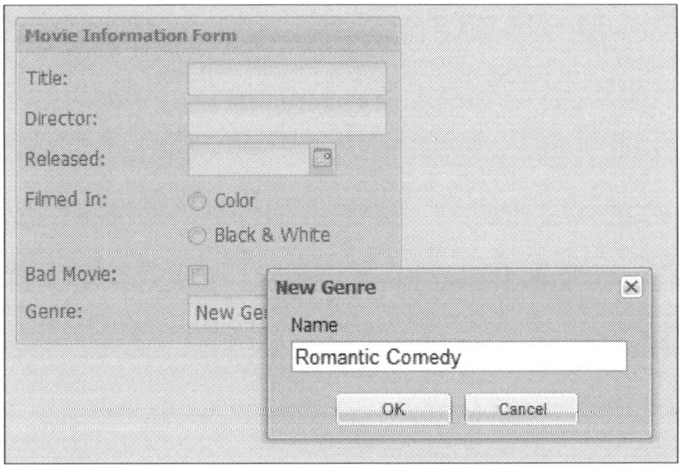


[ A list of valid events to listen for can be found at the bottom of the API documentation page for each Component, along with the arguments the listeners are passed, which are unique to each event. ]

# Buttons and form action

Now, we have quite a complex form with only one problem—it doesn't send data to the server, and we will want a way to reset the form, which was the actual point behind creating our form in the first place. To do this, we are going to add some buttons which will perform these actions.

Our buttons are added to a `buttons` config object, similar to the way that the form fields were added. These buttons really only need two things: the text to be displayed on the button, and the function (which is called the handler) to execute when the button is clicked.

```
buttons: [{
   text: 'Save',
   handler: function(){
      movie_form.getForm().submit({
         success: function(form, action){
            Ext.Msg.alert('Success', 'It worked');
```

```
         },
         failure: function(form, action){
            Ext.Msg.alert('Warning', 'Error');
         }
      });
   }
}, {
   text: 'Reset',
   handler: function(){
      movie_form.getForm().reset();
   }
}]
```

The handler is provided with a function—or a reference to a function—that will be executed once the button is clicked. In this case, we are providing an anonymous function.

# Form submission

Our `FormPanel` has a `url` option that contains the name of the file that the form data will be sent to. This is simple enough—just like an HTML form, all of our fields will be posted to this `url`, so they can be processed on the server side.

```
movie_form.getForm().submit({
   success: function(form, action){
      Ext.Msg.alert('Success', 'It worked');
   },
   failure: function(form, action){
      Ext.Msg.alert('Warning', 'Error');
   }
});
```

Inside our **Save** button, we have an anonymous function that runs the following code. This will run the actual submission function for our form, which sends the data to the server using AJAX. No page refresh is needed to submit the form. It all happens in the background, while the page you are looking at remains the same:

> In order for our form submission to work properly, the HTML page must be run from a web server, not the file system.

The `success` and `failure` options provided to the `submit` call handle the server's response. These are also anonymous functions, but could just as easily be references to functions created earlier on in the code.

Did you notice that the functions have a pair of arguments passed to them? These will be used to figure out what response the server gave. But first, we need to discuss how to provide that response on the server side.

# Talking back—the server responses

When our form is submitted to the server, a script on the server side will process the post data from the form, and decide if a `true` or `false` 'success' message should be sent back to the client side. Error messages can be sent back along with our response, and these can contain messages that correspond to our form field names.

When using forms and server-side validation, a `success` Boolean value is required. An example of a response JSON string from the server would look like this:

```
{
    success: false,
    errors: {
        title: "Sounds like a Chick Flick"
    }
}
```

When the `success` property is set to `false`, it triggers the Ext JS form to read in the error messages from the `errors` property, and apply them to the form's validation to present the user with error messages.

Server-side validation of our form submission gives us a way to look up information on the server side, and return errors based on this. Let's say we have a database of bad movie names, and we don't want users to submit them to our database. We can submit the form to our script, which checks the database and returns a response based on the database lookup of that name.

If we wanted to filter out `chick flicks` the response could look something like this:

```
{
  success: false,
  errors: {
      title: "Sounds like a Chick Flick"
  },
   errormsg: "That movie title sounds like a chick flick."
}
```

The `false` success response triggers the form's error messages to be displayed. An `errors` object is passed with the response. The form uses this object to determine each of the error messages for the fields. A name/value pair exists in the `errors` object for each form field's error.

Our example response also passes an `errormsg property`, which is not used by the form, but is going to be accessed separately to present our own error message in an Ext JS Message Box.

The error objects messages are handled automatically by the form, so let's take the extra error message that we were passing back, and display it in a message box.

```
buttons: [{
    text: 'Save',
    handler: function(){
        movie_form.getForm().submit({
            success: function(form, action){
                Ext.Msg.alert('Success', 'It worked');
            },
            failure: function(form, action){
                Ext.Msg.alert('Warning', action.result.errormsg);
            }
        });
    }
}, {
    text: 'Reset',
    handler: function(){
        movie_form.getForm().reset();
    }
}]
```

Our `submit` form action passes information back to the `success` and `failure` handlers. The first argument is the Ext JS form Component we were using, and the second is an Ext JS action object. Let's take a look at what's available in the Ext JS action object:

| Option | Data type | Description |
|---|---|---|
| `failureType` | String | The type of failure encountered, whether it was on the client or server |
| `response` | Object | Contains raw information about the server's response, including useful header information |
| `result` | Object | Parsed JSON object based on the response from the server |
| `type` | String | The type of action that was performed–either `submit` or `load` |

Now that we know what is available to the `failure` handler, we can set up some simple error checking:

```
failure: function(form, action){
    if (action.failureType == Ext.form.Action.CLIENT_INVALID) {
        Ext.Msg.alert("Cannot submit",
            "Some fields are still invalid");
    } else if (action.failureType === Ext.form.Action.CONNECT_FAILURE)
{
        Ext.Msg.alert('Failure', 'Server communication failure: '+
            action.response.status+' '+action.response.statusText);
    } else if (action.failureType === Ext.form.Action.SERVER_INVALID)
{
        Ext.Msg.alert('Warning', action.result.errormsg);
    }
}
}
```

By checking the failure type, we can determine if there was a server connection error and act accordingly, even providing details about the server's specific error message by inspecting the `result` and `response` properties.

# Loading a form with data

There are three basic ways in which forms are used in a user interface:

- To input data for a separate action—say, Google search
- To create new data
- To change existing data

It's the last option is what we are interested in now. To accomplish this, we need to learn how to load that data from its source (static or database) into our user interface—our form.

# Static data load

We can take data from somewhere in our code, a variable for instance, or just plain static text, and display it as the value in our form field by calling the `setValue` method. This single line of code will set a field's value:

```
movie_form.getForm().findField('title').
            setValue('Dumb & Dumber');
```

Once we start working with larger forms with many fields, this method becomes a hassle. That's why we also have the ability to load our data in bulk via an AJAX request. The server side would work much as it did when we loaded the combo box:

```
<?php
// connection to database goes here

$result = mysql_query('SELECT * FROM movies WHERE id = '.$_
REQUEST['id']);

if (mysql_num_rows($result) > 0) {
  $obj = mysql_fetch_object($result);
  Echo '{success: true, data:'.json_encode($obj).'}';
}else{
  Echo '{success: false}';
}

?>
```

This would return a JSON object containing a success property, and a data object that would be used to populate the values of the form fields. The returned data would look something like this:

```
{
   success: true,
   data:{
      "id":"1",
      "title":"Office Space",
      "director":"Mike Judge",
      "released":"1999-02-19",
      "genre":"1",
      "tagline":"Work Sucks",
      "coverthumb":"84m.jpg",
      "price":"19.95",
      "available":"1"
   }
}
```

To trigger this, we need to use the form's `load` method:

```
movie_form.getForm().load({
   url:'data/movie.php',
   params:{
      id: 1
   }
});
```

Providing the load method with a `url` and `params` config will do the trick. The `params` config represents what is sent to the server side script as post/get parameters. By default, these are sent as post parameters.

# DOM listeners

As mentioned when discussing adding listeners to Components, adding DOM event listeners to the constituent HTML elements of a Component is a different matter.

Let's illustrate this by adding a click listener to the header of the `FormPanel`. When a panel is configured with a `title`, an element which houses that title is created when the Component is rendered. A reference to that element is stored in the panel's `header` property.

The key point here is that no elements exist until the Component is rendered. So we use a listener function on the render lifecycle event to add the click listener:

```
var movie_form = new Ext.FormPanel({
    url: 'movie-form-submit.php',
    renderTo: document.body,
    frame: true,
    title: 'Movie Information Form',
    listeners: {
        render: fuction(component) {
            component.header.addListener({
                click: function(eventObj, el) {
                    Ext.Msg.alert("Click event", "Element id " +
                        el.id + " clicked");
                }
            });
        }
    }
```

Let's take the time to read and understand that code.

We specify a listener function for the render event. The listener function is passed as a reference to the Component which just rendered. At this point, it will have a `header` property. This is an `Ext.Element` object which was talked about in Chapter 2.

We call the `addListener` method of the `Ext.Element` class to add our click listener function. The parameter to this class should be familiar to you. It is a standard `listeners` config object which associates an event name property with a listener function which is called on every mouse click.

# Summary

We have taken the foundation of the classic web application—forms—and injected them with the power of Ext JS, creating a uniquely-flexible and powerful user interface. The form created in this chapter can validate user input, load data from a database, and send that data back to the server. From the methods outlined in this chapter, we can go on to create forms for use in simple text searches, or a complexly validated data entry screen.

# 4

# Menus, Toolbars, and Buttons

The unsung heroes of every application are the simple things like buttons, menus, and toolbars. In this chapter, we will cover how to add these items to our applications.

By following the examples in this chapter we will learn how to use menus, both as components in their own right—either static or floating as popups—and as dependent menus of buttons.

We will then learn how to use toolbars, which contain buttons that call a function on click, or that pop up a submenu on click, or cycle between several submenu options on each click.

The primary classes we will cover in this chapter are:

- `Ext.menu.Menu`: A Container class which by default displays itself as a popup component, floating above all other document content. A menu's child items behave in a similar manner to buttons, and may call a handler function on mouse click. A menu may also be used as a static component within a page.
- `Ext.Toolbar`: A Container class which arranges its child Components horizontally in the available width, and manages overflow by offering overflowed Components in a popup menu.
- `Ext.Button`: The primary handler for button creation and interaction. A Component class which renders a focusable element which may be configured with a handler function which is called upon mouse click, or a menu to display upon mouse click.
- `Ext.SplitButton`: A subclass of button which calls a handler function when its main body is clicked, but also renders an arrow glyph to its right which can display a dropdown menu when clicked.

- `Ext.CycleButton`: A subclass of SplitButton which cycles between checking individual menu options of its configured menu on each click. This is similar to cycling through different folder views in Windows Explorer.
- `Ext.ButtonGroup`: A Panel class which lays out child Components in a tabular format across a configurable number of columns.

# What's on the menu?

We will begin by introducing the Menu class which will be used in all following examples.

We are going to demonstrate usage of the Menu class as both a static component within a page, and as a popup. Both menus will be configured with the same options by using a technique which was suggested in Chapter 2: we define a variable called `menuItems` to reference an array which specifies the menu's items, and use it in both cases.

The Menu class inherits from Container, so any menu options are child Components specified in the `items` config. It also inherits the usual Component config options such as `renderTo`, and the `width` option.

The static menu will be rendered to the document body, and in order for it to be rendered as a visible, static element in the document, we configure it with `floating: false`.

So the configuration we end up with is as follows:

```
new Ext.menu.Menu({
    renderTo: document.body,
    width: 150,
    floating: false,
    items: menuItems
});
```

The popup menu needs no extra configuring aside from its items. We do need to decide when and where to display it. In this case we will add a `contextmenu` (right click) event listener to the document, and show the menu at the mouse event's position:

```
var contextMenu = new Ext.menu.Menu({
    items: menuItems
});
Ext.getDoc().on({
    contextmenu: function(eventObj) {
        contextMenu.showAt(eventObj.getXY());
```

```
    },
    stopEvent: true
});
```

When we run this example, the static menu will be visible. When we right click on the document, the result should be the two menus shown below. Notice how only the second, popup menu has a shadow to indicate that it floats above the document.

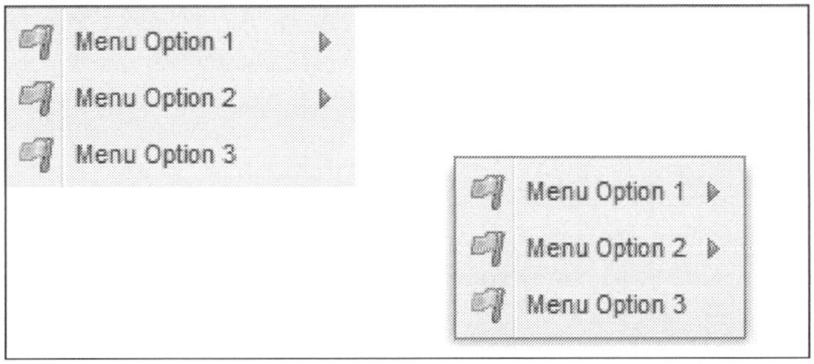


# The menu's items

The `menuItems` variable references an array which should be familiar by now. Just like the items config of a FormPanel used in the previous chapter, it's a list of child Components or config objects. In a menu, a config object with no `xtype` creates a MenuItem Component. The MenuItem class accepts the following config options in addition to those it inherits:

- `icon`: The URL of an image to display as an icon
- `iconCls`: A CSS class name which allows a stylesheet to specify a background image to use as an icon
- `text`: The text to display
- `handler`: A function to call when the item is clicked
- `menu`: A Menu object, or Menu configuration object or an array of menu items to display as a submenu when the item is clicked

Because a menu inherits from Container, it can accept other Components as child items. If some complex, menu option dependent input is required, a menu may be configured with a panel as a child item. The `menu` config of "Menu Option 2" we're creating next contains a FormPanel as its sole child item:

```
{
    text: 'Menu Option 2',
    iconCls: 'flag-green',
    menu: {
```

```
            plain: true,
            items: {
                xtype: 'form',
                border: false,
                bodyStyle: 'background:transparent;padding:5px',
                labelWidth: 70,
                width: 300,
                defaults: {
                    anchor: '100%'
                },
                items: [{
                    xtype: 'combo',
                    editable: false,
                    fieldLabel: 'Select',
                    triggerAction: 'all',
                    store: [ [0, 'One or...'], [1 ,'The other']],
                    value: 0,
                    getListParent: function() {
                        return this.el.up('div.x-menu');
                    }
                }, {
                    xtype: 'textfield',
                    fieldLabel: 'Title'
                }],
                fbar: [{
                    text: 'Submit'
                }]
            }
        }
    }
```

The configurations in the above object will mostly be familiar by now.

There is one extra config we use for the menu which contains the FormPanel.

- `plain`: Specify as `true` so that the menu does not have to show the incised line for separating icons from text

The panel within the menu has the following configs:

`border`: Specify as `false` to produce a panel with no borders.

`bodyStyle`: A CSS style string to apply to the document body. We want to make it transparent to allow the menu to show, and we apply padding.

The ComboBox must render its dropdown list to the menu's element so that clicking on the list does not trigger the menu to hide:

- `getListParent`: This is a function which a ComboBox may be configured with. It must return the HTML element to render the dropdown list into. By default a ComboBox renders its dropdown into the document. We call the `up` function of the `Ext.Element` class to find the ancestor node of the combo's element which is a `DIV` which has the CSS class "x-menu".

The FormPanel as a child of a menu will display like this:

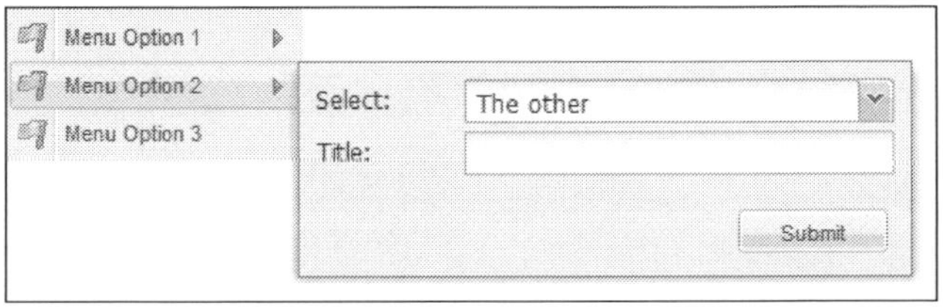


# A toolbar for every occasion

An Ext JS Panel, and every Ext JS Component which inherits from the Panel class (This includes Window, TreePanel, and GridPanel) can be configured to render and manage a toolbar docked above, or below the panel's body—or both if really necessary. These are referred to as the top and bottom toolbars, or `tbar` and `bbar` for short.

Panels and subclasses thereof may also be configured with a footer bar which renders buttons right at the bottom of the panel—below any bottom toolbar.

The Toolbar class is also an Ext JS Component in its own way, and may when necessary be used on its own, or as a child Component of any Container.

Our second example renders a toolbar standalone into the body of the document. We will use all the main button types to illustrate their usage before moving on to add handlers to react to user interaction. The toolbar will contain the following child components:

- A basic button
- A button configured with a menu which is displayed when the button is clicked
- A SplitButton which will display a menu only when its arrow glyph is clicked
- A CycleButton which on click, cycles between three different options
- A pair of mutually exclusive toggle buttons of which only one may be in a "pressed" state at once

```
Ext.onReady(function(){
    new Ext.Toolbar({
        renderTo: Ext.getBody(),
        items: [{
            xtype: 'button',
            text: 'Button'
        },{
            xtype: 'button',
            text: 'Menu Button',
            menu: [{
                text: 'Better'
            },{
                text: 'Good'
            },{
                text: 'Best'
            }]
        },{
            xtype: 'splitbutton',
            text: 'Split Button',
            menu: [{
                text: 'Item One'
            },{
                text: 'Item Two'
            },{
                text: 'Item Three'
            }]
        }, {
            xtype: 'cycle',
            showText: true,
            minWidth: 100,
            prependText: 'Quality: ',
            items: [{
                text: 'High',
                checked: true
            }, {
                text: 'Medium'
            }, {
                text: 'Low'
            }]
        }, {
            text: 'Horizontal',
            toggleGroup: 'orientation-selector'
        }, {
            text: 'Vertical',
```

```
                toggleGroup: 'orientation-selector'
            }]
        });
    });
```

As usual, everything is inside our `onReady` event handler. The `items` config holds our toolbar's entire child Components—I say child Components and not buttons because as we now know, the toolbar can accept many different types of Ext JS Components including entire forms or just form fields—which we will be implementing later on in this chapter.

The result of the above code looks like this:

> The default `xtype` for each element in the `items` config is `button`. We can leave out the `xtype` config element if `button` is the type we want, but I like to include it just for clarity.

# Button configuration

In addition to inherited config options, a button accepts the following configurations which we will be using in the following examples for this chapter:

- `icon`: The URL of an image to display as an icon
- `iconCls`: A CSS class name which allows a stylesheet to specify a background image to use as an icon
- `text`: The text to display
- `handler`: A function to call when the button is clicked
- `menu`: A Menu object, or Menu configuration object, or an array of menu items to display as a submenu when the button is clicked
- `enableToggle`: Specify as `true` to make a single button toggleable between pressed and unpressed state
- `toggleGroup`: A mnemonic string identifying a group of buttons of which only one may be in a "pressed" state at one time
- `toggleHandler`: A function to be called when a button's "pressed" state is changed

# A basic button

Creating a button is fairly straightforward; the main config option is the text that is displayed on the button. We can also add an icon to be used alongside the text if we want to. A handler function is called when the button is clicked.

Here is the most basic configuration of a button:

```
{
    xtype: 'button',
    text: 'Button',
    handler: functionReference
}
```

The following screenshot shows what happens when the mouse is hovered over the **Button** button:

# Button with a menu

A button may be configured to act as a trigger for showing a dropdown menu. If configured with a `menu` option, clicking the button displays a menu below the button. The alignment of the menu is configurable, but defaults to being shown below the button.

Each option within the menu may itself be configured with a `menu` option allowing a familiar cascading menu system to be built very easily. The following is a config for a button which displays a dropdown menu upon click:

```
{
   xtype: 'button',
   text: 'Button',
   menu: [{
      text: 'Better'
   },{
      text: 'Good'
   },{
      text: 'Best'
   }]
}
```

The following screenshot shows what happens when the **Menu Button** is clicked on, and the mouse is hovered over the **Best** option:

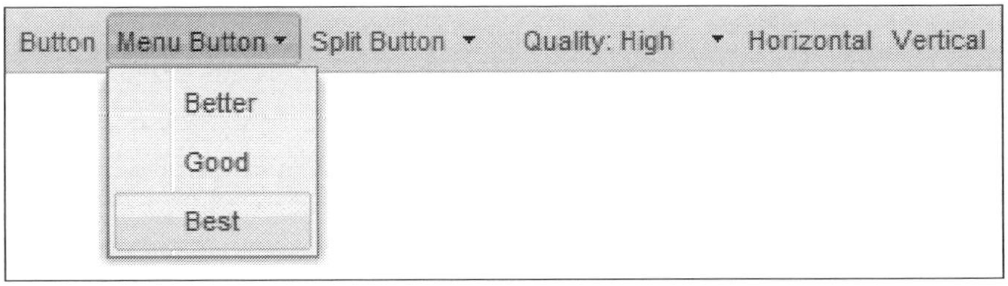


## Split button

A split button may sound like a complex component, but it is no more complex to create than a plain button. By using a split button we get the ability to specify a click handler which is called when the main body of the button is clicked. But we can also configure in a menu which will be displayed when the arrow glyph to the right of the main body is clicked.

```
{
   xtype: 'split',
   text: 'Split Button',
   menu: [{
      text: 'Item One'
   },{
      text: 'Item Two'
   },{
      text: 'Item Three'
   }]
}
```

The following screenshot shows what happens when the **Split Button**'s arrow glyph is clicked:

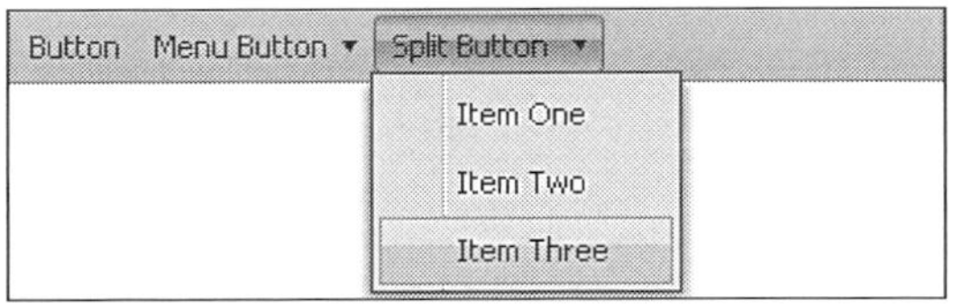


## Toggling button state

Sometimes it is useful to have a button which "sticks" in the pressed state to indicate switching some state within our app. To enable a single button to be clicked to toggle between the pressed and unpressed state, configure the button with `enableToggle: true`.

If a set of buttons are to toggleable, but only one may be pressed at once, configure each button in that set with a `toggleGroup`. This is an ID string which links buttons which enforce this rule.

Toggleable buttons may be configured with a `toggleHandler` function which is called whenever the button's state changes in either direction.

```
{
    text: 'Horizontal',
    toggleGroup: 'orientation-selector'
}, {
    text: 'Vertical',
    toggleGroup: 'orientation-selector'
}
```

This code produces the pair of buttons below in which only one orientation may be selected at once, **Horizontal** or **Vertical**:

# Toolbar item alignment, dividers, and spacers

By default, every toolbar aligns elements to the leftmost side. There is no alignment config for a toolbar, so if we want to align all of the toolbar buttons to the rightmost side, we need to add a fill item to the toolbar. This item is sometimes referred to as a 'greedy spacer'. If we want to have items split up between both the left and right sides, we can also use a fill, but place it between items:

```
{
    xtype: 'tbfill'
}
```

Pop this little guy in a toolbar wherever you want to add space and it will push items on either side of the fill to the ends of the tool bar, as shown below:

We also have elements that can add space or a visual vertical divider, like the one used between the **Menu Button** and the **Split Button**.

The spacer adds a few pixels of empty space that can be used to space out buttons, or move elements away from the edge of the toolbar:

```
{
    xtype: 'tbspacer'
}
```

A divider can be added in the same way:

```
{
   xtype: 'tbseparator'
}
```

# Shortcuts

Ext JS has many shortcuts that can be used to make coding faster. Shortcuts are a character or two that can be used in place of a configuration object. For example, consider the standard toolbar filler configuration:

```
{
   xtype: 'tbfill'
}
```

The shortcut for a toolbar filler is a hyphen and a greater than symbol:

```
'->'
```

Not all of these shortcuts are documented. So be adventurous, poke around the source code that is distributed in the `src` folder of the SDK download, and see what you can find. Here is a list of the commonly-used shortcuts:

| Component | Shortcut | Description |
|---|---|---|
| Fill | '->' | The fill that is used to push items to the right side of the toolbar. |
| Separator | '-' or 'separator' | A vertical bar used to visually separate items. |
| Spacer | ' ' | Empty space used to separate items visually. The space is two pixels wide, but can be changed by overriding the style for the `xtb-spacer` CSS class. |
| TextItem | 'Your Text' | Add any text or HTML directly to a toolbar by simply placing it within quotes. |

# Icon buttons

The standard button can be used as an icon button like the ones we see used in text editors to make text bold or italic—simply a button with an icon and no text. Two steps need to be taken to make an icon button—defining an image to be used as the icon and applying the appropriate class to the button.

```
{
   xtype: 'tbbutton',
   cls: 'x-btn-icon',
   icon: 'images/bomb.png'
}
```

This could just as easily be an icon beside text by changing the style class and adding the `text` config.

```
{
   xtype: 'tbbutton',
   cls: 'x-btn-text-icon',
   icon: 'images/bomb.png',
   text: 'Tha Bomb'
}
```

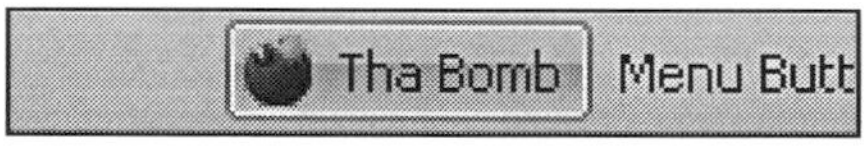


Another method for creating an icon button is to apply a CSS class to it that contains a background image. With this method we can keep the references to images in our CSS instead of our JavaScript, which is preferable whenever possible.

```
{
   xtype: 'tbbutton',
   iconCls: 'bomb'
}
```

The CSS to go along with this would have a background image defined, and the CSS 'important' flag set.

```
.bomb {
    background-image: url( images/bomb.png ) !important;
}
```

## Button events and handlers—click me!

A button needs to do more than just look pretty—it needs to react to the user. This is where the button's handler and events come in. A `handler` is a function that is executed when a button is clicked.

The `handler` config is where we add our function, which can be an anonymous function like below or a method of a class—any function will do:

```
{
    xtype: 'button',
    text: 'Button',
    handler: function(){
        Ext.Msg.alert('Boo', 'Here I am');
    }
}
```

This code will pop up an alert message when the button is clicked. Just about every handler or event in Ext JS passes a reference to the component that triggered the event as the first argument. This makes it easy to work with whichever component that fired this handler, calling the disable method on it.

```
{
    xtype: 'tbbutton',
    text: 'Button',
    handler: function(f){
        f.disable();
    }
}
```

We can take this reference to the button—a reference to itself—and access all of the properties and functions of that button. For this sample, we have called the `disable` function which grays out the button and makes it non-functional.

We can have more fun than just disabling a button. Why don't we try something more useful?

## Loading content on menu item click

Let's take our button click and do something more useful with it. For this example, we are going to add a `config` option named `helpfile` to each menu item that will be used to determine what content file to load in the body of our page:

```
{
   xtype: 'tbsplit',
   text: 'Help',
   menu: [{
      text: 'Genre',
      helpfile: 'genre',
      handler: Movies.showHelp
   },{
      text: 'Director',
      helpfile: 'director',
      handler: Movies.showHelp
   },{
      text: 'Title',
      helpfile: 'title',
      handler: Movies.showHelp
   }]
}
```

Note the `helpfile` config option that we have added to each of the menu items configs. We have made this config property up so that we have a way to store a variable that is unique to each menu item. This is possible because config properties can be anything we need them to be, and are copied into the Component upon construction, and become properties of the Component. In this case, we are using a config property as a reference to the name of the file we want to load.

The other new thing we are doing is creating a collection of functions to handle the menu item click. These functions are all organized into a `Movies` object.

```
var Movies = function() {
    var helpbody;
    return {
        showHelp : function(btn){
            Movies.doLoad(btn.helpfile);
        },
        doLoad : function(file){
            helpbody = helpbody ||
                Ext.getBody().createChild({tag:'div'});
            helpbody.load({
                url: 'html/' + file + '.txt'
            });
        },
        setQuality: function(q) {
            helpbody = helpbody ||
                Ext.getBody().createChild({tag:'div'});
            helpbody.update(q);
```

```
            }
        };
    }();
```

This piece of code is worth reading a few times until you understand it. It illustrates the creation of a singleton object.

Notice that the function has `()` after it. It is called immediately returning an object, instead of a class that could be instantiated.

The `Movies` variable is assigned to reference *whatever that function returns*. It does not reference the function.

The object returned from that function contains three functions. These are the "member functions" of the `Movies` singleton object. It offers utility methods which our example code will use.

All the functions have access to the `helpbody` variable because they were declared within the same function it was declared in. They can use that variable, but it is not available to outside code. This is an important capability of singleton objects built in this slightly confusing manner.

# Form fields in a toolbar

As the Toolbar class inherits from Container, it can be used to house any Ext JS Component. Naturally, form fields and combo boxes are very useful items to have on a toolbar. These are added as child items just as with all Container classes we have encountered so far:

```
{
    xtype: 'textfield'
}
```

In the same way as we created form fields in the last chapter, we add the form fields to the items array, which will place the form fields within the toolbar. Now let's make the form field do something useful, by having it perform the same functionality as our help menu, but in a more dynamic way.

```
{
    xtype: 'textfield',
    listeners: {
        specialkey: Movies.doSearch
    }
}
```

This listener is added directly to the form field's config. For this, we are using a `specialkey` listener, which we used in the previous chapter. This is the listener that is used to capture edit keystrokes, such as *Enter* and *Delete* among others. The `handler` function will be added to our small `Movies` class created earlier:

```
doSearch : function(field, keyEvent){
    if (keyEvent.getKey() == Ext.EventObject.ENTER) {
        Movies.doLoad(field.getValue());
    }
}
```

Now the text field in our toolbar that enables us to type in the name of the text file to load should look like the following. Try typing in some of the samples used in our menu, such as **director** or **title:**

# Buttons don't have to be in a toolbar

Up until now, we have been dealing with buttons in toolbars. But because buttons are part of the Ext JS Components class hierarchy, they can be used as child items of any Container, not just toolbars. When used outside of a toolbar, they are themed in a slightly different way.

A button can be added to the items array, just like we would add a panel or other child components.

```
new Ext.Window({
    title: 'Help',
    id: 'helpwin',
    width: 300,
    height: 300,
    items: [{
        xtype: 'button',
        text: 'Close',
        handler: function(){
            Ext.getCmp('helpwin').close();
        }
    }]
}).load("html/director.txt ").show();
```

The above code fragment would produce the following display:

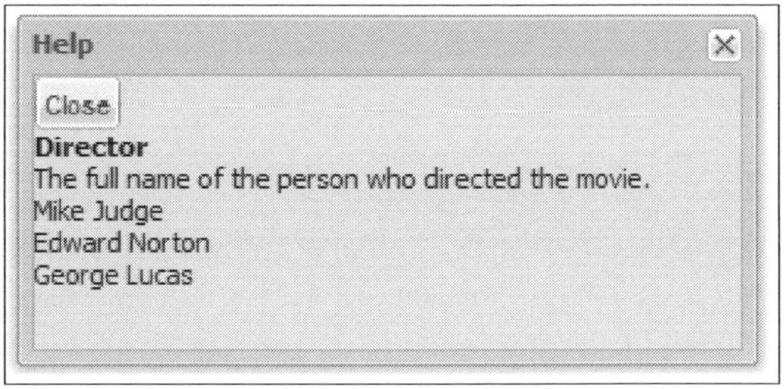


# Toolbars in panels

As mentioned at the beginning of this chapter, toolbars can be configured into all Ext JS Panel classes (Panel, GridPanel, TreePanel, and Window) docked either above or below the panel, body (or both)

Panel classes, such as the window and the grid, have a top and bottom toolbar config, along with a buttons config:

- `tbar`: A toolbar, or toolbar configuration object, or an array specifying toolbar child items. This causes a toolbar to be docked above the panel's body.
- `bbar`: A toolbar, or toolbar configuration object, or an array specifying toolbar child items. This causes a toolbar to be docked below the panel's body.
- `fbar`: Also may be specified as `buttons`. A toolbar, or toolbar configuration object, or an array specifying toolbar child items, which specifies a toolbar to be placed into the panel's `footer` element.

If we wanted to place a toolbar at the top of a window, we would specify a `tbar` config option which references an array of toolbar child config objects like this:

```
new Ext.Window({
    title: 'Help',
    width: 300,
    height: 300,
    renderTo: document.body,
    closeAction: 'hide',
    layout: 'fit',
    tbar: [{
        text: 'Close',
        handler: function(){
            winhelp.hide();
        }
```

```
        },{
            text: 'Disable',
            handler: function(t){
                t.disable();
            }
        }]
    });
```

When this window is activated by clicking the **Director** help menu entry, this produces the following display:

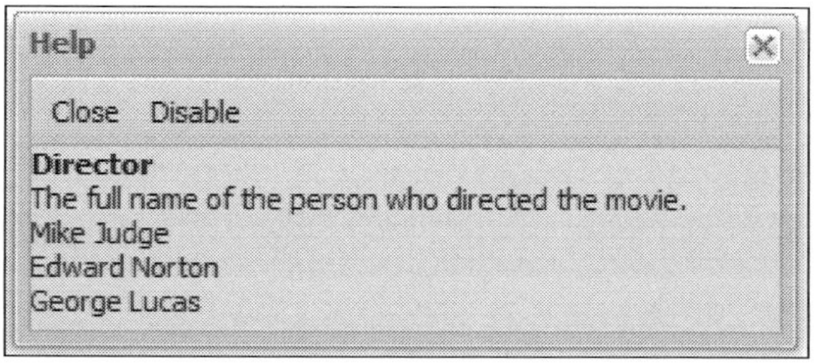


Of course if we wanted that same toolbar on the bottom of the window, we can change from a `tbar` to a `bbar`.

We can also specify a toolbar (or config of a toolbar, or toolbar's items) to be rendered into the footer area of a panel or window. Buttons are themed as normal buttons in a footer bar, and by default are aligned to the right:

```
new Ext.Window({
    title: 'Help',
    width: 300,
    height: 300,
    renderTo: document.body,
    closeAction: 'hide',
    layout: 'fit',
    fbar: [{
        text: 'Close',
        handler: function(){
            winhelp.hide();
        }
    }]
});
```

If the help window was configured in this way, it would display like this:

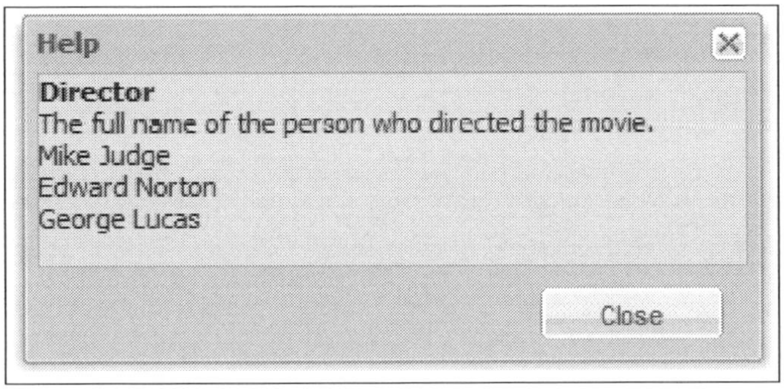


Ext JS also has a custom toolbar for paged grids which contains all of the buttons for moving through pages of results. We will cover this special toolbar in the grid chapter later in this book.

# Toolbars unleashed

As mentioned above, the toolbar class is a special type of Container class which lays out its child components in a particular, preconfigured way. We can use it to house more complex Components, and we can experiment with using different layout types to size and arrange the child Components in different ways. Layouts will be covered in Chapter 7, but we can see some of their power in our final toolbar example.

In the final example, we use the `hbox` (horizontal box) layout to arrange ButtonGroups across the toolbar, and force them to be vertically sized to the size of the highest one, to produce a pleasing, even ribbon effect.

```
new Ext.Panel({
    title: 'Panel with heavyweight toolbar',
    renderTo: document.body,
    width: 600,
    height: 400,
    tbar: new Ext.Toolbar({
        layout: {
            type: 'hbox',
            align: 'stretchmax'
        },
        items: [{
            xtype: 'buttongroup',
            title: 'Group 1',
            columns: 1,
            items: [{
```

```
                text: 'Group 1 Button One',
                handler: handlerFn
            },{
                text: 'Group 1 Button Two',
                handler: handlerFn
            },{
                text: 'Group 1 Button Three',
                handler: handlerFn
            }]
        },{
```

This example will produce output like this:

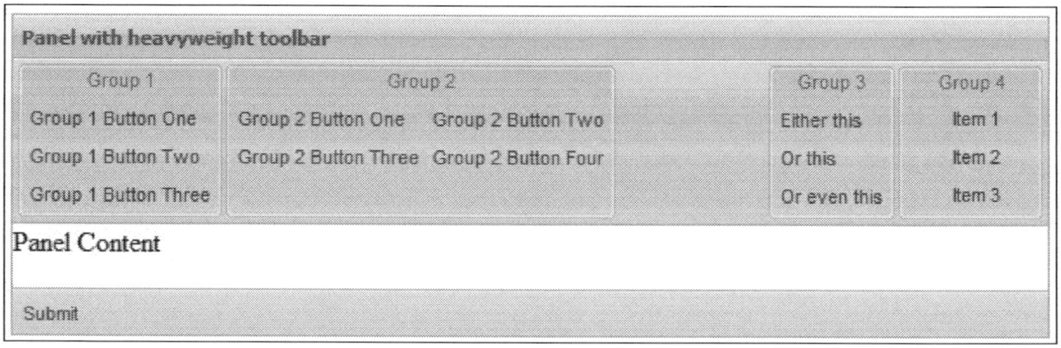


This example illustrates the concept that a toolbar is a Container which may contain any Component, and also that a ButtonGroup is a Container with the same heritage. The first three ButtonGroups contain Buttons; the last one for a slight change of style contains MenuItems.

# Summary

In this chapter, we had the chance to play with a couple of different ways to create toolbar items, including using a config object or its shortcut. The many options available for toolbars make them a useful component for everything from the simplest button bar, to a complex combination of buttons, menus, and form fields. Interacting with the buttons, menus, and form fields is easy using the built-in handlers.

In the next chapter we will get to know one of the most powerful and useful Components in the Ext JS Component family, The GridPanel.

# 5
# Displaying Data with Grids

The grid is, without doubt, one of the most widely-used components of Ext JS. We all have data, and this needs to be presented to the end user in an easy-to-understand manner. The spreadsheet (a.k.a. grid) is the perfect way to do this—the concept has been around for quite a while because it works. Ext JS takes that concept and makes it flexible and downright amazing!

In this chapter we will be:

- Using a GridPanel to display structured data in a user-friendly manner
- Reading data from the server (which provides the data from a database) to display in the grid
- Working with a grid's events and manipulating the grid's features
- Using some advanced data formatting and display techniques for grids
- Paging data in a grid
- Exploring highly efficient grid types for displaying large datasets

We will cover how to define the rows and columns, but more importantly, we will learn how to make the grid a very useful part of our application. We can do this by adding custom rendered cells that contain images, and change styles based on data values. In doing this we are adding real value to our grid by breaking out of the boundaries of simple spreadsheet data display!

# What is a grid anyway?

Ext JS grids are similar to a spreadsheet; there are two main parts to each spreadsheet:

- Columns
- Rows

Here our columns are **Title**, **Released**, **Genre**, and **Price**. Each of the rows contains movies such as **The Big Lebowski**, **Super Troopers**, and so on. The rows are really our data; each row in the grid represents a record of data held in a data store.

# A GridPanel is databound

Like many Ext JS Components, such as the ComboBox we worked with in Chapter 3, the GridPanel class is bound to a data store which provides it with the data shown in the user interface. So the first step in creating our GridPanel is creating and loading a store.

The data store in Ext JS gives us a consistent way of reading different data formats such as XML and JSON, and using this data in a consistent way throughout all of the Ext JS widgets. Regardless of whether this data is originally provided in JSON, XML, an array, or even a custom data type of our own, it's all accessed in the same way thanks to the consistency of the data store and how it uses a separate reader class which interprets the raw data.

Instead of using a pre-configured class such as the `ArrayStore` used in our ComboBox from Chapter 3, we will explicitly define the classes used to define and load a store.

# The record definition

We first need to define the fields which a Record contains. A **Record** is a single row of data and we need to define the field names, which we want to be read into our store. We define the data type for each field, and, if necessary, we define how to convert from the raw data into the field's desired data type.

What we will be creating is a new class. We actually create a *constructor* which will be used by Ext JS to create records for the store.

As the 'create' method creates a constructor, we reference the resulting function with a capitalized variable name, as per standard CamelCase syntax:

```
var Movie = Ext.data.Record.create([
    'id',
    'coverthumb',
    'title',
    'director',
    'runtime',
    {name: 'released', type: 'date', dateFormat: 'Y-m-d'},
    'genre',
    'tagline',
    {name: 'price', type: 'float'},
    {name: 'available', type: 'bool'}
]);
```

Each element in the passed array defines a field within the record. If an item is just a string, the string is used as the name of the field, and no data conversion is performed; the field's value will be whatever the `Reader` object (which we will learn more about soon) finds in the raw data.

If data conversion is required, then a field definition in the form of an object literal instead of a string may contain the following config options:

- `Name`: The name by which the field will be referenced.
- `type`: The data type in which the raw data item will be converted to when stored in the record. Values may be `'int'`, `'float'`, `'string'`, `'date'`, or `'bool'`.
- `dateFormat`: If the type of data to be held in the field is a date type, then we need to specify a format string as used by the `Date.parseDate` function.

Defining the data type can help to alleviate future problems, instead of having to deal with all string type data defining the data type, and lets us work with actual dates, Boolean values, and numbers. The following is a list of the built in data types:

| Field type | Description | Information |
|---|---|---|
| `string` | String data | |
| `int` | Number | Uses JavaScript's `parseInt` function |
| `float` | Floating point number | Uses JavaScript's `parseFloat` function |
| `boolean` | `True/False` data | |
| `date` | Date data | `dateFormat` config required to interpret incoming data. |

Now that the first step has been completed, and we have a simple Record definition in place, we can move on to the next step of configuring a Reader that is able to understand the raw data.

# The Reader

A store may accept raw data in several different formats. Raw data rows may be in the form of a simple array of values, or an object with named properties referencing the values, or even an XML element in which the values are child nodes.

We need to configure a store with a Reader object which knows how to extract data from the raw data that we are dealing with. There are three built in Reader classes in Ext JS.

## ArrayReader

The `ArrayReader` class can create a record from an array of values.

By default, values are read out of the raw array into a record's fields in the order that the fields were declared in the record definition we created. If fields are not declared in the same order that the values occur in the rows, the field's definition may contain a `mapping` config which specifies the array index from which we retrieve the field's value.

## JsonReader

This `JSONReader` class is the most commonly used, and can create a record from raw JSON by decoding and reading the object's properties.

By default, the field's name is used as the property name from which it takes the field's value. If a different property name is required, the field's definition may contain a `mapping` config which specifies the name of the property from which to retrieve the field's value.

## XmlReader

An `XMLReader` class can create a record from an XML element by accessing child nodes of the element.

By default, the field's name is used as the XPath mapping (not unlike HTML) from which to take the field's value. If a different mapping is required, the field's definition may contain a mapping config which specifies the mapping from which to retrieve the field's value.

## Loading our data store

In our first attempt, we are going to create a grid that uses simple local array data stored in a JavaScript variable. The data we're using below in the `movieData` variable is taken from a very small movie database of some of my favorite movies, and is similar to the data that will be pulled from an actual server- side database later in this chapter.

The data store needs two things: the data itself, and a description of the data—or what could be thought of as the fields. A `reader` will be used to read the data from the array, and this is where we define the fields of data contained in our array.

The following code should be placed before the Ext JS `onReady` function:

```
var movieData = [
    [
      1,
      "Office Space",
      "Mike Judge",
      89,
      "1999-02-19",
      1,
      "Work Sucks",
      "19.95",
      1
    ],[
      3,
      "Super Troopers",
      "Jay Chandrasekhar",
```

```
        100,
        "2002-02-15",
        1,
        "Altered State Police",
        "14.95",
        1
      ]
      //...more rows of data removed for readability...//
    ];
  var store = new Ext.data.Store({
    data: movieData, ,
    reader: new Ext.data.ArrayReader({idIndex: 0}, Movie)
  });
```

If we view this code in a browser we would not see anything—that's because a data store is just a way of loading and keeping track of our data. The web browser's memory has our data in it. Now we need to configure the grid to display our data to the user.

# Displaying structured data with a GridPanel

Displaying data in a grid requires several Ext JS classes to cooperate:

- **A** `Store`: As mentioned in Chapter 3, a data store is a client-side analogue of a database table. It encapsulates a set of records, each of which contains a defined set of fields. Full details about data stores are contained in Chapter 15.
- **A** `Record` **definition**: This defines the fields (or "columns" in database terminology) which make up each record in the `Store`. Field name and datatype are defined here. More details are in Chapter 15.
- A Reader which uses a Record definition to extract field values from a raw data object to create the records for a Store.
- A `ColumnModel` which specifies the details of each column, including the column header to display, and the name of the record field to be displayed for each column.
- **A** `GridPanel`: A panel subclass which provides the **controller** logic to bind the above classes together to generate the grid's user interface.

If we were to display the data just as the store sees it now, we would end up with something like this:

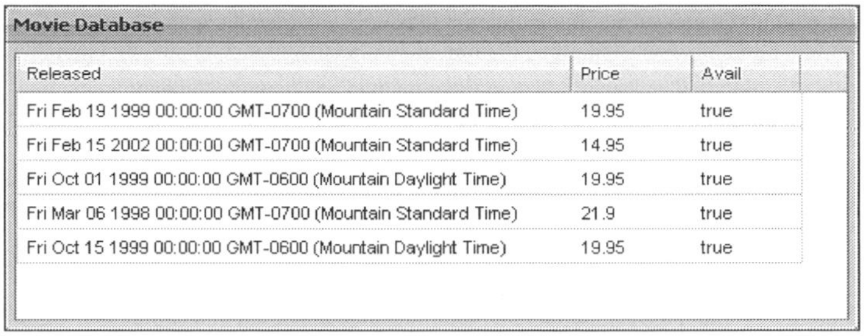
Movie Database
Released
Price
Avail
Fri Feb 19 1999 00:00:00 GMT-0700 (Mountain Standard Time)
19.95
true
Fri Feb 15 2002 00:00:00 GMT-0700 (Mountain Standard Time)
14.95
true
Fri Oct 01 1999 00:00:00 GMT-0600 (Mountain Daylight Time)
19.95
true
Fri Mar 06 1998 00:00:00 GMT-0700 (Mountain Standard Time)
21.9
true
Fri Oct 15 1999 00:00:00 GMT-0600 (Mountain Daylight Time)
19.95
true

Now that is ugly—here's a breakdown of what's happening:

- The **Released** date has been type set properly as a date, and interpreted from the string value in our data. It's provided in a native JavaScript date format—luckily Ext JS has ways to make this look pretty.
- The **Price** column has been type set as a floating point number. Note that there is no need to specify the decimal precision.
- The **Avail** column has been interpreted as an actual Boolean value, even if the raw data was not an actual Boolean value.

As you can see, it's quite useful to specify the type of data that is being read, and apply any special options that are needed so that we don't have to deal with converting data elsewhere in our code.

Before we move on to displaying the data in our grid, we should take a look at how the convert config works, as it can come in quite useful.

# Converting data read into the store

If we need to, we can convert data as it comes into the store, massage it, remove any quirky parts, or create new fields all together. This should not be used as a way to change the display of data; that part will be handled elsewhere.

A common task might be to remove possible errors in the data when we load it, making sure it's in a consistent format for later actions. This can be done using a convert function, which is defined in the 'convert' config by providing a function, or reference to a function. In this case we are going to create a new field by using the data from another field and combining it with a few standard strings.

```
var store = new Ext.data.Store({
  data: movieData,
  reader: new Ext.data.ArrayReader({id:'id'}, [
    'id',
    'title',
```

```
        'director',
        {name: 'released', type: 'date', dateFormat: 'Y-m-d'},
        'genre',
        'tagline',
        'price',
        'available',
        {name:'coverthumb',convert:function(v, rawData){
          return 'images/'+rawData[0]+'m.jpg';
        }}
      ])
    });
```

This convert function when used in this manner will create a new field of data that looks like this:

```
'images/5m.jpg'
```

We will use this new field of data shortly, so let's get a grid up and running.

# Displaying the GridPanel

The class that pulls everything together is the GridPanel. This class takes care of placing the data into columns and rows, along with adding column headers, and boxing it all together in a neat little package.

The movie data store we created isn't much good to anybody just sitting in the computer's memory. Let's display it in a grid by creating a simple GridPanel:

1. Let's add our data store to the following GridPanel code:

```
Ext.onReady(function() {...
var grid = new Ext.grid.GridPanel({
    renderTo: Ext.getBody(),
    frame: true,
    title: 'Movie Database',
    height: 200,
    width: 520,
    store: store,
    colModel: new Ext.grid.ColumnModel({
       defaultSortable: false,
        columns: [
            {header: "Title", dataIndex: 'title'},
            {header: "Director", dataIndex: 'director'},
            {header: "Released", dataIndex: 'released',
```

```
                xtype: 'datecolumn'},
            {header: "Genre", dataIndex: 'genre'},
            {header: "Tagline", dataIndex: 'tagline'}
        ]
    })
});
```

2. Bring this page up in a browser, and here's what we will see:

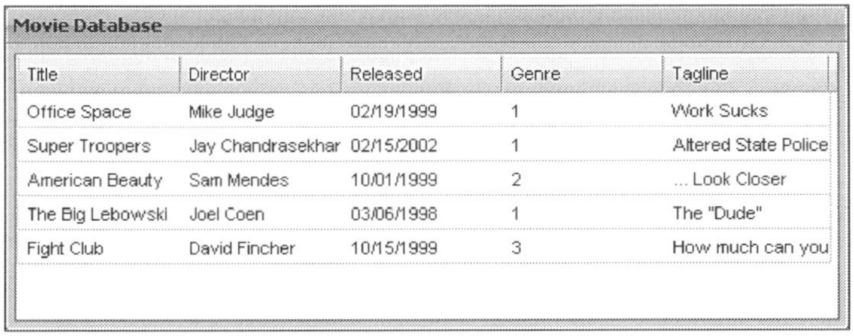
Movie Database
Title
Director
Released
Genre
Tagline
Office Space
Mike Judge
02/19/1999
1
Work Sucks
Super Troopers
Jay Chandrasekhar
02/15/2002
1
Altered State Police
American Beauty
Sam Mendes
10/01/1999
2
... Look Closer
The Big Lebowski
Joel Coen
03/06/1998
1
The "Dude"
Fight Club
David Fincher
10/15/1999
3
How much can you

# How did that work?

All except two of the config options used here should be familiar to us now because they are inherited from base classes such as the panel

Believe it or not, there are only **two** new config options that are really essential to make a GridPanel different from a Panel! They are:

- `store`: This references a store object which provides the data displayed in the grid. Any changes to the store are automatically applied to the UI.
- `colModel`: This is a `ColumnModel` object which defines how the column headers and data cells are to be displayed. It defines a header for each column, and the name of the field to display in that column.

We can almost read through the configuration like a sentence:

> *Render our grid into the body of the document, frame it, and give it a title of 'Movie Database'. The height will be 200 and the width 520; it will use our 'store' data store and have the columns specified.*

This again shows us the benefits of both object-based configuration, and the Ext JS class hierarchy.

The configuration is readable, not a series of parameters whose order must be remembered.

Also, the `renderTo` `frame`, `title`, `height`, and `width` options are all inherited from base classes, and are common to all `Panel` classes. So we will never have to think about these once we have mastered the `Panel` class.

# Defining a grid's column model

The `ColumnModel` class encapsulates a set of column objects, each of which defines an individual column's characteristics. This is a mirror image of the field definitions in the Record definition which specify how to read in a field's value from a raw data object.

The `ColumnModel` works at the opposite end of the data flow. It defines which fields from each record to display (you don't have to show them all), and also how the value from each field is to be converted back into string form for display in the UI.

The `ColumnModel` also maintains defaults to be applied to the columns which it manages, and offers an API to manipulate the columns, and provide information about them.

To define our grid's columns, we configure the `ColumnModel` with an array of `column` config objects. Each of the objects within a `ColumnModel's` `columns` array defines one column. The most useful options within a column definition are:

- `header`: The HTML to display in the header area at the top of the column.
- `dataIndex`: The name of the record field—as defined in the Record definition—to display in each cell of the column.
- `xtype`: The type of column to create. This is optional, and defaults to a basic column which displays the referenced data field unchanged. But to display a formatted date using the default date format, we can specify 'datecolumn'. There are several other column `xtype`s described in the API documentation.

So a `ColumnModel` definition is like this:

```
new Ext.grid.ColumnModel({
    defaultSortable: false,
    columns: [
        {header: 'Title', dataIndex: 'title'},
        {header: 'Director', dataIndex: 'director'},
        {header: 'Released', dataIndex: 'released'},
        {header: 'Genre', dataIndex: 'genre'},
        {header: 'Tagline', dataIndex: 'tagline'}
    ]
})
```

This will create grid column headers that look like the following. We have also set the default of sortable for each column to false by using a master config in the Column Model:

Here are some other useful config options for each column within the column model:

| Option | Description | Usage |
|---|---|---|
| `renderer` | Specifies a function which returns formatted HTML to display in a grid cell | Can be used to format the data for this column into your preferred format. Any type of data can be transformed. We will learn about these in the next few pages. |
| `hidden` | Hides the column | Boolean value defining whether or not the column should be displayed. |
| `hideable` | Allows the UI to offer checkboxes to hide/show the column | If a column must not be hidden (or indeed begins hidden and must not be shown) by the user, set this option to `true`. |
| `width` | Specifies the column width in pixels | The width of the column. Default is 100 pixels; overflowing content is hidden. |
| `sortable` | Specifies whether the column is sortable | Boolean value specifying whether or not the column can be sorted. Overrides the `defaultSortable` configuration of the ColumnModel. |

# Built-in column types

There are several built-in column types, all identified by their own unique `xtype` which provide special formatting capabilities for cell data. The usage of these is illustrated in the example code for this chapter.

## BooleanColumn

Displays the text **true** or **false** (or the locale specific equivalents if you include the correct Ext JS locale file) in the column's cells depending on whether the cell's field value is true or false. It can be configured with alternative true/false display values. Example usage:

```
{
    xtype: 'booleancolumn',
    header: 'Available',
    dataIndex: 'available',
    trueText: 'Affirmative',
    falseText: 'Negative'
}
```

## DateColumn

This displays the cell's field value as a formatted date. By default, it uses the date format `'m/d/Y'`, but it can be configured with a `format` option specifying an alternative format. The value in the column's associated field must be a date object. Example usage:

```
{
    header: "Released",
    dataIndex: 'released',
    xtype: 'datecolumn',
    format: 'M d Y',
    width: 70
}
```

## NumberColumn

Displays the cell's field value formatted according to a format string as used in `Ext.util.Format.number`. The default format string is `"0.00"`. Example usage:

```
{
    header: "Runtime",
    dataIndex: 'runtime',
    xtype: 'numbercolumn',
    format: '0',
    width: 70
}
```

## TemplateColumn

Uses an `Ext.XTemplate` string to produce complex HTML with any fields from within the row's record embedded.

```
{
    header: "Title",
    dataIndex: 'title',
    xtype: 'templatecolumn',
    tpl: '<img src="{coverthumb}" ' +
        'width="50" height="68" align="left">'+
        '<b style="font-size:13px;">{title}</b><br>'+
        'Director:<i> {director}</i><br>{tagline}'
}
```

The tokens in the template (tpl) between braces are field names from the store's record. The values are substituted in to create the rendered value. See the API documentation for the `Ext.XTemplate` class for more information.

### ActionColumn

Displays icons in a cell, and may be configurable with a *handler* function to process clicks on an icon. Example illustrating arguments passed to the handler function:

```
{
    header: 'Delete',
    sortable: false,
    xtype: 'actioncolumn',
    width: 40,
    align: 'center',
    iconCls: 'delete-movie',
    handler: function(grid, rowIndex, colIdex, item, e) {
        deleteMovie(grid.getStore().getAt(rowIndex));
    }
}
```

# Using cell renderers

If the built in column types cannot create the desired output in a grid cell (which is very unlikely given the data formatting capabilities of the `XTemplate` class), then we can write a custom renderer function.

We can do some pretty neat things with cell rendering. There are few limitations to stop us from making the cell look like or contain whatever we want. All that needs to be done is to specify one of the built-in cell formatting functions provided by Ext JS, such as `usMoney`, or we can create our own cell renderer that returns a formatted value. Let's take a look at using the built-in cell renderers first. Then we can experiment with creating our own.

## Formatting data using the built-in cell renderers

Many built-in formatting functions exist to take care of common rendering requirements. One that I use quite often is the date renderer:

```
renderer: Ext.util.Format.dateRenderer('m/d/Y')
```

Some of the built-in renderers include commonly-required formatting, such as `money`, `capitalize`, and `lowercase`.

Here are a few of the renderers that I find most useful:

| Renderer | Description | Usage |
|---|---|---|
| `dateRenderer` | Formats a date for display | Can be used to format the data for this column into our preferred date display format. Any type of date can be transformed. |
| `uppercase` `lowercase` | Upper and lower case conversion | Converts the string to completely upper or lower case text. |
| `capitalize` | Pretty text | Formats a text string to have correct capitalization. |

# Creating lookup data stores—custom cell rendering

We're going to start by taking the 'genre' column, which has a numeric value, and look up that value in the genre data store we created earlier in Chapter 3 to find the textual representation of our genre number.

First, we add a config option to the column model that tells the columns which function to use for rendering each cell's content.

```
{header: 'Genre', dataIndex: 'genre', renderer: genre_name}
```

Now we need to create that function. The function being called by the column is passed the value of its cell as the first argument. The second argument is a cell object, while the third is the record for the current row being rendered, followed by row index, column index, and the store—none of which we will use for this renderer. So let's just specify the first argument as 'val' and leave off the rest.

```
function genre_name(val) {
    var rec = genres.getById(val);
    return rec ? rec.get('genre') : val;
}
```

The renderer function is passed the value of the current cell of data. This value can be compared, massaged, and any actions we need can be performed on it— whatever value is returned by the function is rendered directly to the grid cell. A `queryBy` method is used to filter the data from our genre store and find the matching row of data. It accepts a function that performs a comparison against each row of data, and returns `true` to use the row that matches.

Just for good measure, here is a compacted version of the same function. It's not as easy to read as the first version, but accomplishes the same result.

```
function genre_name(val){
  return genres.queryBy(function(rec){
    return rec.data.id == val;
  }).itemAt(0).get('genre');
}
```

# Combining two columns

The lookup data store is a very useful renderer. However, it's also common for developers to need to combine two columns to form a single cell. For example, to perform a calculation on a pair of columns to figure out a total, percentage, remainder, and so on, or to concatenate two or more text fields into a fancy display.

Let's just take the title of our movie, and append the tagline field underneath the title. The first step will be to hide the tagline column, since it will be displayed along with the title field—we don't need it shown in two places. Hiding the column can be done in our column model, and while the column will be hidden from display, the data still exists in our store.

```
{header: 'Tagline', dataIndex: 'tagline', hidden: true}
```

The next step is our `renderer` function that will take care of combining the fields. Here we will start to use the rest of the arguments passed to the renderer function.

```
function title_tagline(val, x, rec){
  return '<b>'+val+'</b><br>'+rec.get('tagline');
}
```

This function simply concatenates a couple of strings along with the data and returns the modified value. I went ahead and bolded the title in this sample to provide some contrast between the two pieces of data. As you can see, HTML tags work just fine within grid cells. The next step would be to add the renderer config to our column model, referencing the `title_tagline` function that we just created.

```
{header: 'Title', dataIndex: 'title', renderer: title_tagline}
```

This will make the **Title** column look like this:

Title
Director
Released
Genre
Price
Office Space
Work Sucks
Mike Judge
02/19/1999
Comedy
$19.95

# Generating HTML and graphics

Let's get some good visuals by placing an image into each row, which will show the cover art for each movie title. As we just found out, we can use plain HTML within the cell. So all that needs to happen is to create a renderer that grabs our field containing the file name of the image—we created in the store earlier—and write that into an IMG tag as the SRC attribute.

```
function cover_image(val){
  return '<img src="' +val+'">';
}
```

By creating this fairly straightforward function, and setting it as the column renderer, we have an image in our grid:

```
{header: 'Cover', dataIndex: 'coverthumb', renderer:
                                       cover_image}
```

If you make all these renderer additions, the grid should now look like this:

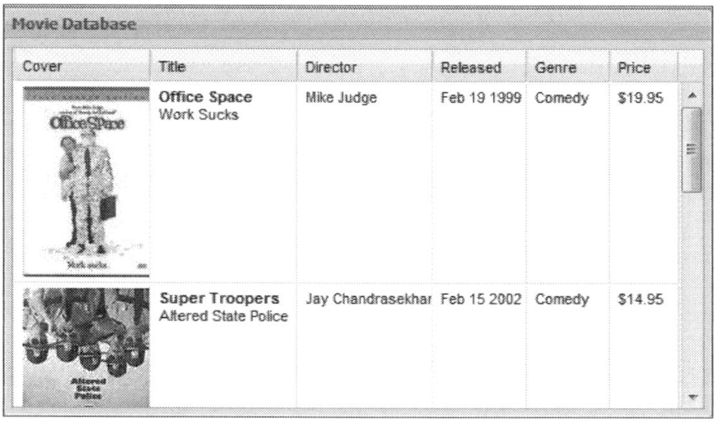


# Built-in features

Ext JS has some very nice built-in features to help complete the spreadsheet-like interface. Columns have built-in menus that provide access to sorting, displaying, and hiding columns:

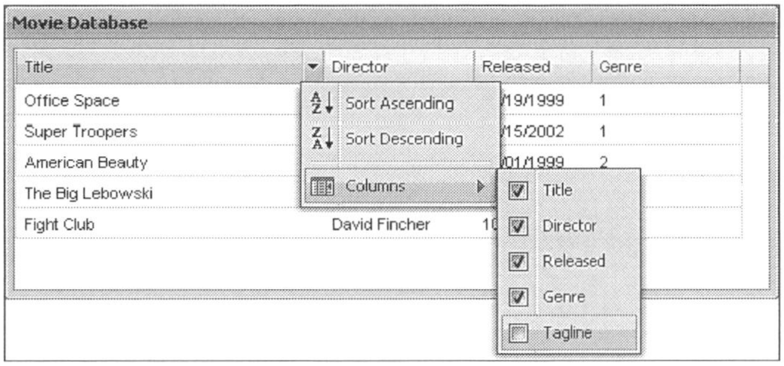


# Client-side sorting

Unless specified as a server-side (remotely) sorted grid, an Ext JS grid is by default able to sort columns on the client side. Server-side sorting should be used if the data is paged, or if the data is in such a format that client-side sorting is not possible. Client-side sorting is quick, easy, and built-in—just set a column's `sortable` config to `true`:

```
{header: 'Tagline', dataIndex: 'tagline', id: 'tagline', sortable:
true}
```

We can also accomplish this after the grid has been rendered; to make this easier and predictable we need to assign an ID to the column as shown above:

```
var colmodel = grid.getColumnModel();
colmodel.getColumnById('tagline').sortable = true;
```

Our column model controls the display of columns and column headers. If we grab a reference to the column model by asking for it from the grid, then we can make changes to the columns after it has been rendered. We do this by using the `getColumnById` handler that the column model provides us with, and which accepts the column ID as the argument.

# Hidden/visible columns

Using the column header menu, columns can be hidden or shown. This can also be changed at a config level, to have columns hidden by default, as shown below:

```
{header: "Tagline", dataIndex: 'tagline', id: 'tagline', hidden:
true}
```

The more exciting way is to do this after the grid has been rendered, by using the functions Ext JS provides:

```
var colmodel = grid.getColumnModel();
colmodel.setHidden(colmodel.getIndexById('tagline'),true);
```

Grabbing a reference to the column model again will allow us to make this change.

# Column reordering

Dragging a column header will allow the user to reorder the entire column into a new order within the grid. All of this is enabled by default as part of the built-in functionality of the grid.

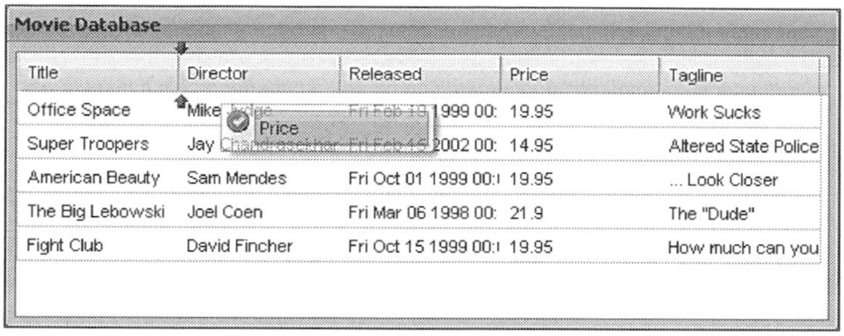


Any column can be dragged to a different order in the grid. This screenshot shows the **Price** column being moved to between the **Title** and **Director** columns.

We can disable this functionality entirely by setting a config option in the GridPanel:

```
enableColumnMove: false
```

This move event—and many other events in the grid—can be monitored and responded to. For example, we could monitor the movement of columns and pop up a message based on where the column was moved to:

```
grid.getColumnModel().on('columnmoved',
  function(cm,oindex,nindex) {
    var title = 'You Moved '+cm.getColumnHeader(nindex);
    if (oindex > nindex){
        var dirmsg = (oindex-nindex)+' Column(s) to the Left';
    }else{
        var dirmsg = (nindex-oindex)+' Column(s) to the Right';
    }
    Ext.Msg.alert(title,dirmsg);
  }
);
```

Many different events can be monitored using the same technique. The grid, data store, and column model each have their own set of events that can be monitored, all of which we will learn about in more detail later in this chapter.

# Displaying server-side data in the grid

With Ext JS we can pull data into our web page in many ways. We started by pulling in local array data for use in the grid. Now we are going to pull the data in from an external file and a web server (database).

# Loading the movie database from an XML file

We have this great movie database now, but each time I want to add a new movie I have to edit the JavaScript array. So why not store and pull our data from an XML file instead? This will be easier to update, and the XML file could even be generated from a database query or a custom script.

Let's take a look at an example of how our XML file would be laid out:

```
<?xml version="1.0" encoding="UTF-8"?>
<dataset>
    <row>
      <id>1</id>
      <title>Office Space</title>
      <director>Mike Judge</director>
      <released>1999-02-19</released>
      <genre>1</genre>
      <tagline>Work Sucks</tagline>
      <price>19.95</price>
      <active>1</active>
    </row>
    <row>
      <id>3</id>
      <title>Super Troopers</title>
      <director>Jay Chandrasekhar</director>
      <released>2002-02-15</released>
      <genre>1</genre>
      <tagline>Altered State Police</tagline>
      <price>14.95</price>
      <active>1</active>
    </row>
  //...more rows of data removed for readability...//
</dataset>
```

The other change we would need to make is to alter the data reader, and set the location of our XML file so that the data store knows where to fetch the data from.

There are four basic changes that need to happen when moving from local to remote data:

- The `url` option, specifying the location of our data needs to be added—this will replace the `data` option that we used to store local data
- The reader is changed from an `ArrayReader` to an `XmlReader` to deal with the differences involved in reading from an XML format instead of an array format
- The `XmlReader` is told which element contains a record or row of data by setting the `record` option
- We will need to call the store's `load` function that tells our data store to pull in the data from the file on the server and parse it into memory

```
var store = new Ext.data.Store({
  url: 'movies.xml',
  reader: new Ext.data.XmlReader({
    record:'row',
    idPath:'id'
  }, Movie),
  autoLoad: true
});
```

Try making these changes and see if your grid still works—there should be no noticeable difference when changing data sources or formats.

Note that to make the change from local to remote data and from an array format to an XML format, the only changes we need to make were to the data store. Ext JS isolates these types of changes by using a common data store that is able to use an external reader to read many formats and store them internally in the same way.

# Loading the movie database from a JSON file

We're in the same boat as XML with this data format. Just changing the reader and setting up some config options will take care of everything.

The JSON rows of data are expected to be in the form of an array of objects—our `movies.json` file will therefore contain data that looks like this:

```
{
  success:true,
  rows:[
    {
      "id":"1",
      "title":"Office Space",
```

```
      "director":"Mike Judge",
      "released":"1999-02-19",
      "genre":"1",
      "tagline":"Work Sucks",
      "price":"19.95",
      "active":"1"
    },{
      "id":"3",
      "title":"Super Troopers",
      "director":"Jay Chandrasekhar",
      "released":"2002-02-15",
      "genre":"1",
      "tagline":"Altered State Police",
      "price":"14.95",
      "active":"1"
    }
    //...more rows of data removed for readability...//
  ]
}
```

The main difference between setting up a JSON reader versus an XML reader, is that the JSON reader needs to know the name of the root element that holds our array of objects (the rows of data). So instead of specifying a `record` config, we need to specify a `root` config:

```
var store = new Ext.data.Store({
  url: 'movies.json',
  reader: new Ext.data.JsonReader({
    root:'rows',
    idProperty:'id'
  }, Movie),
  autoLoad: true
});
```

This grid will have an identical look and the same functionality as the array and the XML grids that we created earlier.

> JSON and arrays are a format native to JavaScript called an Object Literal and Array Literal, and will end up being the quickest formats for the data store (JavaScript) to read, which means that our grid will be displayed much faster than with most other formats, specifically XML.

# Loading data from a database using PHP

The setup for our GridPanel stays the same. But instead of grabbing a static file with the JSON data, we can pull the data from a PHP script that will fetch the data from a database, and format it into JSON that Ext JS is able to read:

```
<?php
// connect to database
$sql = "SELECT * FROM movies";
$arr = array();
If (!$rs = mysql_query($sql)) {
  Echo "{success:false}";
}else{
  while($obj = mysql_fetch_object($rs)){
    $arr[] = $obj;
  }
  Echo "{success:true,rows:".json_encode($arr)."}";
}
?>
```

> The PHP code used in these examples is meant to be the bare minimum needed to get the job done. In a production environment you would want to account for security against SQL injection attacks, other error checking, and probably user authentication—which the example code does not account for.

# Programming the grid

Most of the code we have written so far concerns configuring the grid to be displayed. Often, we will want the grid to do something in response to user input—interaction. One of the common interactions in a grid is to select or move the rows of data. Ext JS refers to this interaction and how it's handled as the "selection model". Let's see how to set up a selection model.

# Working with cell and row selections

Ext JS grids delegate the monitoring of user interaction with the grids rows, cells, and columns to a separate selection model object. The selection model is used to determine how rows, columns, or cells are selected, and how many items can be selected at a time. This allows us to create listeners for these selection events, along with giving us a way to query which rows have been selected.

The built-in selection models are:

- `CellSelectionModel`: This lets the user to select a single cell from the grid
- `RowSelectionModel`: This lets the user select an entire row, or multiple rows from the grid
- `CheckBoxSelectionModel`: This one uses a checkbox to enable row selection

Choosing a selection model is something that depends on your project's requirements. For our movie database, we will use a row selection model, which is the most commonly used type of selection model, and just happens to be the default.

The selection model is defined in the GridPanel config by using the `selModel` config option—the shortform `sm` could also be used.

```
selModel: new Ext.grid.RowSelectionModel({
  singleSelect: true
})
```

We will also pass the selection model a config that specifies single row selections only. This stops the user from selecting multiple rows at the same time.

# Listening to our selection model for selections

Listeners for a grid can be included in many different places depending on the desired interaction. Earlier, we applied a listener to our column model because we wanted to listen for column activity.

Here, we will add a `listener` to the selection model because we want to know when a user has selected a `movie`.

```
sm: new Ext.grid.RowSelectionModel({
  singleSelect: true,
  listeners: {
    rowselect: function(sm, index, record) {
      Ext.Msg.alert('You Selected',record.get('title'));
    }
  }
})
```

The above listener code will result in the following display:

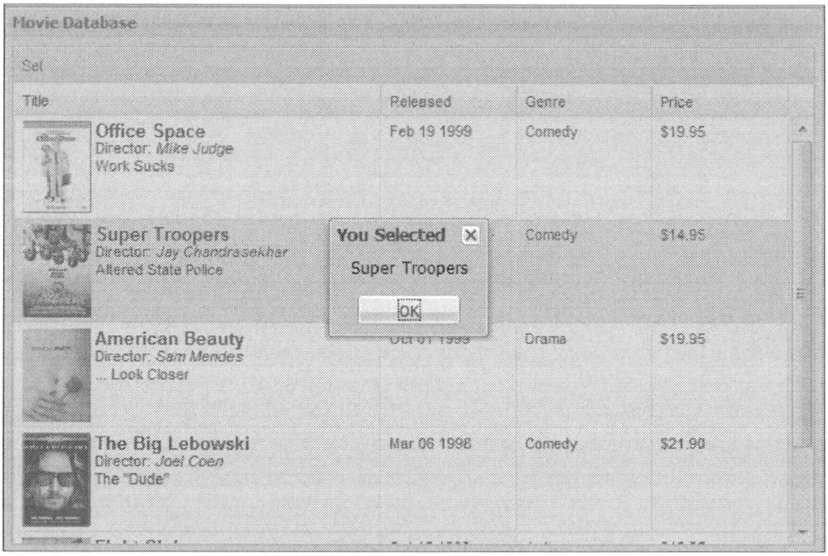


Selecting a row now brings up an alert dialog. Let's take a look at what is happening here:

- A listener is set for the `rowselect` event. This waits for a row to be selected, and then executes our function when this happens
- Our function is passed a selection model, the numeric index of the row selected (starting with zero for the first row), and the data record of the row that was selected
- Using the data record that our function received, we can grab the `title` of the movie selected and put it into a message dialog

# Manipulating the grid (and its data) with code

There are many ways to programmatically manipulate the grid and its data. The key is to understand how the responsibility for managing the grid is broken down between the objects that we use to put a grid together.

In the following discussions we will show use of the store and its associated records for manipulating the data, and use of the selection model for determining how the user is interacting with the grid.

# Altering the grid at the click of a button

Here, we are going to add a top toolbar, which will have a button that brings up a prompt allowing the movie title to be edited. This will use a toolbar and buttons which we explored in Chapter 4, along with the MessageBox from Chapter 2.

```
tbar: [{
  text: 'Change Title',
  handler: function(){
    var sm = grid.getSelectionModel(),
       sel = sm.getSelected();
    if (sm.hasSelection()){
      Ext.Msg.show({
      title: 'Change Title',
          prompt: true,
          buttons: Ext.MessageBox.OKCANCEL,
          value: sel.get('title'),
          fn: function(btn,text){
            if (btn == 'ok'){
              sel.set('title', text);
            }
          }
      });
    }
  }
}]
```

The result of this addition is as follows:

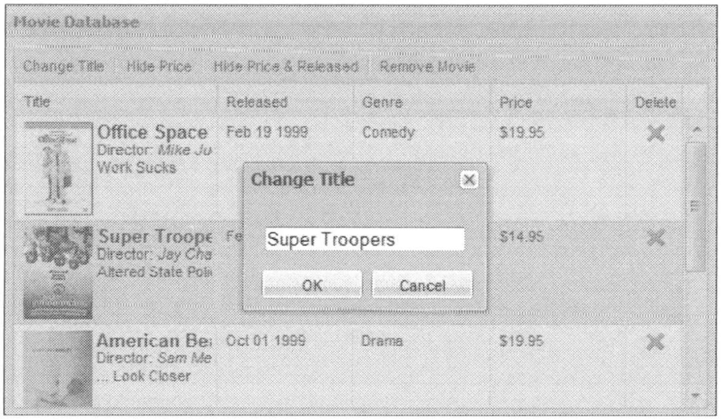

All we are really doing here is changing the data in the data store, which updates the grid automatically. The data in our database on the web server has stayed the same, and the web server has no idea whether anything has changed. It's up to us to communicate this change to the server via an AJAX request or via some other method we may prefer to use. This is covered in the next chapter in case you are wondering.

Let's take a quick look at what's happening here:

- `sm`: The selection model is retrieved from our grid
- `sel`: We used the selection model to retrieve the row that has been selected
- `sel.get`: Using the get method of the currently selected record, we can grab a field's value
- `sel.set`: Using the set method of the currently selected record, we can change a field's value

This basic method can be used to create many fun user interactions. Our limitation is that there are only 24 hours in a day, and sleep catches up with everyone!

# Advanced grid formatting

As we are in the mood to create some user-grid interactions, let us add some more buttons that do fun stuff.

We will now add a button to the top toolbar to allow us to hide or show a column. We will also change the text of the button based on the visibility of the column—a fairly typical interaction:

```
{
  text: 'Hide Price',
  handler: function(btn){
    var cm = grid.getColumnModel(),
        pi = cm.getIndexById('price');
    // is this column visible?
    if (cm.isHidden(pi)){
        cm.setHidden(pi,false);
        btn.setText('Hide Price');
    }else{
        cm.setHidden(pi,true);
        btn.setText('Show Price');
    }
  }
}
```

We have used a new method here—`getIndexById`, which, as you can imagine, gets the column index, which will be a number from zero to one less than the total number of columns. This number is an indicator of where that column is in relation to the other columns. In our grid code, the column `price` is the fourth column, which means that the index is three because indexes start at zero.

# Paging the grid

Paging requires that we have a server-side element (script) which will break up our data into pages. Let's start with that. PHP is well-suited to this, and the code is easy to understand and interpret into other languages. So we will use PHP for our example.

When a paging grid is paged, it will pass `start` and `limit` parameters to the server-side script. This is typical of what's used with a database to select a subset of records. Our script can read in these parameters and use them pretty much verbatim in the database query. The start value represents which row of data to start returning, and the limit specifies how many total rows of data to return from the starting point.

Here is a typical PHP script that would handle paging. We will name the file `movies-paging.php`.

```
<?php
// connect to database
$start = ($_REQUEST['start'] != '') ? $_REQUEST['start'] : 0;
$limit = ($_REQUEST['limit'] != '') ? $_REQUEST['limit'] : 3;
$count_sql = "SELECT * FROM movies";
$sql = $count_sql . " LIMIT ".$start.", ".$limit;
$arr = array();
If (!$rs = mysql_query($sql)) {
  Echo "{success:false}";
}else{
  $rs_count = mysql_query($count_sql);
  $results = mysql_num_rows($rs_count);
  while($obj = mysql_fetch_object($rs)){
    $arr[] = $obj;
  }
  Echo "{success:true,results:".$results.",
        rows:".json_encode($arr)."}";
}
?>
```

This PHP script will take care of the server-side part of paging. So now we just need to add a paging toolbar to the grid—it's really quite simple!

Earlier we had used a top toolbar to hold some buttons for messing with the grid. Now we are going to place a paging toolbar in the bottom toolbar slot (mostly because I think paging bars look dumb on the top).

The following code will add a paging toolbar:

```
bbar: new Ext.PagingToolbar({
  pageSize: 3,
  store: store
})
```

And of course we need to change the `url` of our data store to the `url` of the PHP server-side paging code. A `totalProperty` is also required when paging data. This is the variable name that holds the total record count of rows in the database as returned from the server side script. This lets the paging toolbar figure out when to enable and disable the previous and next buttons among other things.

```
var store = new Ext.data.Store({
  url: 'movies-paged.php',
  reader: new Ext.data.JsonReader({
    root:'rows',
    totalProperty: 'results',
    idProperty:'id'
  }, Movie)
});
```

Instead of autoLoading the store, we kick off the Store's loading process by asking the PagingToolbar to load the first page because it knows what parameters to send, so we do not need to pass any in a programmatic call of the store's load method.

```
grid.getBottomToolbar().changePage(1);
```

The result will look like this:

# Grouping

Grouping grids are used to provide a visual indication that sets of rows are similar to each other, such as being in the same movie genre. It also provides us with sorting that is confined to each group. So if we were to sort by the price column, the price would sort only within each group of items.

# Grouping store

Grouping of data by common values of one field is provided by a special data store class called `GroupingStore`.

The setup is similar to a standard store. We just need to provide a few more configuration options, such as the `sortInfo` and the `groupField`. No changes to the actual data are needed because Ext JS takes care of grouping on the client side.

```
var store = new Ext.data.GroupingStore({
  url: 'movies.json',
  sortInfo: {
    field: 'genre',
    direction: "ASC"
  },
  groupField: 'genre',
  reader: new Ext.data.JsonReader({
    root:'rows',
    idProperty:'id'
  }, Movie)
});
```

We also need to add a `view` configuration to the grid panel. This view helps the grid to visually account for grouped data.

```
var grid = new Ext.grid.GridPanel({
  renderTo: document.body,
  frame:true,
  title: 'Movie Database',
  height:400,
  width:520,
  store: store,
  autoExpandColumn: 'title',
  colModel: // column model goes here //,
  view: new Ext.grid.GroupingView({
    forceFit: true,
    groupTextTpl: '{text} ({[values.rs.length]} {[values.rs.length
> 1 ? "Items" : "Item"]})'
  })
});
```

After making the changes needed for a grouping grid, we end up with something that looks like this:

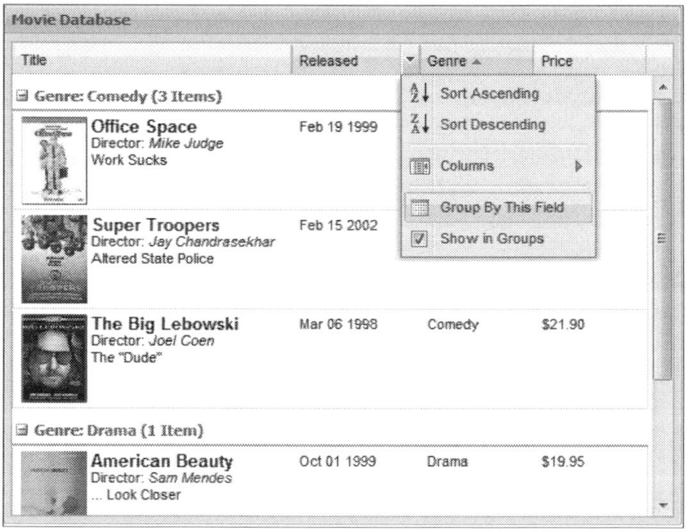


If you now expand the context menu for the column headings, you will see a new item in the menu labeled **Group By This Field** that will allow the user to change the grouping column on the fly.

# Summary

We have learned a lot in this chapter about presenting data in a grid. With this new-found knowledge we will be able to organize massive amounts of data into easy-to-understand grids.

Specifically, we covered:

- Creating data stores and grids for display
- Reading XML and JSON data from a server and displaying it in a grid
- Rendering cells of data for a well formatted display
- Altering the grid based on user interaction

We also discussed the intricacies of each of these elements, such as reading data locally or from a server—along with paging and formatting cells using HTML, images, and even lookups into separate data stores.

Now that we've learned about standard grids, we're ready to take it to the next level, by making our grid cells editable just like a spreadsheet—which is the topic of the next chapter.

# 6
# Editor Grids

In the previous chapter we learned how to display data in a structured grid that users could manipulate. But one major limitation was that there was no way for the users to edit the data in the grid in-line. Fortunately, Ext JS provides an `EditorGridPanel`, which allows the use of form field type editing in-line—which we will learn about it in this chapter. This works much like Excel or other spreadsheet programs, allowing the user to click on and edit cell data in-line with the grid.

In this chapter we will learn to:

- Present the user with editable grids that are connected to a data store
- Send edited data back to the server, enabling users to update server-side databases using the Ext JS editor grid
- Manipulate the grid from program code, and respond to events
- Use tricks for advanced formatting and creating more powerful editing grids

But first, let's see what we can do with an editable grid.

# What can I do with an editable grid?

The `EditorGridPanel` is very similar to the forms we were working with earlier. In fact, an editor grid uses the exact same form fields as our form. By using form fields to perform the grid cell editing we get to take advantage of the same functionality that a form field provides. This includes restricting input, and validating values. Combine this with the power of an Ext JS `GridPanel`, and we are left with a widget that can do pretty much whatever we want.

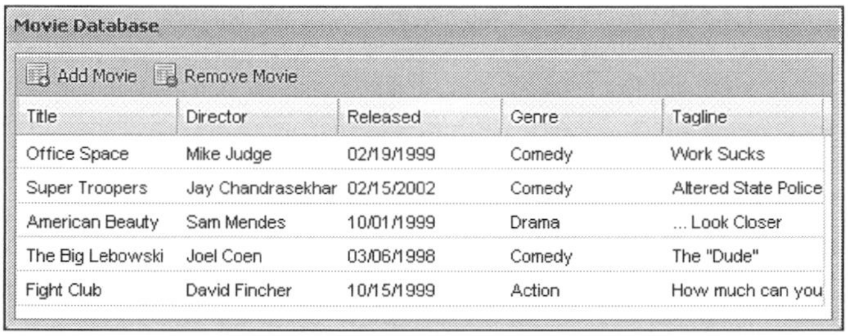


All of the fields in this table can be edited in-line using form fields such as the text field, date field, and combo box.

# Working with editable grids

The change from a non-editable grid to an editable grid is quite a simple process to start with. The complexity comes into the picture when we start to create a process to handle edits and send that data back to the server. Once we learn how to do it, that part can be quite simple as well.

Let's see how we would update the grid we created at the start of Chapter 5 to make the title, director, and tagline editable. Here's what the modified code will look like:

```
var title_edit = new Ext.form.TextField();

var director_edit = new Ext.form.TextField({vtype: 'name'});

var tagline_edit = new Ext.form.TextField({
   maxLength: 45
});

var grid = new Ext.grid.EditorGridPanel({
   renderTo: document.body,
   frame:true,
   title: 'Movie Database',
   height:200,
   width:520,
   clickstoEdit: 1,
```

```
    store: store,
    columns: [
        {header: "Title", dataIndex: 'title',
            editor: title_edit},
        {header: "Director", dataIndex: 'director',
            editor: director_edit},
        {header: "Released", dataIndex: 'released',
            renderer: Ext.util.Format.dateRenderer('m/d/Y')},
        {header: "Genre", dataIndex: 'genre',
            renderer: genre_name},
        {header: "Tagline", dataIndex: 'tagline',
            editor: tagline_edit}
    ]
});
```

There are four main things that we need to do to make our grid editable. These are:

- The grid definition changes from being `Ext.grid.GridPanel` to `Ext.grid.EditorGridPanel`
- We add the `clicksToEdit` option to the grid config—this option is not required, but defaults to two clicks, which we will change to one click
- Create a form field for each column that we would like to be editable
- Pass the form fields into our column model via the `editor` config

The editor can be any of the form field types that already exist in Ext JS, or a custom one of our own. We start by creating a text form field that will be used when editing the movie title.

```
var title_edit = new Ext.form.TextField();
```

Then add this form field to the column model as the `editor`:

```
{header: "Title", dataIndex: 'title', editor: title_edit}
```

The next step will be to change from using the `GripPanel` component to using the `EditorGridPanel` component, and to add the `clicksToEdit` config:

```
var grid = new Ext.grid.EditorGridPanel({
    renderTo: document.body,
    frame: true,
    title: 'Movie Database',
    height: 200,
    width: 520,
    clickstoEdit: 1,
   // removed extra code for clarity
})
```

Making these changes has turned our static grid into an editable grid. We can click on any of the fields that we set up editors for, and edit their values, though nothing really happens yet.

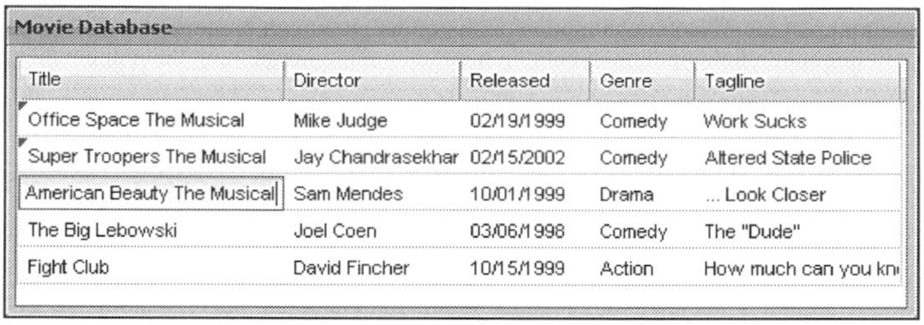


Here we see that some changes have been made to the titles of a few of the movies, turning them into musicals. The editor gets activated with a single click on the cell of data; pressing *Enter*, the *Tab* key, or clicking away from the field will record the change, and pressing the *Escape* key will discard any changes. This works just like a form field, because, well... it is a form field.

The little red tick that appears in the upper-left corner indicates that the cell is 'dirty', which we will cover in just a moment. First, let's make some more complex editable cells.

# Editing more cells of data

For our basic editor grid, we started by making a single column editable. To set up the editor, we created a reference to the form field:

```
var title_edit = new Ext.form.TextField();
```

Then we used that form field as the editor for the column:

```
{header: "Title", dataIndex: 'title', editor: title_edit}
```

Those are the basic requirements for each field. Now let's expand upon this knowledge.

# Edit more field types

Now we are going to create editors for the other fields. Different data types have different editor fields and can have options specific to that field's needs.

Any form field type can be used as an editor. These are some of the standard types:

- `TextField`
- `NumberField`

- ComboBox
- DateField
- TimeField
- CheckBox

These editors can be extended to achieve special types of editing if needed, but for now, let's start with editing the other fields we have in our grid—the release date and the genre.

# Editing a date value

A DateField will work perfectly for editing the release date column in our grid. So let's use that. We first need to set up the editor field and specify which format to use:

```
release_edit = new Ext.form.DateField({
  format: 'm/d/Y'
});
```

Then we apply that editor to the column, along with the renderer that we used earlier:

```
{header: "Released", dataIndex: 'released', renderer:
  Ext.util.Format.dateRenderer('m/d/Y'), editor: release_edit}
```

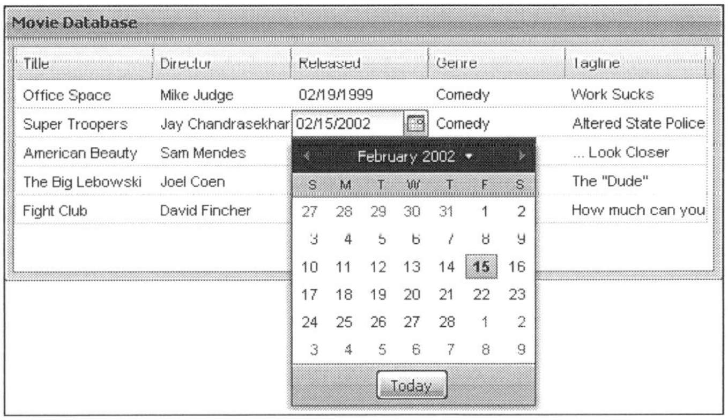


This column also takes advantage of a renderer, which will co-exist with the editor. Once the editor field is activated with a single click, the renderer passes the rendering of the field to the editor and vice versa. So when we are done editing the field, the renderer will take over formatting the field again.

## Editing with a ComboBox

Let's set up an editor for the genres column that will provide us with a list of the valid genres to select from—sounds like a perfect scenario for a combo box.

```
var genre_edit = new Ext.form.ComboBox({
  typeAhead: true,
  triggerAction: 'all',
  mode: 'local',
  store: genres,
  displayField: 'genre',
  valueField: 'id'
});
```

Simply add this editor to the column model, like we did with the others:

```
{header: "Genre", dataIndex: 'genre', renderer: genre_name,
                                        editor: genre_edit}
```

Now we end up with an editable field that has a fixed selection of options.

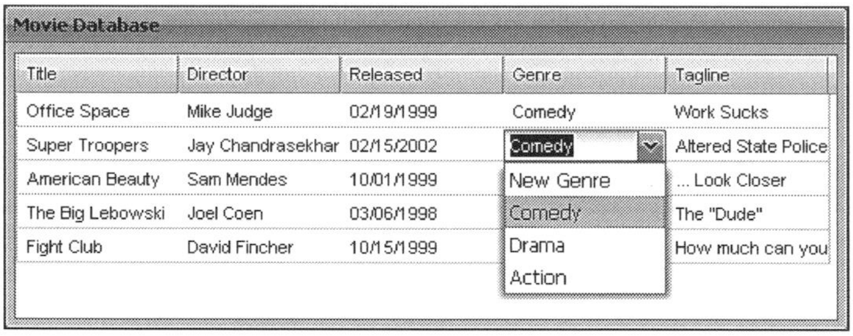


## Reacting to a cell edit

Of course, we now need to figure out how to save all of this editing that we have been doing. I am sure the end user would not be so happy if we threw away all of their changes. We can start the process of saving the changes by listening for particular edit events, and then reacting to those with our own custom handler. Before we start coding this, we need to understand a bit more about how the editor grid works.

### What's a dirty cell?

A field that has been edited and has had its value changed is considered to be 'dirty' until the data store is told otherwise. Records within the data store which have been created, modified, or deleted are tracked, and maintained in a list of uncommitted changes until the store is told that the database has been synchronized with these changes.

We can tell the store to clear the dirty status of a record by calling the commit method. This signifies that we have synchronized the database, and the record can now be considered 'clean'.

Let's imagine `e` as an edit event object. We could restore the edited record to its unmodified, 'clean' state by calling the `reject` method:

```
e.record.reject();
```

Alternatively, we can tell the store that the database has been synchronized, and that the changes can be made permanent:

```
e.record.commit();
```

# Reacting when an edit occurs

To save our users changes to the data store, we are going to listen for an edit event being completed, which is accomplished by listening for the `afteredit` event.

The listener we need is added to the grid panel:

```
var grid = new Ext.grid.EditorGridPanel({
  // more config options clipped //,
  title: 'Movie Database',
  store: store,
  columns: // column model clipped //,
  listeners: {
    afteredit: function(e){
      if (e.field == 'director' && e.value == 'Mel Gibson'){
        Ext.Msg.alert('Error','Mel Gibson movies not allowed');
        e.record.reject();
      }else{
        e.record.commit();
      }
    }
  }
});
```

As with other events in Ext JS, the editor grid listeners are given a function to execute when the event occurs. The function for `afteredit` is called with a single argument: an edit object, which has a number of useful properties. We can use these properties to make a decision about the edit that just happened.

| Property | Description |
|---|---|
| grid | The grid that the edit event happened in |
| record | The entire record that's being edited; other column values can be retrieved using this objects get method |
| field | The name of the column that was edited |
| value | A string containing the new value of the cell |
| originalValue | A string containing the original value of the cell |
| row | The index of the row that was edited |
| column | The index of the column that was edited |

For instance, if we wanted to make sure that movies directed by `Mel Gibson` never made it into our database, we could put a simple check in place for that scenario:

```
if (e.field == 'director' && e.value == 'Mel Gibson'){
  Ext.Msg.alert('Error','Mel Gibson movies not allowed');
  e.record.reject();
}else{
  e.record.commit();
}
```

First, we check to see that the `director` field is the one being edited. Next, we make sure the new value entered for this field is not equal to `Mel Gibson`. If either of these is false, we commit the record back to the data store. This means that once we call the `commit` method, our primary data store is updated with the new value.

```
e.record.commit();
```

We also have the ability to reject the change—sending the changed value into the black hole of space, lost forever.

```
e.record.reject();
```

Of course, all we have done so far is update the data that is stored in the browser's memory. I'm sure you're just dying to be able to update a web server. We will get to that soon enough.

# Deleting and adding in the data store

We are going to create two buttons to allow us to alter the data store—to add or remove rows of data. Let's set up a top toolbar (`tbar`) in the grid to contain these buttons:

```
var grid = new Ext.grid.EditorGridPanel({
  // more config options clipped //,
  tbar: [{
    text: 'Remove Movie'
  }]
}
```

## Removing grid rows from the data store

Let's expand on the **remove** button that we just added to the toolbar in our grid. When this button is clicked, it will prompt the user with a dialog that displays the movie title. If the **Yes** button is clicked, then we can remove the selected row from the data store, otherwise we will do nothing.

```
{
  text: 'Remove Movie',
  icon: 'images/table_delete.png',
  cls: 'x-btn-text-icon',
  handler: function() {
    var sm = grid.getSelectionModel(),
        sel = sm.getSelected();
    if (sm.hasSelection()){
      Ext.Msg.show({
        title: 'Remove Movie',
        buttons: Ext.MessageBox.YESNOCANCEL,
        msg: 'Remove ' + sel.data.title + '?',
        fn: function(btn){
          if (btn == 'yes'){
            grid.getStore().remove(sel);
          }
        }
      });
    };
  }
}
```

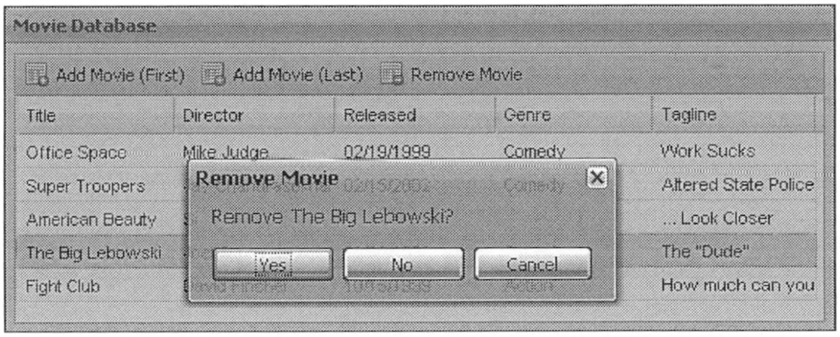

Let's take a look at what is happening here. We have defined some variables that we will use to determine if there were selections made, and what the selections were:

- `sm`: The selection model is retrieved from our grid
- `sel`: We used the selection model to retrieve the row that has been selected
- `grid.getStore().remove(sel)`: Passing the `data store remove` function will remove that record from the store and update the grid

It's as simple as that. The local data store that resides in the browser's memory has been updated. But what good is deleting if you can't add anything—just be patient, grasshopper!

## Adding a row to the grid

To add a new row, we use the record constructor that we create to represent a movie object, and instantiate a new record. We used the `Ext.data.Record.create` function to define a record constructor called `Movie`, so to insert a new movie into the store is as simple as this:

```
{
   text: 'Add Movie',
   icon: 'images/table_add.png',
   cls: 'x-btn-text-icon',
   handler: function() {
      grid.getStore().insert(0, new Movie({
            title: 'New Movie',
            director: '',
            genre: 0,
            tagline: ''
         })
      );
      grid.startEditing(0,0);
   }
}
```

The first argument to the `insert` function is the point at which the record inserted. I have chosen zero, so the record will be inserted at the very top. If we wanted to insert the row at the end we could simply retrieve the row count for our data store. As the row index starts at zero and the count at one, incrementing the count is not necessary because the row count will always be one greater than the index of the last item in the store.

```
grid.getStore().insert(
    grid.getStore().getCount(),
    new Movie({
```

```
            title: 'New Movie',
            director: '',
            genre: 0,
            tagline: ''
        })
    );
    grid.startEditing(grid.getStore().getCount()-1,0);
```

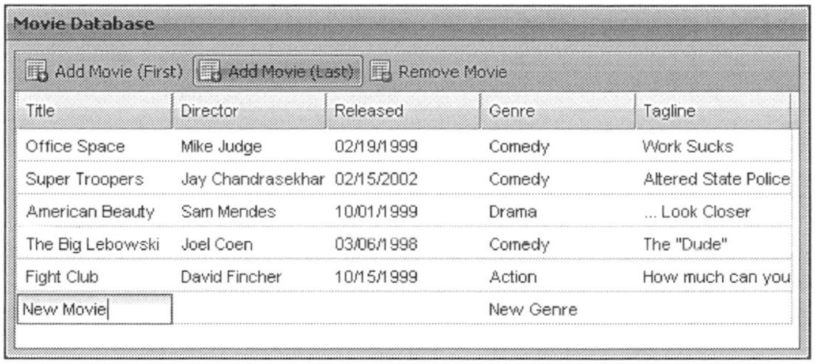


Now let's take a closer look at inserting that record. The second argument is the new record definition, which can be passed with the initial field values.

```
new Movie({
    title:'New Movie',
    director:'',
    genre:0,
    tagline:''
})
```

After inserting the new row, we call the `startEditing` method that will activate a cell's editor. This function just needs a row and column index number to activate the editor for that cell.

```
grid.startEditing(0,0);
```

This gives our user the ability to start typing the movie title directly after clicking the **Add Movie** button. Quite a nice user interface interaction which our end users will no doubt love.

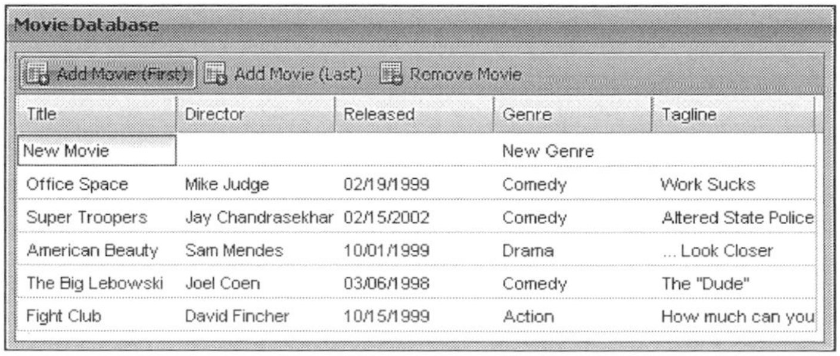

# Saving edited data to the server

Everything we have done so far is related to updating the local data store residing in the memory of the web browser. More often than not, we will want to save our data back to the server to update a database, file system, or something along those lines.

This section will cover some of the more common requirements of grids used in web applications to update server-side information.

- Updating a record
- Creating a new record
- Deleting a record

# Sending updates back to the server

Earlier, we set up a listener for the `afteredit` event. We will be using this `afteredit` event to send changes back to the server on a cell-by-cell basis.

To update the database with cell-by-cell changes, we need to know three things:

- `field`: What field has changed
- `value`: What the new value of the field is
- `record.id`: Which row from the database the field belongs to

This gives us enough information to be able to make a distinct update to a database. We communicate with the server (using Ajax) by calling the connection request method.

```
listeners: {
   afteredit: function(e){
      Ext.Ajax.request({
         url: 'movie-update.php',
            params: {
            action: 'update',
            id: e.record.id,
            field: e.field,
            value: e.value
         },
         success: function(resp,opt) {
            e.record.commit();
         },
            failure: function(resp,opt) {
            e.record.reject();
         }
```

```
            });
        }
    }
```

This will send a request to the `movie-update.php` script with four parameters in the form of post headers. The `params` we will pass into the request methods config as an object, which are all sent through the headers to our script on the server side.

The `movie-update.php` script should be coded to recognize the 'update' action and then read in the `id`, `field`, and `value` data and then proceed to update the file system or database, or whatever else we need to do to make the update happen on the server side.

This is what's available to us when using the `afteredit` event:

| Option | Description |
|---|---|
| grid | Reference to the current grid |
| record | Object with data from the row being edited |
| field | Name of the field being edited |
| value | New value entered into the field |
| originalValue | Original value of the field |
| row | Index of the row being edited—this will help in finding it again |
| column | Index of the column being edited |

# Deleting data from the server

When we want to delete data from the server, we can handle it in very much the same way as an update—by making a call to a script on the server, and telling it what we want to be done.

For the delete trigger, we will use another button in the grids toolbar, along with a confirm dialog to ask the user if they are sure they want to delete the record before actually taking any action.

```
{
  text: 'Remove Movie',
  icon: 'images/table_delete.png',
  cls: 'x-btn-text-icon',
  handler: function() {
    var sm = grid.getSelectionModel(),
        sel = sm.getSelected();
    if (sm.hasSelection()){
      Ext.Msg.show({
```

```
            title: 'Remove Movie',
            buttons: Ext.MessageBox.YESNOCANCEL,
            msg: 'Remove '+sel.data.title+'?',
            fn: function(btn){
              if (btn == 'yes'){
                Ext.Ajax.request({
                   url: 'movie-update.php',
                   params: {
                       action: 'delete',
                       id: e.record.id
                   },
                   success: function(resp,opt) {
                       grid.getStore().remove(sel);
                   },
                   failure: function(resp,opt) {
                       Ext.Msg.alert('Error',
                       'Unable to delete movie');
                   }
                });
              }
          }
        });
      };
    }
  }
```

Just as with edit, we are going to make a request to the server to have the row deleted. The `movie-update.php script` would see that the action is `delete` and the `record id` that we passed; it will then execute the appropriate action to delete the record on the server side.

# Saving new rows to the server

Now we're going to add another button that will add a new record. It sends a request to the server with the appropriate parameters and reads the response to figure out what the `insert id` from the database was. Using this `insert id`, we are able to add the record to our data store with the unique identifier generated on the server side for that record.

```
  {
    text: 'Add Movie',
    icon: 'images/table_add.png',
    cls: 'x-btn-text-icon',
    handler: function() {
```

```
      Ext.Ajax.request({
        url: 'movies-update.php',
        params: {
          action: 'create',
          title: 'New Movie'
        },
        success: function(resp,opt) {
          var insert_id = Ext.util.JSON.decode(
            resp.responseText
          ).insert_id;
          grid.getStore().insert(0,
 new Movie({
              id: insert_id,
              title: 'New Movie',
              director: '',
              genre: 0,
              tagline: ''
            }, insert_id)
);
          grid.startEditing(0,0);
        },
        failure: function(resp,opt) {
          Ext.Msg.alert('Error','Unable to add movie');
        }
      });
    }
}
```

Much like editing and deleting, we are going to send a request to the server to have a new record inserted. This time, we are actually going to take a look at the response to retrieve the `insert id` (the unique identifier for that record) to pass to the record constructor, so that when we start editing that record, it will be easy to save our changes back to the server.

```
success: function(resp,opt) {
  var insert_id = Ext.util.JSON.decode(
    resp.responseText
  ).insert_id;
  grid.getStore().insert(0,
 new Movie({
      id: insert_id,
      title: 'New Movie',
      director: '',
      genre: 0,
      tagline: ''
```

```
        }, insert_id)
    );
      grid.startEditing(0,0);
    }
```

Our success handler accepts a couple of arguments; the first is the response object, which has a property that contains the response text from our `movie-update.php` script. As that response is in a JSON format, we're going to decode it into a usable JavaScript object and grab the `insert id` value.

```
var insert_id = Ext.util.JSON.decode(
  resp.responseText
).insert_id;
```

When we insert this row into our data store, we can use this `insert id` that was retrieved.

# RowEditor plugin

One of the more popular ways to edit data in a grid uses a User Extension called the RowEditor. This extension presents the user with all the editable fields at once, along with save and cancel buttons. This allows editing of all fields within a record before committing all changes at once. Since this is a plugin, we simply need to include the additional JavaScript and CSS files and configure our Grid to use the plugin.

Using this plugin requires that we include the RowEditor JavaScript file, which can be found in the `examples/ux` folder of the Ext JS SDK download. Be sure to include it directly after the `ext-all.js` file.

```
<script src="../ux/RowEditor.js"></script>
```

We also need to include the `RowEditor` styles found in the `ux/css` folder, (the file is called `RowEditor.css`,) along with the two images needed that are found in the `ux/images` folder, called `row-editor-bg.gif` and `row-editor-btns.gif`.

Now we just need to configure the `EditorGrid` to use this plugin.

```
var grid = new Ext.grid.EditorGridPanel({
  // more config options clipped //,
  title: 'Movie Database',
  store: store,
  columns: // column model clipped //,
plugins: [new Ext.ux.grid.RowEditor()]
});
```

From here we have the plugin in place, but it doesn't really do much as far as saving the changes. So let's throw a writable data store in the mix to make this editor plugin much more powerful.

# Writable store

In our final example of this chapter we will combine use of the RowEditor with a writable data store to implement full `CRUD` functionality for movie database maintenance.

First, let's examine how to set up a writable data store. An Ext JS 3.0+ data store understands four operations to perform which require synchronization with a server:

- **Create**: A record has been inserted into the data store
- **Read**: Data store needs to be filled from the server
- **Update**: A record has been modified within the data store
- **Destroy**: A record has been removed from the data store

To enable the data store to perform this synchronization, we configure it with an `API` object which specifies a URL to use for each operation. In our case we use the same PHP script passing a parameter specifying the action to perform:

```
api: {
    create : 'movies-sync.php?action=create',
    read : 'movies-sync.php?action=read',
    update: 'movies-sync.php?action=update',
    destroy: 'movies-sync.php?action=destroy'
},
```

This config option takes the place of the `url` config which we specified when the store was a simple load-only store.

We also need to configure a writer which will serialize the changes back into the format that the reader uses. In our case, we were using a `JsonReader`, so we use a `JsonWriter`. We tell the `JsonWriter` to submit the full record field set upon update, not only the modified fields because the PHP script creates an SQL statement which sets all of the row's columns:

```
writer: new Ext.data.JsonWriter({
    writeAllFields: true
}),
```

We configure the data store to *not* automatically synchronize itself with the server whenever its data changes, as otherwise it would synchronize during row editing, and we want to submit our changes only when we have edited the whole row:

```
autoSave: false,
```

We must not forget to handle exceptions that may happen with the complex operations being performed by the data store. A data store may fire an exception event if it encounters an error, and handling these errors is highly recommended.

It also relays exception events from the communication layer (The Proxy object we mentioned in the last chapter). These will pass a type parameter which specifies whether it was the client or the server which produced the error:

```
listeners: {
    exception: function(proxy, type, action, o, result, records) {
        if (type = 'remote') {
            Ext.Msg.alert("Could not " + action, result.raw.message);
        } else if (type = 'response') {
            Ext.Msg.alert("Could not " + action, "Server's response
could not be decoded");
        } else {
            Ext.Msg.alert("Store sync failed", "Unknown error");
        }
    }
}
```

You can test this error handling by triggering a "deliberate mistake" in the PHP update script. If you submit one of the textual fields containing an apostrophe, the creation of the SQL statement will be incorrect because it concatenates the statement placing the values within apostrophes. The example will display an alert box informing the user of a server side error in an orderly manner.

To configure the UI side of this, all we need to do is create a `RowEditor`, and specify it as a plugin of the grid:

```
var rowEditor = new Ext.ux.grid.RowEditor({
    saveText: 'Update',
    listeners: {
        afteredit: syncStore
    }
});
var grid = new Ext.grid.GridPanel({
    renderTo: document.body,
    plugins: rowEditor,
...
```

The `RowEditor` uses the editors configured into the `ColumnModel` in the same way as our previous examples did. All we need to do is specify a listener for the `afteredit` event which the `RowEditor` fires when the user clicks the **Update** button after a successful edit.

The function to make the store synchronize itself with the server is very simple:

```
function syncStore(rowEditor, changes, r, rowIndex) {
    store.save();
}
```

Running the final example in the chapter, and double-clicking to edit a row will look like this:

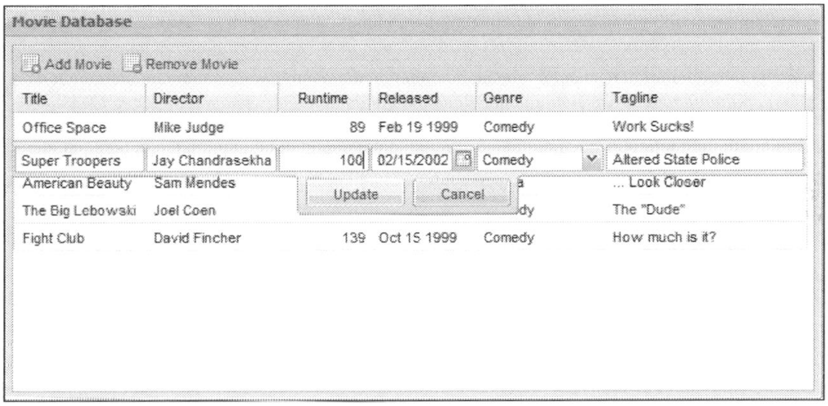

# Summary

The Ext JS Editor Grid functionality is one of the most advanced portions of the framework. With the backing of the `Ext data` package, the grid can pull information from a remote server in an integrated manner—this support is built into the grid class. Thanks to the numerous configuration options available, we can present this data easily, and in a variety of forms, and set it up for manipulation by our users.

In this chapter, we've seen how the data support provided by the grid offers an approach to data manipulating that will be familiar to many developers. The amend and commit approach allows fine-grained control over the data that is sent to the server when used with a validation policy, along with the ability to reject changes. As well as amending the starting data, we've seen how the grid provides functionality to add and remove rows of data.

We've also shown how standard Ext JS form fields such as the ComboBox can be integrated to provide a user interface on top of this functionality. With such strong support for data entry, the grid package provides a very powerful tool for application builders.

For the first time in this book we have utilized a User Extension to create additional functionality that did not previously exist in the Ext JS library. This functionality can be easily shared and updated independent of the Ext JS library, which opens up a huge world of possibilities.

In the next chapter, we'll demonstrate how components such as the grid can be integrated with other parts of an application screen by using the extensive layout functionality provided by the Ext JS framework.

# 7
# Layouts

One of those foundation classes that we have already seen in action is the Container class. We have used panels, and panels are Containers (because they inherit from that base class). They can contain child components. These child components may of course be Containers themselves.

A Container delegates the responsibility for rendering its child components into its DOM structure to a layout manager. The layout manager renders child components, and may, if configured to do so, perform positioning and sizing on those child components.

This is one of the most powerful concepts within the Ext JS library, and it is what turns a collection of forms, grids, and other widgets, into a dynamic, fluid web application which behaves like a desktop application. It takes some time to understand this concept, so let's examine it.

## What is a layout manager?

A **layout manager** is an object which renders child components for a Container.

The default layout manager simply renders child components serially into the Container's DOM, and then takes no further responsibility. No sizing is performed by the default layout manager and so if the Container ever changes size, the child components will not be resized.

Other built-in layout managers, depending on their type and configuration, apply sizing and positioning rules to the child components.

A layout manager may also examine hints configured into the child components to decide how the child component is to be sized and positioned. The form and border layout are examples of this.

To see these principles in action, let's take a look at our first example that will use an `hbox` layout in our panel to arrange two child BoxComponents. The requirement is that the two child boxes are arranged horizontally, with a 50/50 width allocation, and they must fill the container height. The code which creates the panel is:

```
new Ext.Panel({
    renderTo: document.body,
    title: "I arranged two boxes horizontally using 'hbox' layout!",
    height: 400,
    width: 600,
    layout: {
        type: 'hbox',
        align: 'stretch',
        padding: 5
    },
    items: [{
        xtype: 'box',
        flex: 1,
        style: 'border: 1px solid #8DB2E3',
        margins: '0 3 0 0',
        html: 'Left box'
    }, {
        xtype: 'box',
        flex: 1,
        style: 'border: 1px solid #8DB2E3',
        margins: '0 0 0 2',
        html: 'Right box'
    }],
    style: 'padding:10px'
});
```

The layout configuration is an object which specifies not only which layout class is to be used, but also acts as a config object for that class. In this case we use layout type `hbox`, which is a layout that arranges child components as a row of horizontal boxes.

The configuration options are all documented in the API docs, but two that we use here are:

- `padding`: Specifies how much internal padding to leave within the Container's structure when sizing and positioning children. We want them to be inset so that we can visually appreciate the structure.
- `align`: Specifies how to arrange the height of the children. `'stretch'` means that they will be stretched to take up all available height.

The `hbox` layout manager reads hint configurations from the child components when arranging them. Two of the configuration options that we use here are:

- `flex`: A number which specifies the ratio of the total of all flex values to use to allocate available width. Both children have a value of `1`, so the space allocated to each will be `1/2` of the available width.
- `margins`: The top, right, bottom, and left margin width in pixels. We want to see a neat five pixel separation between the two child boxes.

The result of running this example is:

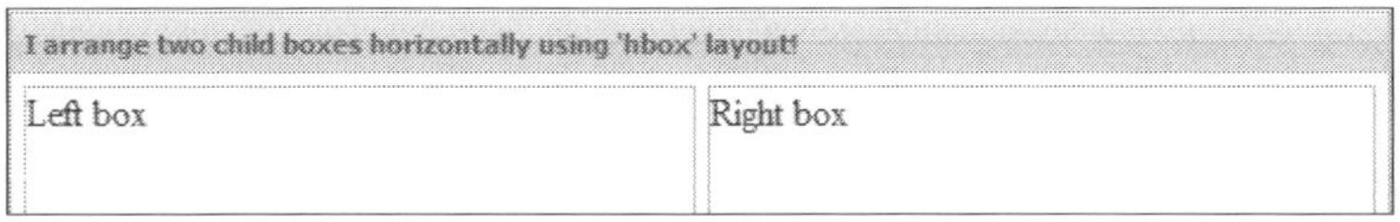


This simple panel is not resizable as we have constructed it. As we are using a layout which applies *rules* to how child items are arranged, if the Panel were to change size, both child items would have their sizes and positions recalculated according to the configuration.

This is the power of the layout system which is an integral part of Container/Component nesting: dynamic sizing.

# So what layouts are available?

While designing your UI, you must first plan how you require any child components within it to be arranged and sized.

With this in mind, you must then plan which layouts to use to achieve that goal. This requires an appreciation of what is available. The layout types built into Ext JS will now be discussed.

## AbsoluteLayout

Type: `'absolute'`. This layout allows you to position child components at X and `Y` coordinates within the Container. This layout is rarely used.

## AccordionLayout

Type: `'acordion'`. This layout may only use panels as child items. It arranges the panels vertically within the Container, allowing only one of the panels to be expanded at any time. The expanded panel takes up all available vertical space, leaving just the other panel headers visible.

Note that this layout does not by default set the child panels' widths, but allows them to size themselves. To force it to size the child panel's widths to fit exactly within the Container, use `autoWidth: false` in the layout config object.

# AnchorLayout

Type: `'anchor'`. This layout manager reads hints from the child components to anchor the widths and heights of the child components to the right and bottom Container borders. This layout reads an optional `anchor` hint from the child items. This is a string containing the width anchor and the height anchor. This layout can be quite useful for form items.

# BorderLayout

Type: `'border'`. This layout manager **docks** child components to the `north`, `south`, `east`, or `west` borders of the Container. Child components must use a `region` config to declare which border they are docked to. There must always be a `region: 'center'` child component which uses the central space between all docked children. `North` and `south` child components may be configured with an initial `height`. `East` and `west` child components may be configured with an initial `width`.

# CardLayout

Type: `'card'`. This layout manager arranges child components in a **stack** like a deck of cards, one below the other. The child components are sized to fit precisely within the Container's bounds with no overflow. Only one child component may be visible (termed **active**) at once. The TabPanel class uses a CardLayout manager internally to activate one tab at a time.

# ColumnLayout

Type: `'column'`. The ColumnLayout manager arranges child components floating from left to right across the Container. Hints may be used in the child components to specify the proportion of horizontal space to allocate to a child. This layout allows child components to wrap onto the next line when they overflow the available width.

# FitLayout

Type: `'fit'`. This layout manager manages only one child component. It handles sizing of the single child component to fit exactly into the Container's bounds with no overflow. This layout is often used in conjunction with a Window Component.

# FormLayout

Type: `'form'`. This is the default layout for FormPanels and FieldSets. It extends AnchorLayout, so has all the sizing abilities of that layout. The key ability of FormLayout is that it is responsible for rendering labels next to form fields. If you configure a field with a `fieldLabel`, it will only appear if the field is in a layout which is using FormLayout.

# HBoxLayout

Type: `'hbox'`. This layout manager arranges child components horizontally across the Container. It uses hints in the child components to allocate available width in a proportional way. It does not wrap overflowing components onto another line.

# TableLayout

Type: `'table'`. This layout manager allows the developer to arrange child components in a tabular layout. A wrapping `<table>` element is created, and children are each rendered into their own `<td>` elements. TableLayout does **not** size the child components, but it accepts `rowspan` and `colspan` hints from the children to create a table of any complexity in which each cell contains a child component.

# VBoxLayout

Type: `'vbox'`. The vertical brother of `'hbox'`, this layout manager arranges child components one below the other, allocating available Container height to children in a proportional way.

# A dynamic application layout

Our first example showed how an individual Container—a panel—which we programmatically render can arrange its child items according to a layout.

To attain a desktop-like application layout, we will use the whole browser window. There is a special Container class called a Viewport which encapsulates the whole document body, and resizes itself whenever the browser changes size.

If it is configured with a size-managing layout, that layout will then apply its sizing rules to any child components. A Viewport uses the `<body>` as its main element. It does not need to be programmatically rendered.

In the remaining layout examples, we will use a Viewport to create a fully dynamic application.

# Our first Viewport

The most common layout manager used in Viewports is the border layout. Applications frequently make use of border regions to represent header, navigation bar, footer, etc. In our examples we will use all five regions (don't forget that only the `center` region is required!).

Border layouts offer split bars between regions to allow them to be resized. It also allows border regions to be collapsed, with the center region then expanding to fill the free space. This offers great flexibility to the user in arranging child components.

Viewports may of course use any layout manager. However, we will be using a border layout in our Viewports from now on.

All our regions will be panels. (Config objects with no xtype generally default to using a panel as the child component). As with all Containers, any component can be used as a child component. We make use of the automatic border display, and the header element which the panel class offers.

In the child components of our border layout example, we specify several hints for the layout manager to use. These include:

- `region`: The border to dock the child component to.
- `split`: This is only used by the border regions, not the center region. If specified as `true`, the child component is rendered with a splitbar separating it from the center region, and allows resizing. Mouse-based resizing is limited by the `minWidth/minHeight` and `maxWidth/maxHeight` hint configs.
- `collapsible`: This is only used by border regions. It specifies that the child component may collapse towards its associated border. If the child component is a panel, a special collapse tool is rendered in the header. If the region is not a panel (only panels have headers), `collapseMode: 'mini'` may be used (see below).
- `collapseMode`: If specified as 'mini', then a mini collapse tool is rendered in the child component's splitbar.
- `margins`: This specifies the margin in pixels to leave round any child component in the layout. The value is a space-separated string of numeric values. The order is the CSS standard of top, right, bottom, left. I recommend use of five pixel margins between border regions to provide visual separation for the user. Remember that where regions adjoin, only one of them needs a margin! This is illustrated in our first example.
- `cmargins`: A margins specification to use when a region is collapsed.

Running the first Viewport example, you should see the following user interface:

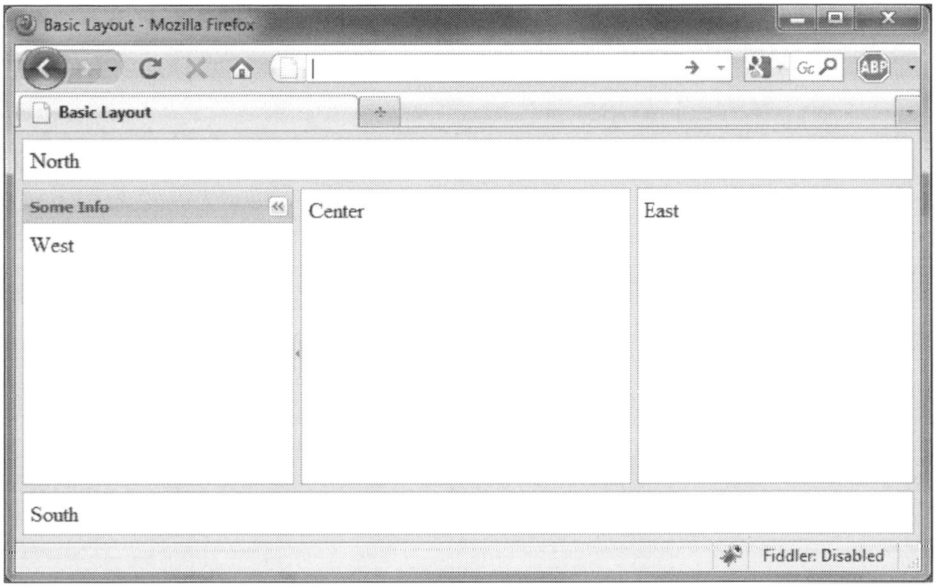


Notice the margins providing visual separation of the regions. Also, notice the **mini** collapse tool in the splitbar of the west region. If you resize the browser, the north and south regions maintain their height, and east and west their width, while the center occupies the remaining space.

Let's examine the code which created this sample layout:

```
var viewport = new Ext.Viewport({
    layout: "border",
    defaults: {
        bodyStyle: 'padding:5px;',
    },
    items: [{
        region: "north",
        html: 'North',
        margins: '5 5 5 5'
    },{
        region: 'west',
        split: true,
        collapsible: true,
        collapseMode: 'mini',
        title: 'Some Info',
        width: 200,
        minSize: 200,
```

```
            html: 'West',
            margins: '0 0 0 5'
        },{
            region: 'center',
            html: 'Center',
            margins: '0 0 0 0'
        },{
            region: 'east',
            split: true,
            width: 200,
            html: 'East',
            margins: '0 5 0 0'
        },{
            region: 'south',
            html: 'South',
            margins: '5 5 5 5'
        }]
    });
```

All the child components are specified by simple config objects. They have a region hint and they use the `html` config which is from the Component base class. The `html` config specifies HTML content for the Component. This is just to indicate which region is which. There are better ways for the child Panels to be given content, which we will see later in this chapter.

Take note of how the north region has a five pixel border all around. Notice then how all the regions under it (west, center and east) have no top border to keep consistent separation.

# Nesting: child components may be Containers

In our third example, we will make the center region into something more useful than a panel containing simple HTML.

We will specify the center child component as a TabPanel. TabPanel is a Container, so it has a single child component. A panel with some simple HTML in this case!

The only difference in this example is that the center config object has an xtype which means it will be used to create a TabPanel (instead of the default panel), and it has an items config specifying child panels:

```
{
    region: 'center',
    xtype: 'tabpanel',
    activeTab: 0,
    items: [{
        title: 'Movie Grid',
        html: 'Center'
    }],
    margins: '0 0 0 0'
}
```

This results in the following display:

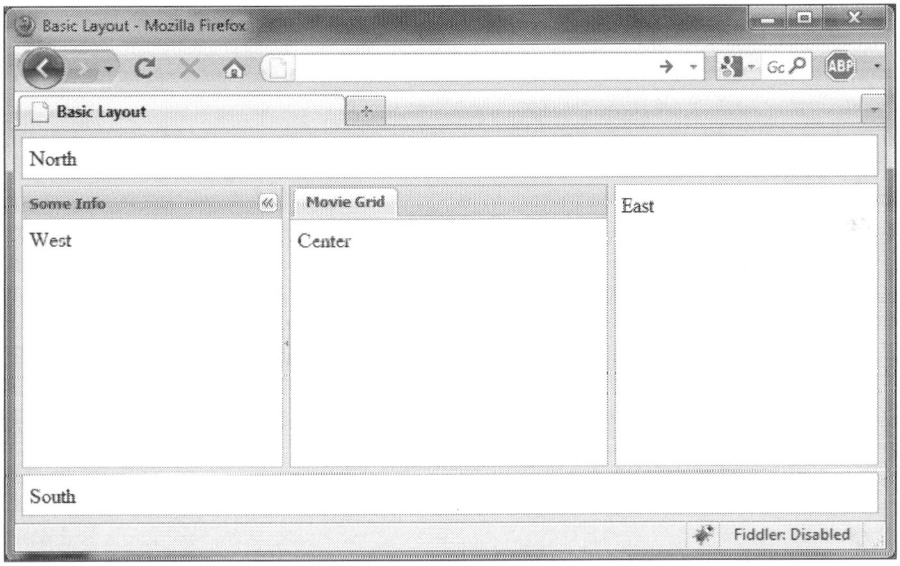


The TabPanel class uses a card layout to show only one of several child components at once. Configure it with an `activeTab` config specifying which one to show initially. In this case it's our 'Movie Grid' panel.

Of course the child component we have configured in our TabPanel is not a grid. Let's add the GridPanel we created in Chapter 5 to our TabPanel to demonstrate the card switching UI which the TabPanel offers:

```
{
    region: 'center',
    xtype: 'tabpanel',
    bodyStyle: '',
    activeTab: 0,
    items: [{
```

```
            title: 'Movie Grid',
            xtype: 'grid',
            store: store,
            autoExpandColumn: 'title',
            colModel: new Ext.grid.ColumnModel({
                columns: [...] // not shown for readability
            }),
            view: new Ext.grid.GroupingView(),
            sm: new Ext.grid.RowSelectionModel({
                singleSelect: true
            })
        },{
            title: 'Movie Descriptions'
        }],
        margins: '0 0 0 0'
    }
```

In this example, we can see that the first child component in the TabPanel's `items` array is a grid. Take note of this to avoid a common pitfall encountered by first time Ext JS users. It can be tempting to overnest child components within extra Container layers, by placing a grid within a panel. Many that attempt to use a grid as a tab first time end up wrapping the grid within a panel like this:

```
    {
        xtype: 'tabpanel',
        items: [{       // Open Panel config with no layout
            items: [{
                xtype: 'grid',  // Panel contains a grid
                ...
            }]
        }]
    }
```

If you read the above code correctly, you can see why it is incorrect and inefficient, and will result in a buggy display.

Recall that the default child Component type to create if no `xtype` is specified is a panel. So that single child Component of the TabPanel is a panel which itself **contains** a grid. It contains a grid, but it has no layout configured. This means that the grid will not be sized, and has an extra Component layer that serves no purpose.

This problem is referred to as **overnesting** and when overnesting is combined with omission of layout configuration, results are unpredictable. Do not think of putting a grid in a tab, think of using a grid as a tab.

Our correctly configured layout will result in the following display:

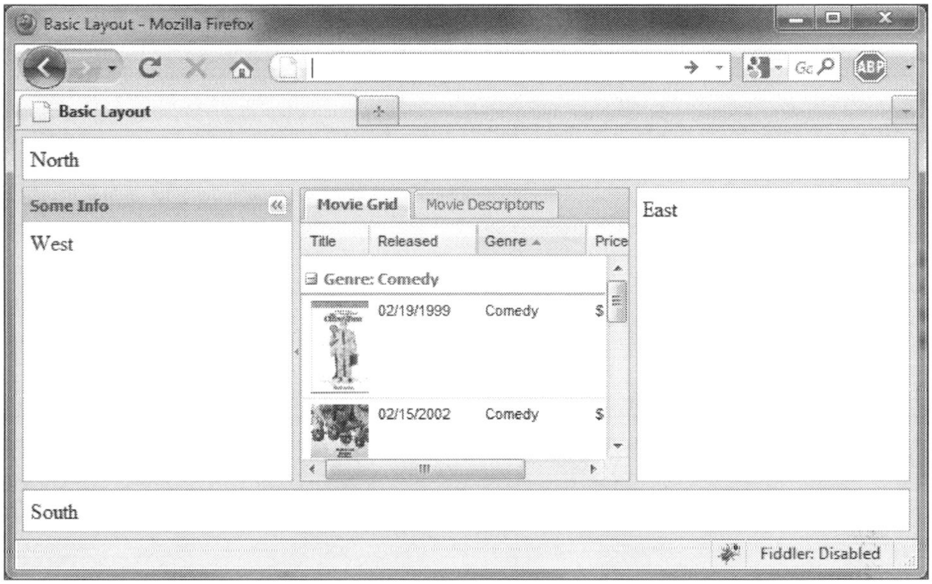


In the above example, the Viewport has sized its center child—the TabPanel—and the TabPanel's card layout have sized its children. The grid is sized to fit as a tab. The second tab is not functional as yet. Let's move on to that next.

# Accordion layout

Now that we have a functioning application of sorts, we can demonstrate another layout manager.

An accordion is a familiar layout pattern in modern web applications. Multiple child components are stacked up vertically with their content areas collapsed. Only one may be expanded at a time.

The accordion layout allows this to be set up very easily. Just use panels as children of a Container which uses the accordion layout, and the panel's headers are used as placeholders which may be clicked to expand the content area:

```
{
    xtype: 'container',
    title: 'Movie Descriptions',
    layout: 'accordion',
    defaults: {
        border: false
```

```
        },
        items: [{
            title: 'Office Space',
            autoLoad: 'html/1.txt'
        },{
            title: 'Super Troopers',
            autoLoad: 'html/3.txt'
        },{
            title: 'American Beauty',
            autoLoad: 'html/4.txt'
        }]
    }
```

Notice that here, we are using `xtype: 'container'` as the accordion. We do not need borders, or toolbars, or a header, so we do not need the complex DOM structure of the panel class; the simple Container will do.

The defaults config is applicable to any Container to provide default configs for child components. In this case, because the TabPanel provides its own borders, we do not want another layer of borders.

Running this example code and selecting the **Movie Descriptions** tab will result in the following display:

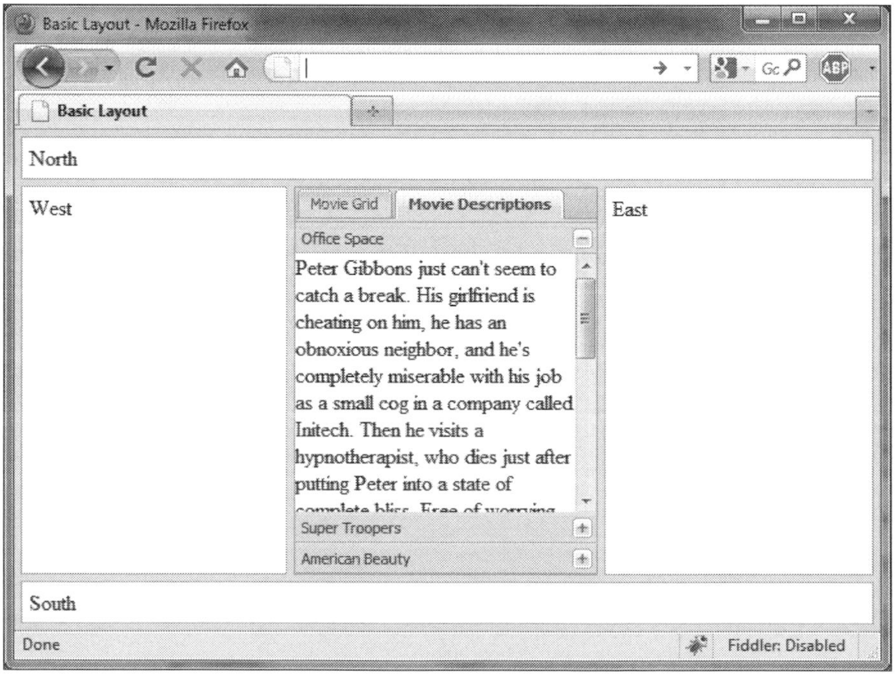

Clicking the headers in the accordion expands the panel's body, and displays the description which was loaded into the child panel using the `autoLoad` config option. This option may be used to load purely decorative HTML.

> Loading HTML in this way only loads HTML *fragments*, not full HTML documents. Scripts and stylesheets will not be evaluated. This option should not be used as a substitute for adding child components if Components are really what is required.

# A toolbar as part of the layout

To make the application more useful, we can add a toolbar to the user interface to add buttons and menus. We encountered these classes in *Chapter 4, Menus, Toolbars, and Buttons*.

We can use a toolbar as the north region of the Viewport. Again, note that we do not put the toolbar inside a north region; we use it as a north region to avoid the overnesting problem.

To ease the clarity of code which creates the Viewport, we create the config object for the toolbar and reference it with a variable:

```
var toolbarConfig = {
    region: 'north',
    height: 27,
    xtype: 'toolbar',
    items: [' ', {
        text: 'Button',
        handler: function(btn){
            btn.disable();
        }
    }, '->', {
    ...
};
```

The config object we create contains the expected `region` and `xtype` properties. Border layout requires that border regions be sized, so we give the toolbar a height of 27 pixels. The items in it, buttons, spacers, separators, fills, and input fields have been covered in Chapter 4.

As with the toolbar examples in Chapter 4, the handling functions are members of a singleton object. In this case, we have an object referenced by a `var Movies` which offers methods to operate our application.

The resulting display will look like this:

# Using a FormPanel in the layout

We can use that empty west region to do something useful now. We can use a FormPanel in the west region to edit the details of the selected movie.

We will configure a listener on the rowselect event of the SelectionModel to load the selected movie record into the FormPanel:

```
sm: new Ext.grid.RowSelectionModel({
    singleSelect: true,
    listeners: {
        rowselect: Movies.loadMovieForm
    }
})
```

The listener function is a member of the Movies object:

```
loadMovieForm: function(sm, rowIndex, rec) {
    editRecord = rec;
    movieForm.getForm().loadRecord(rec);
},
```

The selected record is assigned to the `editRecord` variable which is private to the Movies object. This is so that other member functions can use the record later.

The `getForm` method of the FormPanel returns the BasicForm object which manages the input fields within a FormPanel. The loadRecord method of the BasicForm copies values from the data fields of the record into the form's input fields, using the form fields names to match up the data.

Our example does not handle form submission yet, but it does update the record when you click the **Submit** button. The submit handler function is a member function of the Movies singleton:

```
submitMovieForm: function(){
    if (editRecord) {
        movieForm.getForm().updateRecord(editRecord);
        if (store.groupField &&
                editRecord.modified[store.groupField]) {
            store.groupBy(store.groupField, true);
        }
        movieForm.getForm().submit({
            success: function(form, action){
                Ext.Msg.alert('Success', 'It worked');
            },
            failure: function(form, action){
                Ext.Msg.alert('Warning', action.result.errormsg);
            }
        });
    }
},
```

First we update the record we are currently editing using the `updateRecord` method of the BasicForm. This will automatically update the movie's row in the grid.

However if we modify the field that the grid is grouped by, the store will not detect this and regroup itself, so the above contains code to ensure that the grouping state is kept up to date. If the store is grouped and the `modified` property of the record (see the API docs for the `Record` class) contains a property named after the store's group field, then we explicitly tell the store to regroup itself. As usual, a modification of the store causes automatic update of the grid UI.

If we change the genre of the first movie, and **Submit** it, the resulting display will look like this:

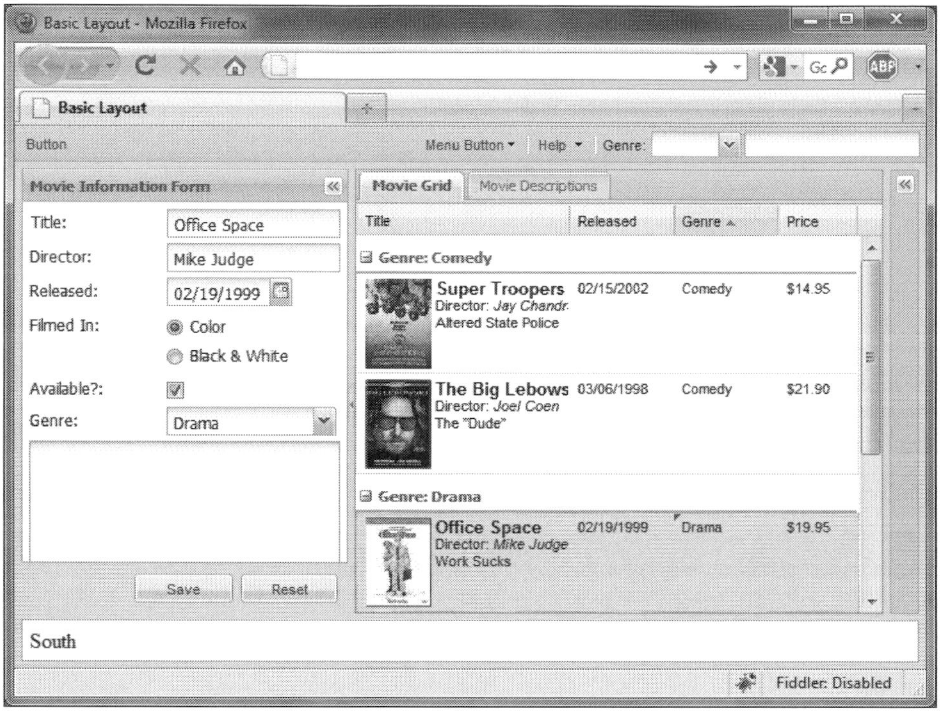


The form you see above shows how the FormLayout class will render labels attached to its child components. The FormLayout class injects into each child component, a reference to the Component's `<label>` element.

FormPanels, and all Containers which use FormLayout may be configured with options which modify how labels are displayed.

> These configuration options are read from the Container's config, not the `layout` config object.

- `hideLabels`: Set to `true` to hide all field labels in the Container.
- `labelWidth`: The width in pixels to allow for labels. All labels within the Container will be of this width.
- `LabelSeparator`: A string specifying a separator to be appended to the end of each label. This defaults to `":"`. To indicate that no separator is required, specify this as `new String()`.

- `labelAlign` - A string, one of `"left"`, `"right"` or `"top"`. It specifies whether to align the label text left justified towards the left margin of the Container, right justified towards the input field, or above the field.
- `LabelPad`: Defaults to 5. The left padding in pixels to apply to field labels.

This example also illustrates the inheritance of the FormLayout manager. It inherits from and illustrates the abilities of AnchorLayout.

# AnchorLayout

One very dynamic and useful layout is the anchor layout, which is enabled by default within a form panel—we used this layout unknowingly in the Chapter 3. It is used to allow the form fields within the form panel to expand and contract based on the size of that panel. Until now we have only used it to control width and it is only percentage based, but it is much more flexible than that.

The single line input fields in the example form use only a width anchor. They are configured with

```
anchor: '100%'
```

This means that the child component always occupies the full container width. You can verify this by dragging the west region's splitbar.

We can also use the anchor layout to adjust the height of the textarea in our 'Movie Information Form' so it fills the remaining space. By measuring the used space, and setting that as the amount of space to subtract, we get a textarea that sizes itself to the available space. We will also want to remove the fixed height that was set earlier.

```
{
  xtype: 'textarea',
  name: 'description',
  hideLabel: true,
  emptyText: 'Description',
  labelSeparator: '',
  anchor: '100% -185'
}
```

I have also added an 'emptyText' config to this field to give it a label of sorts. The anchor can be specified in either pixels or percentage—if pixels, then the field will be sized to 100 percent of the container, minus the amount of pixels specified, positive numbers will add pixels. Percentage numbers are based on the size of the entire container.

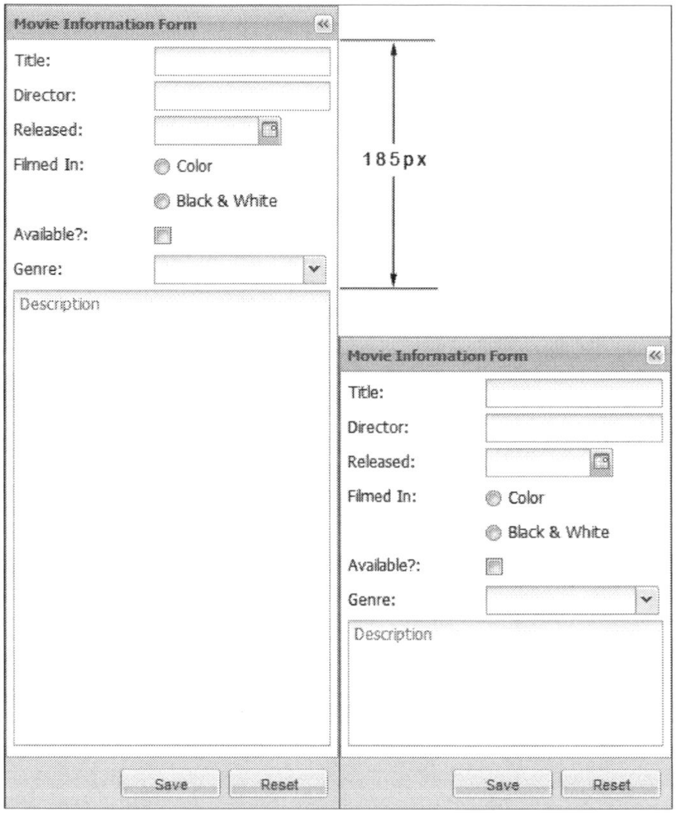


This layout uses the available height. A more reliable way of doing this which does not use hardcoded values is illustrated in the next example.

# More layouts

In our final example we add some more interactivity to the application, which demonstrates the dynamic nature of Ext JS layouts. We also add some further nested layouts to illustrate that nesting of Containers can be continued to any depth.

In this example we add another child item to the TabPanel. Because we do not need a header, or borders or toolbars, we add a Container:

```
{
    xtype: 'container',
    title: 'Nested Layout',
    layout: 'border',
    items: [{
        region: 'north',
        height: 100,
        split: true,
        margins: '5 5 0 5',
        html: 'Nested North'
    },{
        region: 'center',
        html: 'Nested Center',
        margins: '0 5 5 5'
    }]
}
```

We choose a border layout with only two child panels as the regions. They are configured with margins to achieve visual separation, and separated by a splitbar. To make more use of these panels, remember that they can be configured with a `layout`, and child `items` of their own.

# Vbox layout

In this last example, the west FormPanel is now configured with two child components. It uses the `vbox` layout manager to distribute its available vertical space between them:

```
layout: {
    type: 'vbox',
    align: 'stretch',
    padding: 5
},
```

The align config specifies that all child components are to be stretched to the full width of the Container. The padding config specifies the internal padding width of the Container to separate its contents from its border.

The top Component is a Container which uses `layout: 'form'` to render the single line input fields with their labels. This takes up whatever height it needs. Its `autoHeight` config means that it will not be sized by any layout manager.

The second Component is the TextArea and is configured with `flex: 1` which means that it is allocated any remaining vertical space.

# Hbox layout

Let's play with the hbox layout and a pair of grids by laying them out horizontally. One of the items will take 25 percent of the space, and the other will take the remaining 75 percent. We can construct this type of layout using the hbox layout and flex config option in each panel within this layout.

```
{
  title: 'Filter Test',
  xtype: 'container',
  layout: 'hbox',
  align: 'stretch',
  items: [{
    autoHeight: true,
    border: false,
    flex: 1,
    title: 'Genre Filter',
    xtype: 'grid',
    columns: [{header: 'Genre',dataIndex: 'genre',id: 'genre'}],
    store: genres,
    autoExpandColumn: 'genre'
  },{
    autoHeight: true,
    border: false,
    flex: 3,
    title: 'Movie Filter Results',
    ref: 'filteredGrid',
    xtype: 'grid',
    store: store,
    autoExpandColumn: 'title',
    columns: [
      /* movie grid column model */
    ]
  }]
}
```

The flex number we define represents the distribution of space for each panel within the total available area, so if we have 1 in the first panel, and 3 in the second, then the 1 would represent 25 percent of the space, and 3 would represent 75 percent. This could easily be changed to thirds instead of quarters by changing the 3 to 2. Whatever the total number is, Ext JS will take care of dividing up the space properly.

The example above would result in a layout that looked like the following:

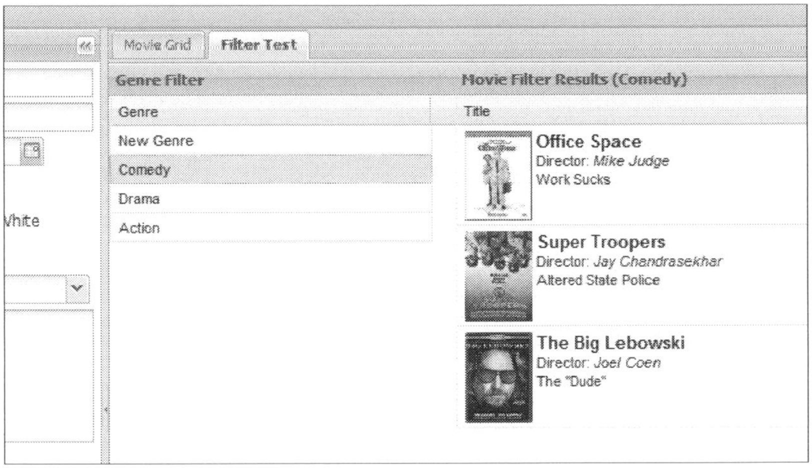


Our next important config is **align**, which sounds a bit different than it actually is. This represents where the panels will vertically align themselves, if within a horizontal layout, and vice versa. Here are the options available for the align config:

| Option | Layout | Description |
|---|---|---|
| `left` | `VBox` | This is the default alignment, which stacks all the items against the left side of the container. |
| center | VBox | Aligns all items in the center of the container. |
| stretch | VBox/HBox | Stretches all items to fill the space available |
| stretchmax | VBox/HBox | Stretches all the items to the width/height of the largest item. |
| top | Hbox | Stacks all the items against the top edge of the container. |
| middle | HBox | Aligns all items in the middle of the container. |

Most of the times I find myself using the stretch align option. There is also a pack config that can be used to align items in the same direction of the layout, so for instance a Hbox layout with the pack set to 'start' would align all our items to the left side of the container.

# Dynamically changing components

The user interactions available in this example illustrate how we can programmatically manipulate layouts and child items.

We have configured `rowclick` and `rowdblclick` event listener into the grid:

```
listeners: {
    rowdblclick: Movies.showFullDetails,
    rowclick: Movies.showFullDesc
},
```

The handlers are methods of the Movies singleton object. We want the single click handler to only perform its functionality if not followed quickly by another click (a double click gesture).

To do this, the Movies singleton creates a `DelayedTask` which is configured with the method to load the movie information panel. The click handler function schedules this to execute with a 200 millisecond delay.

The double click handler cancels that task before performing its functionality . It also illustrates how we can add new Components to existing Containers:

```
showFullDetails : function(grid, rowIndex){
    showDescTask.cancel();
    if (moreInfo.isVisible()){
        moreInfo.collapse();
    }
    var record = store.getAt(rowIndex),
        tabId = 'movie-desc-' + record.id,
        movieTab = mainTabPanel.getComponent(tabId);
        if (!movieTab) {
            movieTab = mainTabPanel.add({
                id: tabId,
                title: record.get("title"),
                closable: true,
                autoLoad: 'html/'+record.id+'.txt'
            });
        }
    mainTabPanel.setActiveTab(movieTab);
},
```

The `showFullDetails` method collapses the `moreInfo` panel to release more space to the center region. It then generates an ID for the movie information tab based upon the clicked movie's ID. Then it looks up that ID from the TabPanel using the `getComponent` method. If nothing was found, then it adds a new panel config object to the TabPanel configured with the generated ID, the movie title, and an autoLoad URL. Then it asks the TabPanel to activate that tab.

Basically, this shows the movie description, but it does not create a new tab every time you click the movie.

# Adding new components

Several Ext JS layout managers allow new child components to be added even after they are rendered. These include:

- AbsoluteLayout
- AccordionLayout
- AnchorLayout
- CardLayout
- ColumnLayout
- ContainerLayout
- FormLayout
- HBoxLayout
- VBoxLayout

New child components can be appended to a Container using the `add` method, or inserted within existing child components using the `insert` method.

To illustrate this, the first button in the toolbar in this example adds a new single line input to the FormPanel to allow editing of the movie's price:

```
addPriceInput: function(btn) {
    btn.disable();
    var fieldCtr = movieForm.getComponent('field-container');
    fieldCtr.add({
        xtype: 'numberfield',
        fieldLabel: 'Price',
        anchor: '100%',
        name: 'price',
        minValue: 10,
        allowNegative: false
    });
    movieForm.doLayout();
}
```

Many new child components can be added or inserted at one time. The Container's DOM is only updated when the Container's `doLayout` method is called.

The Container class's `doLayout` method uses the Container's layout manager to ensure that all child components are rendered and sized according to configuration.

In this case, the whole `movieForm` needs to be laid out because the field container will change height.

# Summary

In this chapter we learned of the importance of layout managers to the Container/Component nesting scheme.

We learned how different layout managers use different rules, and read different hint configs from child components to lay out child components.

We learned how to nest Containers to any level.

We also learned how to add new Components to existing Containers.

# 8

# Ext JS Does Grow on Trees

Hierarchical data is something that most developers are intimately familiar with. The root-branch-leaf structure is the underlying feature for many user interfaces, from the file and folder representations in Windows Explorer to the classic family tree showing children, parents, and grandparents. The `Ext.tree` package enables developers to bring these data structures to the user with only a few lines of code, and provides for a range of advanced cases with a number of simple configuration options.

Although the default Ext JS icon set shows tree nodes as files and folders, you are not restricted to the file system concept. The icons and text of the items, or nodes in your tree, can be changed based on the dynamic or static data used to populate it—and without requiring custom code. How about a security screen showing permission groups containing a number of users, with icons showing a photo of each user, or a gallery showing groups of photos, or image previews in the icons? Ext JS's tree classes put all of these scenarios within your grasp. In this chapter, you will learn about:

- Creating and configuring an `Ext.tree` instance
- Populating an `Ext.tree` with various types of data
- Dragging and dropping tree nodes
- Sorting & filtering a tree
- Creating context menus to provide options on nodes
- Customizing an `Ext.tree` in advanced scenarios

# Planting for the future

Ultimately, the Ext JS tree doesn't care about the data you're displaying, because it's flexible enough to deal with any scenario that you can come up with. Data can be instructed to load upfront, or in logical bursts, which can become a critical feature when you've got a lot of information to load. You can edit data directly in the tree, changing labels and item positions, or you can modify the appearance of the overall tree or of each individual node, all of which will contribute to a customized end user experience.

The Ext JS tree is built on top of the Component model, which underlies the whole Ext JS framework. This means that developers receive the benefits of working with the familiar Component system, that users get a consistent and integrated interface experience, and that you can be sure your tree will work seamlessly with the rest of your application.

# From tiny seeds...

In this chapter, we'll see how you can build a tree from first principles with a minimal amount of code. We'll also discuss the unique data structure that is used to populate the tree, and the way in which clever use of that data can let you harness important configuration options. The Ext JS tree natively supports advanced features such as sorting, and drag-and-drop, so we'll be discussing those as well. But if you need a truly highly customized tree, we'll also explore the way in which configuration options, methods, and events can be overridden or augmented to provide it.

The tree itself is created via the `Ext.tree.TreePanel` class, which in turn contains many `Ext.tree.TreeNodes` classes. These two classes are the core of the Ext JS tree support, and as such will be the main topics of discussion throughout this chapter. However, there are a number of other relevant classes that we'll also cover. Here's the full list from the `Ext.tree` package:

| **Classes** | **Description** |
|---|---|
| `AsyncTreeNode` | Allows `TreeNode` children to be loaded asynchronously |
| `DefaultSelectionModel` | Standard single-select for the `TreePanel` |
| `MultiSelectionModel` | Provides support for multiple node selection |
| `RootTreeNodeUI` | Specialized `TreeNode` for the root of `TreePanel` |
| `TreeDragZone` | Provides support for `TreeNode` dragging |
| `TreeDropZone` | Provides support for `TreeNode` dropping |
| `TreeEditor` | Allows node labels to be edited |
| `TreeFilter` | Filter support for `TreePanel` child nodes |

| Classes | Description |
|---|---|
| TreeLoader | Populates a TreePanel from a specified URL |
| TreeNode | The main class representing a node within a TreePanel |
| TreeNodeUI | Provides the underlying renderer for the TreeNode |
| TreePanel | A tree-like representation of data—the main tree class |
| TreeSorter | Supports sorting of nodes within a TreePanel |

Ouch! Fortunately, you don't have to use all of them at once. `TreeNode` and `TreePanel` provide the basics, and the rest of the classes are bolted on to provide extra functionality. We'll cover each of them in turn, discussing how they're used, and showing a few practical examples along the way.

# Our first sapling

By now, you're probably thinking of the various possibilities for the Ext JS tree, and want to get your hands dirty. Despite the fact that the `Ext.tree` classes are some of the most feature-rich available in the framework, you can still get everything up and running with only a few lines of code.

In the examples that follow, we'll assume that you have a blank-slate HTML page ready and waiting, with all of the Ext JS dependencies included. Most of the code we will use builds on what came before, to make sure that we're only working with bite-sized pieces. Bear this in mind when you look at them in isolation.

It is best practice to put the JavaScript in a separate file and wrap it in an `Ext.onReady` call. However, you can also do it according to your individual coding style.

# Preparing the ground

First, we need to create a containing `<div>` element on our HTML page. We will be rendering our `TreePanel` into this container. So we have to set it to the size we want our tree to be:

```
<div id="treecontainer" style="height:300px; width:200px;"></div>
```

The JavaScript for the tree can be broken down into three parts. Firstly, we need to specify the manner in which it's going to be populated. The `Ext.tree.TreeLoader` class provides this functionality, and here we're going to use it in the simplest manner:

```
var treeLoader = new Ext.tree.TreeLoader({
   dataUrl:'http://localhost/samplejson.php'
});
```

The `dataUrl` configuration parameter specifies the location of the script that is going to supply the **JavaScript Object Notation (JSON)** used to populate our tree. I'm not going to get into the details of the structure of JSON now; let's save that for later. The `dataUrl` parameter is also aliased as the `url` parameter, which you may prefer to use for consistency with other parts of Ext JS.

Each tree requires a root node, which acts as a great-granddaddy for all of its descendants. To create that root node, we use the `Ext.tree.AsyncTreeNode` class:

```
var rootNode = new Ext.tree.AsyncTreeNode({
   text: 'Root'
});
```

The reason we're using `AsyncTreeNode`, rather than the basic `TreeNode` that is also available, is because we're fetching our nodes from the server and are expecting child nodes to be populated branch-by-branch rather than all at once. This is the most typical scenario for a tree.

> `AsyncTreeNode` uses AJAX on-the-fly to ensure your users aren't waiting too long for your data to load and for the first nodes to be rendered.

Finally, we create the tree itself, using the `Ext.tree.TreePanel` class:

```
var tree = new Ext.tree.TreePanel({
   renderTo:'treecontainer',
   loader: treeLoader,
   root: rootNode
});
```

This is just a matter of passing the root node and the `TreeLoader` in as configuration options, as well as using the `renderTo` config to specify that we'd like the `TreePanel` rendered into our `treeContainer` element.

Again, you should remember that you need to wrap all of this code in a call to `Ext.onReady`, to make sure that the DOM is available when our code runs.

# A tree can't grow without data

We've seen that it only takes eleven lines of code to create a tree interface using Ext JS. You can see an example of the finished product here:

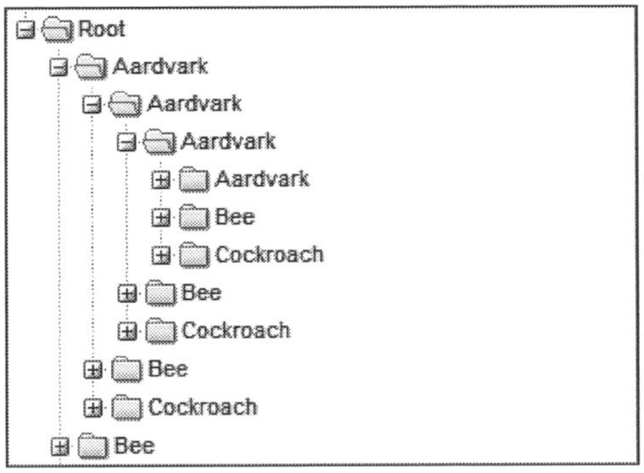


I guess it doesn't look like much, but we've got quite a bit of functionality for our 11 lines of code. We've got a consistent and attractive look and feel, with asynchronous remote loading of child nodes. To be fair, it's not as simple as that, because we skimmed over a crucial part of building an Ext JS tree—the data.

# JSON

The standard `TreeLoader` supports JSON in a specific format—an array of node definitions. Here's a cut-down example:

```
[
   { id: '1', text: 'No Children', leaf: true },
   { id: '2', text: 'Has Children',
     children: [{
       id: '3',
       text: 'Youngster',
       leaf: true
     }]
   }
]
```

The `text` property is the label of the node as it appears in the tree. The `id` property is used to uniquely identify each node, and will be used to determine which nodes are selected or expanded. Using the `id` property can make your life a whole lot easier if you're using some of the advanced features of the `TreePanel`, which we'll see later. The `children` property is optional. The `leaf` property can be thought of as marking a node as either a folder or a file. As a `leaf`, the file is contained within the folder. In the tree, `leaf` nodes will not be expandable and won't have the plus icon that identifies folders.

## A quick word about ID

By default, `TreeNodes` are assigned an automatically-generated ID, meaning that the ID configuration property is actually optional. The generated ID is a text string in the form `ynode-xx`, with `xx` being replaced by a number. IDs can be useful for retrieving a node you have previously referenced. However, it is quite likely that you'd want to assign the ID value yourself. Whenever you expand a node with children to trigger an asynchronous load of data from the server, your server script needs to know exactly which node was clicked in order to send its children back. By explicitly setting the ID, you'll find it a lot easier to match nodes with their actions when you're working with the server.

## Extra data

Although the `id`, `text`, and `leaf` properties are the most commonly used properties, the way in which they are populated by JSON isn't exclusive to them. In fact, any configuration property of a `TreeNode` can be initialized by JSON, which will prove to be a useful trick when we begin to explore the other features of the tree. You're also able to include application-specific data; perhaps your nodes are products and you want to hold the price of them. Any property that isn't recognized as a `TreeNode` config option will still be included on the `TreeNode.attributes` property for later access.

# XML

With Ext JS 3.0, loading XML into your tree is now handled by an official extension to the framework. This means that while you don't get the same level of API documentation as you would with a fully integrated part of Ext JS, XML loading is still a properly supported feature.

The `XmlTreeLoader` class is the extension in question, and in its simplest form can be used in exactly the same way as a standard `TreeLoader`. Given the following XML document:

```
<?xml version="1.0" encoding="ISO-8859-1"?>
<nodes>
  <node text="No Children" id="1" leaf="true" />
  <node text="Has Children" id="2" leaf="false">
    <child text="Youngster" id="3" leaf="true" />
  </node>
</nodes>
```

We can simply create an `XmlTreeLoader` as follows:

```
var treeLoader = new Ext.ux.tree.XmlTreeLoader({
      dataUrl:'http://localhost/samplexml.php'
});
```

This can slot into our previous example without changing any of the rest of the code.

In most situations, you're not going to have XML that's structured like this, so the `XmlTreeLoader` class does provide a means to use any kind of XML document in a tree. By overriding the `processAttributes` method of the `XmlTreeLoader`, you can examine each XML node as it's being processed and tweak the corresponding `TreeNode`. As with JSON, extra attributes on an XML node get added as attributes on the tree node for easy access and additionally, any inner text of an XML node gets added as the `innerText` attribute. For example:

```
Ext.CustomXmlTreeLoader = Ext.extend(Ext.ux.tree.XmlTreeLoader, {
   processAttributes : function(node){
    // prefix the node ID to the node text
    node.text = node.id + " " + node.text;
    // OR the XML node contents added as innerText attrib
    node.text = node.innerText;
    // OR extra XML attrib added as a node attrib
    node.text = node.appSpecificValue;
  }
});
```

Using an `XmlTreeLoader` in your code makes building trees with XML just as easy as it is with JSON.

# Tending your trees

We're now going to discuss the main features that you can bolt on to your tree to make it a little bit more useful. Drag-and-drop, sorting, and node editing, are the kinds of things that lift the `TreePanel` from being a clever way of displaying data, to being a great way of manipulating it.

# Drag and drop

Ext JS takes care of all of the drag-and-drop UI for you when you're using a `TreePanel`. Just add `enableDD: true` to your configuration, and you'll be able to rearrange nodes with a drop target graphic, and add them to folders, with a green plus icon to indicate what you're about to do.

> The `TreePanel` doesn't care about just its own nodes. If you've got more than one `TreePanel` on the page, then you can happily drag-and-drop branches or leaves between them.

But that's only half the story. When you refresh your page, all of your rearranged nodes will be back to their starting positions. That's because the `TreePanel` doesn't automatically know how you want to persist your changes, and in order to educate it, we've got to hook into some events.

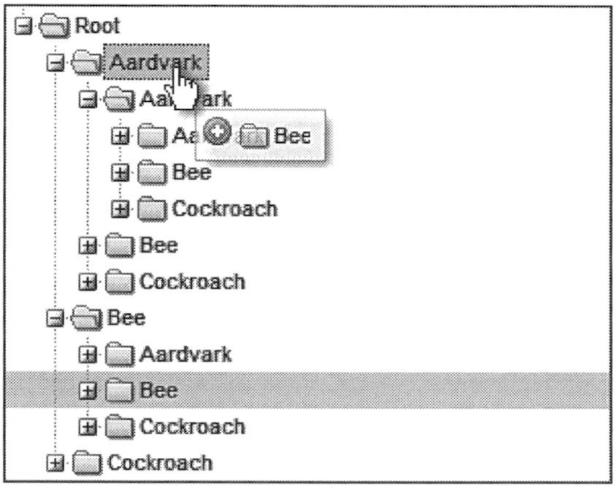


The `beforemovenode` event of the `TreePanel` fires at just the right time for us—after the mouse button is released to signify we want to do a drop, but before the `TreePanel` UI is updated to reflect that. We are most likely to add code such as the following to tell the server about node move events:

```
tree.on('beforemovenode', function(tree, node,
                                   oldParent, newParent, index) {
   Ext.Ajax.request({
      url: 'http://localhost/node-move.php',
      params: {
         nodeid: node.id,
         newparentid: newParent.id,
         oldparentid: oldParent.id,
         dropindex: index
      }
   });
});
```

Augmenting our previous code, we're adding a new event handler for the `beforemovenode` event. The handler function is called with a few useful arguments:

- `tree`: The `TreePanel` that raised the event
- `node`: The `TreeNode` being moved
- `oldParent`: The previous parent of the node being moved
- `newParent`: The new parent of the node being moved
- `index`: The numerical index where the node was dropped

We use these arguments to form the parameters of an AJAX call to the server. As you can pull out pretty much any information you need about the current state of the tree, your server-side script can perform any action that it needs to.

In some cases, that could include canceling the move action. If the logic you place within the `beforemovenode` handler fails, you need to roll back your changes. If you're not doing an AJAX call, this is pretty straightforward—just return `false` at the end of the handler and the action will be canceled. For AJAX though, it's more difficult, because the `XMLHttpRequest` happens asynchronously, and the event handler will proceed with its default action, which is to allow the move.

In these circumstances, you need to make sure that you provide a failure handler for your AJAX request, and pass enough information back to that failure handler to allow it to manually return the tree to its previous state. As `beforemovenode` provides a lot of information through its arguments, you can pass the necessary data to take care of these error events.

# Sorting

We can sort nodes in a `TreePanel` in a very flexible manner by using the `TreeSorter`. Again, building on our previous code, we can create a `TreeSorter` such as this:

```
new Ext.tree.TreeSorter(tree, {
    folderSort: true,
    dir: "asc"
});
```

As `TreeSorter` assumes a couple of defaults—specifically, that your leaf nodes are marked with a property called `leaf` and that your labels are in a property called `text`—we can perform an alphabetical sort very easily. The `dir` parameter tells the `TreeSorter` to sort in either ascending (with the `asc` value) or descending (`desc`) order, and the `folderSort` parameter indicates that it should sort leaf nodes that are within folders—in other words, the whole tree hierarchy.

If you've got data that isn't simple text, you can specify a custom method of sorting with the `sortType` configuration option. `sortType` takes a function as its value, and that function will be called with one argument: a `TreeNode`.

The purpose of the `sortType` function is to allow you to cast a custom property of the `TreeNode`—presumably something you've passed from the server and that is specific to your business needs—and convert it to a format that Ext JS can sort, in other words, one of the standard JavaScript types such as `integer`, `string`, or `date`.

This feature can be useful in cases where data passed to the tree is in a format that isn't conducive to normal searching. Data generated by the server might serve multiple purposes, and hence may not always be right for a particular purpose. For example, we may need to convert dates into a standard format—from US style MM/DD/YY to YYYYMMDD format that is suitable for sorting—or maybe we need to strip extraneous characters from a monetary value so that it can be parsed as a decimal.

```
sortType: function(node) {
   return node.attributes.creationDate
}
```

In the previous example, we return some custom data from our node, and because this value is a valid JavaScript date, Ext JS will be able to sort against it. This is a simple demonstration of how the `sortType` option can be used to allow the `TreeSorter` to work with any kind of server data.

# Editing

There are many scenarios in which editing the value of your nodes can be useful. When viewing a hierarchy of categorized products, you may wish to rename either the categories or the products in line, without navigating to another screen. We can enable this simple feature by using the `Ext.tree.TreeEditor` class:

```
var editor = new Ext.tree.TreeEditor(tree);
```

The defaults of the `TreeEditor` mean that this will now give your tree nodes a `TextField` editor when you double-click on their label. However, as with basic drag-and-drop functionality, enabling this feature doesn't automatically mean that your changes will be persisted to the server. We need to handle the event that fires when you've finished editing the node:

```
editor.on('beforecomplete', function(editor, newValue, originalValue)
{
   // Possible Ajax call?
});
```

The beforecomplete event handler gets called with three arguments:

- editor: The editor field used to edit the node
- newValue: The value that was entered
- originalValue: The value before you changed it

However, it is important to note that the editor parameter is no ordinary Ext.form.Field. It is augmented with extra properties, the most useful of which is editNode, a reference to the node that was edited. This allows you to get information such as the node ID, which would be essential in making a server-side call to synchronize the edited value in the database.

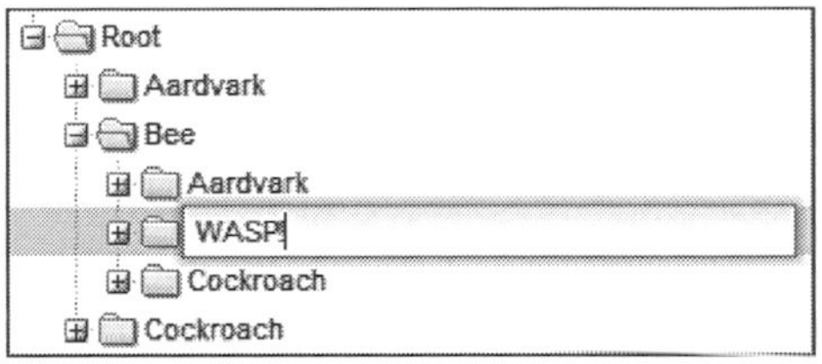


As with the beforemovenode event of the TreePanel, beforecomplete allows cancellation of the edit action by returning false at the end of its handler processing. AJAX requests will need to provide a failure handler to manually restore the edited value.

This has been a quick overview of how to create a very simple inline editor. There are also means of using this class to create more complicated features. The TreeEditor constructor can take up to two optional parameters on top of the single mandatory parameter as shown in the previous example. These are a field configuration object and a configuration object for the TreeEditor. The field config can be one of two things: a field config object to be applied to the standard TextField editor, or an already created instance of a different form field. If it is the latter, it will be used instead of the default, which means that you can add NumberField, DateField, or another Ext.form.Field in a similar manner.

The second parameter allows you to configure the TreeEditor, and is more for fine-tuning rather than introducing any exciting functionality. For example, we can use cancelOnEsc to allow the user to cancel any editing by pressing the *Escape* key, or use ignoreNoChange to avoid firing completion events if a value has not changed after an edit.

# Trimming and pruning

There a few other tricks that the `TreePanel` supports, which assist in the creation of rich applications. Varying selection models, node filtering, and context menus are commonly-used features in many solutions. So let's take a look at these now.

# Selection models

In our previous example code, we dragged and edited `TreeNodes` to alter them immediately. But nodes can also be selected for further processing. The `TreePanel` uses a single selection model by default. In our previous code, we've already done everything we need to enable node selection. As with many aspects of the tree, simply selecting the node doesn't do anything; instead we need to hook in to some of the features provided to manipulate the selection.

A great example of this would be to select a node and have an information panel automatically populated with further details of that node. Perhaps you have a tree of named products, and clicking a node will display the price and stock level of the selected product. We can use the `selectionchange` event to make this happen. Again, using our previous code as a starting point, we could add the following:

```
tree.selModel.on('selectionchange', function(selModel, node) {
   var price = node.attributes.price;
});
```

The second node argument that is passed to the `selectionchange` event makes it very easy to grab any custom attributes in your node data.

What if we want to allow multiple nodes to be selected? How can we do that, and how can we handle the `selectionchange` event in that configuration? We can use `Ext.tree.MultiSelectionModel` when creating our `TreePanel`:

```
var tree = new Ext.tree.TreePanel({
      renderTo:'treeContainer',
      loader: treeLoader,
      root: rootNode,
      selModel: new Ext.tree.MultiSelectionModel()
   });
```

Configuration is as simple as that. Although handling the `selectionchange` event is very similar to the default selection model, there is an important difference. The second argument to the event handler will be an *array* of nodes rather than a single node. We can see multiple selected nodes in this screenshot:

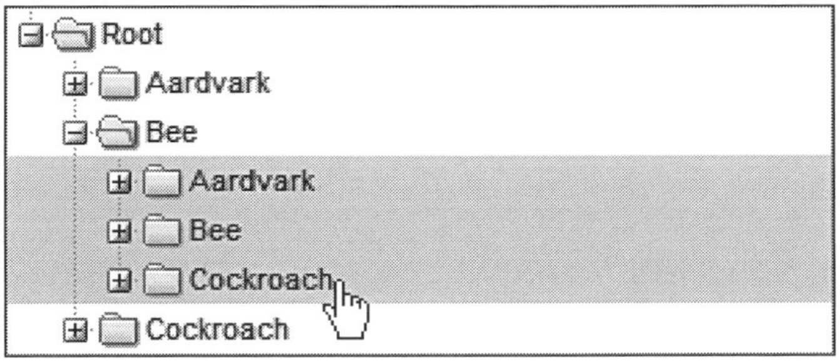


Selection models don't just expose the means of retrieving selection information. They also allow manipulation of the current selection. For example, the `MultiSelectionModel.clearSelections()` method is useful for wiping the slate clean after you have finished handling an event involving multiple nodes. `DefaultSelectionModel` has methods (`selectNext` and `selectPrevious`) for navigating the tree, moving up or down the node hierarchy as required.

# Round-up with context menus

We've already covered a lot of the functionality that the `TreePanel` can provide, so let's consolidate a little bit with a practical example. Adding a context menu that appears when you right-click a `TreeNode` is a trivial task with Ext JS. However, it can be an extremely useful means of adding shortcuts to your interface. We'll be building on the code that has been used in the previous sections. First, let's create the menu, and then we'll hook it up to the `TreePanel`:

```
var contextMenu = new Ext.menu.Menu({
   items: [
      { text: 'Delete', handler: deleteHandler },
      { text: 'Sort', handler: sortHandler }
   ]
});
tree.on('contextmenu', treeContextHandler);
```

The `TreePanel` provides a `contextmenu` event which fires when the user right-clicks on a node. Note that our listeners are not anonymous functions as they have been in the previous examples—instead they have been split off for easy reading.

First, the `treeContextHandler` that handles the `contextmenu` event:

```
function treeContextHandler(node) {
   node.select();
   contextMenu.show(node.ui.getAnchor());
}
```

The handler gets called with a node argument, so we need to select the node to allow us to act upon it later. We then pop up the context menu by calling the `show` method with a single parameter that tells the pop-up menu where to align itself—in this case it's the text of the `TreeNode` we've clicked on.

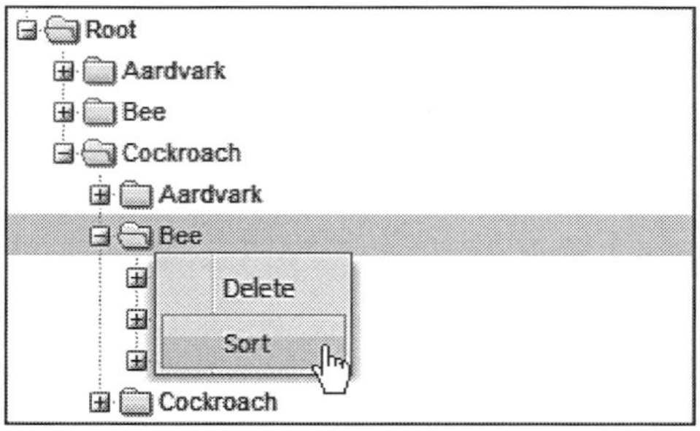


# Handling the menu

We've got two context menu entries—**Delete** and **Sort**. Let's first take a look at the handler for **Delete**:

```
function deleteHandler() {
   tree.getSelectionModel().getSelectedNode().remove();
}
```

Using our previous knowledge of selection models, we get the node that we selected in the `treeContextHandler`, and simply call its `remove()` method. This will delete the node and all of its children from the `TreePanel`. Note that we're not dealing with persisting this change to the server, but if this was something that you needed to do, `TreePanel` has a `remove` event that you could use a handler for to provide that functionality.

The handler for our **Sort** menu entry is given here:

```
function sortHandler() {
   tree.getSelectionModel().getSelectedNode().sort(
      function (leftNode, rightNode) {
         return (leftNode.text.toUpperCase() < rightNode.text.
toUpperCase() ? 1 : -1);
      }
   );
}
```

Again, we use the selection model to get the selected node. Ext JS provides a `sort` method on the `TreeNode` that takes a function as its first parameter. This function gets called with two arguments: the two nodes to compare. In this example, we are sorting by the node's `text` property in descending order, but you can sort by any custom node attribute you like.

> You can use this sorting method in conjunction with a `TreeSorter` without issues. That's because `TreeSorter` only monitors the `beforechildrenrendered`, `append`, `insert`, and `textchange` events on the `TreePanel`. Any other changes will be unaffected.

The **Delete** context menu action will completely remove the selected node from the `TreePanel`, while the **Sort** action will order its children according to their text label.

# Filtering

The `Ext.tree.TreeFilter` class is marked as "experimental" in Ext JS 3.0, so I'm going to touch upon it only briefly, however it has been in the framework since Ext JS 2.0 so I wouldn't shy away from using it. `TreeFilter` is here to stay. It's designed for scenarios where the user needs to search for nodes based on a particular attribute. This attribute could be the text, the ID, or any custom data that was passed when the node was created. Let's take the context menu that we just built and use it to demonstrate filtering. First, we have to create the `TreeFilter`:

```
var filter = new Ext.tree.TreeFilter(tree);
```

You need to go back to the configuration for the context menu and add a new entry to the `items` configuration property:

```
{ text: 'Filter', handler: filterHandler }
```

We now need to create a `filterHandler` function that performs the filter action:

```
function filterHandler() {
   var node = tree.getSelectionModel().getSelectedNode();
   filter.filter('Bee', 'text', node);
}
```

As with our other handler functions, we start by getting the currently selected node in the tree, and then call the `filter` function. This function takes three arguments:

- The value to filter by
- The attribute to filter on; this is optional and defaults to `text`
- The starting node for the filter

We pass the selected node as the starting node for the filter, which means that the node we right-clicked on in order to pop up the menu will have its children filtered by the specified value.

Our aardvark, bee, and cockroach examples don't really require this level of filtering, but there are other situations in which this could prove to be a useful user feature. Online software documentation, with multiple levels of detail, could be represented in a tree and a `TreeFilter` could be used to search by topic. In a more advanced scenario, you could use checkboxes or pop-up dialogs to get the user's input for the filter, providing a much more flexible experience.

# The roots

Although we've demonstrated a number of powerful techniques using the Ext tree support, its real strength lies in the wealth of settings, methods, and hook points that the various classes expose. We've already reviewed a number of ways of configuring the `TreePanel` and `TreeNode` classes, which give access to a number of powerful features. However, there are more configuration options that can be used to tweak and enhance your tree, and we're going to review some of the more interesting ones now.

# TreePanel tweaks

By default, there are a number of graphical enhancements enabled for the `TreePanel` which, depending on your application requirements, may not be desirable. For example, setting `animate` to `false` will prevent the smooth animated effect being used for the expansion and contraction of nodes. This can be particularly useful in situations where nodes will be repeatedly expanded and collapsed by a user and slower animated transitions can be frustrating.

As `TreePanel` extends from `Ext.Panel`, it supports all of the standard `Panel` features. This is easy to remember, because it means that support for toolbars at the top and the bottom (via the `tbar` and `bbar` config options), separate header and footer elements, and expand/collapse functionality for the `Panel` are all supported. The `TreePanel` can also be included in any `Ext.ViewPort` or `Ext.layout`.

# Cosmetic

In terms of purely cosmetic options, `TreePanel` provides the `lines` option, which when set to `false` will disable the guidelines that show the hierarchy of the `TreeNodes` within the panel. This can be useful if you're creating a very simple tree for which lines would just clutter the interface.

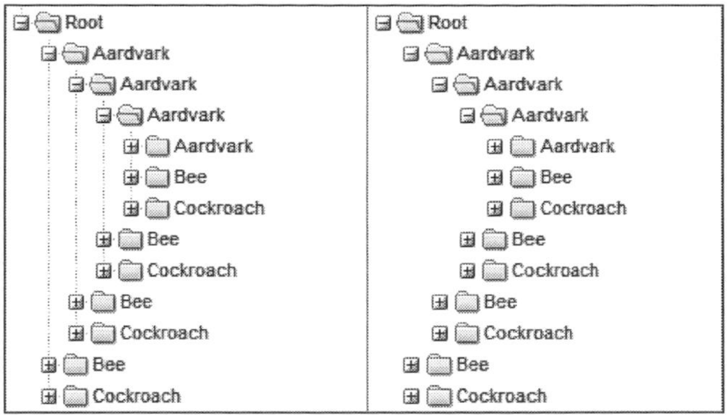


`hlColor` is applicable for drag-and-drop enabled trees, and controls the start color for the fading highlight (supplied as a hex string, such as 990000) which is triggered when a node is dropped. This can be completely disabled by setting `dlDrop` to `false`. Setting `trackMouseOver` to `false` will disable the highlight that appears when you hover over a node.

# Tweaking TreeNode

In many cases, you won't be manually creating `TreeNodes`, other than your root node, so you might think that the configuration options aren't of much use to you. Not so, because it's not just the `id` and `text` properties from your JSON that are used when generating nodes—any property in your JSON that matches with a `config` option on the `TreeNode` will be used to create the node. Say you have a JSON that is like this:

```
[
    { text: 'My Node', disabled: true, href: 'http://extjs.com'}
]
```

You'll get a node that starts off as disabled, but when enabled will act as a link to the Ext JS website.

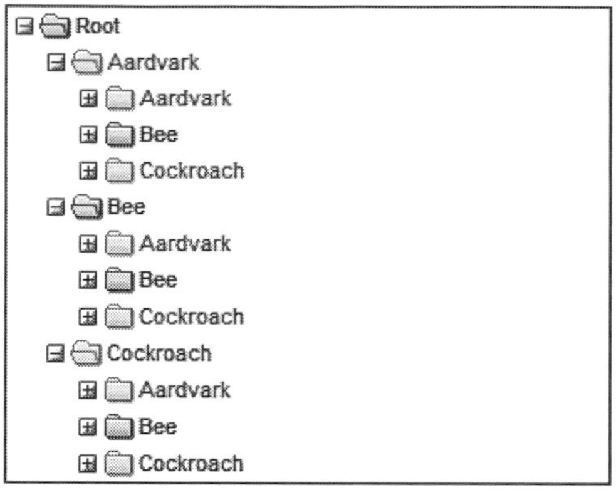


This feature is extremely useful for passing application-specific information to your `TreeNodes`. For example, your server logic may dictate that particular nodes cannot have children. Setting `allowChildren: false` means that the node can't be used as a drop target for a node that is being dragged. Similarly, you can set individual nodes to be disallowed for dragging by using the `draggable: false` option. We can set the status of a checkbox on the node by using `checked: true`. In fact, simply specifying the `checked` option—whether `true` or `false`—will cause the checkbox to appear next to the node. These configuration options allow you to set the behavior of your nodes based on some server logic, but do not require any manual handling in order to see your preferences enacted.

There are a few other useful configuration options available for `TreeNode`. You can provide custom icons by using the `icon` option, or provide a CSS styling hook by using the `cls` option. The `qtip` option lets you provide a pop-up tooltip, perhaps providing a description of the node, while the text label shows its name.

# Manipulating

Once the `TreePanel` is configured, we can begin to work with its nodes. The panel mostly allows for navigation of the hierarchy, starting at a selected node and moving to a parent or child, or up and down the current branch. We can also select nodes or expand them by their path, which could be used to search for specific nodes.

The `expandAll` and `collapseAll` methods are pretty self-explanatory, and can be useful for resetting the tree to a default state. Each method takes a single Boolean parameter to state whether the change should be animated or not.

The `expandPath` method's first parameter is the "path" of a node. The path uniquely identifies the node within the hierarchy, and takes the form of a string which fully qualifies the location of a node in the tree. For example, a path could look like this:

```
/n-15/n-56/n-101
```

Here, we have a representation of the location of the node with the ID `n-101`. `n-15` is the root node, with a child `n-56`; and `n-101` is in turn a child of `n-56`. If you're familiar with XPath, then this notation will be well-known to you. If you're not familiar with XPath then you can think of it as a postal address or a web IP address—a unique way of referring to this node.

By passing this value to `expandPath`, the tree will drill down to the specified node, expanding branches as necessary. Imagine the following code:

```
Ext.Msg.prompt('Node', 'Please enter a product name',
                function(btn, text){
    if (btn == 'ok'){
        var path = GetNodePathFromName(text);
      tree.expandPath(path);
    }
});
```

The `GetNodePathFromName` function could parse the node path string and and return the node ID, enabling quick navigation of the tree based on the user's input. Alternatively, `TreePanel.getNodeById` could be used in a similar way. Rather than expanding the node, further manipulation could occur.

In some circumstances, you may need to perform the reverse action, that is, you have a node but you need to get the path for it. `TreeNode.getPath` is provided for just this purpose, and can be used as a means of storing the location of a node.

# Further methods

The `TreeNode` has a number of other useful methods as well. We've already covered `sort` and `remove`, but now we can add some basic utility methods such as `collapse` and `expand`, `enable` and `disable`, as well as some handy extras such as `expandChildNodes` and `collapseChildNodes`, which can traverse all child nodes of an arbitrary root, and change their expansion states. The `findChild` and `findChildBy` methods allow both simple and custom searching of child nodes, as shown in the following example where we search for the first node with a price attribute of `300`:

```
var node = root.findChild('price', 300);
```

In some cases you may need to mass-manipulate the attributes of your node hierarchy. You can do this by using the `TreeNode.eachChild` method:

```
root.eachChild(function(currentNode) {
   currentNode.attributes.price += 30;
});
```

As the first parameter to `eachChild` is a function, we can perform any logic that is required of our application.

# Event capture

We've already demonstrated a couple of methods of watching for user interaction with the tree, but there are many events available as hooks for your custom code. Earlier, we discussed the use of the `checked` configuration option on a `TreeNode`. When the node checkbox is toggled, the `checkchange` event is fired. This could be useful for visually highlighting the check status:

```
tree.on('checkchange', function(node, checked) {
   node.eachChild(function(currentNode) {
      currentNode.ui.toggleCheck();
   });
}
```

We're propagating the check down through the children of the `TreeNode`. We could also highlight the nodes in question to clearly show that their check status has changed, or perform some other logic, such as adding information about the newly checked nodes to an informational display elsewhere on the page.

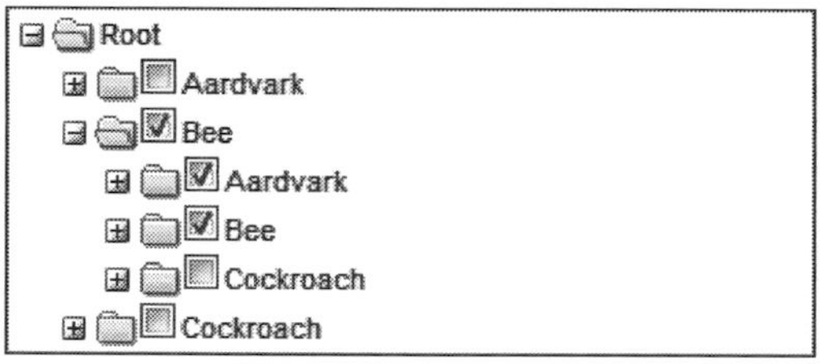


A more common use of the `TreePanel` events is to verify changes or persist them to a server-side store. For example, a tree of categorized products may have some logical restrictions—certain bargain categories may specify the maximum price of a product. We could use the `beforeappend` event to check for this:

```
tree.on('beforeappend', function(tree, parent, node) {
   return node.attributes.price < parent.attributes.maximumPrice;
});
```

This example demonstrates a pattern that you have seen throughout Ext JS—returning `false` from an event handler will cancel the action. In this case, if the price of the node being added is greater than the `maximumPrice` assigned to its parent, the function will return `false`, and the node will not be added.

# Remembering state

In many applications, `TreePanel` instances are used as navigation aids, showing a hierarchical structure, with its nodes being HTML links to node detail pages. In this scenario, if a user wishes to view multiple node detail pages, one after the other, the default behavior of the `TreePanel` can lead to frustration. This is because the tree doesn't save its state between page refreshes, so any expanded node will be rendered as collapsed when the user navigates back to the page. If the user needs to drill down to the branch they are interested in every time they navigate back to the tree, they are quickly going to lose patience with the interface. To try and avoid this situation, we can use some of Ext's state management features.

## StateManager

Now that we have a good grasp of the way we can manipulate the `TreePanel`, working out how we can save and restore its state should be fairly straightforward. Essentially, what we need to do is record each expansion of a `TreeNode`, and when the page reloads, "playback" those expansions. We can use `Ext.state.Manager` with a `CookieProvider` to store our expansion. We can initialize this with:

```
Ext.state.Manager.setProvider(new Ext.state.CookieProvider());
```

This is standard fare for setting up a state provider. We now need to establish exactly what we're going to store, and the logical choice would be the path of the last expanded node. This means that we can simply expand out that path and present the user with the last part of the hierarchy they were interested in. Here's a naive implementation of that idea:

```
tree.on('expandnode', function (node){
Ext.state.Manager.set("treestate", node.getPath());
});
```

In this code, we simply handle the `expandnode` event of the `TreePanel` to record the path, using `TreeNode.getPath`, of any node that is expanded. As we overwrite that value on each expansion, the `treestate` should hold the path of the last node that was expanded. We can then check for that value when the page is loaded:

```
var treeState = Ext.state.Manager.get("treestate");
if (treeState)
   tree.expandPath(treeState);
```

If `treestate` has previously been recorded, we use that to expand the tree out to the last-expanded node.

## Caveats

As mentioned, this is a naive implementation. It doesn't handle cases where the user expands, collapses a node, and then navigates away and back. In such cases, the collapse of the node wouldn't be saved. So when we restore the state, the user will see it expanded again. By handling the `collapsenode` event, we could take this issue into account. We also have a problem with the expansion of multiple nodes. If more than one branch is expanded our code will only expand the one the user clicked most recently. Storing an array of expanded nodes is one approach that could address this shortcoming.

# Summary

Getting a feature-rich tree interface such as `Ext.tree.TreePanel` up and running in eleven lines of code is pretty impressive, and we've shown that it is possible. Over and above that, this chapter has demonstrated that the strength of the `TreePanel` is not simply in its ease of use, but in the way we can use its wealth of configuration options to deliver application-specific functionality.

The use of asynchronous loading is an important feature of the `TreePanel`, because it provides a way of consuming large amounts of dynamic data in a scalable fashion. It's also handled transparently by `Ext.tree`, which means that the implementation is as beneficial for the developer as it is for the end user. And no matter what backend you're using, a custom `Ext.tree.TreeLoader` can consume JSON and XML in any format.

Despite all of their power, the `Ext.tree` classes still manage to feel pretty lightweight in use. It's easy to tame that power by using the configuration options, the methods, and the events that the `TreePanel` and `TreeNode` provide, but it's not just about these classes. `TreeSorter` and `TreeNodeUI` are key parts of the puzzle, adding functionality and allowing customization for a standardized look and feel.

As the `Ext.TreePanel` extends the `Panel`, which in turn extends the `BoxComponent`, we get all of the strong component and layout support that comes from a full-fledged Ext JS component. `BoxComponent` support will be particularly interesting as we move forward, because it means that trees can easily be included in various configurations within an `Ext.Window`, which just happens to be our next topic.

# 9
# Windows and Dialogs

In the olden days of the Web, users of traditional backend systems would spend their time crunching data in list and form-based interfaces. Pick an item from a list of customer orders, then navigate to a detail form, rinse, and repeat. The trouble is that we're talking about thousands of entries in a list, and lots of detail in the forms. The chances are that in our customer order example, we might even need sub-forms to show all of the information that is available, and each time we move to another screen we're refreshing the whole page and getting the entire data all over again.

That's fine; it's how the Web works. But in a data processing scenario, where your users are going back and forth throughout the day, there's a real benefit in optimizing the speed at which screens appear and data is refreshed. As we've seen, the Ext JS grid plays a key part in this, by bringing AJAX-powered paging and sorting of Grid Views into play, to replace the old-style static lists.

Now we're going to take a look at the other part of the puzzle—Ext JS window and dialog support. These classes allow developers to present any kind of information to their users, without forcing the users to navigate to another screen. By popping up as an overlay on top of the current page, a window, or dialog can present detailed data in the form of grids, tree, images, and text. We can also use them in a simplified form to show informational alerts or to quickly capture user data.

- Understand the difference between `Ext.Window` and `Ext.MessageBox`
- Use built-in Ext JS methods to show familiar popups
- Use `Ext.MessageBox` to create customized popup dialogs
- Create `Ext.Windows` with Layouts and child Components
- Tweak the configuration of a window for advanced usage
- Use Window Managers in multi-window applications

# Opening a dialog

In this chapter, we'll talk about the main `Ext.Window` and `Ext.MessageBox` classes, both of which have extensive applications in our enhanced user interface. While the `Window` itself is designed to be a flexible, multipurpose component, the `MessageBox` is a more focused solution. It is used in a similar way as standard JavaScript pop ups such as `alert` and `prompt`, albeit with many more behavioral and presentational options available for it.

`Ext.Window` is another fully-blown `Ext.Container`, giving it a wealth of underlying settings which will be familiar from the other parts of the Ext JS framework. It also hints at the types of interfaces that we can build in a window, given that we can set the internal `layout` of a `Container` to a range of different options.

We're also going to cover some extra classes which help us to manipulate multiple windows: `Ext.WindowGroup` and `Ext.WindowManager`. In advanced applications, we can use more than one window to present drill-down views of information, or we can allow the user to view more than one record at a time in separate windows. Window groups assist with these applications, giving us the power to act upon many windows at once.

Despite the fact that dialogs build on `Ext.Window`, we're going to address dialogs first. That's because the dialogs abstract away many of the powerful options of `Ext.Window`, making it a cut-down version of the superclass.

# Dialogs

As previously mentioned, dialogs can be likened to the prompt and alert functions that are available in most browser implementations of JavaScript. Although the appearance of those pop ups is controlled by the browser and the operating system, and their behavior is limited to the most common cases, these restrictions don't apply to the Ext JS dialogs.

> Although the dialog class is actually `Ext.MessageBox`, Ext JS provides a shorthand version—`Ext.Msg`. This shorthand version can make your code a little more concise, but it's up to you which one you use, as they're both functionally equivalent.

Let's take a look at the ready-made pop ups that Ext JS makes available to us.

# Off the shelf

We've talked about how Ext provides a replacement for the JavaScript alert, so let's have a look at that first:

```
Ext.Msg.alert('Hey!', 'Something happened.');
```

The first thing to notice is that `Msg.alert` takes two parameters, whereas the standard alert takes only one. The first allows you to specify a title for the alert dialog, and the second specifies the body text. The previous code results in a `messagebox` as follows:

As you can see, it performs very much the same function as a standard alert but with that familiar Ext JS look and feel. We can also convey a little bit more information by using the title bar. Showing `Msg.alert` doesn't temporarily halt script execution in the same way that a normal alert will; be aware of this when using the Ext version. Later, we'll look at ways to use callbacks to replicate that halt functionality should you need it.

> You can only use a single `Ext.MessageBox` at a time. If you try to pop up two boxes at the same time, the first will be replaced by the second. So in some cases, you'll want to check for the presence of an existing dialog in case you inadvertently overwrite the message it is presenting.

Let's take a look at another replacement, the `Ext.Msg.prompt`. This allows the capture of a single line of text in the same way the JavaScript prompt does. However, instead of simply returning a value, it gives you a few more options. Here's a comparison of doing the same thing with each method:

```
var data = prompt('Tell me something');

Ext.Msg.prompt('Hey!', 'Tell me something', function(btn, text){
    if (btn == 'ok'){
        var data = text;
    }
}, this, false, '');
```

Again, `Msg.prompt` allows you to pass a title as the first argument, and the body text is the second. The third argument is a callback function that will be called when a button—either **OK** or **Cancel**—is clicked in the prompt. The callback has two arguments: the button that was clicked and the text that was provided by the user. You can use these as demonstrated in the example code.

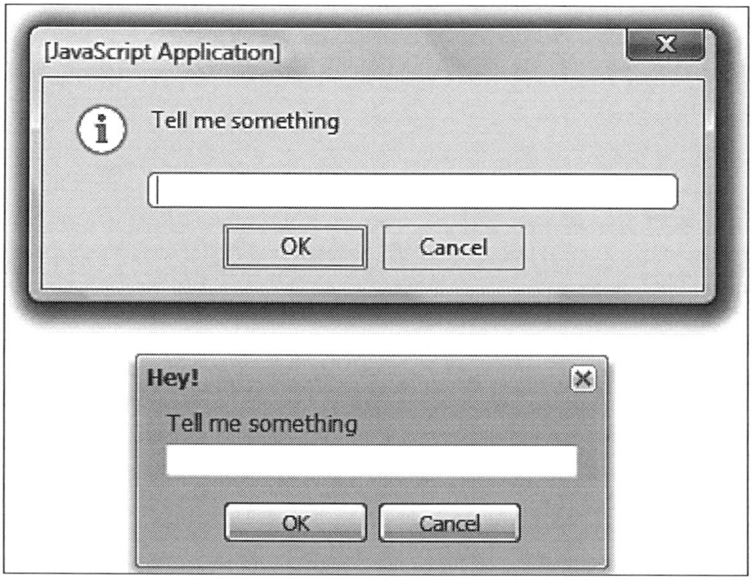


Note the other three options that come after the callback function are scope, multiline, and initial value, respectively. The multiline argument is interesting—accepting a Boolean value, it allows a more flexible capture of text than the standard prompt.

## Confirmation

Our final replacement `messagebox` is for the confirm pop up, which allows the user to choose between confirming an action or rejecting it. The code should be pretty familiar by now:

```
Ext.Msg.confirm('Hey!', 'Is this ok?', function(btn, text){
   if (btn == 'yes'){
      // go ahead and do more stuff
   } else {
      // abort, abort!
   }
});
```

Again we're using the title, body text, and callback arguments that we saw in the `Msg.prompt`, so there are no surprises here. An interesting difference between this and the standard confirm is that whereas the standard confirmation gives the options **OK** and **Cancel**, the Ext JS one gives the user the choice of **Yes** and **No**. This is arguably a better default, particularly when you use a question in the body text of the confirm `messagebox`.

# It's all progressing nicely

There's a fourth standard `messagebox` which is included with Ext JS—one that isn't just a replacement for a basic JavaScript pop up. This is the progress dialog. `Ext.Msg.progress` isn't designed to be used independently like the other Ext message boxes, and doesn't need user input. In fact,you could trigger it like this:

```
Ext.Msg.progress('Hey!', 'We\'re waiting...', 'progressing');
```

But then you're going to be waiting for a while, because you'll get a modal dialog which never progresses anywhere. The first two arguments are the title and body text as in the previous examples, while the third is the text that will appear in the progress bar.

So, if we don't want to be stuck with an eternal progress bar, how can we get things moving? The `Ext.Msg.updateProgress` method is provided just for this purpose. Here's an example which illustrates its use:

```
var count = 0;

var interval = window.setInterval(function() {
   count = count + 0.04;

   Ext.Msg.updateProgress(count);

   if(count >= 1) {
      window.clearInterval(interval);
      Ext.Msg.hide();
   }
}, 100);
```

This is a very contrived example, in which we're calling `updateProgress` every 100 milliseconds via a timer, and incrementing the progress using the count variable every time. The first argument to `updateProgress` is a value between zero and one, with zero representing start and one representing finish, the second allows you to update the progress bar text, and the third lets you change the body text. Updating the text can be handy if you'd like to provide additional feedback to the user, even if this is just to show a percentage representation—"x% complete"—of the current progress.

Back in our example code, note that you must also call `Ext.Msg.hide` in order to clear the progress dialog from the screen—`updateProgress` doesn't handle this for you, even if you set the current progress to a value greater than one.

The four included message boxes—alert, prompt, confirm, and progress—are the foundation of the Ext JS dialog support, but we can also tweak their functionality to support some custom scenarios.

# Roll your own

The four methods for creating message boxes that we've just covered, alert, prompt, confirm, and progress, are essentially shortcuts to a fifth method: `Ext.Msg.show`. This method takes a configuration object as its single argument, and the configuration options within this object allow the creation of a messagebox that supports all of the features available via our shortcut methods. The simplest example of this method is as follows:

```
Ext.Msg.show({
   msg: 'AWESOME.'
});
```

This is a closer replication of the JavaScript alert than the standard Ext JS one—but it's not as functional. Something a little better would be:

```
Ext.Msg.show({
   title: 'Hey!',
   msg: 'Icons and Buttons! AWESOME.',
   icon: Ext.MessageBox.INFO,
   buttons: Ext.MessageBox.OK
});
```

Now we've got our title back as well as our button, but there's an icon as well.

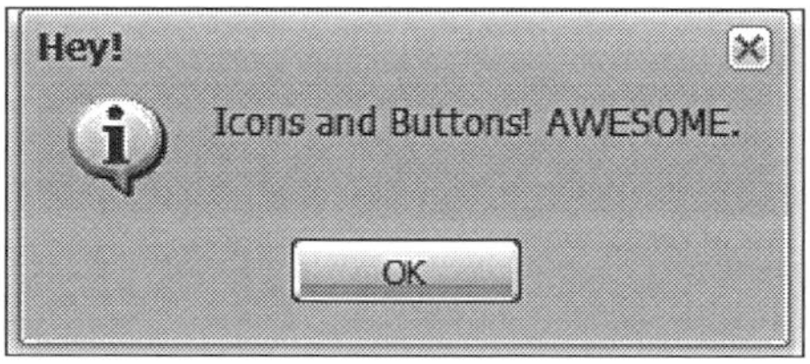


The means of configuring buttons and icons is interesting: pass in one of the constants that Ext JS provides, and you'll get a pre-configured button or a CSS class that shows an icon. Here's the list of the icon constants:

- `Ext.Msg.ERROR`
- `Ext.Msg.INFO`
- `Ext.Msg.QUESTION`
- `Ext.Msg.WARNING`

And the button constants:

- `Ext.Msg.CANCEL`
- `Ext.Msg.OK`
- `Ext.Msg.OKCANCEL`
- `Ext.Msg.YESNO`
- `Ext.Msg.YESNOCANCEL`

This variety of ready-made options provides you with a fair bit of flexibility when it comes to the appearance of your message boxes, but we can go further. As mentioned, the icon constants are simply strings representing CSS class names. For example, `Ext.Msg.QUESTION` provides the `ext-mb-question` string. This ties in to the Ext JS stylesheets and provides the styles for a question icon. The logical conclusion is that we can provide our own strings in place of these constants, allowing full customization of the icon areas.

The button constants are a bit less flexible, and contain object literals specifying how the dialog buttons should be displayed. For example, `Ext.Msg.YESNOCANCEL` contains the following (represented in JavaScript Object Notation for easy reading):

```
{ cancel:true, yes: true, no:true }
```

This is to specify that all of the `yes`, `cancel`, and `no` buttons should be included. You can use this to selectively turn off particular buttons, but you can't change the order or add new buttons in this manner. This means that providing custom button definitions in this way is of limited use.

> In addition to accepting the `Ext.Msg` button constants, the `show` method options will also accept a standard Ext JS button configuration object.

However, we can tweak the dialog in other ways. It's possible to supply `Ext.Msg.show` with `width` and `height` options to restrict the dimensions of your pop up. This could be handy in a situation where you have a long message to display and would like to prevent it from stretching to one long line across the screen.

The `show` configuration object also allows us to use the `cls` option to specify a CSS class to apply to the container of the dialog. A developer could use this to target any child objects of the container by using custom CSS rules, potentially paving the way for multiple dialogs that have totally different appearances. Do you need to provide a bright-pink pop up for your users? This configuration option allows you to do this.

## Behavior

So far, the configuration options for `Ext.Msg.show` have addressed appearance, but there are a few options that can also adjust behavior. If we use the `progress` property, then we can replicate the standard Ext JS progress dialog:

```
Ext.Msg.show({progress:true});
```

By using this in tandem with other options such as `title` and `msg`, you can create a custom progress dialog.

Similarly, the `prompt` and `multiline` options allow the creation of a custom input pop up:

```
Ext.Msg.show({prompt:true, multiline:true});
```

Here, we create a pop up that accepts multiple lines of input. But by omitting the `multiline` value or setting it to `false`, we can limit the pop up to a single line. Again, using the other configuration options for `Ext.Msg.show` allows us to expand this sample code into a fully-featured input dialog.

Another option that changes the default behavior of a pop up is `modal`. This option allows you to specify whether the user can interact with the items behind the pop up. When set to `true`, a semi-transparent overlay will prevent interaction.

As we have discussed earlier, the `Ext.Msg` pop ups don't block script execution in the same way as standard JavaScript pop ups. This means that we need to use a callback to trigger code after the dialog is dismissed. We can do this using `show fn` configuration option, which gets called with two arguments: the ID of the button that has been clicked, and the text entered into the text field in the dialog (where the dialog includes an input field). Obviously, for a simple alert prompt, you're not going to receive any text back, but this function does provide a consistent means of consuming callbacks across the whole range of dialogs that you can build using `Ext.Msg.show`.

We briefly touched on the fact that the `Ext.Msg` messageboxes are actually customized `Ext.Window`. If you think we're able to tweak `Ext.Msg` a lot...wait till you see what `Ext.Window` can let us do.

# Windows

Any computer user will be familiar with the concept of windows: informational panels that appear on the screen to provide more data on the current user's actions. We can replicate this concept using the `Ext.Window` class, a powerful component that supports many advanced scenarios.

# Starting examples

We can open a window using a very minimal amount of code:

```
var w = new Ext.Window({height:100, width: 200});
w.show();
```

Running this gives you an empty pop up window that in itself is...well, completely useless; but it does show off a few of the interesting default features of an `Ext.Window`. Straight out of the box, without any configuration, your window will be draggable, resizable, and will have a handy close icon in the upper right corner of the dialog box. It's still not a very impressive demonstration, however, because our window doesn't actually show anything.

The easiest way to populate a window is by using plain old HTML. Here's an extended example that demonstrates this feature:

```
var w = new Ext.Window({
   height: 150, width: 200,
   title: 'A Window',
   html: '<h1>Oh</h1><p>HI THERE EVERYONE</p>'
});
w.show();
```

We've added two new configuration options here. First, a `title` option that allows you to set the text in the title bar of the window, and second, an `html` option that accepts a string of raw HTML that will be displayed in the window.

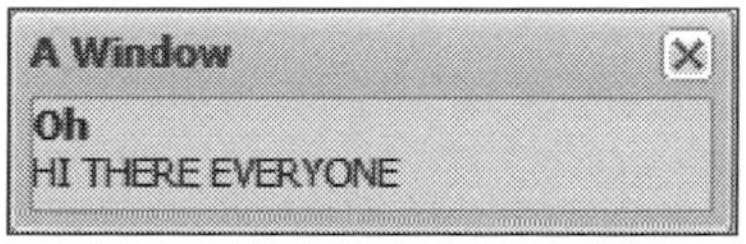


The use of this approach is immediately apparent—we can go back to basics and inject whatever HTML we require directly into the content area of the window. This allows us to tweak our window right down to the markup level, and provide lots of CSS hooks for styling. Even so, it's not the truly integrated experience that we've come to expect from Ext JS. However, another configuration option lets us take a more familiar approach.

# Paneling potential

Remember that `Window` is a subclass of `Panel`, and `Panel` has all kinds of interesting tricks up its sleeve. The `items` configuration option accepts an array of configuration objects or component instances:

```
var w = new Ext.Window({
   items:[
      { xtype: 'textfield', fieldLabel: 'First Name'},
      new Ext.form.TextField({fieldLabel: 'Surname'})
   ]
});
w.show();
```

In the previous example we have added two `textfields`, the first one using "lazy" `xtype` initialization, and the second one using standard object initialization. These two items will be added to the window's internal panel, but the manner in which they are displayed can be controlled based on the window's layout property.

# Layout

Ext JS defines a number of layout models within the `Ext.layout` package, and each of these layouts is used with a panel to allow the components within it to be arranged in a specific manner. In our previous example, we showed how we can add a couple of textboxes to a window, but we can also enhance the appearance of the window simply by using the appropriate layout. In this case, we need `Ext.layout.FormLayout`, which provides support for field labels and the general spacing and positioning you'd expect from an edit form:

```
var w = new Ext.Window({
   layout: 'form',
   items:[
      { xtype: 'textfield', fieldLabel: 'First Name'},
      new Ext.form.TextField({fieldLabel: 'Surname'})
   ]
});
w.show();
```

We use the `layout` configuration option to specify that we want to use a `form` layout, and immediately the difference in appearance becomes clear. In the next screenshot, the first dialog box does not use a layout, and the second one does:

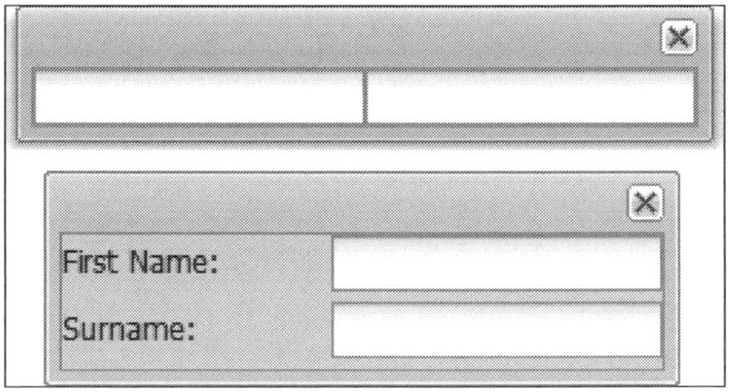


This is not a feature of `Ext.Window`; it comes straight from the `Ext.Container` superclass. But the fact that `Window` supports this feature is extremely important for an application developer—especially when you consider how long it would take to create a rich form using our previous HTML injection technique. The other layouts within the `Ext.layout` package provide many more approaches to windows design, expanding the scenarios that a window can support.

# Configuration

In addition to the various ways of filling the window's content area, we also have a great deal of flexibility when it comes to the appearance and behavior of each pop up. There are many configuration options provided by the `Ext.Window` superclass hierarchy, which starts with `Ext.Panel`, while also having a wealth of options of its own.

## When I'm cleaning windows

In our very first window example, I demonstrated how we get a number of great features for free—resizing, dragging, and a close button. In some situations you may prefer to prevent this behavior with the configuration option `resizable` set to `false`. Dragging is often just a matter of preference, and in most cases there's little harm in leaving it enabled. That said, there are times when it's simply not a necessary functionality, so I prefer to disable it by using the `draggable` option set to `false`.

```
var w = new Ext.Window({
   height:50,
   width: 100,
   closable: false,
   draggable: false,
   resizable: false
});
w.show();
```

When using a form window, it's often preferable to have text buttons explaining that different actions will, for example, either save a record, or cancel any changes that have been made, and in such cases, the **close** icon can be disabled by having the `closable` option set to `false`. There's a second option that gives a little bit more control over this behavior: `closeAction` can be set to either `hide` or `close`, with `hide` simply causing the window to vanish, but not destroying it, and `close` actually removing the window from the DOM. This is an important difference if you think you're going to be re-using the window later, as simply hiding and re-showing it is more efficient than re-creating the window every time.

## The extras

With the default functionality under control, we can begin to review the ways we can further tweak and augment the features of the `Ext.Window`. We've already demonstrated the use of the `height` and `width` options that set the fixed dimensions of the window and crop any content that exceeds these dimensions.

We do have another option. The `autoHeight` and `autoWidth` config settings, which are both Booleans, allow you to fill your window with components without having to worry about ensuring that your `height` and `width` values are absolutely correct. This is a really useful tool during development; when it's unlikely that you know the exact dimensions of whatever you're creating, just set `autoHeight` and `autoWidth` to `true` and forget about it. Even better, these options can be used separately, so that you can set your `width`, but have the `height` automatically calculated. This is useful if you're putting dynamic content into a window, because you will need to make sure that it doesn't stretch the window off the sides of your screen.

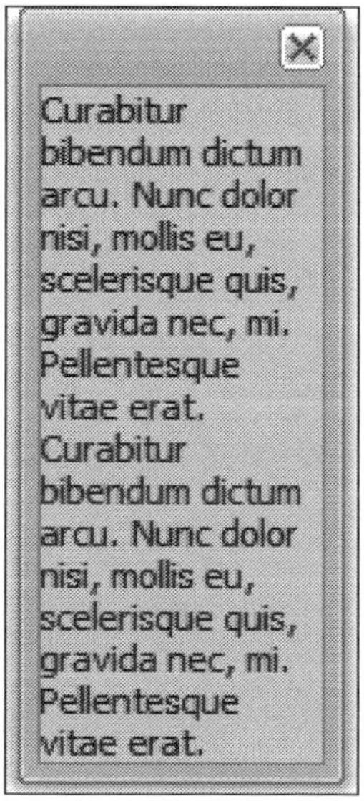

## Desktopping

The most pervasive example of a windowing system is the computer desktop, with multiple windows representing applications or elements of the filesystem. In such systems, users are allowed to hide windows for later use, or minimize them; they're also able to expand windows to fill the screen, or maximize it (also referred to as maximizing the window). These are familiar terms, and are of course supported by `Ext.Window` via the `maximizable` and `minimizable` Boolean configuration options.

These features are disabled by default, but they are fully-featured and work in much the same way as their desktop equivalents. When set to `true`, new icons appear in the upper right of the window that are similar in appearance to the ones on the Windows operating system. `Maximizable` allows the window to be expanded to fill the whole of the browser viewport, as expected, but `minimizable` is a little trickier. Ext JS doesn't know where you want the window to vanish to—on the Windows operating system it would be the task bar, but for other operating systems it could be somewhere else. So you've got to provide the minimize functionality yourself. Ext only gives you the icon and a minimize event that must be handled in a manner appropriate to your application. Later in this chapter, we'll provide a brief example on how this can be achieved using the events available for the `Ext.Window` class.

## Further options

Ext JS Windows support another means of cutting down the real-estate of your window, and this is built right into the framework. The `collapsible` Boolean adds another button to the upper right of the window and allows the user to shrink it down to cause only the title bar to be shown. A second click expands the window back to its original state.

We can also use the `expandOnShow` configuration to specify that a hidden window will always be expanded to its full dimensions when it is shown. This is useful for windows that have been previously hidden and need to be brought back to the user's attention.

## Framing our window

Along with the standard title bar and body content area, we also have the ability to add further content areas to a window. Some of these areas can be fully customized, and some are a little bit more restrictive, but together they provide yet another method for creating functional windows.

Every window has the built-in capability to add toolbars to the top and the bottom, thanks to its `Ext.Panel` inheritance. These toolbars can include any valid toolbar items, be it buttons, menus, or text. In addition, we can use the `footer` element to contain some further buttons via the `buttons` configuration option.

Depending on your requirements, you may choose to use one or more of these content areas to provide tools allowing your users to manipulate and consume the information within the window. A typical example would be to create a window with a form layout, which then includes the **Save** and **Cancel** buttons within the footer. This reflects the typical style of a data entry form, and will be positioned automatically by Ext JS with little configuration being required.

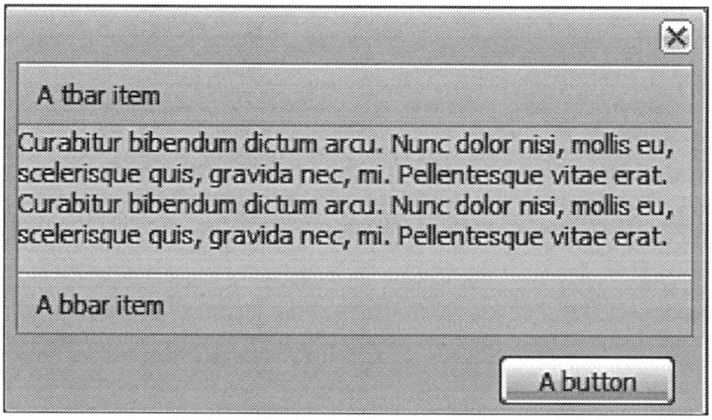


# Manipulating

When our windows are on-screen, we have a range of methods that we can use to change their position, appearance, and behavior. In fact, we've already used one of these methods in our examples—`show`—which is used to display the window in the first place. Although we've always used `show` in its most simple form, it can take up to three arguments—all of which are optional.

```
myWin.show('animTarget', function() { alert('Now Showing'); }, this);
```

Firstly, we can specify an element, or the ID of an element, to form the starting point from which the window should animate when opening. This cosmetic effect can also be specified using the `animateTarget` configuration option. The second argument is a callback function, fired when the rendering of the window is complete, and the third argument is simply the scope for the callback. It turns out the `show` method isn't that basic after all!

The obvious companion to `show` is `hide`. Indeed, it takes the same arguments, and will cause the window to vanish from the screen for later use. If you're sure that you don't want to use the window later then it's probably better to use the `close` method, which will remove it from the DOM and destroy it.

The functionality delivered by the `close` and `hide` methods have already been demonstrated—it is provided by the window's close icon. There are a few more methods that allow programmatic control over items, that we've already covered, such as the `minimize` and `maximize` methods. This basic functionality is augmented by the `restore` method, which is used after `maximize` to return the window to its previous dimensions, and `toggleMaximize`, which is simply a shortcut to switch between `maximize` and `restore`. And in terms of setting the window back to its defaults we can also use the `center` method, which sets the window in the middle of the browser's viewport.

We can further manipulate the position of our windows: `alignTo` allows a developer to programmatically move a window next to a specified element. This method has three parameters:

- The element to align to—as a string or full element
- The position to align with—as detailed in the `Element.alignTo` documentation, and briefly discussed in Chapter 10, *Effects*
- A positioning offset, specified as an `[x,y]` array

This method is useful when you have an application with a dynamic workspace—you need to ensure that your windows appear in the correct place in relation to other items being displayed. A useful compliment to this feature is the `anchorTo` method, which takes the same arguments and allows a window to remain anchored to another element, even when the browser window has been resized or scrolled.

While many of the `Ext.Window` methods simply give a developer access to existing functionality via their code, there are a few additional ones that provide for advanced scenarios or for features that would be laborious to code by hand.

# Events

Pretty much all of the actions we've covered so far have their own events that serve as hooks for your custom code. `Minimize` is one which we've explicitly mentioned earlier, because you have to handle this event if you want the minimize icon to do anything. Ideally, you'd expect the window to be stored in some kind of 'taskbar'-style area for later retrieval.

```
var w = new Ext.Window({
   height: 50,
   width: 100,
   minimizable: true
});
w.on('minimize', doMin);
w.show();
```

In the previous example, we're creating a new window, which we set as `minimizable`, and then add an event listener for the `minimize` event. We then show the window on the screen. Our `doMin` event handling function looks like this:

```
function doMin() {
   w.collapse(false);
   w.alignTo(document.body, 'bl-bl');
}
```

We simply tell our window to collapse down to the title bar (passing in a parameter of `false` simply indicates that we don't want to animate the collapse) and then use the `alignTo` method, which we've discussed previously. With the parameters we've chosen, the window's bottom left will be aligned to the bottom left of the document body—just like the first window in a taskbar would be.

Of course, with further windows, you'd end up with an overlapping stack in the bottom-left; not ideal for a real world application. However, it does show how the minimize event can be handled, and can be used as an alternative to the collapse method.

# State handling

State handling with windows is a relatively simple process. Windows are fully integrated with the standard Ext JS state management facilities via the `stateful` configuration flag. Assuming that we want to track the position, minimize status, size, and z-order of a window through page refreshes and user sessions, we can use code such as this:

```
var w = new Ext.Window({
   stateId: 'myWindowStateId' // a unique stateId is always required
   stateful: true,
   stateEvents:['resize'] // track the resize event
});
```

We use the `stateEvents` option to set an array of window events, which will cause the component to save its state. Unlike state handling with the `TreeNodes` in *Chapter 8, Ext JS Does Grow on Trees*, we don't need to hook into the `beforestatesave` event this time around. The window component will look after itself, and automatically set its configuration to reflect its previous state.

# Window management

In a rich Internet application, it can be desirable to allow the user to have many windows open simultaneously, reviewing a variety of information without having to navigate to separate pages. Ext JS allows for this: you can create any number of non-modal windows and manipulate them as you see fit. However, we face a problem when using a multitude of windows—how do we manage them as a group? For example, the users may wish to clear their workspace by minimizing all open windows. We can achieve this functionality, and more, by using a **window group**.

# Default window manager behavior

When you create an `Ext.Window`, it will automatically be assigned to a default `Ext.WindowGroup` which, by default, can always be referred to via the `Ext.WindowMgr` class. However, you can create as many additional `WindowGroups` as your application requires, assigning windows to them via the `manager` configuration option.

Why would your application require a method of grouping windows? Well, multiple windows are affected by z-order, in that they can be stacked on top of each other. We can use `WindowMgr.bringToFront` to bring a particular window to the top of the stack, perhaps if it has been updated with new information and we want to draw the user's attention to this. In some situations, this would be the same as using `Ext.Window.toFront`. However, the `WindowMgr` approach will respect the z-order grouping of individual `WindowGroups`, and so is a safer method when building a large application with many windowing options.

The grouping and z-ordering of windows is a confusing topic, so let's put these advanced features into a real-world context.

# Multiple window example

We're going to build a very basic simulation of a customer service application. Our user will be the supervisor of a live chat system, where customers who are online can ask questions and get answers straight away. The supervisor will take some of these questions, but they also monitor the status of other agents who are dealing with customer sessions. We'll only be interested in the windowing aspect of this application, so it's going to be filled with a lot of dummy data to illustrate our point.

Here's a screenshot of a simple application developed to support this:

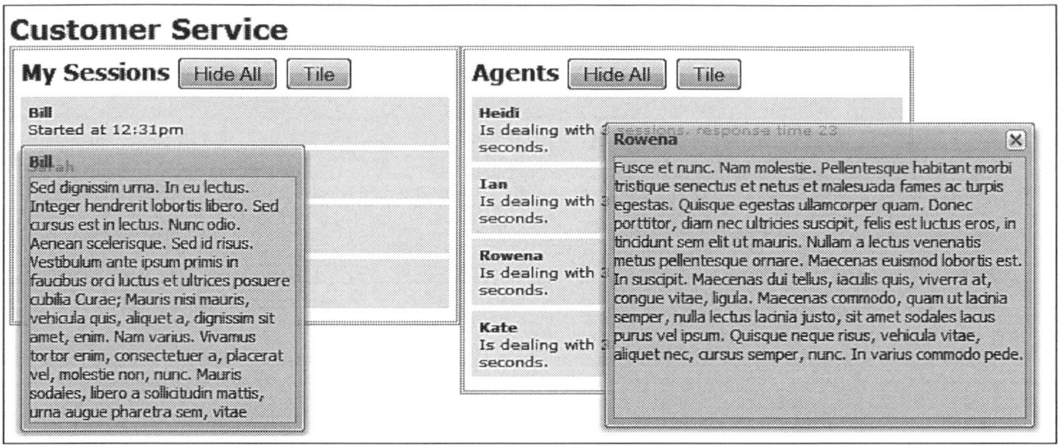


The lists have deliberately been left plain to avoid the need for extra JavaScript code—an application such as this could really benefit from grids or data views displaying the sessions and agents, but we really don't need them just to demonstrate our windowing code.

We're going to use a JavaScript object literal to structure our example. Here's the shell:

```
var customerService = {

    sessionsGroup : null,
    agentsGroup : null,

    init : function() {
}
};
Ext.onReady(customerService.init, customerService);
```

We have a couple of local variables that will hold our window groups, and an empty `init` function that gets called, with the `customerService` object as its scope, from the `Ext.onReady` statement. Now that we've got our JavaScript skeleton, we need to take a look at the markup that is going to power our customer service app:

```
<div id="mySessions">
    <h2>My Sessions
        <button id="hideSessions">Hide All</button>
        <button id="tileSessions">Tile</button>
    </h2>
    <div id="s-p1">
        <h3>Bill</h3>
```

```
        <p>Started at 12:31pm</p>
        <div class="content"></div>
    </div>
</div>
<div id="agents">
    <h2>Agents
        <button id="hideAgents">Hide All</button>
        <button id="tileAgents">Tile</button>
    </h2>
    <div id="a-h1">
        <h3>Heidi</h3>
        <p>Is dealing with 3 sessions...</p>
        <div class="content"></div>
    </div>
</div>
```

This is the HTML that will go straight into the body of our document. We've got two main containers—`mySessions` and `agents`—which then contain `h2` tags with a few buttons, and some div tags. For example, within `mySessions`, we have the div `#s-p1`, containing an `h3`, a paragraph, and another div with the `content` class. The `#s-p1` div is one of many that could appear within `mySessions`, these divs being named as `#s-xxx`, with `xxx` being a unique identifier for that session.

Within agents, we have a similar structure with slightly different IDs—for example, the `agent` divs are named as `#a-xxx`. The various IDs in HTML are extremely important for our JavaScript, as they'll be used to hook up event handlers, as we'll see in a moment. Let's take a look at our full `init` function (note that each code snippet will build on what came before).

```
init : function() {
    var s = Ext.select;
    var g = Ext.get;
    this.sessionsGroup = new Ext.WindowGroup();
    this.agentsGroup = new Ext.WindowGroup();

    s('#mySessions div').on('click', this.showSession, this);
    s('#agents div').on('click', this.showAgent, this);
}
```

The first two lines of the previous block of code are just shortcuts to clean up our code—we're storing references to the Ext functions in a variable with a smaller name. Nothing fancy about it. The next two lines see us creating two distinct window groups—one that will hold our session information windows, and one for the agent information windows.

The next few lines make more sense given the HTML we discussed previously. We use our shortcut to `Ext.select` to add event listeners to all of the divs within `#mySessions`—handled by the `showSession` function—and within `#agents`—handled by `showAgent`. The third argument to the `on` function ensures that we maintain scope when the handlers are called. Let's take a look at the `showSession` function:

```
showSession : function(e){
   var target = e.getTarget('div', 5, true);
   var sessionId = target.dom.id + '-win';
   var win = this.sessionsGroup.get(sessionId);

   if(!win) {
      win = new Ext.Window({
         manager: this.sessionsGroup,
         id: sessionId,
         width: 200,
         height: 200,
         resizable: false,
         closable: false,
         title: target.down('h3').dom.innerHTML,
         html: target.down('.content').dom.innerHTML
      });
   }

   win.show();
   win.alignTo(target);
}
```

There's a lot happening here. The first line ensures that our target variable contains the session div that was clicked on, regardless of whether it was actually one of the session's child elements that was clicked. We then store a unique `sessionId` by taking the ID of the target session div and appending `-win` to it. Finally, we check if the session window group already has a reference to the window that we're about to create, by looking it up using the unique `sessionId`.

If the window doesn't exist then we need to create it. Most of the configuration options shown will be familiar from earlier in this chapter, but take note of our explicit assignment of the `sessionsGroup` as the managing group for this window. We're also using the `sessionId` as the ID for the window rather than relying on the automatically-generated ID that will be used by default. With the `title` and `html` options, we're using the `Ext.Element` DOM traversal facilities to assign the text of the session div's `h3` and `div.content` elements respectively.

We're now sure that the `win` variable holds a valid reference to a window, so we can go ahead and show the window. After we do so, we want to align it with the div that was clicked to show it, so the window's `alignTo` function is called. That's a whistle-stop tour of the `showSession` function. The `showAgent` function is almost identical, but refers to `agentsGroup` rather than `sessionsGroup`. Together these two functions make sure that our session and agent windows pop up successfully, so it's now time to take a look at how our `WindowGroups` can be used to manage them as a unit.

## Customer service WindowGroups

We can add two lines to our `init` function that use window groups to perform a clearout of our customer service workspace:

```
g('hideSessions').on('click', this.sessionsGroup.hideAll);
g('hideAgents').on('click', this.agentsGroup.hideAll);
```

We can add event listeners to our `hideSessions` and `hideAgents` buttons that are directly handled by the `hideAll` functions of the `sessionsGroup` and `agentsGroup`. This short code snippet allows us to hide all of the agent or session windows with a click on the associated button. In a similar vein, we're going to add a couple more event listeners to our other buttons that will cause our windows to be tiled across the screen—organized into an easy overview:

```
g('tileAgents').on('click', this.tileAgents, this);
g('tileSessions').on('click', this.tileSessions, this);
```

This time the events are handled by `tileAgents` and `tileSessions` that look like this:

```
tileAgents : function(e) {
   this.sessionsGroup.hideAll();
   this.tile(this.agentsGroup);
},
tileSessions : function(e) {
   this.agentsGroup.hideAll();
   this.tile(this.sessionsGroup);
}
```

Again, we call the `hideAll` function to make sure that the other set of windows is cleared from the screen. When we've prepared the workspace, we can then pass the relevant window group to the `tile` function:

```
tile : function(group) {
   var previousWin = null;
   group.each(function(win){

      if(previousWin) {
         if(win.getEl().getWidth() + previousWin.getEl().getRight() >
            Ext.getBody().getWidth()) {
            win.alignTo(document.body, 'tl-tl',
                        [0, previousWin.getEl().getHeight()]);
            } else {
            win.alignTo(previousWin.getEl(), 'tl-tr');
         }
         } else {
         win.alignTo(document.body, 'tl-tl');
      }
      previousWin = win;
   });
}
```

The key here is the `WindowGroup.each` function, which allows us to loop through every window assigned to the group and perform further actions and calculations. In this case, if it's our first iteration, then we align the window to `document.body`. For further iterations, the windows are aligned to the previous window in the loop, taking care to add a vertical offset if the window would have pushed off the rightmost side of the screen.

`hideAll` and `each` are useful ways of manipulating multiple windows. In this example, we've shown how two distinct groups of windows can be handled with very little coding overhead.

# Summary

The `Ext.Window` is one of the most fundamental aspects of a rich Ext JS application. Many of the other big components within the framework, such as the grid and tree, can display information in an easily consumable and browsable manner, but the chances are that if you need to display or manipulate a record with a lot of information, do so without disrupting the user's workflow by navigating to a different page, you're going to want to use a window.

The great thing is that `Window` is flexible enough to slot straight into any application you may want to build with it. For ultimate power, simply fill it with custom HTML, or to create an integrated experience use Ext components. The fact is that the window subclasses panel provides you with the ability to construct complex pop ups by using the most suitable `Ext.layout`—be that of a form, or an accordion, or whatever—and have it look and feel the same as the rest of your application.

Although windows and dialogs will most likely have a place in your application, they should be used with care. There's a tendency to identify a requirement for displaying extra information and simply popping it up in the user's face; it could be that a less disruptive interface would be more suitable. Ultimately, `Window` and `Msg` sit alongside the other parts of Ext JS as tools that can be easily integrated into any application that requires them.

# 10
# Charting New Territory

With the 3.x branch of the Ext JS library, charting was introduced in the form of a Flash file that renders different types of charts based on the configuration we provide. This Flash file is part of the YUI library.

In this chapter we are going to start off with a basic pie chart, and move on to more complicated charts from there. For me, the pie chart is the easiest to set-up, and some of the others such as line or bar can take more configuration and data manipulation to get a basic chart displayed. We will chart various data points from our grid of movies that we finished up with in Chapter 7 (Layouts) and create some imaginary data to play with the more advanced features of charting.

In this chapter we will learn to:

- Place a chart within our layout/application
- Load charts with data from a data store
- Create custom-styled charts

## Just another component

Because of Ext JS's standardized component hierarchy, charts will slot easily into your application with no fuss. All chart classes extend the `BoxComponent` base class, and so may simply be used as child components of containers.

And providing the data for them to analyze is simple too. Charts are backed by a standard Ext JS data store, a class which we already know about. We just need to inform a chart which fields of the store's record it will be working with.

Future versions of Ext JS will eliminate the usage of Flash for creating charts, and replace it with solutions based upon web standards such as SVG and VML. However, because of the separation of the data from the presentation, and the strong component hierarchy, this will mean minimal changes to application code. The new charts will still use familiar data stores, and will still be regular components.

There are a handful of charts built right into Ext JS, along with a base class that could be used to create other charts that might be supported by the YUI Chart Flash file. Additional information about the YUI Charting library can be found on its web site. The reference material found on the YUI Charting site (`http://developer.yahoo.com/yui/charts/`) can be particularly useful for styling charts.

The following chart types are built into the Ext JS library:

- Pie
- Bar
- Line
- Column
- Stacked bar
- Stacked column

The first chart we create—the pie—we simply need to add a PieChart component to our layout within a panel, bind it to our store, and setup some basic config options.

# What the flash?

Behind the creation of the Flash elements used in Ext JS Charts is the *swfobject* library. Sitting on top of the *swfobject* library is the FlashComponent class which normalizes the *swfobject* methods into a class that the Ext JS containers can deal with. We will not need to use this class directly, but it is always a good thing to know what we are dealing with.

One thing we will want to do before using the charts is set the Chart URL. This is a path that is set to the location of the `charts.swf` file that comes with Ext JS located in the resources folder. By default the Charts URL is set to a `charts.swf` file that is hosted on Yahoo's servers. This is similar to the spacer image URL that we had to set in Chapter 2.

```
Ext.chart.Chart.CHART_URL = '../resources/charts.swf';
```

Now the charts will use a local resource instead of pulling down the `charts.swf` from Yahoo every time.

> If charts are being used on an Intranet application that does not have external Internet access, then the Chart URL must be set, otherwise charts will appear blank.

Setting the Chart URL to a local resource also allows us to use images in the styling of the charts without having to create a `crossdomain.xml` file. If for some reason we needed to use the Yahoo hosted version of `charts.swf` and are styling the charts with images, then a simple `crossdomain.xml` file should be created and placed in the root of our web site. The file contents should look like this:

```
<?xml version="1.0"?>
<!DOCTYPE cross-domain-policy SYSTEM "http://www.macromedia.com/xml/
dtds/cross-domain-policy.dtd">
<cross-domain-policy>
    <allow-access-from domain="yui.yahooapis.com"/>
</cross-domain-policy>
```

# A slice of data—pie charts

In order to create a pie chart summarizing the genre makeup of our movie collection, we need to go through our data store that contains our movie data and summarize the data into another store that is used just for the chart. Of course if we already have summarized data in a store, this step is not needed, and the store can be used directly in the chart and shared between components.

The first thing we need to do is create a store for our chart to use:

```
var chartStore = new Ext.data.JsonStore({
    fields: ['genre','total'],
    root: 'data'
});
```

A very basic Json store with two fields will work just fine, since all we need to do is store the genre name, and a count of how many movies are in each genre. We are going to massage the data that exists in our movie database store to get the summary data to populate our PieChart's store. A little function should do the job just fine.

```
var loadPieChartFn = function(s){
  var tmpData = {}, genreData = [];
  s.each(function(rec){
    var genre = genre_name(rec.get('genre'));
    (tmpData[genre])? ++tmpData[genre] : tmpData[genre] = 1;
  });
  for (genre in tmpData){
    genreData.push({
      genre: genre,
      total: tmpData[genre]
    });
  }
  chartStore.loadData({data:genreData});
};
```

This function takes a store as the only argument (which is always the first argument passed to a store's listeners) and summarizes the data, updating our pie chart with the summarized data. It loops through the five rows of the movie store, and creates a new data store containing three rows:

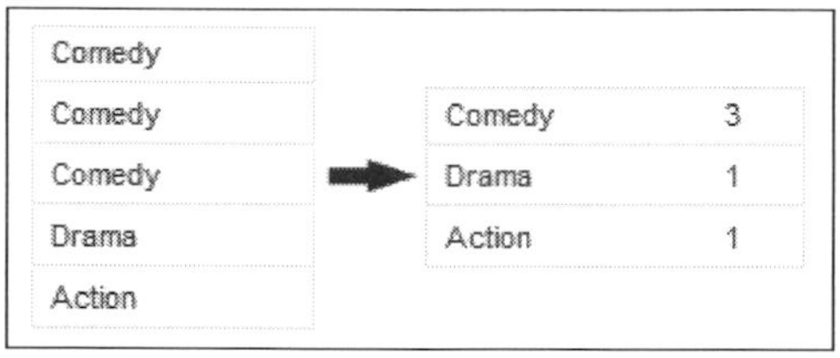


We also need to make sure the chart store is updated when the movie store is updated—tie them together. To do this we just need to call this function whenever the store is changed:

```
listeners: {
    load: loadPieChartFn,
    add: loadPieChartFn,
    remove: loadPieChartFn,
    update: loadPieChartFn,
    clear: loadPieChartFn
}
```

Easy as pie, now our chart store is tied to our movie store.

# Chart in a layout

To add the chart to our layout we are going to split up the west region used in our final example in Chapter 7 making it into a border layout with a north and center region within it. This west region previously just contained our movie form. The movie form will become the new center region and our pie chart will be in a north region.

```
{
    region: 'west',
    layout: 'border',
    xtype: 'container',
    split: true,
    width: 250,
    minSize: 250,
    split: true,
    margins: '0 0 5 5',
    collapseMode: 'mini',
    items: [{
```

```
        region: 'north',
        items: // chart is the sole item,
        split: true,
        height: 250
    }, movieForm ]
}
```

Now we have a split up west region with a 250 pixel tall panel in the north position where we can place our pie chart. The pie chart will need to be added as one of the items of this north panel; since it is a `BoxComponent` type, it cannot be used directly in layouts but instead has to be nested in a panel or rendered directly to a dom node. Well go ahead and do the following.

# Pie chart setup

The next step is to tell the pie chart what store to use and which fields in the store hold the data it needs.

The config options we need to add to our pie chart to get it plumbed up are the *store* of course, along with *dataField* and *categoryField*. The *dataField* is set to the name of the field that holds our genre count, and the *categoryField* is the field that holds the name of the genre.

```
{
    region: 'north',
    items: {
        xtype: 'piechart',
        store: chartStore,
        dataField: 'total',
        categoryField: 'genre'
    },
    split: true,
    height: 250
}
```

This will produce a nice simple pie chart integrated into our layout.

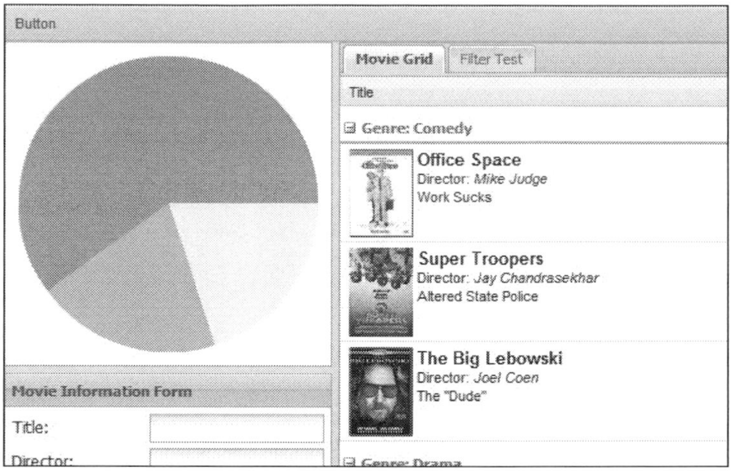


Our pie chart is quite simple now; the default settings have some generic colors for the slices, and no labels or legend, along with a basic mouseover. Let's go ahead and fix this chart up so it looks presentable.

# Styling the pie slices

The overall styling in the charts is done through the *extraStyle* config option, which is an object that contains all of the settings that determine what color, font, sizing and such are used in our charts, along with animation and positioning of different elements of the chart. We can also override the default styles by setting the *chartStyle* config, but we will cover that in more detail later in this chapter. For now, let's modify the *extraStyle* config to keep the styles on a per chart basis.

We will also be styling the series, which is the display portion of each segment of data. In this case, the series refers to each of the slices in the pie. Now pie charts have very few options, so don't expect a huge change. We'll start by adding a legend using the *legend* config object.

```
{
    xtype: 'piechart',
    store: chartStore,
    dataField: 'total',
    categoryField: 'genre',
    extraStyle: {
        padding: 2,
        animationEnabled: true,
```

```
            legend: {
                display: 'bottom'
            }
        }
    }
```

The display config option accepts either 'left', 'right', 'top', or 'bottom' as the value, placing the legend accordingly, which is all it takes to get a legend up and going. While we were at it, I also added padding of two pixels. This padding is the space around the edges of the pie chart, bringing the chart closer to the edges of its container, along with enabling animation, which makes the pie pieces animate to different sizes when the values change. We end up with a chart that looks like the following:

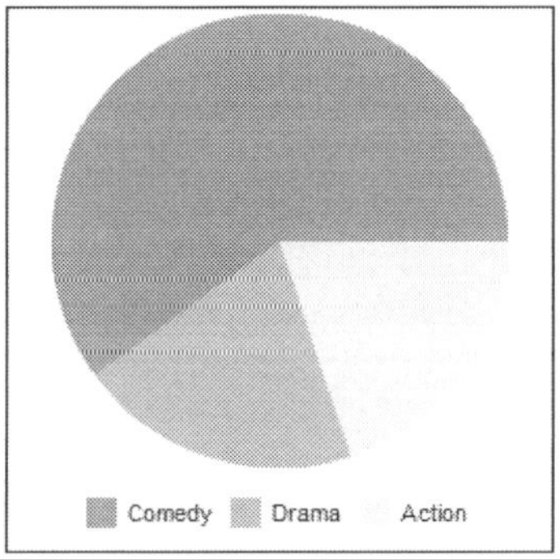


Another chart styling we will want to adjust is the *series* styles. These *series* styles apply to the individual points of data represented in the chart. Since there can be multiple series in one chart (not in the pie chart though), this config accepts an array. Each object in the array has a *style* config, which is another object containing the styles for that series.

```
    {
        xtype: 'piechart',
        store: chartStore,
        dataField: 'total',
        categoryField: 'genre',
        series: [{
            style:{
                showLabels: true,
                colors:[0x953030, 0xFF8C40, 0xFFDB59, 0x8DC63F, 0xFFFFFF]
            }
        }],
        extraStyle: {
            padding: 2,
            animationEnabled: true,
```

```
            legend: {
                display: 'bottom'
            }
        }
    }
```

The *showLabels* config is pretty self explanatory; just set it to `true` to show the percentage labels on the pie pieces. With the *colors* config we just need to set a color that is used for each piece of the pie chart. These colors can be defined as a hex number like in the example above or a hex string like we often use in HTML and CSS.

This change results in a much better looking pie chart:

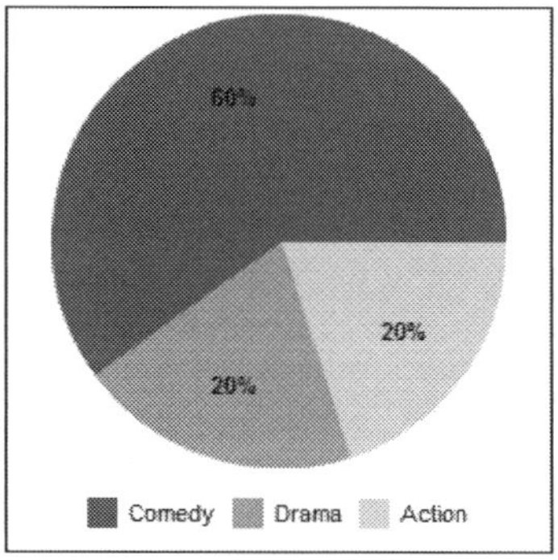


A nice fall theme makes me want to carve a pumpkin, eat some candy, then go outside and rake leaves. Much better than the default hospital colors! With this set of colors we created, if there are more than five data points—since we only defined five colors—the colors will repeat.

> More details on styling can be found in the YUI Charts basic styling section of their site: `http://developer.yahoo.com/yui/charts/#basicstyles`

# Bar and column charts

Why don't we move on to the bar and column charts, where we can re-use the same data, displaying it in a bar or column format instead of a pie? For the most part, these charts display data in the same fashion, so we can re-use the same store without change.

Both the bar and column charts are set up the same way since they are just horizontal and vertical versions of the same chart. We will need to set the `xField` or `yField` depending on the chart type, just like we had set the `dataField` and `categoryField` in the pie chart.

```
{
    xtype: 'barchart',
    store: chartStore,
    xField: 'total',
    series: [{
      yField: 'genre',
      style:{
        color:0x953030
      }
    }]
}
```

This will give us a simple bar chart showing the summary of genres, though the grid lines will look a little funny, since they are automatically calculated by the YUI Charts Flash file, which doesn't always get things right. To get the grid lines to make sense, we need to set up a `xAxis` with a `NumericAxis` that will set the grid lines at whatever interval we tell it to.

```
{
    xtype: 'barchart',
    store: chartStore,
    xAxis: new Ext.chart.NumericAxis({majorUnit: 1}),
    xField: 'total',
    series: [{
       yField: 'genre',
       style:{
          color:0x953030
       }
    }]
}
```

The `majorUnit` setting defines the distance between the full height grid lines, and the `minorUnit` setting added later will set the small ticks along the bottom edge. This will give us a bar chart like the one shown as follows:

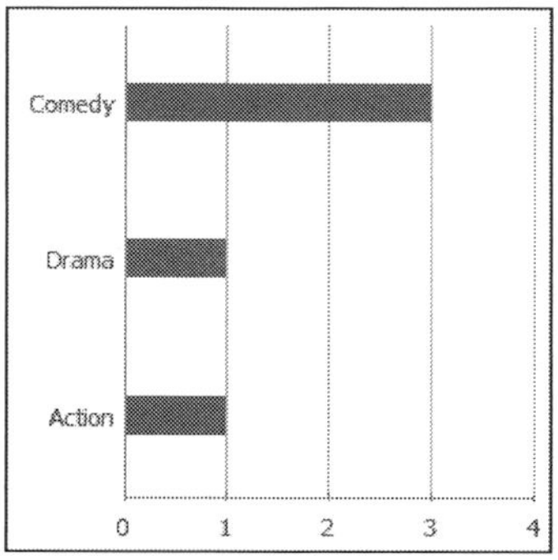


# From bar to column

Switching out a bar chart for a column chart just involves changing the `xtype` and switching the x's to y's and vice versa.

```
{
  xtype: 'columnchart',
  store: chartStore,
  yAxis: new Ext.chart.NumericAxis({majorUnit: 1}),
  yField: 'total',
  series: [{
    xField: 'genre',
    style:{
      color:0x953030
    }
  }]
}
```

This change results in a column chart as follows:

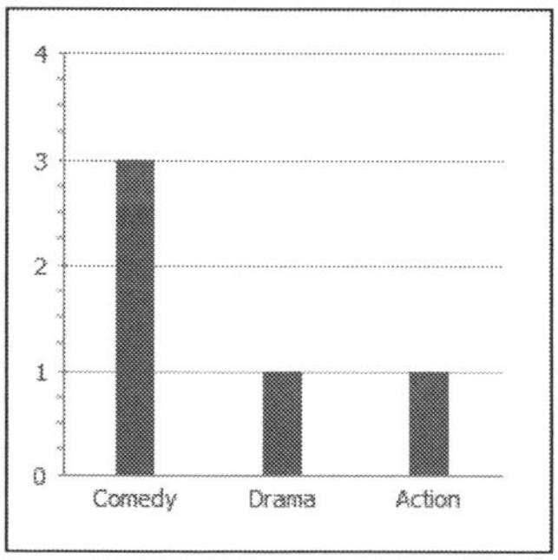

# Add some style

Now that we have learned how easy it is to go from bar to column, let's get back to our bar chart and do some styling. We can style both the x and y axis separately using the *xAxis* and *yAxis* objects in the *extraStyles* object.

```
{
    xtype: 'barchart',
    ...
    extraStyle: {
        padding: 2,
        animationEnabled: true,
        xAxis: {
            majorGridLines: {
                color: 0xEBEBEB
            },
            minorTicks: {
                color: 0x0000ff
            }
        },
        yAxis: {
            labelRotation: -45
        }
    }
}
```

Setting both the `majorGridLines` and `minorTicks` color properties inside the *xAxis* to a very light grey will mute the colors of the grid lines in our bar chart. The *yAxis* gets a `labelRotation` of -45, which is the number of degrees off vertical to rotate the text.

This results in a chart like the following:

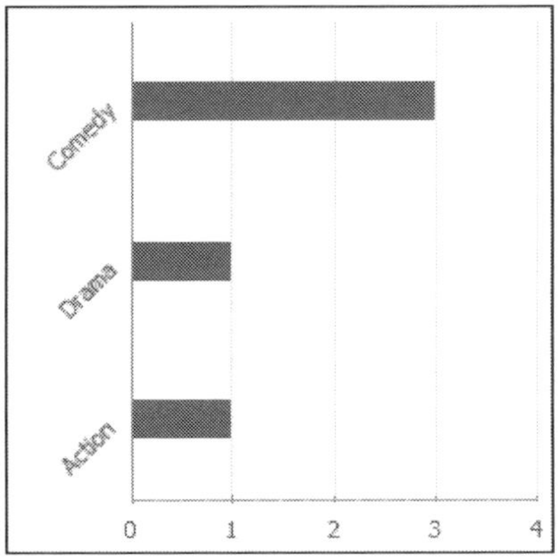

Many more styles are available for the charts, so take a look into the documentation provided by Yahoo on their YUI Charts reference site.

# Stack them across

Sometimes we need to display multiple values that relate to the same data point, or need to be grouped together for some reason or another. For these cases we can use the **StackedBarChart** or **StackedColumnChart**. In order to experiment with these types of charts, we will need to sample our data a bit differently so we can pull together more series of data.

What we're going to do is group our movies by their release year, and see how many movies fall into each genre per year. For this, let's create another function to transform the data into our **chartStore** along with adding some new fields to our charts store to hold the counts from each genre.

```
var chartStore = new Ext.data.JsonStore({
    fields: ['year','comedy','drama','action'],
    root: 'data'
});
```

Now the data transformation function needs to count all genres separately and record the number of movies in each genre grouped by year.

```
var loadChartFn = function(s){
  var tmpData = {}, yearData = [];
  s.each(function(rec){
    var genre = genre_name(rec.get('genre')),
      rel_year = rec.get('released').format('Y');
    if(!tmpData[''+rel_year]){
      tmpData[''+rel_year] = {Comedy:0,Drama:0,Action:0};
    }
    tmpData[''+rel_year][genre]++;
  });
  for (year in tmpData){
    yearData.push({
      year: year,
      comedy: tmpData[year].Comedy,
      drama: tmpData[year].Drama,
      action: tmpData[year].Action
    });
  }
  chartStore.loadData({data:yearData});
};
```

This will convert the data like so:

| | |
|---|---|
| Comedy | 1999 |
| Comedy | 2002 |
| Comedy | 1998 |
| Drama | 1999 |
| Action | 1999 |

→

| | Comedies | Dramas | Action |
|---|---|---|---|
| 1999 | 1 | 1 | 1 |
| 2002 | 1 | 0 | 0 |
| 1998 | 1 | 0 | 0 |

# Get to the stacking

Now that we have multiple points of data, we need to add more objects to the *series* array—one for each of the data points, comedy, drama, and action. We're also adding a new option to the series items called *displayName*, which will be used in the legend we are going to add to this chart later on.

```
series: [{
   xField: 'comedy',
   displayName: 'Comedy',
    style:{
       color:0x953030
    }
},{
    xField: 'drama',
    displayName: 'Drama',
    style:{
       color:0xFF8C40
    }
},{
    xField: 'action',
    displayName: 'Action',
    style:{
       color:0xFFDB59
    }
}]
```

Changing the *xtype* on our chart to a *stackedbarchart* from *barchart* and adding a *stackingEnabled* flag set to `true` will complete the process, giving us a nicely stacked bar chart.

```
xAxis: new Ext.chart.NumericAxis({majorUnit: 1, minorUnit: .25,
stackingEnabled: true})
```

This produces a chart that will look like the following:

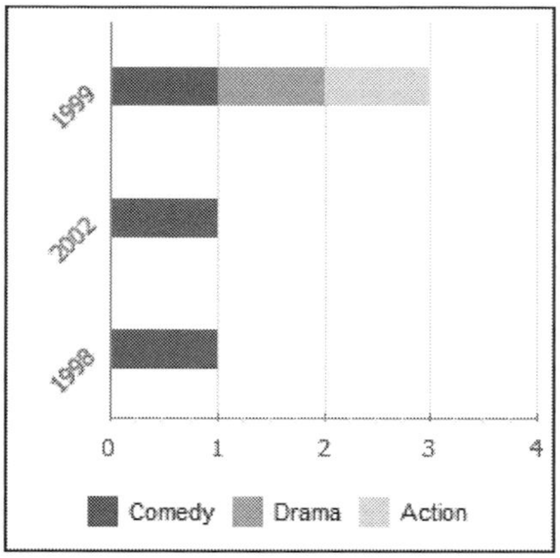


Of course I took this opportunity to also enable the legend on the bottom, since it was not entirely clear looking at the chart what the three stacked colors represented. Just like we did in our first pie chart, setting the *legend* to *display* 'bottom' in the `extraStyle` config is all we need, since we set `displayName` earlier in the series (without the `displayName` set, the legend would display 0, 1, and 2).

```
extraStyle: {
    ...
    legend: {
        display: 'bottom'
    }
}
```

Turning this same chart into a non-stacked bar chart with multiple series just involves removing the `stackingEnabled` config in the `xAxis` (or setting it to `false`).

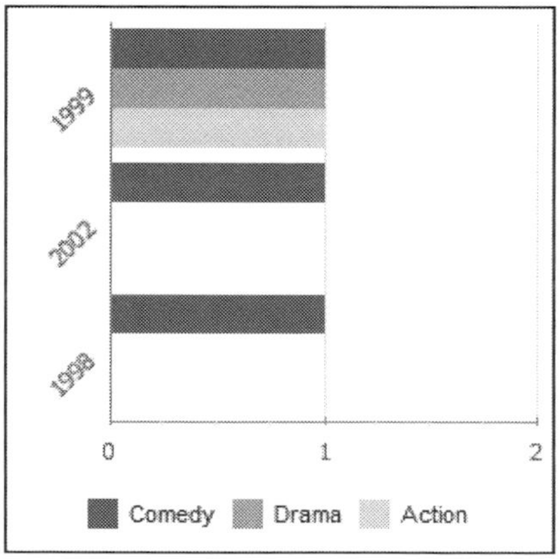

# Charting lines

The line chart can be used in much the same way as a column chart, however there is no bar variation of the line chart, as it can only draw lines horizontally. Switching the xtype to 'linechart' and swapping the x's for y's and vice versa will give us a line chart. Also remember to remove the *stackingEnabled* option, as this is not compatible with line charts.

```
{
    xtype: 'linechart',
    store: chartStore,
    yAxis: new Ext.chart.NumericAxis({majorUnit: 1, minorUnit: .25}),
    xField: 'year',
    series: [{
       yField: 'comedy',
       displayName: 'Comedy',
         style:{
             color:0x953030
         }
    },{
          ...
    }],
    extraStyle: {
        padding: 2,
        animationEnabled: true,
        yAxis: {
            majorGridLines: {
                color: 0xEBEBEB
            },
            minorTicks: {
                color: 0xEBEBEB
            }
        },
        xAxis: {
            labelRotation: -45
        },
        legend: {
            display: 'bottom'
        }
    }
}
```

With these simple changes, we now have a line chart that looks like so:

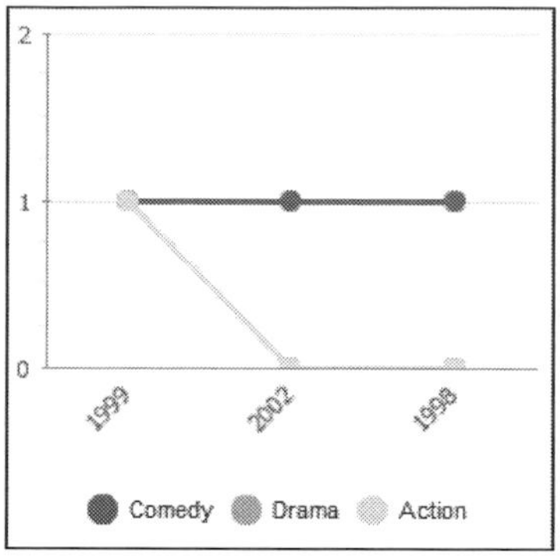


It would appear from this graph that I consistently added comedies to my movie collection. Note that the **Drama** and **Action** lines overlap, causing the **Drama** line to be hidden below **Action**.

# Tooltips

By default, a very generic tooltip exists on the chart, but we have the ability to change this to whatever we want using the `tipRenderer` config. The `tipRenderer` accepts a function as the value, which needs to return a text string to use for the tooltip text. The default is this boring information, which is nothing we can't glean from the chart itself. I want more.

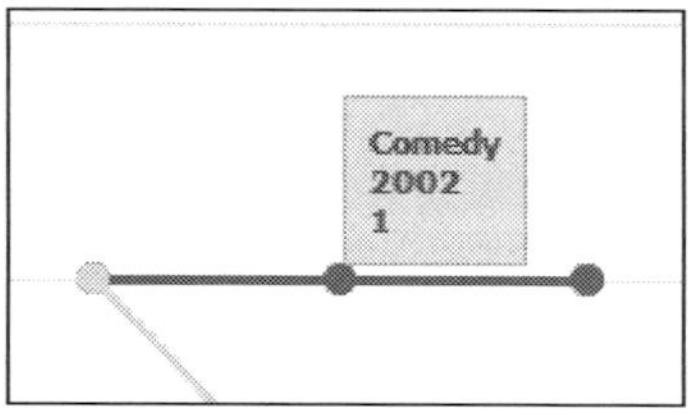


[ Tooltips can be styled just like the other components of a chart using the options available in the `extraStyles` config object. ]

What if we were informed by the tooltip which movie titles made up the data at this particular point on the chart? Now that would be useful. Our function just needs to return a string; other than that requirement we can do whatever we need to, like in this case where we will loop through our movies to get the titles of each movie in the appropriate genre, filmed in the corresponding year.

```
{
    xtype: 'linechart',
    ...
    tipRenderer : function(chart, record, index, series){
        var genre = series.displayName,
            genre_id = genres.getAt(genres.find('genre',
genre)).get('id'),
            year = record.get('year'),
            movies = [];

        store.each(function(rec){
            if(rec.get('genre') == genre_id &&
rec.get('released').format('Y') == year){
                movies.push(rec.get('title'));
            }
        });

        if (movies.length) {
            return movies.join(', ');
        }else{
            return 'None';
        }
    }
}
```

The `tipRenderer` function is called with four arguments passed, the chart, current record of the charts store, the index of the series, and the specific series config. We can use this information to get the details we want from the other stores, which results in a tooltip like the following:

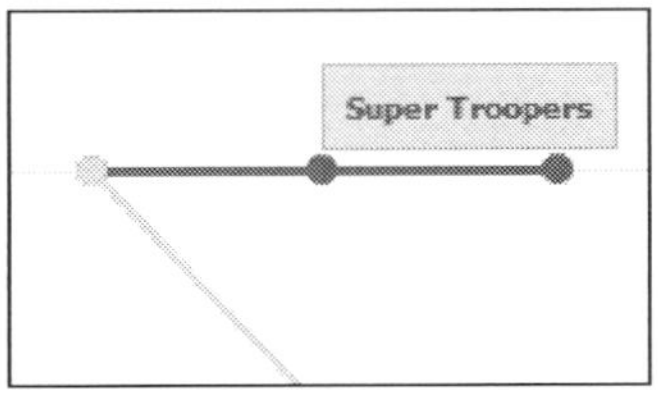


Now we know which movies make up the statistics for the points on the chart. Very useful information now!

# A real world example

For the last example we will use some real-world data and create a simple version of a commonly used application.

The dataset is taken from a cyclist racing a 10 mile time trial. Every two seconds his bike computer records a GPS location, and the racer's heart rate. It records current speed in meters per second based upon elapsed time and GPS fix. The recorded data is provided as an XML file containing a series of **trackpoints**:

```
<Trackpoint>
  <Time>2010-08-03T18:11:35.000Z</Time>
  <Position>
    <LatitudeDegrees>53.060790784657</LatitudeDegrees>
    <LongitudeDegrees>-1.0703133791685104</LongitudeDegrees>
  </Position>
  <AltitudeMeters>66.4000015258789</AltitudeMeters>
  <DistanceMeters>4.050000190734863</DistanceMeters>
  <HeartRateBpm>
    <Value>89</Value>
  </HeartRateBpm>
  <Extensions>
    <TPX>
      <Speed>4.057000160217285</Speed>
    </TPX>
  </Extensions>
</Trackpoint>
```

We will create a line chart tracking speed and heart rate to help the cyclist's coach plan his training.

First we define a `TrackPoint` record definition which extracts the data from the above XML element:

```
var TrackPoint = Ext.data.Record.create([
    { name: 'lon', mapping: 'Position/LongitudeDegrees', type: 'float'
},
    { name: 'lat', mapping: 'Position/LatitudeDegrees', type:
'float'},
    { name: 'elevation', mapping: 'AltitudeMeters', type: 'float' },
    { name: 'distance', mapping: 'DistanceMeters', type: 'float' },
    { name: 'time', mapping: 'Time', type: 'date', dateFormat: 'c' },
    { name: 'heartRate', mapping: 'HeartRateBpm>Value', type: 'int' },
    { name: 'speed', mapping: 'Extensions/TPX/Speed', type: 'float',
        convert: function(v) {
            return v * 2.23693629;  // Metres/sec to miles/hour
        }
    },
    { name: 'elapsed', mapping: 'Time', type: 'date',
        convert: (function() {
            var start;
```

```
                return function(v, raw) {
                    v = Date.parseDate(v, 'c');
                    if (!start) {
                        start = v;
                    }
                    return new Date((v.getTime() - start.getTime()));
                }
            })()
        }
    ])
```

The `mapping` configs specify an Xpath to the element containing the field's value. Where a field must be *calculated*, we configure a `convert` function which is passed the mapped value, and the raw data element.

After loading the store, we extract the GPS fixes to create a Google map using one of the many user extension classes available for Ext JS.

To create a multi-line chart, we must define a *series definition* for each line:

```
heartRateSeries = {
    yField: 'heartRate',
    style: {
        color: 0xff1100,
        size: 8
    }
},
speedSeries - {
    yField: 'speed',
    axis: 'secondary',
    style: {
        color: 0x00aa11,
        size: 8
    }
}
```

We are plotting two lines using the Y axis, while the elapsed time is on the X axis. Each series must specify which field provides its value, and the style for the line points. Optionally, you may specify which axis to bind the value to if, as in this case where we are using two X axes with different measures on each. Heart rate will be red, and speed will be green.

Then we define the axes for the chart. In our previous examples we only defined one X axis and one Y axis. To use two we specify an axes array, and designate one as the secondary axis:

```
    xAxis: new Ext.chart.TimeAxis({
        title: 'Elapsed time',
        labelRenderer: function(date) {
            return date.format("H:i:s");
        }
    }),
    yAxes: [
        new Ext.chart.NumericAxis({
            minimum: 40,
            maximum: 220,
            title: 'Heart rate',
            position: 'left'
        }),0
        new Ext.chart.NumericAxis({
            minimum: 0,
            maximum: 40,
            majorUnit: 5,
            title: 'Speed\nMPH',
            position: 'right',
            order: 'secondary'
        })
    ]
```

To get the chart displayed in its region is all we need. The last example should produce a display like this:

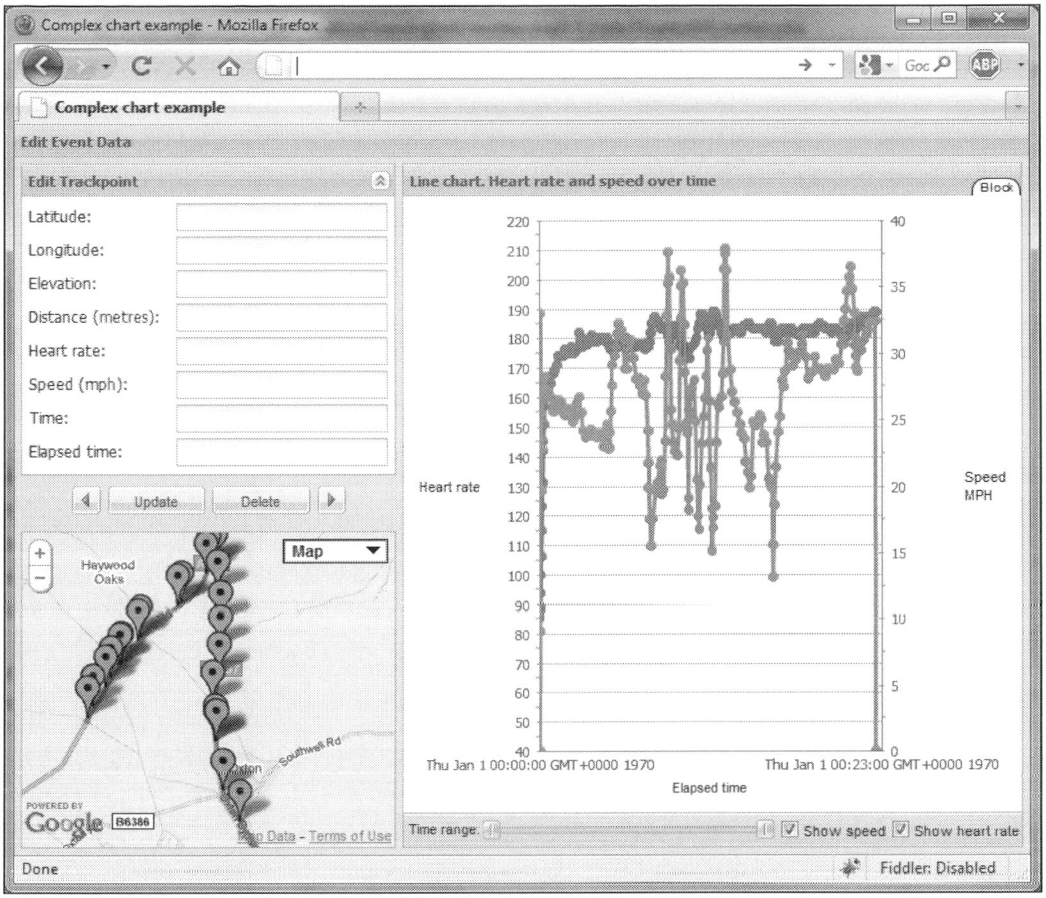

# Dynamically changing the data store

As with all store backed widgets, changes to the data store are immediately reflected in the user interface. This example uses a twin slider control to "zoom in" to a particular time segment of the race. The maximum value is set to the maximum elapsed time, and when the slider positions are changed, the data store is filtered to filter out datapoints outside the slider's time range. The chart will change as the slider fires its change event. To prevent too many updates *during* sliding, we use the `buffer` option on the change listener to add a 50 millisecond delay:

```
timeSlider = new Ext.slider.MultiSlider({
    flex: 1,
    values: [0, 0],
    plugins : [
        Ext.ux.SliderThumbSync,
```

```
        new Ext.slider.Tip({
            getText: function(thumb) {
                var start = new Date(thumb.slider.thumbs[0].value *
1000),
                    end = new Date(thumb.slider.thumbs[1].value *
1000);
                return '<b>' + start.format("i:s") + ' to ' +
end.format('i:s') + '</b>';
            }
        })
    ],
    listeners: {
        change: function() {
            var v = timeSlider.getValues();
            store.filterBy(function(rec) {
                var e = rec.get("elapsed").getTime() / 1000;
                return (e >= v[0]) && (e <= v[1]);
            });
        },
        buffer: 50
    }
})
```

We can also edit `Trackpoints` to correct any data, or remove points. For example, we might want to remove the zero mph trackpoints from the beginning.

To facilitate this, we have enabled *selection* of records by using the mouse events provided on the chart items. Ext Charts *relay* all the events offered by Yahoo Charts. The event names are converted to lower case, and stripped of any redundant 'event' suffix.

Mouse event handlers are passed an event which contains the following properties:

- `Component`: The chart firing the event
- `index`: The index of the record corresponding to the item
- `item`: The data item providing the value (The record's data object)
- `seriesIndex`: The series which rendered the item
- `type`: The event type
- `x`: The X position within the chart object
- `y`: The Y position within the chart object

We add an itemclick listener to load the associated TrackPoint record into the editing form in the west region:

```
listeners: {
    itemclick: function(evt) {
        editTrackpoint = store.getAt(evt.index);
        trackpointEditForm.getForm().loadRecord(editTrackpoint);
        trackpointEditForm.getForm().findField(evt.seriesIndex ?
'speed' : 'heartRate').focus();
    }
}
```

The editing form allows us to change certain values within the `TrackPoint`, and then update the store, or to delete the `TrackPoint` from the store. The chart will update immediately.

# Programatically changing the styles

We can also change the displayed style of existing series in a chart. We have two checkboxes to show and hide the heart rate trace and the speed trace. Each checkbox is configured with a check listener which updates the style property of its associated series definition object, and then refreshes the chart:

```
listeners: {
    check: function(cb, checked) {
        speedSeries.style.visibility = checked ? 'visible' :
'hidden';
        window.chart.refresh();
    }
}
```

# Summary

In this chapter, we have seen how easy it can be to get a basic chart working, and switching between the different chart types can also be quite easy depending on the type of chart. We learned how to give a chart the data it needs to draw bars, lines, and pie slices by adding a store to the chart and loading it with data. Then we styled the chart to fit our needs. From here we now have a foundation to start graphing more complex data into charts and if you're unlucky, you will soon be creating charts for the company board meetings.

# 11
# Effects

The easiest thing to do when writing a software application is to switch into programmer mode—to focus on the code, and not on the end user experience. The architecture of a system is extremely important, but if the user is not satisfied with their interactions with the system, then the project can only be seen as a failure.

Ext JS contributes to solving this issue by providing many slick components that react well to user input and maintain a consistent look and feel across the entire framework. "Feel" is a very fuzzy word when it comes to software design; the way a link acts when you hover over it or the way in which a window appears onscreen can be the difference between a pleasurable experience and a confusing one.

Many of Ext JS's components have transitional animations built-in by default, allowing you to smoothly expand a `treenode` rather than suddenly pop it open, or to shrink down a window to a specified button that can be used to reactivate it later.

Features like this aren't just an added layer on top of the rest of the Ext framework; they're baked in at a low level to provide a consistent experience for both the developer and the end user.

In this chapter, we'll discuss:

- The range of built-in Ext JS options for animation and effects
- Creating custom animations and tweaking the existing ones
- Using multiple animations together
- Other Ext JS visual effects such as masking and tooltips

## It's elementary

The `Ext.Element` underlies many of the feature-rich widgets in Ext JS; indeed the `Ext.Component.getEl` method reflects the fact that widgets such as windows form fields and toolbars are supported by this fundamental building block.

`Ext.Element` mixes many methods from `Ext.Fx`, the class that is designed to provide slick transitions and animations for HTML elements and components alike. We're going to discuss the exciting possibilities that `Ext.Fx` provides, and also talk about the way in which it works together with `Ext.Element`.

# Fancy features

Along with building blocks of animation, we're going to examine various pieces of eye candy that you can find dotted around the Ext framework. There are a number of classes that provide added functionality to give your users feedback or assistance when they're using your application, and many components support these features straight out of the box. We can also use them in a standalone manner to create rich tooltips, mask items that are in the process of loading new data, or highlight individual parts of the screen to draw the user's attention to them.

# It's OK to love

In truth, many of the functions we're going to cover in this chapter are superficial in nature. They add some whizz-bang transitions that are not strictly essential. There are two lines of defense for criticism. Firstly, a good developer understands that users are not machines—they're people—and a little bit of whizz-bang is good for everyone. Secondly, and perhaps more scientifically, it's much better to have a transition to signify a change than simply have something appear. A transition draws the eye and gives the user the opportunity to consume the visual cue that was presented.

A sudden change on screen results in a "what happened" response; a smooth transition provides a hint as to what's going on. As we tour the various features of `Ext.Fx`, bear in mind that they can be used for more than just being eye-candy; they're great for adding value to your user experience.

# Fxcellent functions

`Ext.Fx` is presented as a standalone class, architecturally independent of `Ext.Element`, but in reality it cannot be used on its own. Instead, it is automatically mixed into the methods and properties of the `Ext.Element` class, so that each action from `Ext.Fx` is available for each `Ext.Element` instance. The examples that follow will illustrate this point.

# Methodical madness

As mentioned earlier, `Ext.Fx` has a range of methods that are called upon to perform the magic. Each of these methods is available for `Ext.Element` instances. So in the examples that follow, we're going to assume that you have a div element with an ID of "target" on your ready-to-go HTML page.

# Fading

The term "fading" is used in `Ext.Fx` to refer to a change in opacity—from 100 percent opaque to 0 percent (fade out) and vice versa (fade in). In other words, we're making something disappear and reappear—but as this is the *Effects* chapter, the transition is animated. The two methods that perform these transitions are `Ext.Fx.fadeOut` and `Ext.Fx.fadeIn`, and both support simple zero-argument usage:

```
Ext.get('target').fadeOut();

window.setTimeout(function() {
Ext.get('target').fadeIn();
}, 3000);
```

This usage will cause the target element to fade away slowly until it is completely invisible. The timeout happens three seconds later and causes the target to slowly re-appear, or fade in, until it is fully visible again.

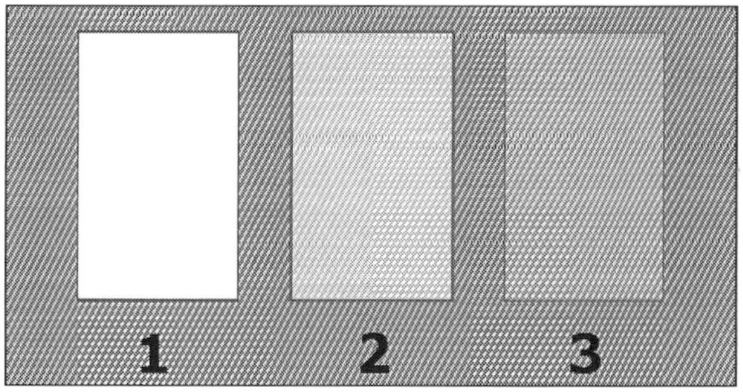


You can tweak the behavior of these methods using the `endOpacity` configuration option. This allows you to specify that the element will not fade out to complete invisibility, which can be useful if you simply want to indicate that an item is now less important. Alternatively, you can use it to dictate that an item will not return to total solidity:

```
Ext.get('target').fadeOut({endOpacity:0.25});

window.setTimeout(function() {
Ext.get('target').fadeIn({endOpacity: 0.75});
}, 3000);
```

In the example just given, the initially-solid item is supposed to fade out to one quarter opacity before being restored after three seconds to only three quarters opacity.

In addition to the configuration options such as `endOpacity` that are specific to individual effects methods, there are also a number of common options shared by all `Ext.Fx` methods. These allow you to tweak the behavior of your effects even further. We'll discuss these later in this chapter.

# Framing

Framing is reminiscent of a video game radar "ping". It radiates out from the point of origin, fading away with distance. A great use of this feature is to highlight a particular element on the screen—and the `Ext.Fx.frame` method also allows us to ensure that the user's attention is drawn by using multiple "pings". The simplest way of using it is without arguments:

```
Ext.get('target').frame();
```

This causes the target element to radiate a single light blue ping to draw attention to the element, which may be useful in some scenarios. However, to make sure that the user knows about a more important event, we could use something like this:

```
Ext.get('target').frame('ff0000', 3);
```

The first argument is the hexadecimal color of the framing effect, in this case, an angry red. The second argument specifies the number of times the ping is to be repeated. So here, we're using three red pulses to indicate that something pretty bad is about to happen:

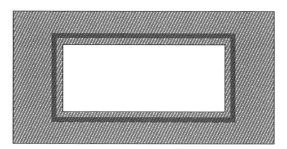

These are the real strengths of the `frame` method: repetition, and the ability to use different colors to represent different situations and priorities.

# Woooo: ghosting

Ghosts!-or rather ghosting—this is the term Ext JS gives to fading an element while it moves in a specified direction. This effect is used to give the impression that an element is transitioning from one area to another, for example the act of paging through a number of images could trigger ghosting when the **next** or **previous** link is selected. The default usage of `ghost` causes the element to drop-down while fading out.

```
Ext.get('target').ghost();
```

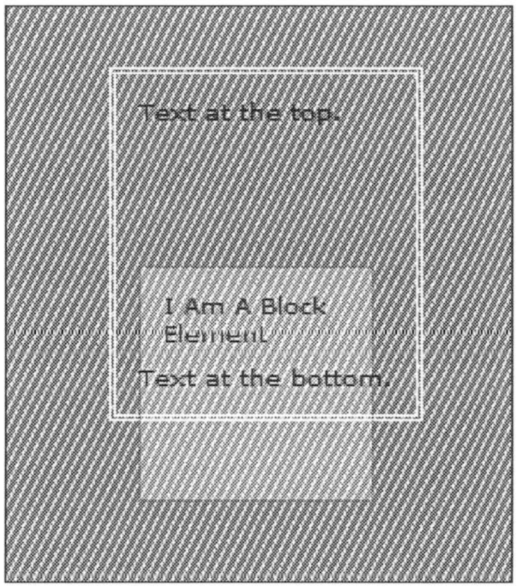


The default settings could be used to discard elements that are no longer needed—perhaps deletion of events could be signified with a call to `Ext.Fx.ghost`. As mentioned previously, we can also cater to other situations by specifying different directions for the ghosting depending on the situation. The standard `Ext.Fx` anchor points, used in animation and alignment, can also be used with the ghost method:

```
Ext.get('target').ghost('tr');
```

Here, we indicate that the target will ghost out in the direction of its upper-right corner, but any anchor point is accepted. We'll talk more about anchoring later in the chapter. But it is this parameter that would allow us to replicate the paging functionality which was described earlier, that is, we can use left and right anchor points to move the ghost in the relevant directions.

## Highlighting

If you're familiar with the term "Web 2.0", then you may also have heard of the "yellow fade technique". A quick web search will turn up numerous references to this JavaScript technique, which became popular when Web 2.0 was first becoming a buzzword. Typically used when an action has been completed and the user has been redirected to a new page, this effect causes a portion of the page—often an error message—to have its background highlighted in a different color. The highlight slowly fades away over a few seconds. Traditionally, the highlighted color has been a friendly yellow, but for error messages, we might favor something stronger. Having said that, yellow is the default for `Ext.Fx.highlight`:

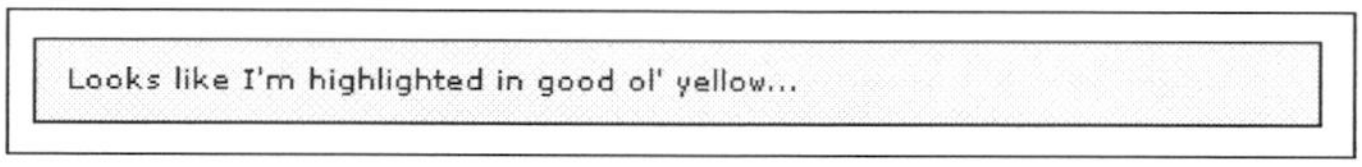
Looks like I'm highlighted in good ol' yellow...

This is triggered by the following basic code:

```
Ext.get('target').highlight();
```

Ext JS takes highlighting to the next level. While the standard usage affects the CSS background color of the target element, you can choose any CSS property, such as the color or border color. You can also specify the `endColor` of the highlight. In our second and more complex example, we can cause the text itself to start out white and end up green:

```
Ext.get('target').highlight('ffffff',{
    attr: 'color',
    endColor: '00ff00'
});
```

This is an extremely flexible method that can be used to highlight large portions of a page—perhaps a fieldset in a form, or just a block of text—perhaps in an online spellchecker. The point to be noted is that we can use it to respond and react to user input, and use its flexibility to indicate the state of our system in a noticeable manner.

## Huffing and puffing

`The puff` method of `Ext.Fx` tries to replicate the look of a `puff` of smoke slowly dissipating into the air. While some of the `Ext.Fx` effects are used to highlight areas, puff is used to transition an element off the screen. To do this, the element expands while becoming more transparent, eventually fading away completely. `Puff` doesn't have any special options of its own, so the default usage is pretty obvious:

```
Ext.get('target').puff();
```

`Puff` could be used with a quick transition to dismiss a window from the workspace, or a slower transition could illustrate the removal of an element, maybe an image from a gallery. However, there is one important point to note about this method: when used within the document flow, it will affect the position of the elements around it.

Although absolutely-positioned windows will not affect their surroundings, in our gallery example, it is possible that when you use `puff`, you'll get unexpected results as the expanding dimensions push your other images out of the way.

Developers who are aware of the potential side effects of using `Ext.Fx.puff` can add it to their toolkit, providing another interesting method of creating dynamic transitions in their applications.

# Scaling the Ext JS heights

Scaling is one of the few Ext JS effects that have a specific use, rather than simply being an overlay on top of another action. It changes the dimensions of an element using a smooth transition, which has numerous applications. We can expand text areas to give more space for user input; we can replicate, maximize, and restore effects seen in the windowing applications; we can change the focus of a workspace by shrinking one portion and expanding another. The basic usage of `Ext.Fx.scale` looks like this:

```
Ext.get('target').scale(50, 150);
```

In this example, the target element will be smoothly-scaled to a width of 50 pixels and a height of 150 pixels. Both of these options also accept null values, which indicate that they should not be changed. This is useful if you want to restrict the scale only horizontally or vertically.

> `Ext.Fx.scale` works only with those elements that have their display style set to block, to allow the width and height changes to take effect. Using it on inline elements won't trigger an error, but you will not see any change in the dimensions of the element, either.

# Sliding into action

Within Ext JS, sliding refers to the transition of an element into or out of view. This is the same effect used in the `Ext.Fx.ghost` method, so we've seen it in action already. But in reality, there are two methods that fall under this heading—`Ext.Fx.slideIn` and `Ext.Fx.slideOut`.

We can use these methods to either drop out an element that is no longer required, or introduce a new element onto the screen. An obvious application for this would be addition and deletion of records, where new items `slideIn` to the list and deleted items `slideOut`.

```
Ext.get('target').slideOut();
window.setTimeout(function() {
Ext.get('target').slideIn();
}, 3000);
```

In the previous example, we move the target out of view, and three seconds later bring it back in. By default, elements will `slideIn` and `slideOut` from their top edge, but the first argument to both functions allows you to use anchors to specify the direction of the movement:

```
Ext.get('target').slideOut('tr');
```

Here, we dictate that the target will `slideOut` to the top right. As with `Ext.Fx.puff`, you must be aware of the elements that surround the item you're sliding; text and other non-absolutely-positioned elements may be pushed around during the slide.

## Switching from seen to unseen

The `switchOff` method is another means of removing an element from the screen. This one combines two actions: firstly the element fades slightly to acknowledge the start of the effect, and then the element slowly collapses from the top and the bottom until it disappears. This two-stage effect means it can be used to draw the user's eye before the real vanishing act takes place. We can use `Ext.Fx.switchOff` in the following way:

```
Ext.get('target').switchOff();
```

As you can see, there are no unique arguments for this method, so it would seem that you're stuck with the default effect. But later we'll discuss the configuration options that are available for all of the `Ext.Fx` methods—the secret to complete control over your effects.

`switchOff` comes in pretty handy in situations where you'd like to cause an element to vanish without user interaction. For example, you might have some kind of monitoring screen on your website that displays the current visitors to your site, and tracks them as they move between pages. When their session expires, they will be removed from the list. Rather than simply transitioning off the screen you can highlight to the user that this is about to happen using `switchOff`: a quick flash to indicate that the action is about to occur, and then the actual collapse transition.

## Shifting

The `Ext.Fx.shift` method may sound like a function in the same vein as `ghost` and `slideOut`, but in actual fact it's a little different. There's no default behavior associated with the method, so simply call it in this fashion:

```
Ext.get('target').shift();
```

This will have no effect. Instead, `shift` must be supplied with a literal containing one or more values from the following:

- `width`
- `height`
- `x`
- `y`

By setting one of these values and passing it to `shift`, we can cause the target element to move to the `x, y` coordinates and resize to the `width, height` dimensions—in the smooth manner which we've come to expect of `Ext.Fx`. Here's an example:

```
Ext.get('target').shift({
    x: 5,
    y: 300,
    width: 300,
    height: 200
});
```

In this example, our target element will move to a position of five pixels from the left and 300 from the top of the viewport, and will resize to 300 x 200 pixels. These changes happen simultaneously, with the element resizing as it moves.

Effectively, `shift` is a version of `Ext.Fx.scale` that adds the ability to reposition the element. This is a great mechanism for re-organizing a workspace—shifting panels of data from a place of prominence to a place more unobtrusive, and doing so in a smooth, dynamic manner.

# And now, the interesting stuff

All of the methods that we've just covered have some broad similarities. But each of them has certain distinct differences which make them applicable as solutions for a range of very different problems. We're now going to discuss how an extra feature of `Ext.Fx` can tweak and tailor the effects that we've already reviewed.

In many of the previous examples, the functionality on offer is slightly limited. What's been glossed over until now is that each of the methods we've discussed also accepts a standard configuration object that provides a host of common options to bring their full functionality to your fingertips.

# The Fx is in

We've briefly touched upon the way in which anchoring options are used within `Ext.Fx`; for example, methods such as a ghost accepting a string representing the direction in which to move. Over the next few pages, we'll not only discuss this in detail, but we'll also go over the numerous configuration options that are common to all of the `Ext.Fx` methods.

# Anchoring yourself with Ext

Specifying directions, anchors, alignment, and more is all based around a scheme of anchor positions. These are used by Ext JS's animation system to determine the direction of movement, and they have a pretty simple naming convention:

| Anchor Position String | Description |
|---|---|
| tl | Top-left corner (the default) |
| T | Center of the top edge |
| tr | Top right corner |
| l | Center of the left edge |
| r | Center of the right edge |
| bl | Bottom-left corner |
| b | Center of the bottom edge |
| br | Bottom-right corner |

These options allow eight-way movement when using methods such as `Ext.Fx.ghost`. But the same concept is seen in methods such as `Ext.Element.alignTo` and `Ext.Element.anchorTo`, where two anchor points can be combined, and the "?" character can be used to dictate that the alignment will be constrained to the viewpoint.

In short, it pays to familiarize yourself with the Ext JS anchor positions, as you'll almost certainly use them in your application—either to move elements or to just bend them to suit your many needs. More than that, `Ext.Components` has underlying elements. So you'll most likely use these features when developing a solution with rich widgets.

Now, back to the topic at hand—taming the `Ext.Fx` class.

# Options

As mentioned earlier, each of the `Ext.Fx` methods we've covered can take an optional configuration literal as its last parameter, which provides 11 settings for tweaking your effects. The simplest is probably `duration`, which specifies how long the effect should last. This is useful for ensuring that your transitions last long enough for your users to catch them. Although the default durations of each effect are usually pretty sensible, there are many use cases for overriding this value. Here's an example of using duration, and indeed the configuration option argument in general:

```
Ext.get('target').switchOff({
    duration: 10
});
```

In this example, we pass a standard object literal to the `switchOff` method, and the duration property is set to `10`, indicating that the `switchOff` should take place over ten seconds.

With the default behavior of some of the `Ext.Fx` methods, you end up with some sub-optimal transitions. For example, many of the effects that cause an element to vanish will actually just leave a big gap where the element used to be. This is because they complete the transition by setting the visibility of the element to hidden, rather than removing it from the DOM or from the document flow. We can rectify this using two more configuration options: `remove` and `useDisplay`.

The first, `remove`, signifies that we'd like to completely destroy the element when the transition has completed. The second, `useDisplay`, means that the element will be hidden using `display:none` rather than `visibility:hidden`, so that it will no longer affect the nodes around it. Using `remove` and `useDisplay` together is redundant. If the node is completely removed, it makes no difference how it's hidden. If you're planning on re-using or re-showing the element in question, then stick with `useDisplay`; otherwise you may as well be tidy (and avoid potential memory leaks) and use `remove`.

The configuration options also allow us to dictate what else happens when the effect has completed. We have two options that control the look of our element: `afterCls` and `afterStyle`, which allow a CSS class or raw CSS rules to be applied to the element at the end of our transition. This can be used to add a permanent change to the element in question, perhaps highlighting it as a newly-introduced item.

We have two more options that give us the power to perform further actions when the effect has completed: `callback`, which allows us to specify a function to be called at the end of the transition, and `scope`, which is the scope of the callback function. For example:

```
Ext.get('target').switchOff({
   callback: function() {
      alert('Effect complete!');
   }
});
```

The `Ext.Fx` class handles the queuing of effects automatically, so don't use this to trigger another effect. Instead, use it to trigger actions associated with the animation.

# Easy does it

Our next configuration option is `easing`. In animation terminology, `easing` refers to the means by which the transition *eases* from a stop to movement and back to a stop again. By default, Ext JS effects will abruptly start and stop, but by using the `easing` option, we can specify how it will accelerate and decelerate at the start and end of the effect respectively.

> The easing effects supported by Ext JS vary depending on which adapter you're using. If you're using the Ext JS Base adapter, then you'll get the full works.

A basic example of this in action is the `easeBoth` value. This causes the animation to gradually speed up and then slow down in order to provide a smooth-looking transition:

```
Ext.get('target').scale(50, 150, {easing: 'easeBoth'});
```

Here, we're applying the easing option to the scale effect, and by using `easeBoth`, we can have a less jarring movement as it progresses. There are many more easing options:

- `easeNone`
- `easeIn`
- `easeOut`
- `easeBoth`
- `easeInStrong`
- `easeOutStrong`
- `easeBothStrong`

- `elasticIn`
- `elasticOut`
- `elasticBoth`
- `backIn`
- `backOut`
- `backBoth`
- `bounceIn`
- `bounceOut`
- `bounceBoth`

That's a list of the options supported by Ext JS Base. Those like `bounceIn` provide a bit of a spring to the effect, which is perhaps more useful in a gaming application than in data entry, but the beauty of having such a wide choice is that you are likely to find something that fits your requirements.

The final few configuration options apply to the way your current effect interacts with other effects that may occur within its lifetime. For example, `block` will specify that no other effects are queued up while this one is running, which is useful in scenarios where triggering further changes could adversely affect your application's state. The `block` option tells all other effects to "bide your time" until things have calmed down.

```
Ext.get('target').shift({
   x: 5,
   y: 300,
   width: 300,
   height: 200,
   block: true
});
```

Here, we see an interesting usage of the `Ext.Fx.shift` method, in which the shift-specific configuration options are augmented by the common `Fx` ones.

We also have the `stopFx` and `concurrent` options. `stopFx` allows us to cancel all effects that get triggered after this one, while `concurrent` specifies whether subsequent effects will run in parallel with this one, or will be queued up until after this one has completed. By default, they'll queue up and run in sequence, but there are situations in which you will be able to apply multiple effects at a time, and we'll talk more about that in the next few sections.

# Multiple effects

Most of the time, you'll use effects one at a time on different elements to achieve the look you're after, but in some circumstances, it can be useful to use multiple effects. There are a few different ways of handling this scenario, and in the next few sections, we're going to review these ways. We're also going to see how we can influence any running effects from our code.

## Chaining

An easy way to set up a second effect to run after your first is completed is to use the chaining method. As each of the main `Ext.Fx` methods return the `Ext.Element` that was the target of the effect, you can then call further `Ext.Element` methods, including those provided by `Ext.Fx`:

```
Ext.get('target').slideIn().highlight();
```

As you can see from this example, we're calling `slideIn` followed by `highlight`, which indicates that `highlight` will be added to the effects queue to run after `slideIn` completes.

## Queuing

Queuing is the default behavior for effects set up either by method chaining, or by multiple calls. The following code sample is functionally identical to our previous example:

```
Ext.get('target').slideIn();
Ext.get('target').highlight();
```

In both cases, the `highlight` effect will be queued up behind `slideIn`. This negates the need for any complicated timing or callback-based set-ups to trigger effects that run sequentially.

## Concurrency

Although queuing is default, we also have the option of running effects in parallel by using the previously discussed `concurrent` configuration option. This gives us the opportunity to combine effects—for example, we could `highlight` an element as it scales up:

```
Ext.get('target').scale(300, 200 ,{
    concurrent:true
}).highlight();
```

This provides a very powerful capacity for customization.

## Blocking and Ext.Fx utility methods

There are a number of extra methods within the `Ext.Fx` class that aren't directly responsible for creating effects. Instead, they can be used to manage and monitor effects that are already in the queue. A great example of this is the `stopFx` method, which is as simple as it sounds—we can call it to cancel any animations that are currently running. It also clears the effects queue, and primes the element for user interaction or further manipulation.

Interestingly, `stopFx` returns the target `Ext.Element`, allowing the developer to chain up further methods. Perhaps you have set up a `slideIn` that is subsequently canceled and replaced with `slideOut`:

```
Ext.get('target').stopFx().slideOut();
```

Such code is useful if we need to interrupt an animation to give the control back to the user—an ability that can be crucial in giving the user the response they require. However, in other circumstances you may want to prevent the user from interfering with the current state of the application, and if that's the case, we have the `hasFxBlock` method. Typically, this is used to make sure that the user can't queue up the same effect many times—we can prevent additional effect calls to the element if `hasFxBlock` returns true.

# Elemental

As we've seen, the `Ext.Element` is the key to using `Ext.Fx`. It's important that, when rolling your own custom versions of Ext JS, you make sure that you include `Ext.Fx` if you want to be able to use its methods for `Ext.Element`. However, even when used standalone, `Ext.Element` has a number of methods all of its own that can provide some interesting possibilities for animation.

# Making a move

There are many methods on `Ext.Element` that can be used to manipulate a target element, but some of them have a free extra. Pass in a `true` value as the last parameter, and the manipulation will be animated.

```
Ext.get('target').moveTo(300, 500, true);
```

In this case, the target element will move to a location 300 pixels from the left and 500 from the top of the viewport. But, because of this last parameter, it will not simply jump to that location, but will smoothly transition to the specified point.

In addition to simply passing in `true` as the third parameter, we can pass in a full configuration object instead. This uses the same animation options for `Ext.Fx` that we discussed earlier in the chapter.

> `Ext.Element` animations can be used at the same time as the ones from `Ext.Fx`, but they are not guaranteed to support the queuing features that are always available with the `Ext.Fx` methods.

There are many methods, such as `setOpacity` and `scroll` that can be used in this fashion to provide the means for adding simple transitions. This is a good foundation, which `Ext.Fx` builds upon.

There's another piece of the animation puzzle that we're yet to touch upon: `Ext.Element.animate`. This is the generic means of applying animations to an element, and is a shortcut to the same underlying methods that are used by all of the `Ext.Element` methods that support animation.

Advanced applications of this method involve using the `Ext.lib.anim` entries that register all of the stock animation types available to Ext JS, and adding new registered animation handlers to support custom scenarios. In most cases, using the stock `Ext.Element` methods or the `Ext.Fx` methods will be sufficient, even for advanced cases.

## Using Ext components

The animations which are available on `Ext.Element` are particularly interesting when you consider that many `Ext.Components`, such as the `Window` or `FormPanel`, have an underlying element as their container. This means that you can apply these effects to full components as well as to standard elements, providing an added utility for these methods.

# Reveal all

Although we've covered `Ext.Fx` and the other animation techniques that Ext JS offers in depth, we've still got a few more features to cover when it comes to showing off with the framework. There are a number of Ext classes that provide a little extra sparkle to the top of the standard solutions. We've got `LoadMask` that allows you to mask off a portion of the screen while it's being refreshed, and `QuickTip` that offers a rich, configurable tooltip system.

These classes open up a new range of options when it comes to creating compelling user-experiences, and we're going to examine them in detail over the next few pages. A key feature of each is that they are reasonably simple to use, which is partly the reason why you'll want to use them in many of your Ext JS applications.

# You're maskin', I'm tellin'

The `Ext.LoadMask` class has a couple of different use cases. We can use it to simply display a message that keeps the user informed, or we can use it to prevent interaction with a component that is being refreshed.

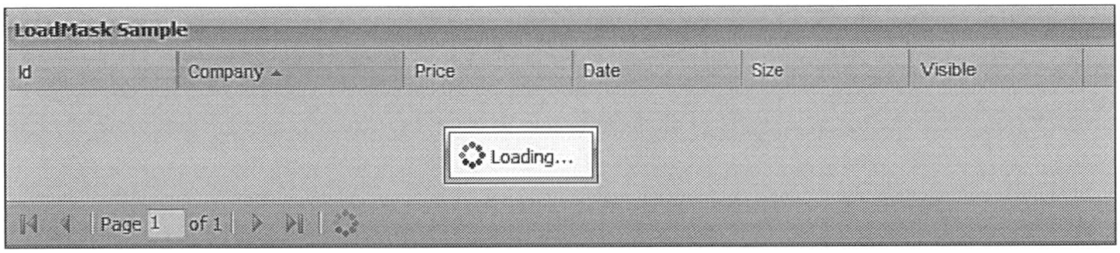


Let's look at the first scenario, which is using an `Ext.LoadMask` to simply overlay an element with a message:

```
var target = Ext.get('target');
var mask = new Ext.LoadMask(target);
mask.show();
```

In the previous example, once we have obtained an element using `Ext.get`, we pass it into the `Ext.LoadMask` constructor and call the `show` method on the `LoadMask` instance. There is also an optional second parameter for the `Ext.LoadMask` constructor, a configuration object with four properties:

| Property Name | Description |
|---|---|
| `Msg` | The loading message to be displayed in the center of the mask |
| `msgCls` | The CSS class to use for the loading message container |
| `removeMask` | Boolean; set to True to destroy the mask after the load is complete |
| `store` | Discussed later |

When creating a load mask in this way, we can dismiss it by calling the `mask.hide` method. Although this masking approach is pretty straightforward, it's also a little verbose. So in some cases, it's better to use the shortcut method that `Ext.Element` provides:

```
Ext.get('target').mask('Loading...', 'x-mask-loading');
```

In this example, we're explicitly passing the message text and message CSS class as the first and second arguments respectively. This allows us to replicate the functionality provided by a basic `Ext.LoadMask` call, as shown in the first example, but they're both optional. When you're done with the mask, you can hide it by calling the `unmask` method of your `Ext.Element` instance. If you have stored a reference to the mask, you can call the `hide` method of that instance instead.

## Data binding and other tales

Although it initially seems that the `Ext.Element` approach is better, there are actually a few compelling reasons for using the full `LoadMask`. The most interesting reason is that it can be tied to a specified `Ext.data.Store` instance, allowing you to automatically mask and unmask your element based on when the store is loading. This cuts down on your code when showing the mask, but it also negates the need to hook up an event listener for your load complete events. Let's take a look at how this feature can be used:

```
var slowStore = GetSlowStore();

var mask = new Ext.LoadMask(Ext.get('target'), {
   store:slowStore
});

slowStore.load();
```

We're not interested in how to create a store, so that's been hidden away in a function call. All we care about is that our example store is going to take a couple of seconds to finish loading. We instantiate a new `LoadMask` with an element as the first constructor parameter and a configuration literal as the second one. The `store` property accepts our `slowStore` as its value.

Now that everything's set up, we simply call the `load` method of the store. This will mask over our target element, and in a few seconds when it has finished loading, the mask will automatically be dismissed.

## Considering components

As we've seen, there are a number of ways of manually masking elements, and you could use any of these approaches to the `Ext.Elements` that underlie many `Ext.Components`. However, it's important to note that some components provide this functionality for you, cutting down on the code that you need to write in order to enable this feature in your applications. For example, the `Ext.grid.GridPanel` has a Boolean `loadMask` configuration option, which not only masks the panel but also automatically ties in to the data source that is feeding the `GridPanel`. So `GridPanel` has this handy feature baked right in!

# QuickTipping

It's often very useful to be able to supply further information for a button or form field, just in case your users are unclear as to its purpose. In many cases, it's impractical to put this information inline, next to the item in question, simply because it would make the interface highly cluttered. In this situation, tooltips are a great alternative to inline information, and with Ext JS these little pop-up snippets can contain any HTML that you'd like to show.

The `Ext.QuickTips` class is a singleton that provides a very easy method of creating rich tooltips. It allows you to put your `QuickTip` setup information directly into the markup of your page—a great method for reducing the configuration required. In many cases, having the description text within your main HTML makes the most sense. This approach is supported by the use of a number of extra attributes for any HTML element that you'd like to tie the `QuickTip` to, with `ext:qwidth`, `ext:qtitle` and `ext:qtip` being the most commonly-used:

```
<input type="text" ext:qtitle="Information" ext:qtip=
                 "This field can contain text!" ext:qwidth="200" />
```

We need to activate the global `QuickTips` handler before this starts working:

```
Ext.QuickTips.init();
```

It's also worth mentioning that nonstandard attributes will cause your HTML document to fail validation—so bear that in mind if your application requires valid HTML. After completing these two steps, you'll end up with the tooltip as shown in the following screenshot:

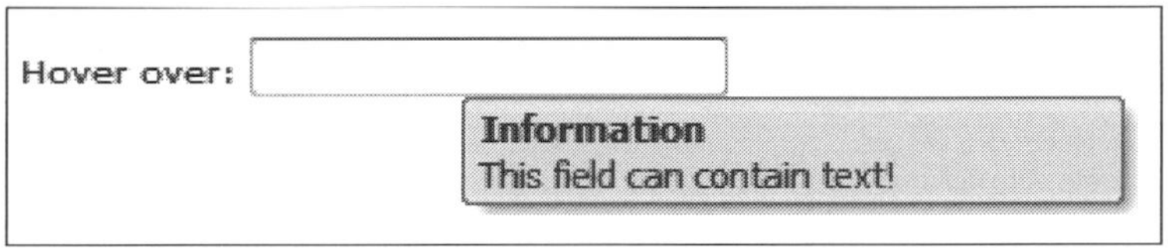


Along with using markup-based tooltips, we can also programmatically create more customizable ones with the `Ext.ToolTip` class. This provides a range of configuration options to change the behavior and appearance of the tooltips, and also allows you to pull tooltip data from an external source, by using the power of AJAX.

The simplest usage of this class is as follows:

```
new Ext.ToolTip({
   target: 'tipTarget',
   html: 'This is where our information goes!'
});
```

The constructor for `Ext.ToolTip` accepts a configuration literal as its only argument, and here we're using the mandatory `target` property to specify which element will trigger the tooltip; in this case it will be the one with the ID `tipTarget`. Note that we're using a string to refer to the ID, but in fact you can pass in an `Ext.Element` reference or a standard HTML node. We're then setting the `html` property to the text that we'd like to show in the tooltip. As the name of the property indicates, you can add any extra markup you like, even images.

`Ext.ToolTip` has a number of other interesting options, such as the ability to tweak the time it takes for the tooltip to appear and then vanish, by using the `showDelay` and `hideDelay` configuration properties. This can be useful if you need the tooltip to appear promptly when the user hovers over its associated element, or if you want to make sure that the information is on-screen long enough to be taken in.

We've also got the ability to set the title of the tooltip in the same way as we did with the markup-based solution, that is, by using the `title` option. In fact, many of the options, such as `title`, come from the fact that `Ext.ToolTip` is a subclass of `Ext.Panel`. This means that we can use features such as the `autoLoad` configuration option to grab content from a URL, or use the `closable` option, to force the user to dismiss the tooltip using a close widget.

A great feature introduced in Ext JS 3.0 allows **anchoring** of a tooltip—providing a means of letting your tooltips actually point at the object they refer to. By using the `anchor` configuration option with a value of `top`, the tooltip appears below the target element with a guiding arrow protruding from the top of the tooltip element. You can also use the `anchorOffset` to tweak where the arrow appears on the tooltip's edge.

This feature is only supported when you're using the tooltip inside a container that is using the `AnchorLayout` layout manager, so bear that in mind when using this anchoring technique.

`QuickTips` and `ToolTips` are great examples of Ext JS classes that aren't *essential* to an application, but provide a layer of functionality that can take your solution from something ordinary to something highly usable.

# Summary

There's a fine line between visual cues and annoying effects. Although we've reviewed many of the Ext JS features that allow you to gear your application towards either extreme, this chapter has only been about the tools and not how you should use them.

That said, we've also looked at a couple of examples that illustrate just how useful eye candy can be when helping out your users. By providing a little something extra when you're deleting a record or closing a data display, you can turn a potentially confusing experience into one that is supported by gradual changes in visual state, rather than immediate shifts from one click to another.

The key is to ensure that those gradual changes aren't too gradual, that your animations aren't in-your-face, and that they aren't triggered every time the user presses a button. Software applications are about getting things done, and having portions of the page whizzing around the screen isn't likely to help with that.

Ext JS isn't just about these fancy effects, though. We've demonstrated a couple of classes that are utility tools with style. `ToolTips` and `LoadMasks` are genuinely useful in many scenarios, and could rarely be used in an "in-your-face" manner.

Using `ToolTips` can add a lot of value to a busy application, removing clutter by moving inline text into pop ups, and providing unified and attractive assistance to your users. Images, and even HTML links, can provide more information than could possibly be shown next to a form field.

The other class which we covered, `LoadMask`, can form a critical part of a system, ensuring not only that your users are prevented from interrupting a load operation, but also that the mask that appears is attractive, consistent, and can contain customized information that keeps the users informed.

In the next chapter, we're going to take a look at one of the most typical examples of Web 2.0 glitz: drag-and-drop. In a typical Ext JS manner, we're going to see how it's not only simple to use, but also powerful in its functionality.

# 12
# Drag-and-drop

In the world of software development, desktop applications are still number one. Although websites and, latterly, web applications are developing rapidly using frameworks such as Ext JS, they are yet to reach the level of complexity that we see in our most extensive desktop programs.

Drag-and-drop, the subject matter of this chapter, is a good example of this. Moving items across the screen using the mouse on a standard computer desktop is all-pervasive; it is available for a great many actions and it is available in virtually every application, even if this is in a limited form.

Part of the reason for this is that implementing drag-and-drop using JavaScript is pretty hard. Coming up with a consistent methodology for turning any element into a draggable widget that can then be placed on another element, have it work in every browser, have it support scrolling, and take into account iframes is, to say the least, problematic.

At the start of the Web 2.0 revolution, we started to see some more consistent implementations of drag-and-drop appearing—ones that fulfilled many of the criteria we've just outlined. But even then, the Web didn't start using it in such a free and easy manner as the desktop, perhaps because of the poor use cases that were used as demonstrations for this new functionality. After all, does anyone really want to work with a drag-and-drop shopping cart system?

This chapter will cover:

- An overview of how drag-and-drop works in Ext JS
- A simple example to illustrate how to set up drag-and-drop
- Using drag-and-drop with Ext JS components
- Managing advanced drag-and-drop features such as scrolling, proxies, and metadata

# Drop what you're doing

The implementation of drag-and-drop that Ext JS provides succeeds on many levels. It is cross-browser and easy to use, but more importantly, it is used in multiple widgets within the framework, such as the `GridPanel` and `TreePanel`, making it easy to implement in useful real world applications.

In addition, the `Ext.dd` package contains a number of classes that allow you to create simple drag-and-drop features with ease—shopping carts included. There is sufficient granularity to support more advanced scenarios as well, providing you with a means of creating custom drag-and-drop solutions that are fully integrated into your Ext application.

In this chapter, we'll review the `Ext.dd` package and ways in which it can extend your toolkit, but we'll also be looking at how to extend the drag-and-drop functionality provided by the various Ext components.

# Life's a drag

There are clearly two parts to creating a working drag-and-drop feature—the dragging, and the dropping. As these are two separate operations, we'll handle them separately for our simple use case.

## Sourcing a solution

The first part we need to look at is the drag action. Ext will enable this using the `Ext.dd.DragSource`, which actually makes the whole thing a breeze. Assume that you've got a `<div>` element on your page with an ID `dragMe`:

```
new Ext.dd.DragSource("dragMe");
```

That's all you need to get up and running!

Try running this code and grab hold of your element. You can now drag it around the page, but there's a little bit more to it than that. Ext JS provides a few extra features by default, which will be demonstrated by this code.

## Approximating

When you begin dragging the element, you'll see that you don't actually drag the full element as you would in some drag-and-drop implementations that you might have seen. Instead, Ext JS automatically provides a `proxy`—a lightweight representation of whatever element you're dragging. This facility is provided by Ext in the form of the `Ext.dd.StatusProxy` class.

If you're using an element with a little bit of text in it, you'll see that Ext uses that as the contents of the status proxy, but that's as far as it goes in trying to replicate your element when creating a visualization of the drag action. The dimensions of your element will be discarded, and the proxy will try and fit the content in as best as it can. But if you've got a lot of data inside your element you may find that the status proxy is somewhat out of shape.

What's the advantage of having a status proxy, rather than just using the element itself? Well, one thing that you'll also see from our demonstration code is that Ext provides a small **no-entry** icon as you move the proxy around, which changes to a green tick when you move the proxy over a valid drop point, as we'll see shortly. But the great thing is that using a proxy will give you this indicator for free.

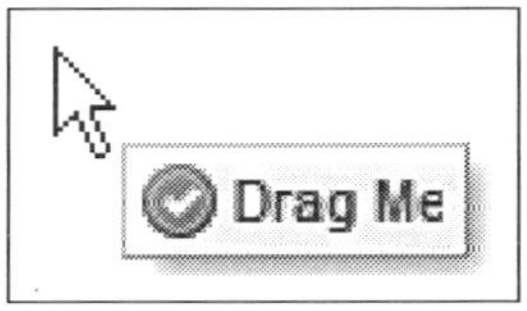


Another advantage of using the status proxy instead of the full element is that it's much more workable, both in terms of processing power and in terms of the actual stuff you're going to be dragging across the screen; moving a 10 column, 200 row table isn't going to be smooth and isn't going to look good either. A status proxy makes for a neat solution to these kinds of problems, and has some bonus features too—as we'll see later.

## Snap!

Another built-in feature of the `Ext.dd.DragSource` is the action that occurs when you drop the element in a place that isn't a valid drop target—that is, when the proxy's red **no entry** sign is showing. It immediately "snaps" back to where it came from, highlighting the original element in light-blue to notify the user that it has returned to its original position.

# Drop me off

Now that we've managed to drag something around, we can move to the second part of the plan—dropping. The idea is that we have a `drop target`—an element that triggers the green tick in the proxy to signify that you can drop the proxy into it.

In order to do this, we make use of the `Ext.dd.DropTarget` class, in pretty much the same way as we used `DragTarget`:

```
new Ext.dd.DropTarget("dropHere");
```

The `DropTarget` constructor accepts a mixed element object—in this case, the ID of an element on our page—and defines that element as a valid target for any drop operations. Running these two examples together will illustrate the changing status of the drag proxy icon—from red to green, when it's hovering over a drop target.

# But wait: nothing's happening!

The tricky thing about this kind of basic drag-and-drop is that nothing really happens when you perform the drop action. In fact, the dragged element just snaps back to its source just as it would if you'd dropped it when the proxy icon was red.

The trick lies in providing a function that overrides the `DropTarget.notifyDrop` method. By default, this method has no implementation and simply returns `false`, causing the dragged element to snap back to its source. By writing a little bit of custom code, we can make the drop action complete in whichever way we see fit.

> Why is this step necessary? Surely Ext JS should know that we want to drag that over to there. There are so many variations of drag-and-drop that it's impossible for Ext to understand what you're trying to do. Instead, it makes it trivial to add your own actions to drag-and-drop operations.

We're going to take a look at some sample code that hooks into this facet of the drag-and-drop support by creating a simple example that causes the dragged element to be inserted within the drop target. This is probably the behavior that you expected to see with the default setup. Although it won't be that useful within itself, it should help fill in some of the gaps.

Assuming that we have the same code as in our previous few examples, with a `DragSource` and a `DropTarget`, we now need to add an implementation of `notifyDrop` to the `DropTarget`:

```
new Ext.dd.DragSource('drag');
new Ext.dd.DropTarget('drop', {
   notifyDrop: function() { return true; }
});
```

This simple addition, which overrides the default implementation of `notifyDrop`, returns `true` and signifies that we do not wish the drag target to snap back to its original position. This is enough to partially fulfill our expectations of what our drag-and-drop code should have done in the first place. The drag source can be released over the drop target without snapping back to its original position. However, we do need to do a little more work to actually make the element move into the target, and we'll look at how to do this, shortly.

# Interacting the fool

While the previous examples are interesting in the abstract sense—they give us an idea of how the Ext JS drag-and-drop system works—they aren't going to be setting your newest development alight. For that, we need to consider how multiple drag targets and drop targets can interact, and how we can set up more complicated systems for dragging around items of data.

# Zones of control

We've seen how to hook up a single draggable item, but often, you'll want to have a number of elements ready to be moved around the screen. The solution here is to use `Ext.dd.DragZone` and `Ext.dd.DropZone` to enable the movement of multiple nodes. We're going to replicate a simple to-do list application, which will allow the user to move items from one list to another. However, this functionality will be seriously limited, allowing us to focus only on the relevant topics. First, we need to set up some basic HTML:

```
<h1>Today</h1>
<ul id="today">
   <li>Shopping</li>
   <li>Haircut</li>
</ul>
<h1>Tomorrow</h1>
<ul id="tmrw">
   <li>Wash car</li>
</ul>
```

We've got two lists, one with the `id` of `today` and one with the `id` of `tmrw`. Our user will be able to move items between the two lists to simulate reorganization of their next few day's tasks. Our first snippet of JavaScript will use the `Ext.dd.DragZone` to set these lists as containers of draggable items. Remember that your JS code needs to go inside an `Ext.onReady` call.

```
new Ext.dd.DragZone('today');
new Ext.dd.DragZone('tmrw');
```

This looks pretty straightforward, but there is one sticking point. Testing the code at this point will highlight the fact that it doesn't actually enable any functionality—nothing happens. Along with setting up the DragZone, we need to explicitly say which child nodes within those DragZone instances are going to be draggable.

> Why the extra step? In complex applications, we may have many nested child nodes. So automatically setting all of them up as draggable could cause performance problems and unexpected behavior. Instead, we could do so manually, avoiding these potential issues.

In order to make our list items draggable, we need to register them with the Ext.dd.Registry:

```
var drags = document.getElementsByTagName('li');
for(var i =0; i< drags.length; i++){
   Ext.dd.Registry.register(drags[i]);
}
```

This is a pretty naïve implementation, simply registering all of the <li> elements on the page, but it should give you an idea of what is required. If you test the code now, you'll see that all of the items can be dragged around as you'd expect. So we need to move on to providing a place to drop them:

```
var cfg = { onNodeDrop: drop }
new Ext.dd.DropZone('tmrw', cfg);
new Ext.dd.DropZone('today', cfg);
```

We create a cfg object, which holds configuration data common to both of our Ext.dd.DropZone instances. The onNodeDrop method of DropZone is called by DropZone.notifyDrop automatically when it realizes that you've dropped a registered node. In this case, we're pointing to a function called drop that will override the existing, empty implementation of onNodeDrop. The new implementation looks like this:

```
// dropNodeData-drop node data object
// source-drag zone which contained the dragged element
// event-the drag drop event
// dragNodeData-drag source data object
// this-destination drop zone
function drop(dropNodeData, source, event, dragNodeData) {
var dragged = source.dragData.ddel;
   var sourceContainer = source.el.dom;
   var destinationContainer = this.getEl();
   sourceContainer.removeChild(dragged);
```

```
        destinationContainer.appendChild(dragged);
        return true;
    }
```

We use the arguments passed to this function to get hold of three elements:

- The item that is being dragged
- The list that it came from
- The list it's being dragged to

With this information, we can remove the item from the source list and then append it to the destination list. We then return a value `true` to prevent the item's proxy from snapping back to its point of origin.

## Changing our lists

With this sample code, we've demonstrated the use of Ext JS drag-and-drop functionality in a practical manner. It's a very simple application, of course, but it's good. We can see how the powerful aspects of the `Ext.dd` package can be applied in a straightforward manner.

Later, we'll see how many aspects of the Ext JS framework support drag-and-drop with very little configuration, and how the knowledge of the working of underlying classes is essential if such support is to be shaped to your requirements.

# Registering an interest

We've already discussed how the child nodes of a `DragZone` must be registered in the `Ext.dd.Registry` before they can be dragged around. This extra step can be a little painful, and we'll see ways around this later, but for now, let's concentrate on the advantages you get when a node is added to the `Ext.dd.Registry`.

In our previous examples, we used the `Ext.dd.Registry.register` method with a single parameter: the element to be registered. However, `register` also takes a second, optional parameter that allows you to add an extra metadata object to the item being dragged around. This metadata can be leveraged in any way you see fit for your application, but a possible use would be to pass "compatibility" information to the drop event. Imagine you are producing an application that lets you assemble a "virtual outfit" by dragging and dropping items of clothing. We could use metadata to make sure that only items of clothing from the "summer" range can be combined, by including range information as part of the drag data. There are many different applications for the metadata facility, but because it's just an arbitrary object, it really is up to you to decide how it can be used.

Although there is overhead associated with the use of `Ext.dd.Registry`, we've shown that it also has important benefits, which, depending on the needs of your application, could outweigh the hassle of writing extra registration code.

# Extreme drag-and-drop

One of the great things about drag-and-drop in Ext JS is that you can use it with many of the supplied Ext Components without having to delve into the guts of how they work. We're going to examine the use of drag-and-drop to create a master-detail layout with the `Ext.DataView` and the `Ext.FormPanel`. This way, we can demonstrate the integration of drag-and-drop with commonly-used components. Much of what we're going to cover will be familiar to you from our previous example, but the application of that knowledge will be slightly different.

We're going to be working with some very simple HTML:

```
<div id="people"></div>
<div id="detail"></div>
```

The `people` `<div>` will contain our `DataView`, listing a group of people pulled from a store. The `detail` `<div>` will contain the form that we can drag items onto.

# DataView dragging

The first step is to create our `Ext.DataView`, and enable the dragging of its nodes. The code to initialize the view looks like this:

```
var personView = new Ext.DataView({
   tpl: '<tpl for=".">' +
         '<div class="person">' +
            '<h1>{name}</h1>' +
            '<div><img src="img/{image}" alt="{name}" /></div>' +
```

```
            '</div>' +
        '</tpl>',
    itemSelector: 'div.person',
    store: personStore
});
personView.render('people');
```

You'll notice that the implementation of the `personStore` isn't shown, but it needs to have an ID, name, image, city, and country items within its records in order to support what we're going to do. Note that within our template, we're showing a header containing the `name` of the person and an `image` representing them.

Based on our experience with list items, we can set up a `DragZone` for the `DataView` container, and register the `<div>` elements with a class `person`, using the `Ext.dd.Registry`. If you try this approach, you'll see why it's not the right one for this particular application—it simply doesn't work! The `person` nodes can't be dragged around as you'd expect.

The reason for this lies with the `Ext.dd.Registry`. As the children of a `DragZone` need to be registered with the `Ext.dd.Registry` before they can be dragged around, we would need to ensure that every possible child—in our case the `<h1>` and `<img>` tags—is registered. This is clearly not a very practical solution, and so we must take a different approach.

# Dealing with drag data

We need to deal with this issue on a slightly higher level. Rather than dealing with each individual child node, we will look at overriding the default behavior of `Ext.dd.DragZone` in order to achieve our goal.

The `getDragData` method of the `DragZone` class is called whenever a `mousedown` occurs within the `DragZone` container. This means that we can use it to listen for the start of a drag event no matter which child node is clicked. In our circumstances, we'll examine the target of the `mousedown` event and navigate up through the DOM until we find the `person` node that represents the item we really want to use in our drag operation. So the code for setting up our `DragZone` would look like this:

```
new Ext.dd.DragZone(personView.getEl(), {
    getDragData : function(e) {
        var container = e.getTarget('div.person', 5, true);
        return {
            ddel : container
        }
    }
});
```

As mentioned earlier, we get the `person` container node from the `mousedown` event, and we use it to populate the `ddel` property of the object that is returned from `getDragData`. Earlier in the chapter, when dealing with dropping a node onto a `DropZone`, we looked at the `dragData.ddel` property to find the node that was being dropped. This is the same data, but from the other point of view—this is how it gets populated.

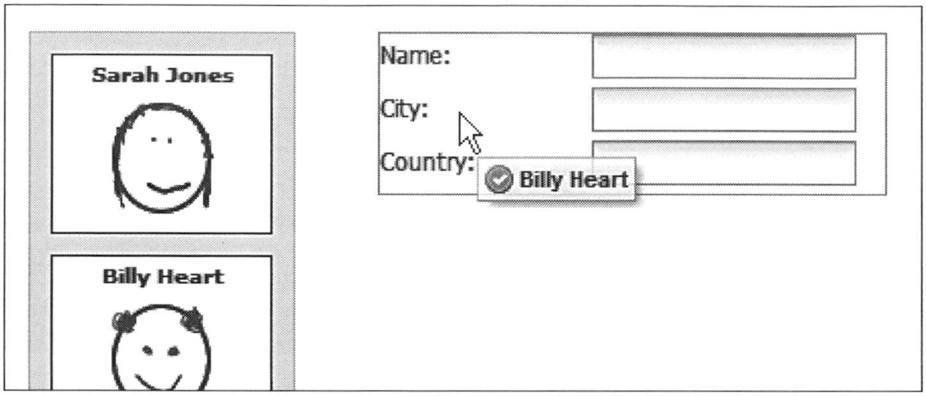


Now we've got our `DataView` working as we expected, but there are a couple of interesting additions that we can make at this point. Let's examine those now.

# Proxies and metadata

When we specified the `ddel` property in `getDragData`, we were essentially populating the proxy that was going to follow the mouse pointer as we dragged our node around. This is a useful consideration. Consider the following code:

```
return {
   ddel : container.down('h1').dom
}
```

Now, instead of our proxy appearing as the full node, it'll only appear as the `<h1>` tag within our node. When we've talked about proxies before, we've mentioned that dragging a cut-down version of the full item can be a very useful approach, and this is how it can be achieved when using `DragZones`.

We also have the option of passing extra data into the drag by using other properties of `dragData`. In fact, any information that we add to the object will be available when the item is dropped. Here's what we're going to do in our example code:

```
return {
   ddel : container.down('h1').dom,
   record : personView.getRecord(container.dom)
}
```

We can actually pass the record associated with the item that was clicked as a data item in our drag operation. This is going to come in very handy when we come to populate our `FormPanel`.

## Dropping in the details

This is the other side of the coin—handling the drop action that is triggered when we release a dragged node from our `DataView`. The concepts behind this will be familiar from our previous examples. We need to create a `DropTarget` from the `FormPanel` and then override its `notifyDrop` method to dictate what will happen when the drop action occurs.

Let's take a look at the code for our `FormPanel`:

```
var detailForm = new Ext.form.FormPanel({
   width: 250,
   height: 80,
   defaultType: 'textfield',
   items: [
      { fieldLabel: 'Name', name:'name' },
      { fieldLabel: 'City', name:'city' },
      { fieldLabel: 'Country', name:'country' }
   ]
});
```

This is all pretty standard stuff, but note that the names of the form fields match up with the names of the fields in our data record that was used to populate the drag node. We can now set up the `DropTarget`:

```
new Ext.dd.DropTarget(detailForm.body.dom, {
   notifyDrop  : function(source, e, data){
      var record = source.dragData.record;
      detailForm.getForm().loadRecord(record);
      return true;
   }
});
```

Note that we can grab the full record straight from the `dragData` on the drag source, and load it into the form. That's the strength of being able to put any data we like into `dragData`, and here it shows how we can populate the form with a minimum amount of code.

# Drag-drop groups

We started off our tour of `Ext.dd` by looking at how individual nodes could be moved around the screen and placed in designated containers. From there, we described the methods used to enable dragging for many nodes at once, and how these could be dropped within containers with child nodes.

When you're dealing with lots of draggable elements, there's a third facility that can be used to make sure that your nodes behave in the way you'd expect: drag-drop groups. `DragSource`, `DragZone`, `DropTarget`, and `DropZone` accept the configuration option `ddGroup` that in turn accepts a string identifier indicating which group you'd like to assign your instance to.

But what does this configuration option actually do, in practical terms, and what new features does it provide for your applications? Well, strictly speaking, it means that a drag-drop class instance will only be able to interact with other drag-drop instances in the same group, but that's a rather dry way of explaining it. Let's look at a real-world use case.

# Nursing our drag-drop to health

Imagine that you have a screen in your application with four separate containers, each of which is specified as both `DragZone` and `DropZone`. Without drag-drop groups, the default behavior here would be that the user could drag from any one of these defined areas to any of the other three.

In many cases, you're likely to want to limit these kinds of interactions. Let's say that containers one and two represent today and tomorrow's appointments for a doctor, and containers three and four are appointments for a nurse. Appointments for the doctor can't be transferred to the nurse, and ones for the nurse can't be given to the doctor. So the application needs to implement this restriction.

We could do this very easily by specifying a `ddGroup` of "doctor" for containers one and two, and `ddGroup` of "nurse" for containers three and four. This would mean that an attempt to drag a nurse appointment into a doctor container would fail, as the nurse drag-drop objects are not allowed to interact with items outside their own drag-and-drop groups.

This kind of advanced functionality becomes essential when you're writing applications that make extensive use of drag-and-drop. We don't need to write code to check whether the drop target is correct, as drag-drop groups take care of this for us.

# It's all in the details

We've had a good overview of the main classes within the `Ext.dd` package now. So it's time to start looking at some of the interesting configuration options, properties, methods, and events that allow us to tweak the behavior of the drag-and-drop classes.

# Configuration

The "big four" of `Ext.dd`—`DragSource`, `DragZone`, `DropTarget`, and `DropZone`—are notable within the Ext JS framework for being important classes that don't really offer much in the way of configuration options. That's because, despite being important, they're all relatively simple to set up: designate a linked node and away you go. That said, we've already covered one option that all of these classes support—`ddGroup`—and there are a couple more common options available.

The `dropAllowed` and `dropNotAllowed` options are both strings that dictate the CSS classes to be passed to the drag source when the respective conditions are `true`. For example, if the item is hovering over an invalid drop target, then the class specified by `dropNotAllowed` will be used.

`DropTarget` and `DropZone` have the `overClass` option in common. This allows you to change the CSS class applied to the drop target element when a drag source moves over it. This is blank by default, and so is a useful method of augmenting the graphical cue provided by the status proxy.

# It's all under control

The drag-and-drop support within Ext JS is structured a little differently than the rest of the framework. Typically, to add in your own behavior, you will handle events that a class fires off, as we've seen when discussing the `TreePanel` and other components. With `Ext.dd`, there are very few events to handle. Instead, a number of abstract methods are provided for the developer to override.

> Ext JS describes these methods as "abstract methods", a concept rarely seen in Javascript as it is not strictly supported. Here, the term simply refers to an empty implementation that needs to be replaced by the developer in order to achieve the desired functionality.

We've already seen how the `notifyDrop` and `onNodeDrop` methods for `DropZone` need to be overridden to complete the drop process, but there are plenty of other abstract methods that we can hook in to. In fact, even for the drop action, there are a number of similar-sounding methods available for use in certain situations:

- `notifyDrop`
- `onContainerDrop`
- `onNodeDrop`

On the face of it, all of these could apply to the same scenario: handling the action performed when an item is dropped on a target. The trick is that the first three are actually related. On `DropZone`, `notifyDrop` isn't actually abstract; instead, it simply establishes whether `onNodeDrop` or `onContainerDrop` will be called. It's these two methods that need to be overridden if you want to perform a drop action.

# Managing our movement

The `Ext.dd` package includes a `DragDropMgr` class, which is generally intended for use as an internal helper for the framework itself. However, there are a few interesting points to note about the class. Let's briefly review the way that this manager can fit into your own applications.

# Global properties

As `DragDropMgr` is used to track all of the drag-and-drop manipulations that occur, we can use it to globally change the way those manipulations are handled. For example, the `clickPixelThresh` property can be changed to set the minimum number of pixels that the mouse needs to move before a drag is initiated. This can be useful in situations where your drag targets also accept a click event—you may wish to increase this value to prevent accidental drags.

Similarly, the `clickTimeThresh`, normally set to 1000 milliseconds or 1 second, dictates the delay time between clicking an element and starting the drag. This could be decreased to make the start of the process seem more responsive, or increased if it's interfering with other actions.

We can also fine-tune the way in which the drop action is handled. By default, the drag-and-drop mode is set to `POINT`, where the position of the mouse pointer is used to determine whether the object being dragged is within the drop target. We can change this behavior to `INTERSECT` mode:

```
Ext.dd.DragDropMgr.mode = Ext.dd.DragDropMgr.INTERSECT;
```

This means that the edges of the drag source and drop target are used to establish interaction. If the two items overlap them, then the drop target is considered valid. This can be handy if the items you wish to drag are going to be large as it could be easier for the user to simply make the edges touch rather than move the mouse pointer directly over the target.

These properties are only likely to be used in edge cases, but would come in handy as part of our toolkit.

# Scroll management

One very slick part of the drag-and-drop puzzle that can be handled automatically is scrolling a container while trying to drag an item into an off-screen region. The `Ext.dd.ScrollManager` means that you can either drag items off bounds from the document body, or cause an element with scrollbars to shift as you drag the elements within it. Setting this facility up is pretty simple:

```
Ext.dd.ScrollManager.register('myContainer');
```

With this code, we've set up the `myContainer` element to be scroll-managed. Note that the scrolls occur in short bursts as you reach the edges of the container. We can tweak the behavior of the scroll as well, by setting the `ddScrollConfig` of the element to be registered.

```
var el = Ext.get('myContainer');
   el.ddScrollConfig = {};
Ext.dd.ScrollManager.register(el);
```

The `ddScrollConfig` consists of a configuration object containing a number of options. The bursts of scrolling are animated by default, and it can be disabled by setting `animate` to `false`, or can have its duration changed by setting `animDuration` to a value other than the default of 0.4 seconds:

```
el.ddScrollConfig = {
   animDuration: 0.2 // anim takes 0.2 seconds to complete
};
```

We can increase the frequency of scroll bursts by setting the frequency to a millisecond value, and change the amount of pixels by which to scroll by using the increment option. We can also control the width of the trigger area on both the horizontal and the vertical sides by using the `vthresh` and `hthresh` options, which are both specified as pixel numbers.

Although the `Ext.dd.ScrollManager` performs a simple purpose and does so with very little code, the utility of this class should not be underestimated. Setting up this functionality manually would be taxing, and it is such a crucial part of drag-and-drop that without `ScrollManager`, we'd be hand-coding it in every application we write. So while `Ext.dd.ScrollManager` is a fairly simple utility class, it's the one that makes many common drag-and-drop scenarios a great deal easier to develop.

# Dragging within components

As we've seen previously, there are a couple of components that offer drag-and-drop support completely out of the box. It's important to remember that these features exist. Given our new drag-and-drop knowledge, we could implement them from scratch. Instead, we'll quickly review the main Ext components that have this facility baked in.

## TreePanel

The default `Ext.TreePanel` not only enables drag-and-drop via the provided configuration option, but exposes a number of events, such as `beforenodedrop`, that allow us to hook our own functionality into the component.

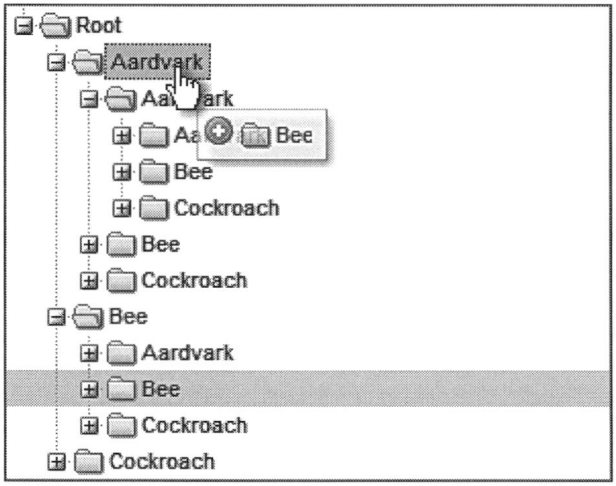


By using AJAX requests, we can persist the results of our drag-and-drop actions to the server for retrieval later. If you're using multiple `TreePanel` instances, you can even drag-and-drop between them, and restrict the direction of movement using the `enableDrag` and `enableDrop` configuration options.

## GridPanel

The `Ext.grid.GridPanel` also provides drag-and-drop support out of the box with the use of the `enableDragDrop` configuration option. Setting this to `true` will allow you to begin dragging rows out of your grid. But you would still need to provide a custom `DropTarget` for the row destination. This could even be another `GridPanel`, but it means that you'll have to leverage the knowledge you gained earlier in this chapter to really put grid drag-and-drop to good use.

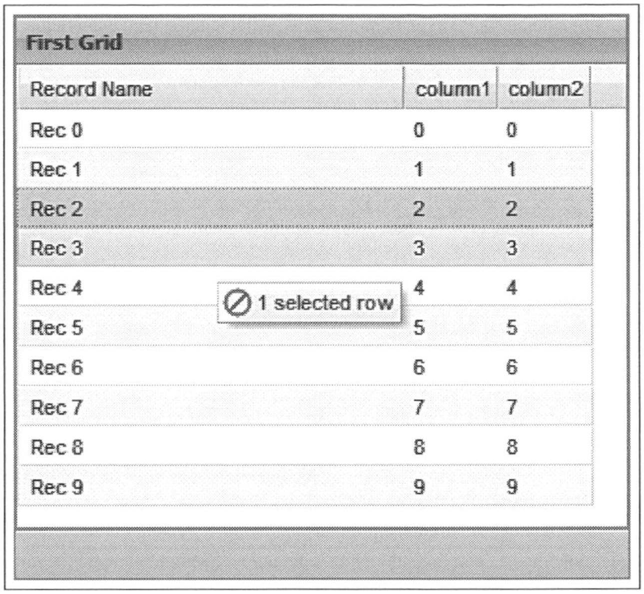


The custom `Ext.grid.DragZone` is also provided to facilitate these actions, giving you a shortcut to both the data being dragged and the grid that holds it. This class means that there's a bit less heavy lifting required when you want to drag rows within your application.

# Using it in the real world

There are many cases where drag-and-drop is actually a barrier for the user—such as when adding an action that takes longer to complete than the more standard approach. Why drag-and-drop something when clicking it could be just as effective? The visual cue of the drag-and-drop status proxy may look great in a screenshot, but in a real-world situation there may be a more logical approach.

That said, the visual element of drag-and-drop is still its most important feature. There is no better way of organizing a list or a tree of information than by pulling it around the screen using the mouse. When completing tasks like these, a graphical representation of what's going on will not only help your users to get the job done more quickly, but when backed by Ext JS, could also turn out to be the least development-intensive approach as well.

`Ext.dd` is a package that doesn't supply any widgets of its own. Instead it supports other segments of the framework and works as a behind-the-scenes facilitator of exciting end user functionality. As such, it can be a little difficult to come to grips with it, especially as it provides a variety of approaches to solve similar issues.

In this chapter, we've covered all of the major pieces of the Ext JS drag-and-drop puzzle. So, when you do come up with a problem that can be tackled using drag-and-drop, you can use `DragZones`, `DropTargets`, and `StatusProxies` to achieve the look and feel that your application requires.

# Summary

It feels as if our knowledge of drag-and-drop on the Web has come pretty far from our understanding in the earlier chapters. We started off by discussing some of the typical demonstrations of drag-and-drop, which were developed to show off the Web 2.0 functionality. Some of those demonstrations suffered from a lack of real utility, but they were undeniably compelling. We showed how to create a few 'fancy but pointless' effects of our own to get a grasp of the underlying concepts of the `Ext.dd` package, and then quickly expanded our knowledge to harness the drag-and-drop classes that allow our applications to take advantage of this feature.

The wide range of in-built support that Ext provides is only part of the story, albeit a very important part. The `TreePanel`, for example, certainly wouldn't be as impressive a component were it not for its ability to rearrange nodes within a hierarchy using simple drag-and-drop. But the other part of our tale is just as interesting—the ways in which we can customize that built-in functionality and then replace, extend, and implement our own solutions, which would enable the next level of desktop-like interactivity.

# 13
# Code for Reuse: Extending Ext JS

In this chapter, we'll discuss how we can create our own custom components by extending the Ext JS library. We'll talk about how we can create our own namespaces, differentiating our custom components from others. We'll also discuss some other core object-oriented concepts (just enough to understand what we need here) and the concept of Event-driven application architecture.

This chapter covers:

- Object-oriented design as applied to Ext JS library
- Inheritance and method overriding
- Defining custom namespaces
- Creating custom components
- Event-driven application architecture
- Xtypes
- Lazy instantiation on application performance
- Object-oriented JavaScript

Over the last several years, we've seen a drastic shift with regards to client-side scripting in browser-based web applications. JavaScript has become the de facto standard in client-side scripting, with support for it built into every major browser available.

The issue in the past, with cross-browser development, has always been in each browser's implementation of the Document Object Model. Microsoft's Internet Explorer, having taken the majority share of the browser marketplace, helped to gather support for a modern Document Object Model, to which all other browsers had to adapt. However, after the release of Internet Explorer 6, Microsoft halted new development of their browser for several years, other than to provide security fixes. Added to this was Microsoft's play to try and create new standards. Rather than implementing JavaScript, Internet Explorer actually implemented JScript, which ran JavaScript files, but had a slightly different implementation that never garnered momentum (other than in Internet Explorer), possibly because it did not adhere to the ECMAScript standard. This created several issues. The **World Wide Web Consortium (W3C)** had created a standard for the Document Object Model, which companies like Mozilla and Opera adhered to and furthered. Yet Internet Explorer (the dominant browser) was stagnant.

These events led to very hard times for client-side developers, as a great deal of time and effort went into creating client-side code that was cross-browser compliant. Netscape and Internet Explorer had been waging the browser war over several versions, slowly growing more divergent in their standards acceptance, with cross-browser development consistently becoming more of a challenge. The landscape had changed, in that a large degree of client-side development had become relegated to basic form validation and image rollovers, because few developers were interested in investing the time and effort necessary to write large, cross-browser compliant, client-side applications.

Enter Web 2.0. Circa 2005, the buzzword of the day was AJAX, or Asynchronous JavaScript and XML. AJAX wasn't a new technology, but its use had been fairly minimal and obscure. Developers with a deep knowledge of JavaScript, looking to create greater and more dynamic websites, had begun to implement the technology as a way of reinvigorating the client-side movement, creating richer and more interactive user experiences.

This renewed interest in client-side scripted applications, but with the same issues existing around cross-browser compatibility. Several cross-browser JavaScript libraries (Dojo, Prototype, Yahoo UI, and so on) had begun life, in response to minimizing the previous woes involved in cross-browser, client-side development. The developers of these libraries, with their knowledge of JavaScript, had kept pace with the changes in this language as well. JavaScript had travelled well beyond the confines of a solely procedural scripting language, with full support for object-oriented development. In developing their libraries, these developers took full advantage of an object-oriented style of development that JavaScript's prototype-based model allowed, creating small objects of functionality that could build upon one another to provide extensive resources of reusable code.

> In the coming pages, I will often use the words object and class interchangeably, because it seems a little easier to understand. Technically, JavaScript is a classless language, and our objects are built with JavaScript's prototype-based programming model.

# Object-oriented programming with Ext JS

Ext JS is a perfect example of this shift. The Ext JS library is an extensive collection of packages of classes of reusable code: small pieces of functionality that can be taken on their own, or combined to create some truly fantastic client-side magic. An additional part of its beauty is the ability to extend the library further, creating our own custom components as extensions of those already present. This gives us the ability to create our own reusable pieces of code. We can write our own objects, as extensions of the library. This means that we don't have to write all of our functionality on our own, as much of this work has already been done for us. We expand upon the foundation, providing our own custom functionality.

## Inheritance

To gain a full understanding of what we need to do, we have to understand one of the key concepts of object-oriented programming—*inheritance*.

As we write our own components, these components will usually *inherit* from some other component of Ext JS, extending that component's functionality by providing our own properties and overriding the component's existing behavior. We create a new class, as an extension of an existing Ext JS class and inheriting that parent class's properties and methods, which we can then override to create new functionality without completely reinventing the wheel.

# Break it down and make it simple

Confused yet? It's a lot to take in. Let's break this down into a basic example that may clarify a few things. Say we are writing a Customer Resource Management application for a company. This company has `salespeople`, who have `clients` (and client `contacts`), and the company also has `vendors` that they do business with, who also have `contacts`. Here we've identified three similar objects within our application. If we take these objects down to the base level, we notice that each of these objects is a `Person` (the `Clients` and `Vendors` would more clearly be `Companies`):

- Salesperson
- Client Contact
- Vendor Contact

Each one of these `Person` objects will share some basic attributes and methods, because each person has a `name`, an `email address`, a `phone number`, and an `address`. We'll create a quick class diagram to visually represent the `Person` object:

> Class diagrams, and UML diagramming in general, are a great way to visually represent different programming constructs. A full explanation is outside the purview of this text, but I highly recommend that you become familiar with them. Our diagrams here show the class name, the attributes, and methods of the class.

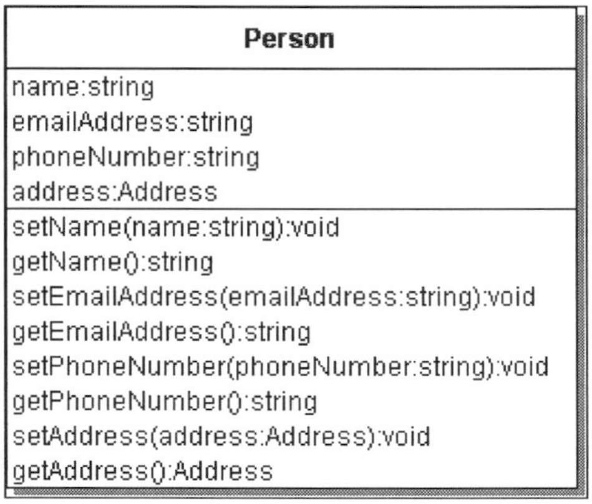

Person
name:string
emailAddress:string
phoneNumber:string
address:Address
setName(name:string):void
getName():string
setEmailAddress(emailAddress:string):void
getEmailAddress():string
setPhoneNumber(phoneNumber:string):void
getPhoneNumber():string
setAddress(address:Address):void
getAddress():Address


Note that the `Person` object has four attributes: `name`, `emailAddress`, `phoneNumber`, and `address`. Also note that the `address` attribute is, in itself, another object. We've included some simple methods for the object as well, to get and set our attributes.

Each one of these objects also has its own object-specific properties such as a `salesPersonID`, a `clientContactID`, or a `vendorContactID`.

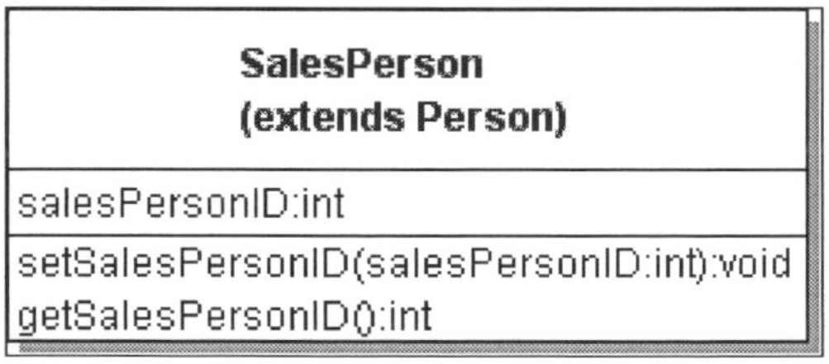

Note that in our diagram of the `SalesPerson` object, you do not see any of the `Person`-specific properties and methods. Because `SalesPerson` extends (*inherits*) the `Person` object, all of the properties and methods of the `Person` object become a part of the `SalesPerson` object as well. We can now create a `SalesPerson`.

```
var sp = new SalesPerson();
```

This creates a new instance of the `SalesPerson` object, with all of the attributes and methods of the `SalesPerson` object, including those of the parent `Person` object, by extension.

# Sounds cool, but what does it mean?

By default, the `SalesPerson` object, being an extension of `Person`, allows you to set a name to the `SalesPerson` in the following manner:

```
SalesPerson.setName('Zig Ziggler')
```

You don't have to reference the methods, or the attributes, by calling on the object's (`SalesPerson`) parent object (`Person`) directly because, through *inheritance*, `SalesPerson` is a `Person`.

## Now, what was this overriding stuff?

Through inheritance, all of the methods and attributes of a parent object become the child's as well. However, there will be times when you may want the child object's method to be different from that of its parent. For example, let's say our `Person` object had its own `validate()` method, which has validated all of the attributes and returned its own error array, but your `SalesPerson` object has some additional attributes to validate as well. By defining a `validate()` method within the `SalesPerson` object, you are overriding the `validate()` method of its **Person** parent object.

```
validate: function() {
  // Some validation code here
}
```

But, in this case, you would want total attribute validation; both the internal object-specific properties, as well as those of the parent object. So here, you would also need to call the `validate()` method of the parent object:

```
validate: function() {
  var errorArr =
ourObjects.salesperson.superclass.validate.call(this);
  // The salesperson specific validate stuff, appending the errorArr
  return errorArr;
}
```

These are the basic pieces of OO that we need to understand so that we can begin to create our own custom classes with Ext JS. Well, almost...

# Understanding packages, classes, and namespaces

There are a few final pieces of the object-oriented puzzle we need, in order to keep a solid grasp of our goals. We've talked about how Ext JS is a large collection of objects extending other objects, but it's also important to understand a few other pieces of basic OO terminology, and how they help in keeping things organized.

## Packages

A **package** is a collection of `classes` that share something in common. For instance, the `Ext.data` package is a collection of classes for dealing with data, such as the different types of data Stores, Readers, and Records. The `Ext.grid` package is a collection of classes for the various grid objects, including all of the different grid types and selection models. Likewise, the `Ext.form` package contains classes for building forms, to include all of the classes of the different field types.

## Classes

A **class** is what we call a specific JavaScript object, defining that object's attributes and methods. Going back to our previous examples, `Person` and `SalesPerson` would both be written as class objects, and both would probably be part of the same package.

## Namespaces

Classes are a part of packages, and packages generally have their own namespace. **Namespaces** are containers of logically grouped packages and class objects. As an example, the Ext JS library falls into the `Ext` namespace. Forms within Ext JS fall into the `Ext.forms` namespace, where `forms` is a package of the various classes used to make up forms. It's a hierarchal relationship, using dot notation to separate the namespace from the package from the class. Variables from one namespace must be passed into another namespace, so applying a namespace helps to encapsulate information within itself. `Ext.grid`, `Ext.form`, and `Ext.data` are all custom namespaces.

## What's next?

Now that we have our terminology down, and a basic understanding of these core object-oriented concepts, we can finally get down to applying them within the context of creating Ext JS custom components.

# Ok, what do we extend?

Typically, we'll be writing an application and will see ourselves writing the same basic piece over and over again. Or, we may be lucky to identify it early enough that we can just choose the best piece and move forward right away. It usually comes down to deciding which Ext JS component is the best one to extend.

Let's revisit our previous scenario, a Customer Resource Management system. We know that we have several `Person` objects within our application. From a display perspective, we will probably need something to display a person's contact details.

There are several different components for the display of information, and we must choose the right one. A grid object would work, but a tabular display across so many different values might clutter our application, and in this scenario, we probably only need to see the details of one person at a time. A `PropertyGrid` is a little different from a standard grid, but we're just going to output a name and an address. We really don't need the user to see the field names so much as the data itself. We can pretty much eliminate the DataView as well, for the same reasons as rejecting the grid. We really need only one record at a time.

This brings us to a form or a panel. Forms imply editing of information, so for a display-only application you really come back to a panel. Panel objects are extremely versatile objects, being the core of many other objects within Ext JS. The body of a window object is a panel. The different pieces of an Accordion are panel objects. The bodies of the tabs in a TabPanel are panel objects. Creating a custom component that extends the panel object opens the doors to a variety of different display options within an Ext JS application.

# Creating a custom namespace

We want to create our custom components within their own custom namespace for encapsulation, quick reference, and to help us organize our code. It may be that our packages or class may be named the same as other packages and classes already within Ext JS. A custom namespace prevents conflicts from occurring between classes of the same name, as long as each is defined within its own separate namespace. A common naming convention for user-defined objects is to use the `Ext.ux` namespace.

```
Ext.namespace('Ext.ux');
```

Because we're going to create a collection of display panels for our CRM application, we'll really set our namespace apart from the rest.

```
Ext.namespace('CRM.panels');
```

We need to place this line at the top of each class definition template.

# Our first custom class

First, let's take a look at a fairly simple script that takes a single record of information and lays it out in a panel on the screen.

```
// ch13ex1.js
  var userData = [

  {ID:1,FIRSTNAME:'John',LASTNAME:'Lennon',EMAIL:'john@beatles.com',
PASSWORD:'apple1',ADDRESSTYPE:'Home (Mailing)',STREET1:'117 Abbey Road
',STREET2:'',STREET3:'',CITY:'New York',STATE:'NY',ZIP:'12345',PHONETY
PE:'Cell',PHONE:'123-456-7890'},
  {ID:2,FIRSTNAME:'Paul',LASTNAME:'McCartney',
EMAIL:'paul@beatles.com',PASSWORD:'linda',ADDRESSTYPE:'Work
(Mailing)',STREET1:'108 Penny Lane',STREET2:'',STREET3:'',
CITY:'Los Angeles',STATE:'CA',ZIP:'67890',PHONETYPE:'Home',
PHONE:'456-789-0123'},
  {ID:3,FIRSTNAME:'George',LASTNAME:'Harrison',
EMAIL:'george@beatles.com',PASSWORD:'timebandit',
ADDRESSTYPE:'Home (Shipping)',STREET1:'302 Space
Way',STREET2:'',STREET3:'',CITY:'Billings',STATE:'MT',
ZIP:'98765',PHONETYPE:'Office',PHONE:'890-123-4567'},
  {ID:4,FIRSTNAME:'Ringo',LASTNAME:'Starr',
EMAIL:'bignose@beatles.com',PASSWORD:'barbie',
ADDRESSTYPE:'Home (Mailing)',STREET1:'789 Zildizhan Pl',
STREET2:'',STREET3:'',CITY:'Malibu',
STATE:'CA',ZIP:'43210',PHONETYPE:'Home',PHONE:'567-890-1234'}
  ];

   var userDetail = new Ext.Panel({
     applyTo: 'chap13_ex01',
     width: 350,
     height: 250,
     title: 'Chapter 13 Example 1',
     bodyStyle: 'padding:10px',
     data: userData[0],
     tpl: new Ext.XTemplate([
       '<img src="/resources/images/s.gif" width="21" height="16"
                         /><b>{FIRSTNAME} {LASTNAME}</b><br />',
```

```
        '<img src="/resources/images/icons/silk/database_edit.gif"
width="16" height="16" id="emailEdit_{ID}" class="iconLnk" align="Edit
Email Address" border="0" />{EMAIL}<br />',
        '<img src="/resources/images/icons/silk/database_edit.gif"
width="16" height="16" id="phoneEdit_{ID}" class="iconLnk" align="Edit
Phone" border="0" />{PHONE} ({PHONETYPE})<br />',
        '<b>{ADDRESSTYPE} Address</b><br />',
        '<img src="/resources/images/icons/silk/database_edit.gif"
width="16" height="16" id="addrEdit_{ID}" class="iconLnk" align="Edit
Address" border="0" />{STREET1}<br />',
        '<tpl if="STREET2.length &gt; 0">',
        '<img src="/resources/images/s.gif" width="21" height="16"
/>{STREET2}<br />',
        '</tpl>',
        '<tpl if="STREET3.length &gt; 0">',
          '<img src="/resources/images/s.gif" width="21" height="16"
                                                      />{STREET3}<br />',
        '</tpl>',
        '<img src="/resources/images/s.gif" width="21" height="16"
                                                  />{CITY}, {STATE} {ZIP}'
      ])
    });
```

What we have here is a simple array of data objects, and a panel definition. We're passing a single data item into the panel's configuration, defining an `XTemplate` for the record's display when the panel is rendered.

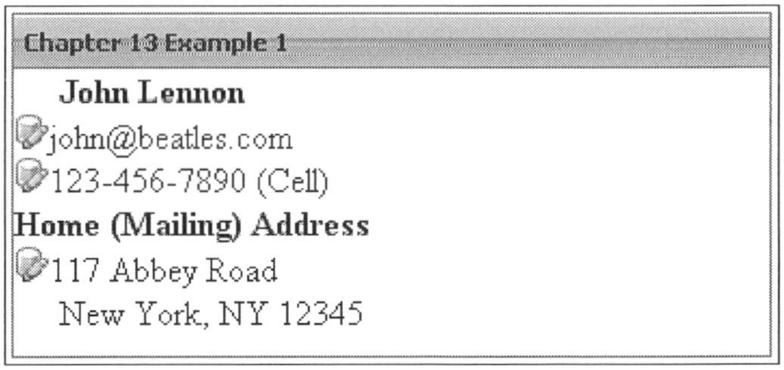


Turning this into a reusable component is very easy, as the majority of our code will just be moved into our custom class definition. First, we'll create a new class template, `ContactDetails.js`, and define its initial class declaration as extending the `Ext.Panel` class. Ext JS actually provides custom methods for extending components.

**Example 2**:

```
ContactDetails.js
```

```
Ext.namespace('CRM.panels');

CRM.panels.ContactDetails = Ext.extend(Ext.Panel,{
  // The panel definition goes here
});
```

Our next step is to begin defining the custom properties and methods of our component. We begin with the default properties that are specific to our component. Some of these properties may be overridden in our object configuration, but these defaults allow us to only pass in what we might need to change for our individual application.

```
width: 350,
height: 250,
bodyStyle: 'padding:10px',
data: {
  ID: 0,
  FIRSTNAME: '',
  LASTNAME: '',
  EMAIL: '',
  ADDRESSTYPE: 'Home (mailing)',
  STREET1: '',
  STREET2: '',
  STREET3: '',
  CITY: '',
  STATE: '',
  ZIP: '',
  PHONETYPE: 'Home',
  PHONE: ''
},
tpl: new Ext.XTemplate([
   '<img src="/resources/images/s.gif" width="21" height="16"
                    /><b>{FIRSTNAME} {LASTNAME}</b><br />',
   '<img src="/resources/images/icons/silk/database_edit.gif"
width="16" height="16" id="emailEdit_{ID}" class="iconLnk" align="Edit
Email Address" border="0" />{EMAIL}<br />',
   '<img src="/resources/images/icons/silk/database_edit.gif"
width="16" height="16" id="phoneEdit_{ID}" class="iconLnk" align="Edit
Phone" border="0" />{PHONE} ({PHONETYPE})<br />',
   '<b>{ADDRESSTYPE} Address</b><br />',
   '<img src="/resources/images/icons/silk/database_edit.gif"
width="16" height="16" id="addrEdit_{ID}" class="iconLnk" align="Edit
Address" border="0" />{STREET1}<br />',
```

```
    '<tpl if="STREET2.length &gt; 0">',
      '<img src="/resources/images/s.gif" width="21" height="16"
                                            />{STREET2}<br />',
    '</tpl>',
    '<tpl if="STREET3.length &gt; 0">',
      '<img src="/resources/images/s.gif" width="21" height="16"
                                             />{STREET3}<br />',
    '</tpl>',
    '<img src="/resources/images/s.gif" width="21" height="16"
                                      />{CITY}, {STATE} {ZIP}'
]),
```

> Pit stop!
>
> Does anything look familiar here? Yes, it should, especially after looking at the 'records' within `userData`. A class is an object, just like each 'record' in the `userData` array is an object. At its most base level, an object is a collection of name/value pairs. The only true difference is that a class will also have functions as the `value` of an attribute `name` of the object, and the object can be referenced by its class (the name of the class). Each of these name/value pairs forms the constructor of the `ContactDetails` class.

# Overriding methods

Continuing to build our first custom class, we get into overriding methods. As we have previously mentioned, we can override a method of our parent class by defining a method of the same name in the child class. A key component of the Panel class is the `initComponent()` method, which (as the name suggests) initializes the Panel component. Most methods will never need to be overridden, but sometimes we'll need to override a specific method to add to, or change, the default behavior of a component.

```
initComponent: function(){
  CRM.panels.ContactDetails.superclass.initComponent.call(this);
    if (typeof this.tpl === 'string') {
    this.tpl = new Ext.XTemplate(this.tpl);
  }
},
```

> Ext JS uses `superclass` as the programmatic reference to the object's parent class object, as `CRM.panels.ContactDetails` is a subclass of its parent (superclass) `Ext.Panel`.

With our component, we needed a way to apply a new `XTemplate` to our component, should one be passed into our `ContactDetails` class. As a developer can pass in the template configuration via the `tpl` argument, instead of an actual `XTemplate` object, it is important to validate that input and adjust accordingly. Our first action is to call the `initComponent()` method of our parent Panel class, and then adjust the value of the `tpl` argument as needed.

# Understanding the order of events

In our last example (Example 2), we used the `initComponent()` method to apply our `XTemplate` to our Panel object, by writing an overriding method for the `initComponent()` method that supersedes the inherited Panel (parent) class.

```
// Overriden parent object method
initComponent: function(){
  CRM.panels.ContactDetails.superclass.initComponent.call(this);
  if (typeof this.tpl === 'string') {
    this.tpl = new Ext.XTemplate(this.tpl);
  }
},
```

Here, we've called the `initComponent()` method of our parent Panel (super) class. After that, we verify that we have a value for our `tpl` attribute and cast it to an `XTemplate` if only a string was passed in for the variable, before the method of our component.

```
update: function(data) {
  this.data = data;
  this.tpl.overwrite(this.body, this.data);
}
```

The `update()` method takes an argument of data (a `record` object from our array), applies that argument to the component's `data` attribute, and then applies the component's `XTemplate` to the 'body' of the component. This is a custom method of the component, not an overridden method of the parent panel class. What's important to our discussion is the need for this method.

# When can we do what?

Our `XTemplate` does not get immediately applied to our component, as it isn't able to overwrite the panel body until the panel body has actually been rendered. This is what we mean by 'order of events', and can initially be very confusing, until you put a little thought into it. For instance, say we had dynamically tried to apply a custom ID argument as part of our constructor:

```
id: 'ContactDetails_' + this.data.ID,
```

This would have broken our component. Why? Because `this.data` is also an item within our constructor, and doesn't actually exist until the component is instantiated into memory. The same thing would have happened, if we had tried to apply our `XTemplate` within the `initComponent()` method:

```
initComponent: function(){
  CRM.panels.ContactDetails.superclass.initComponent.call(this);
  this.tpl.overwrite(this.body, this.data);
},
```

This would have failed when `initComponent()` begins the process of creating the component. The component, at this stage, still isn't part of the browser's Document Object Model, so there isn't any 'body' for the `XTemplate` to be applied to yet. Getting a handle on the 'order of events' is one of the biggest challenges in learning Ext JS, if you don't know about it, and the order of events may be different with different Ext JS classes as well.

# What is an event-driven application?

Now we get down to the real juice. One huge barrier to cross, when transitioning from a procedural programming style into object-oriented development, is understanding the **event-driven** application model. Not all OO programs are event-driven, but the paradigm is definitely shifting in that direction, and Ext JS is no exception. This is a concept that most JavaScript developers have known for years, as the browser itself forces us into an event-driven model, as each action of the browser is an event. Basically, the flow of an application is determined by sensing some change of state or user interaction, called an **event**. When the event occurs, the application *broadcasts* that the event has taken place. Another piece of the application (a *listener*, also known as an *observer*) is listening for the event broadcast. When it sees that the event has been broadcast, it then performs some other action.

Our `ContactDetails` class is no different. As an extension of the Panel class, it automatically contains all of the events and event listeners that are a part of the Panel class. An event, `render`, was previously defined. The process of building the display of the panel fires off a 'broadcast' of the render event.

```
this.fireEvent('render');
```

The `Ext.Panel` object has already defined an event listener for the `render` event. Once the `render` event has been handled, it calls the `onRender()` method.

```
this.addListener('render',this.onRender,this,
          {ct:this.ct,position:this.position});
```

An event has been reached, which is then broadcast. An event listener is listening for that broadcast. Upon hearing the broadcast, it executes additional pre-configured actions that have been defined for that event. Understanding this process plays a key part in how we develop event-driven applications, and our own applications with Ext JS.

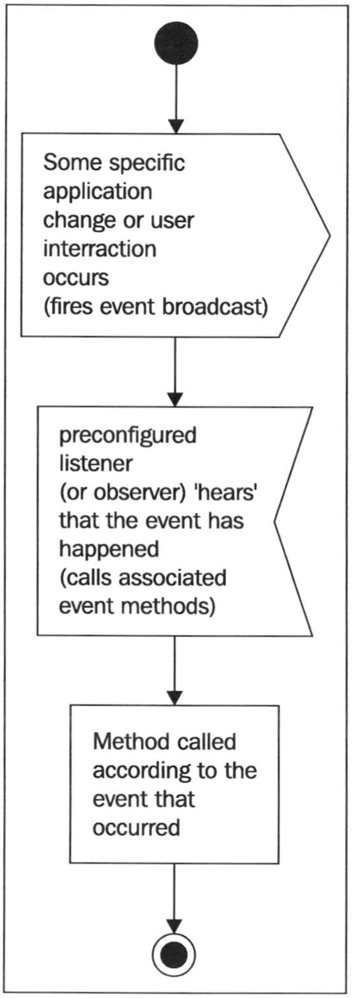

# Creating our own custom events

We may just as easily apply our own custom events within our Ext JS applications. Other developers can add listeners to new events that we've registered with our applications or we can add our own listeners to kick-off other methods within our custom component.

For example, let's create a new `update` event within our custom component. We'll adjust our `initComponent()` method to register our new event:

```
initComponent: function(){
  CRM.panels.ContactDetails.superclass.initComponent.call(this);
  if (typeof this.tpl === 'string') {
    this.tpl = new Ext.XTemplate(this.tpl);
  }
  this.addEvents('update');
},
```

This new code is all it takes to register our new event. We'll also go ahead and register a new, internal **event listener**, which we'll use to call a new method that we'll write in a moment:

```
initComponent: function(){
  CRM.panels.ContactDetails.superclass.initComponent.call(this);
  if (typeof this.tpl === 'string') {
    this.tpl = new Ext.XTemplate(this.tpl);
  }
  this.addEvents('update');
  this.addListener({
    update:{
      fn: this.onUpdate,
      scope: this
    }
  });
},
```

What this states is that whenever the update event is broadcast, our application will turn around and call the `onUpdate()` method of our `ContactDetails` component.

```
onUpdate: function(data){
  console.log('in onUpdate');
}
```

The `onUpdate()` method, in this case, only outputs a short message to the debugging console, which you can see if you are debugging your application in Firefox with the Firebug plugin (*console* is not supported in Internet Explorer). The final step is having the update event broadcast. We already have an `update()` method, so it would make sense for us to broadcast the *update* once it's completed:

```
update: function(data) {
  this.data = data;
  this.tpl.overwrite(this.body, this.data);
  this.fireEvent('update', this.data);
},
```

Here we broadcast our update event by calling the Ext JS's `fireEvent()` method, and passing along our data as the argument to any method listening for the update event. We can have any number of event listeners configured for a particular event, either internal to the component, or externally within a script referencing our custom component.

# Our first custom component: complete

Here's the final component we've been constructing. At this point in time, we don't really need the custom update event. We'll leave it in, as it may be useful later, and we'll just remove the `onUpdate()` method for now. We can have events that are registered within our applications that are never listened for. They are available for convenience, should we want to use them, but they are otherwise ignored, which is fine.

```
// ContactDetails.js
Ext.namespace('CRM.panels');

CRM.panels.ContactDetails = Ext.extend(Ext.Panel,{
  width: 350,
  height: 250,
  bodyStyle: 'padding:10px',
  data: {
    ID: 0,
    FIRSTNAME: '',
    LASTNAME: '',
    EMAIL: '',
    ADDRESSTYPE: 'Home (mailing)',
    STREET1: '',
    STREET2: '',
    STREET3: '',
    CITY: '',
    STATE: '',
```

```
      ZIP: '',
      PHONETYPE: 'Home',
      PHONE: ''
    },
    tpl: new Ext.XTemplate([
       '<img src="/resources/images/s.gif" width="21" height="16"
                         /><b>{FIRSTNAME} {LASTNAME}</b><br />',
       '<img src="/resources/images/icons/silk/database_edit.gif"
width="16" height="16" id="emailEdit_{ID}" class="iconLnk" align="Edit
Email Address" border="0" />{EMAIL}<br />',
       '<img src="/resources/images/icons/silk/database_edit.gif"
width="16" height="16" id="phoneEdit_{ID}" class="iconLnk" align="Edit
Phone" border="0" />{PHONE} ({PHONETYPE})<br />',
       '<b>{ADDRESSTYPE} Address</b><br />',
       '<img src="/resources/images/icons/silk/database_edit.gif"
width="16" height="16" id="addrEdit_{ID}" class="iconLnk" align="Edit
Address" border="0" />{STREET1}<br />',
       '<tpl if="STREET2.length &gt; 0">',
         '<img src="/resources/images/s.gif" width="21" height="16"
                                              />{STREET2}<br />',
       '</tpl>',
       '<tpl if="STREET3.length &gt; 0">',
         '<img src="/resources/images/s.gif" width="21" height="16"
                                             />{STREET3}<br />',
       '</tpl>',
       '<img src="/resources/images/s.gif" width="21" height="16"
                                           />{CITY}, {STATE} {ZIP}'
     ]),
    initComponent: function(){
      CRM.panels.ContactDetails.superclass.initComponent.call(this);
      if (typeof this.tpl === 'string') {
        this.tpl = new Ext.XTemplate(this.tpl);
      }
      this.addEvents('update');
    },

    onRender: function(ct, position) {
      CRM.panels.ContactDetails.superclass.onRender.call
                                   (this, ct, position);
      if (this.data) {
        this.update(this.data);
      }
    },
    update: function(data) {
      this.data = data;
      this.tpl.overwrite(this.body, this.data);
```

```
        this.fireEvent('update', this.data);
      }
    });
```

With our new custom component, we now have a new way of calling it into our applications as well.

```
// ch13ex2.js
  var userData = [
    {ID:1,FIRSTNAME:'John',LASTNAME:'Lennon',
EMAIL:'john@beatles.com',PASSWORD:'apple1',
ADDRESSTYPE:'Home (Mailing)',
STREET1:'117 Abbey Road',STREET2:'',STREET3:'',
CITY:'New York',STATE:'NY',ZIP:'12345',PHONETYPE:'Cell',
PHONE:'123-456-7890'},
  {ID:2,FIRSTNAME:'Paul',LASTNAME:'McCartney',
EMAIL:'paul@beatles.com',PASSWORD:'linda',
ADDRESSTYPE:'Work (Mailing)',
STREET1:'108 Penny Lane',STREET2:'',
STREET3:'',CITY:'Los Angeles',STATE:'CA',ZIP:'67890',
PHONETYPE:'Home',PHONE:'456-789-0123'},
  {ID:3,FIRSTNAME:'George',LASTNAME:'Harrison',
EMAIL:'george@beatles.com',PASSWORD:'timebandit',
ADDRESSTYPE:'Home (Shipping)',STREET1:'302 Space Way',STREET2:'',STREE
T3:'',CITY:'Billings',STATE:'MT',ZIP:'98765',
PHONETYPE:'Office',PHONE:'890-123-4567'},
  {ID:4,FIRSTNAME:'Ringo',LASTNAME:'Starr',
EMAIL:'bignose@beatles.com',PASSWORD:'barbie',
ADDRESSTYPE:'Home (Mailing)',STREET1:'789 Zildizhan Pl',
STREET2:'',STREET3:'',CITY:'Malibu',STATE:'CA',ZIP:'43210',PHONETYPE:
'Home',PHONE:'567-890-1234'}
  ];

   var userDetail = new CRM.panels.ContactDetails({
     applyTo: 'chap13_ex01',
     title: 'Chapter 13 Example 1',
     data: userData[0]
   });

   updateContact = function(event,el,data){
    userDetail.update(data.data);
  }

   Ext.get('actionLink').on('click',updateContact,this,
                                  {data:userData[1]});
```

We've taken an anchor element, with an `id` of `actionLink`, from our calling page, and given it an `onclick` event that updates the data of our `ContactDetails` object, `userDetail`. Clicking on the **Update Data** link on the page changes the contact details from `John` over to `Paul`.

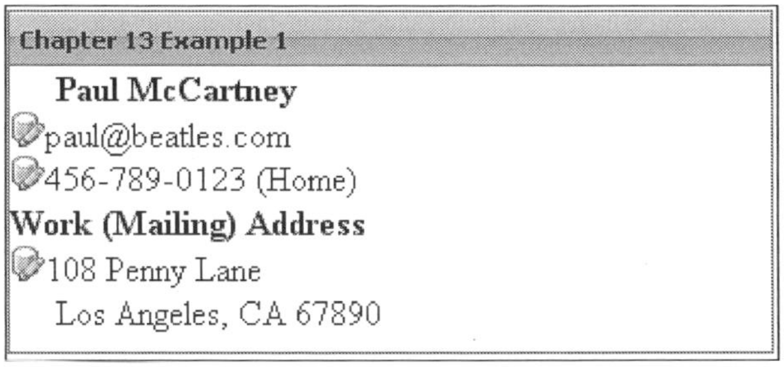


# What's next? Breaking it down

Ok, we've now created our first custom component. That was fairly painless. But, looking back at what we've done, it looks as if we've pushed ourselves into a small corner again. As it stands, every aspect of our application that requires contact information would have to display the name, e-mail address, phone number, and address of our contact, every time. What happens if we require only the address? Or just the name, or e-mail, or the phone number?

Well, this is where we refactor, creating even more custom components. For our purposes, we'll quickly break this down into two components: one for `UserDetail`, and another for `AddressDetail`.

**Example 3**: `UserDetail.js`

```
// UserDetail.js
Ext.namespace('CRM.panels');

CRM.panels.UserDetail = Ext.extend(Ext.Panel,{
  width: 350,
  height: 125,
  bodyStyle: 'padding:10px',
  data: {
    ID: 0,
    FIRSTNAME: '',
    LASTNAME: '',
    EMAIL: '',
    ADDRESSTYPE: 'Home (mailing)',
    STREET1: '',
    STREET2: '',
```

```
      STREET3: '',
      CITY: '',
      STATE: '',
      ZIP: '',
      PHONETYPE: 'Home',
      PHONE: ''
    },
    split: false,
    tpl: new Ext.Template([
       '<img src="/resources/images/s.gif" width="21" height="16"
                          /><b>{FIRSTNAME} {LASTNAME}</b><br />',
       '<img src="/resources/images/icons/silk/database_edit.gif"
width="16" height="16" id="emailEdit_{ID}" class="iconLnk"
align="Edit Email Address" border="0" />{EMAIL}<br />',
       '<img src="/resources/images/icons/silk/database_edit.gif"
width="16" height="16" id="phoneEdit_{ID}" class="iconLnk"
align="Edit Phone" border="0" />{PHONE} ({PHONETYPE})<br />'
     ]),
     initComponent: function(){
      CRM.panels.UserDetail.superclass.initComponent.call(this);
      if (typeof this.tpl === 'string') {
        this.tpl = new Ext.XTemplate(this.tpl);
      }
     },
    update: function(data) {
      this.data = data;
      this.tpl.overwrite(this.body, this.data);
    }
});
Ext.reg('userdetail',CRM.panels.UserDetail);
```

**Example 3**: `AddressDetail.js`

```
Ext.namespace('CRM.panels');
CRM.panels.AddressDetail = Ext.extend(Ext.Panel,{
  width:350,
  height:125,
  bodyStyle: 'padding:10px',
  data: {
    ID: 0,
    FIRSTNAME: '',
    LASTNAME: '',
    EMAIL: '',
    ADDRESSTYPE: 'Home (mailing)',
    STREET1: '',
```

```
        STREET2: '',
        STREET3: '',
        CITY: '',
        STATE: '',
        ZIP: '',
        PHONETYPE: 'Home',
        PHONE: ''
      },
      split: false,
       tpl: new Ext.XTemplate([
         '<b>{ADDRESSTYPE} Address</b><br />',
        '<img src="/resources/images/icons/silk/database_edit.gif" 
    width="16" height="16" id="addrEdit_{ID}" class="iconLnk" align="Edit 
    Address" border="0" />{STREET1}<br />',
        '<tpl if="STREET2.length &gt; 0">',
          '<img src="/resources/images/s.gif" width="21" height="16" 
                                                 />{STREET2}<br />',
        '</tpl>',
        '<tpl if="STREET3.length &gt; 0">',
          '<img src="/resources/images/s.gif" width="21" height="16" 
                                                 />{STREET3}<br />',
        '</tpl>',
        '<img src="/resources/images/s.gif" width="21" height="16" 
                                             />{CITY}, {STATE} {ZIP}'
      ]),
      initComponent: function(){
        CRM.panels.AddressDetail.superclass.initComponent.call(this);
        if (typeof this.tpl === 'string') {
          this.tpl = new Ext.XTemplate(this.tpl);
        }
      },
      update: function(data) {
        this.data = data;
        this.tpl.overwrite(this.body, this.data);
      }
    });
    Ext.reg('addrdetail',CRM.panels.AddressDetail);
```

By breaking these into two separate components, we can now use either piece in any area of our application, independently.

**Example 3**: `ch13ex3.js`

```
var userData = [
    {ID:1,FIRSTNAME:'John',LASTNAME:'Lennon',EMAIL:'john@beatles.
com'
,PASSWORD:'apple1',ADDRESSTYPE:'Home (Mailing)',STREET1:'117 Abbey
Road',STREET2:'',STREET3:'',CITY:'New York',
STATE:'NY',ZIP:'12345',PHONETYPE:'Cell',PHONE:'123-456-7890'},
  {ID:2,FIRSTNAME:'Paul',LASTNAME:'McCartney',
EMAIL:'paul@beatles.com',PASSWORD:'linda',
ADDRESSTYPE:'Work (Mailing)',STREET1:'108 Penny
Lane',STREET2:'',STREET3:'',CITY:'Los Angeles',STATE:'CA',
ZIP:'67890',PHONETYPE:'Home',PHONE:'456-789-0123'},
  {ID:3,FIRSTNAME:'George',LASTNAME:'Harrison',
EMAIL:'george@beatles.com',PASSWORD:'timebandit',
ADDRESSTYPE:'Home (Shipping)',STREET1:'302 Space Way',
STREET2:'',STREET3:'',CITY:'Billings',STATE:'MT',ZIP:'98765',
PHONETYPE:'Office',PHONE:'890-123-4567'},
  {ID:4,FIRSTNAME:'Ringo',LASTNAME:'Starr',
EMAIL:'bignose@beatles.com',PASSWORD:'barbie',
ADDRESSTYPE:'Home (Mailing)',STREET1:'789 Zildizhan Pl',
STREET2:'',STREET3:'',CITY:'Malibu',STATE:'CA',ZIP:'43210',
PHONETYPE:'Home',PHONE:'567-890-1234'}
  ];

  var userDetail = new CRM.panels.UserDetail({
    applyTo: 'chap13_ex03a',
    title: 'User Detail',
    data: userData[0]
  });

  var addrDetail = new CRM.panels.AddressDetail({
    applyTo: 'chap13_ex03b',
    title: 'Address Detail',
    data: userData[0]
  })

  updateContact = function(event,el,data){
    userDetail.update(data.data);
    addrDetail.update(data.data);
  }
   Ext.get('actionLink').on('click',updateContact,this,
                                    {data:userData[1]});
```

> Best Practice
>
> Ok, looking at our two custom components, it's fairly obvious that they are essentially the same object with different `XTemplates` applied, and it would probably be best for them to have their own parent class of overloaded, template-applying methods, and just be repositories of the `XTemplate` defaults and our `xtypes`. But, for our examples, we're going to try and keep it simple for now.

# Using xtype: the benefits of lazy instantiation

In our previous example, a new line was added to the bottom of each class file:

```
Ext.reg('userdetail',CRM.panels.UserDetail);
```

What we've done here is register our new custom component as an `xtype`. Well, what does that mean exactly? An `xtype` is a component container element, registered with the Ext JS library, registering the component with the Component Manager, for lazy object instantiation. What this means is that we can use the `xtype` as a quick object identifier, when laying out our applications, and that these types of objects are only loaded into browser memory when they are actually used. This can greatly improve the overall performance of our application, especially when a view may contain many objects. We should use `xtype` wherever possible while writing object configuration, so that objects that might not immediately be displayed won't take up valuable memory resources. Next, we'll look at this in practice.

# Using our custom components within other objects

Now that we've created our custom components, we can add them to any other container object within Ext JS. We can now use our `xtype` to refer to the component type, for lazy instantiation, and we can get all of the benefits of modular design. Let's apply our two new components with a border layout, for side-by-side viewing.

**Example 4**: `ch14ex4.js`

```
var ContactDetail = new Ext.Panel({
  title: 'Contact Details',
  applyTo: 'chap13_ex04',
  width: 400,
  height: 125,
```

```
    layout: 'border',
    frame: true,
    items:[{
      region: 'west',
      xtype: 'userdetail',
      width: 200,
      data: userData[0]
    },{
      region: 'center',
      xtype: 'addrdetail',
      width: 200,
      data: userData[0]
    }]
  });
```

We have identified the west and center regions of our `BorderLayout` as belonging to the `UserDetail` and `AddressDetail` class types respectively. If this layout were part of a window object, these two classes wouldn't even be loaded into memory until the window was shown, helping to reduce browser memory usage.

# Summary

Extending the various classes of the Ext JS library is the best way to place ourselves on a fast track to Rapid Application Development, by allowing us to easily create modular, reusable components. Within this chapter, we've discovered some of the most powerful aspects of the Ext JS library.

We had a brief overview of object-oriented development with JavaScript, and then covered how object-oriented program design applies to the Ext JS library. We spent a little time covering some of the basics of object-oriented programming such as inheritance, method overriding, and some basic terminology.

We then began applying some of these concepts within Ext JS such as defining custom namespaces, creating custom components, and overriding methods of our object's parent (super) class.

We followed up by giving a small explanation of event-driven application architecture, and applied that by writing a custom event and listener for our custom component.

Finally, we covered `xtypes` and the importance of lazy instantiation on application performance, and then modified our code to use `xtypes` for our new custom components to add them into other Ext JS object containers. In the next chapter we'll discuss how to write and use plugins, and how a plugin differs from a component.

# 14
# Plugging In

Like any good development library, there are ways we can inject our own functionality into it, interacting with the components without modifying them directly. This injection happens by way of the plugins config option that every component has available to it. Each widget in Ext JS that inherits from the Component class has the ability to use plugins, which is pretty much everything, from panels to grids to form fields and everything in between.

In this chapter we will learn to:

- Structure a typical plugin
- Use plugins within components or widgets
- Have a plugin interact with its owner
- Learn advanced plugin techniques

## What can we do?

What can we do with a plugin, and what are the use cases? The usage of a plugin has a very broad range because of how much freedom we are given in the code. There are plugins that simply change the way a selection model on a tree work, make a text field use uppercase, or alter the appearance of a slider. The more complex plugins can create expanding grid rows or visual row editors and much more. There are very few limitations when it comes to plugins.

For our example, we are going to be creating a plugin that will filter our grid-based user input from a text field. We can add some fun features to this, such as case sensitivity and highlighting the target text. We will also cover how to inject items into the owner components layout.

# How it works

Before we jump in and write a plugin, let's take a quick look at how a plugin interacts with its host Component. The plugin itself is generally extended from a base class like the observible class. However we don't need to extend from a particular class to make a plugin, it can be as simple as an empty object, or a singleton.

> The component that is using the plugin is referred to as the host component.

The important part is to have the right methods available, which are called in the following order:

- Constructor: Here we receive and can change the configuration of the plugin, since this method is called when the plugin is first instantiated. This method can be omitted if we don't plan on having any configurable options for our plugin.
- Init: This method is called after the host component is initialized, which is after the config has been processed and the owner component has set up all of its dependencies such as toolbars or form fields. Though the host Components pieces are configured at this point, they are not necessarily rendered yet, so attaching event based render listeners will be needed depending on what we are trying to do.

Another part of this process that does not belong on the list above, but should be noted, is that we can attach listeners to events on the owner component within the `init` method. So for instance, we can attach a function to execute when the owner component has rendered, or a store has loaded, and so on.

# Using a plugin

Of course the other half of this puzzle is actually using the plugin. When we create our component, say a grid for instance, we need to specify a 'plugins' config, which contains an array of instances (or configs) of plugins. So we can either add the plugins using the following format:

```
{
  title: 'Movie Grid',
  xtype: 'grid',
  ...
        plugins: [new Ext.ux.PluginName()],
  ...
}
```

Or we have the option of passing a plugin config using a `ptype` like the following:

```
{
  title: 'Movie Grid',
  xtype: 'grid',
  ...
        plugins: [{ptype:'plugin-name'}],
  ...
}
```

The `ptype` for the plugin must be registered when we create the plugin, but we will learn more about this soon. Let's get coding.

# Plugin structure

There are two main ways to structure our plugin code:

- **singleton**: Our plugin can be created as a singleton class and used across multiple components, though any variables used in the plugin would be shared between each usage. This can be incredibly lightweight, but also has many limitations.
- **observible/object**: Extending from the observible class in Ext JS is the most common method for creating plugins; it offers the most flexibility, though comes with the cost of more overhead. This can be simplified by extending JavaScript's Object constructor.

The singleton plugin structure can be very useful; however most cases will use an instantiation of a class, so I want to focus on creating the most common form of a plugin—extending observible.

The structure created for our new plugin will look very similar to the way we extend components. We are essentially doing the same thing, just adding the specific methods that need to exist when this component is used as a plugin. The following is the basic structure used for a plugin, which we will use as a starting point:

```
Ext.ns('Ext.ux');

Ext.ux.PluginName = Ext.extend(Ext.util.Observable, {
    constructor: function(config){
        // here we can add or alter the config
        Ext.ux.PluginName.superclass.constructor.call(this);
    },
    init: function(cmp){
        // here we can interact with the host component
    }
});

Ext.preg('plugin-name',Ext.ux.PluginName);
```

Notice the constructor and init methods—these two make the foundation of a plugin, and in fact the `init` method is required for a plugin to function. Having a constructor method is not needed if we don't want to have a configurable plugin. The `init` method on the other hand is where the plugin gets its first reference to its instantiated host component, so this is where most of the heavy lifting is performed.

```
Ext.ux.PluginName = Ext.extend(Ext.util.Observable, {
    constructor: function(config){
        // here we can add or alter the config
        Ext.ux.PluginName.superclass.constructor.call(this);
    },
    init: function(cmp){
        // here we can interact with the owner component
    }
});
```

A single argument is passed into the init method, which is a reference to the instance of the host component. From within this init method, we can now call methods on the host component, or add listeners, but the first thing I like to do is create a reference to this host component reference that is scoped within our plugin. This way we have easy access to the host component.

```
Ext.ux.PluginName = Ext.extend(Ext.util.Observable, {
    constructor: function(config){
        // here we can add or alter the config
        Ext.ux.PluginName.superclass.constructor.call(this);
    },
    init: function(cmp){
        this.hostCmp = cmp;
        // here we can interact with the host component
    }
});
```

Now it becomes free for all, and we can pretty much do whatever we want, but for the sake of this example, let's create a simple plugin that gives us a grid filter window. We are going to add this plugin we are creating on to the main movies grid in our movie database example code from Chapter 10.

# First signs of life

This is the point when our plugin starts to come to life, when we are able to actually do something. First lets make our plugin create and show a window when the owner grid is rendered.

In the plugins init method, we can create our window and attach on render listener to the owner grid which will show the window. The constructor method is not needed at this point, but if your sample code already has it, it will not cause any problems to leave it in.

```
Ext.ns('Ext.ux');

Ext.ux.GridSearchWindow = Ext.extend(Ext.util.Observable, {
    /* constructor method not needed at this point */
    init: function(cmp){
        this.hostCmp = cmp;
        this.hostCmp.on('render', this.onRender, this, {delay:200});
    },
    onRender: function(){
        this.win = new Ext.Window({
            width: 200,
            height: 120,
            x: 300, y: 300,
            title: 'Grid Search',
            layout: 'fit',
            closable: false,
            constrain: true,
            renderTo: this.hostCmp.id
        });
        this.win.show();
    }
});

Ext.preg('gridsearchwin',Ext.ux.GridSearchWindow);
```

Now that we have a basic plugin, we need to add it to the grid using the plugins config.

```
{
  title: 'Movie Grid',
  xtype: 'grid',
  ...
        plugins: [{ptype:'gridsearchwin'}],
  ...
}
```

When our movie grid is created, a window will be displayed that is constrained to our grids panel area.

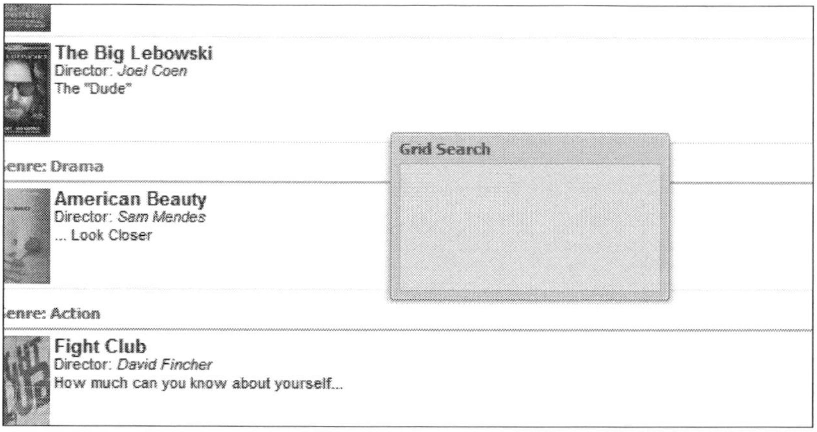


In our example we are waiting for the host grids render event to show the window, but there is no technical reason we need to do this. In our case it's just because of the constrain feature and positioning, our window could just as easily be displayed directly in the init method of our plugin if it was not constrained and initially positioned.

> As our window uses constrain along with an initial x and y position, we must delay the `onRender` event from firing to give our grid time to figure out its size and place the window properly within.

# The search form

With our window up and running—opening along with the grid—we can start to add some form fields and buttons to perform the search features of our plugin.

```
Ext.ux.GridSearchWindow = Ext.extend(Ext.util.Observable, {
    ...
    onRender: function(){
        this.win = new Ext.Window({
            width: 200,
            ...,
            renderTo: this.hostCmp.id,
            items: this.getFormConfig(),
            buttons: [{
                text: 'Find',
                handler: this.doSearch,
```

```
                scope: this
            }, '->', {
                text: 'Clear',
                handler: this.clearSearch,
                scope: this
            }]
        });
        this.win.show();
    },
    doSearch: function(){
        var s = this.hostCmp.getStore();
        s.filter(this.win.field.getValue(),this.win.value.
getValue(),true);
    },
    clearSearch: function(){
        this.hostCmp.getStore().clearFilter();
    },
    getFormConfig: function(){
        return {
            xtype: 'form',
            bodyStyle: 'padding: 5px;',
            border: false,
            labelAlign: 'right',
            labelWidth: 60,
            items: [{
                fieldLabel: 'Column',
                xtype: 'combo',
                ref: '../field',
                triggerAction: 'all',
                displayField: 'display',
                valueField: 'field',
                mode: 'local',
                width: 110,
                value: 'title',
                store: {
                    xtype: 'jsonstore',
                    fields: ['display','field'],
                    root: 'data',
                    data: {data:[]}
                }
            },{
                fieldLabel: 'Find',
                xtype: 'textfield',
                ref: '../value',
```

```
                    width: 110
                }]
            }
        }
    });
```

The new methods we added are `doSearch`, `clearSearch`, and `getFormConfig`—the first two are methods for our search and clear buttons to use, however the `getFormConfig` method returns an object containing the config used to create the actual form, which will give us a basic window and form like the following:

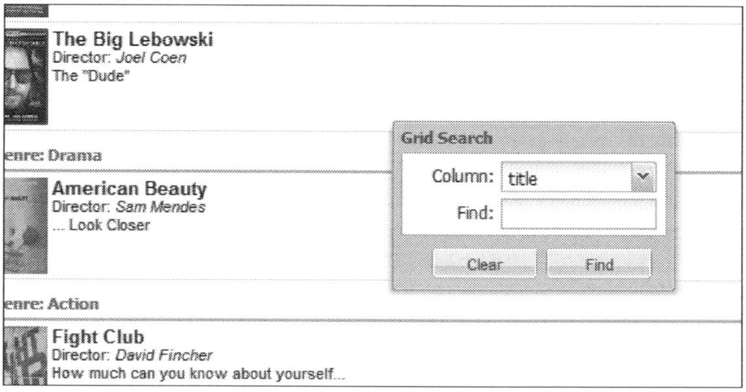


# Interacting with the host

Our start of a plugin looks good now, but let's go to the next step and interact some more with our host component by reading it's configuration and interacting with some of it's features.

One of the first things we did is assign the host component to a property on the local scope:

```
this.hostCmp = cmp;
```

So at any point within our plugin we have access to the host components methods through this property in the scope, in this case it's a grid. This reference to the grid works just like any other component reference—so we are going to take a look at the host grids column model and create some combo box options based on that.

We know that the grid component has a columns property that contains the column configuration, so let's grab it from the `initialConfig` object. We will add a `getColumnsData` method that can encapsulate our logic.

```
getColumnsData: function(){
    var flds = [];
    Ext.each(this.hostCmp.initialConfig.columns, function(itm){
        flds.push({
            display: itm.header,
            field: itm.dataIndex
        });
    }, this);
    return {
        data: flds
    };
}
```

This method now returns a chunk of data in the format of an object literal that can be used with a store—specifically, the store for our forms combo box. By looping through all of the columns and pushing each into a new array, then returning that array inside the 'data' property of an object, we can use it directly in our combo box's store. Modify the form configuration from above to use the following:

```
{
                fieldLabel: 'Column',
                xtype: 'combo',
                ref: '../field',
                triggerAction: 'all',
                displayField: 'display',
                valueField: 'field',
                mode: 'local',
                width: 110,
                value: 'title',
                store: {
                    xtype: 'jsonstore',
                    fields: ['display','field'],
                    root: 'data',
                    data: this.getColumnsData()
                }
            }
```

Now we have a window that has options available in the combo box, and can search the grid.

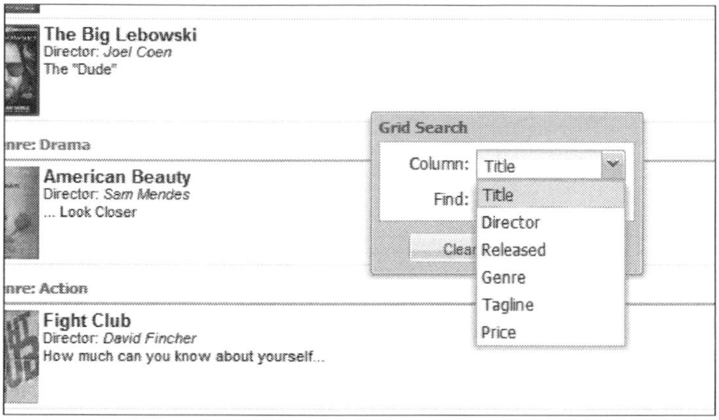


That is exactly how easy it is to create a plugin, which is both easy to distribute or share and gives us many opportunities to add extra features to components with minimal code.

# Configurable plugins

Like many other components in Ext JS, we can provide our plugin with a configuration when we instantiate it. This lets us customize our plugins on a case per case basis. Any configuration options that are passed in with the plugins config are copied into the scope of the plugin.

In order for our config options to be copied into the scope, a constructor method must exist that handles this.

```
        constructor: function(config){
            Ext.apply(this,config);
            Ext.ux.GridSearchWindow.superclass.constructor.
    call(this,config);
        }
```

Now we can go ahead and add an option to our plugins config. I am adding a fields array that lists the fields I want to be included in the combo box used to select the field to search.

```
    {
      title: 'Movie Grid',
      xtype: 'grid',
      ...
```

```
        plugins: [{
    ptype:'gridsearchwin',
    fields: ['title','tagline']
  }],
  ...
}
```

Now we will have a 'fields' attribute in our plugins scope that we can utilize within any scoped methods such as the `init` method or the `getColumnsData` method that we are going to modify now.

```
    getColumnsData: function(){
        var flds = [], flen = this.fields?this.fields.length:0;
        Ext.each(this.hostCmp.initialConfig.columns, function(itm){
            if (flen === 0 || (flen > 0 &&
this.fields.indexOf(itm.dataIndex) >= 0)){
                flds.push({
                    display: itm.header,
                    field: itm.dataIndex
                });
            }
        }, this);
        return {
            data: flds
        };
    }
```

By adding some simple checks around the statement that adds columns to our combo box's data, we can filter out the unwanted options. There is also a check for whether the fields configuration exists or not. This will produce the following:

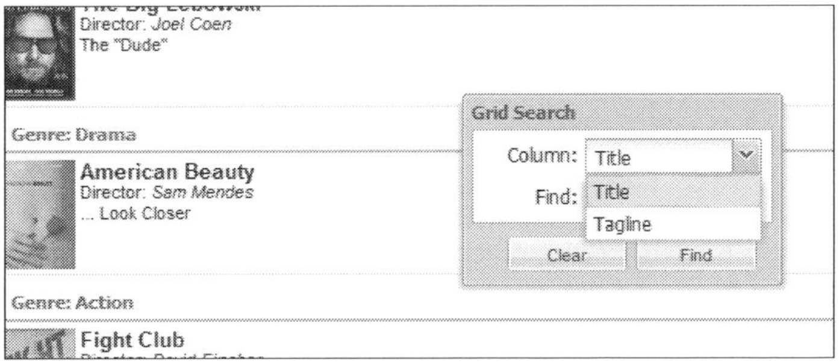

# Extra credit

For that extra little cherry on top, we can add simple text highlighting to our grid search plugin by first adding the appropriate CSS to our document.

```
.highlight { background-color: #ffff80; }
```

Then we will need a function that will wrap all of the grid cell renderers in our grid with a highlighting function.

```
    wrapRenderers: function(){
        var cm = this.hostCmp.getColumnModel();
        Ext.each(cm.config,function(col,i){
            var origFn = cm.getRenderer(i),
            vid = this.win.value.id,
            hlFn = function(){
                var a = arguments, sv = Ext.getCmp(vid).getValue();
                val = origFn(a[0],a[1],a[2],a[3],a[4],a[5]);
                if (sv && val.replace) {
                    val = val.replace(new RegExp('(' + sv + ')',
'gi'), '<span class="highlight">$1</span>');
                }
                return val;
            };
            cm.setRenderer(i, hlFn);
        },this);
    }
```

And last but not least, call this new method when the store loads to apply the new renderers to the grid:

```
    init: function(cmp){
        this.hostCmp = cmp;
        this.hostCmp.on('render', this.onRender, this, {delay:200});
        this.hostCmp.getStore().on('load', this.wrapRenderers, this);
    }
```

This will give us some pretty sweet search term highlighting.

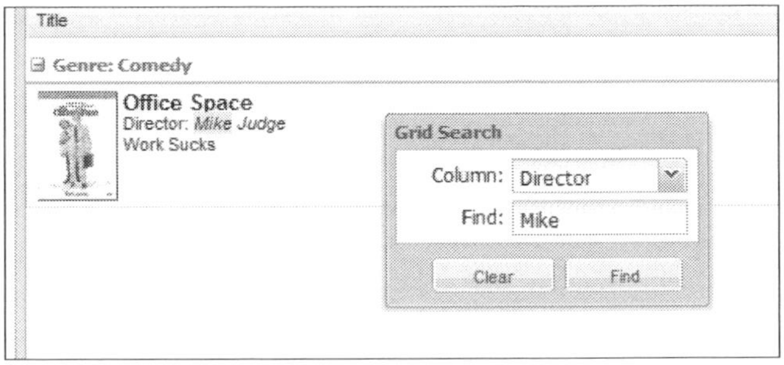


That's all!

# Summary

In this chapter we have learned how to create the most common form of a plugin, the form I find myself using most often, which is extending the observible class. We were able to attach our own code to events on the host component and create a distinct, separate functionality that interacts with the host component like it was a built in feature.

# 15
# It's All About the Data

Ext JS is an extremely powerful, cross-browser library, providing any developer with a beautiful and consistent set of tools for laying out browser-based applications. But there's a lot more here than just pretty boxes and grids. As the title says, *It's All About the Data*! An application without data is really nothing more than an interactive static page, and our users are going to want to manipulate real information. One of the wonders of web applications is that they've taken computing full circle and back to the days of the client/server application model. Ext JS's AJAXified objects provide us with the means to work with real-time data straight from the server, and in this chapter we'll cover the many different ways in which you can retrieve from and post data to your Ext JS based applications.

In this chapter, we cover:

- Understanding data formats
- The data Store object
- Finding data
- Filtering data
- Dealing with Recordset changes
- The DataWriter
- Many objects use a Store

## Understanding data formats

We have dozens of component objects available to us within Ext JS, and most of them can take dynamic data from the server. It's all in knowing what kind of data a component can take, and what formats are acceptable.

# Loading HTML into a panel

You've probably noticed that many components are basically just a box. `TabPanel` instances, `Accordion` instances, and the content area of a `Window` are all just large boxes (a `<div>` element), or `Panel` instances. Each of these unique objects has its own methods and properties, yet each of them extends the `Ext.Panel` object.

Applying dynamic data to a basic `Panel` is super simple, because it takes the simplest of formats: straight text or HTML. Our first example will load a simple HTML page into a `Panel`. First, we'll need the rendering page, and a container element for our content:

```
...     <div id="mainContent">
          <div id="chap15_ex01"></div>
        </div>...
```

Here, we have shown what will go inside the `<body>` tag of our example HTML page. Next, we'll need a server-side template to call for content:

```
<b>William Shakespeare:</b> <i>Poet Laureate</i><br />
```

The last thing we'll need is the actual script to create our example `Panel`:

**Example 1**: `scripts\chapter15_01.js`

```
Ext.onReady(function(){
  var example1 = new Ext.Panel({
    applyTo:'chap15_ex01',
    title:'Chapter 15: Example 1',
    width:250,
    height:250,
    frame:true,
    autoLoad:{
      url:'example1ajax.html'
    }
  });
});
```

Calling the `ch13ex1.html` template in the browser will run this basic script. Let's look over the code to see what we're doing:

1. We wait until the DOM is rendered (`Ext.onReady()` function).
2. We create a new `Ext.Panel` object, rendered to the `chap13_ex01` element (a `<div>` on the rendered page).
3. We load in the contents of the external URL `example1ajax.html`.

It is very simple to pull in an HTML template as content for a `Panel` item. But we would really like dynamic data. Let's build on this example, and pull in data from an application server. We can use the same `autoLoad` attribute to call an application server processing page to return data.

> Ext JS is a client-side scripting library and, as such, you can use any server-side programming language that you feel comfortable with. You may have noticed that some earlier examples in this book are coded in PHP. Examples within this chapter, and the next, require the Adobe ColdFusion server to process the dynamic data, and require you to download and install the free Developer's Edition to run the examples. At this point, we're using ColdFusion to illustrate two different points:
>
> - That any server-side processor can feed data to Ext JS.
> - That not every application server, or remote application, will return data in a standard format. Our examples of Custom Data Readers, later in this chapter, will iterate this point further.
>
> The free Adobe ColdFusion Developer's Edition server is available at `http://www.adobe.com/products/coldfusion`. Review the sample `README.txt` file for more detailed instructions on accessing the example files for this chapter.

For Example 2, we'll change our `<div> id` to `chap15_ex02`, and use the `chapter15_02.js` file to load the data using a different approach, which now reads as follows:

**Example 2**: `scripts\chapter15_02.js`

```
var example2 = new Ext.Panel({
  applyTo:'chap15_ex02',
  title:'Chapter 15: Example 2',
  width:250,
  height:250,
  frame:true,
  autoLoad:{
    url:'Chapter15Example.cfc',
    params:{
      method:'example2',
      returnFormat:'plain',
      id: 1
    }
  }
});
```

You'll notice that the URL is now calling an Adobe ColdFusion Component (CFC), passing in some parameters to get its results. We have a very basic CFC, which runs a small query based on the passed parameters to generate the content that is passed back through the AJAX call.

**Example 2**: `Chapter_15\Chapter15Example.cfc`

```
<cfcomponent output="false">
  <cffunction name="example2" access="remote" output="false"
returntype="string">
    <cfargument name="id" type="numeric" required="true" />
    <cfset var output = "" />
    <cfset var q = "" />
    <cftry>
      <cfquery name="q" datasource="cfbookclub">
        SELECT firstName,
            lastName,
            bio
        FROM Authors
        WHERE authorID = <cfqueryparam cfsqltype="cf_sql_integer"
value="#ARGUMENTS.id#" />
      </cfquery>
      <cfif q.recordcount>
        <cfsavecontent variable="output"><cfoutput>
          <b>#q.firstName# #q.lastName#</b><br />
          <i>#Replace(q.bio,"\n","<br />","all")#</i><br />
        </cfoutput></cfsavecontent>
      </cfif>
      <cfcatch type="database">
        <!--- Place Error Handling Here --->
      </cfcatch>
    </cftry>
    <cfreturn output />
  </cffunction>
</cfcomponent>
```

As the purpose of this book isn't to teach you a server-side language, let's break this down in the simplest way. The CFC takes an argument of `id`, which is passed into a query of the `Authors` table. If a record is returned from the query, a basic string is returned in a predetermined format. The AJAX call (`autoLoad`) is passing several parameters:

- The method to run within the CFC
- The format type to return (plain text, in this case)
- The method arguments (in this case `id`)

## Gotchas with remote data

You must remember that you should call data only via AJAX from the domain of your site. Attempting to reference data from a site outside of your domain will error out at the browser level, as it's considered to be cross-site scripting. **Cross-site scripting** is a means of delivering malicious scripts to an unsuspecting user, generally from outside of the site that they're visiting. Most modern browsers now have built-in facilities to prevent this type of attack. Ext JS does provide facilities for bypassing this restriction, via the `Ext.data.ScriptTagProxy`, but this should only be used if you are confident of the security of the data you are requesting, and its effect on your application.

## Other formats

Ext JS has the capability to consume external data in a variety of formats:

<table>
<tr><th>Format</th><th>Example</th></tr>
<tr><td>Plain Text</td><td>Eric Clapton is a consummate guitarist</td></tr>
<tr><td>HTML</td><td><b>Jimi Hendrix is considered, by some, to have been one of the finest blues guitarists that ever lived</b></td></tr>
<tr><td>JSON</td><td><pre>{
  'members': 4,
  'band': [
    {'id':1,'first_name':'John',
     'last_name':'Lennon'},
    {'id':2,'first_name':'Paul',
     'last_name':'McCartney'},
    {'id',3,'first_name':'George',
     'last_name':'Harrison'},
    {'id':4,'first_name':'Ringo',
     'last_name':'Starr'}
  ]
};</pre></td></tr>
<tr><td>XML</td><td><pre><band>
  <members>4</members>
  <member>
    <firstname>Jimmy</firstname>
    <lastname>Page</lastname>
  </member>
  <member>
    <firstname>Robert</firstname>
    <lastname>Plant</lastname>
  </member>
  ...</pre></td></tr>
</table>

| Format | Example |
|---|---|
| JavaScript Array | `var PinkFloyd = [ ['1','David','Gilmour'], ['2','Roger','Waters'], ['3','Richard','Wright'], ['4','Nick','Mason'] ]` |

The format that you choose may be decided according to the Ext JS object you are using. Many developers like to use XML, as many databases (MS SQL, Oracle, MySQL, PostgreSQL, and DB2 to name a few) can return it natively, and many RESTful web services use it. Although this is a good thing, especially when working with varying external applications, XML can be very verbose at times. Data calls that return small sets of data can quickly clog up the bit stream because of the verbosity of the XML syntax. Another consideration with XML, is the browser engine. An XML data set that looks fine to Mozilla Firefox may be rejected by Internet Explorer, and Internet Explorer's XML parsing engine is slow as well. JSON, or JavaScript Object Notation, data packages tend to be much smaller, taking up less bandwidth. JSON is often preferred over XML for exactly these reasons. If the object you're using can accept it, a simple array can be even smaller, although you will lose the descriptive nature that the JSON or XML syntaxes provide.

# The data Store object

Most Ext JS objects (and even `Panel` instances, with some additional work) take data as **Records** or **Nodes**. Records are typically stored within a data `Store` object. Think of a `Store` as being similar to a spreadsheet, and each record as being a row within the spreadsheet, or as a table in your server-side database, with each record representing a row in that table.

The *data* package contains many objects for interacting with data. You have several different `Store` subclasses:

- `JsonStore`: `Store` object specifically for working with JSON data
- `ArrayStore`: `Store` object for working with arrays
- `XMLStore`: `Store` object for working with XML
- `GroupingStore`: `Store` object that holds 'grouped' datasets

Any `Store` will require some kind of Reader object to parse the inbound data, and again the data package has several Reader subclasses:

- `JsonReader`: For working with JSON datasets
- `ArrayReader`: For working with JavaScript arrays
- `XmlReader`: For working with XML datasets

> The `TreePanel` object doesn't use a traditional data `Store`, but has its own specialized `Store` called a `TreeLoader`, which is passed into the configuration through the `loader` config option. The `TreeLoader` accepts simple arrays of definition objects, much like those expected by an `ArrayReader`. See the Ext JS API (`http://www.extjs.com/deploy/dev/docs/?class=Ext.tree.TreeLoader`) for more information.

# Defining data

`Store` objects are easily configured, requiring the source of the data and a description of the expected records. Our applications know to expect data, but we have to tell them what the data is supposed to look like. Let's say, for instance, that our application manages media assets for our site. We would have a server-side object that queries a folder in our file system and returns information on the files that the folder contains. The data returned might look something like this:

```
{
    files: [
        {name: 'beatles.jpg', path:'/images/', size:46.5, lastmod:
                                                    '2001-12-21
00:00:00'},
        {name: 'led_zeppelin.jpg', path:'/images/', size:43.2,
                              lastmod: '2001-12-21 00:00:00'},
        {name: 'the_doors.jpg', path: '/images/', size:24.6, lastmod:
                                            '2001-12-21 00:00:00'},
        {name: 'jimi_hendrix.jpg', path: '/images/', size:64.3,
                                lastmod: '2001-12-21 00:00:00'}
    ]
}
```

This is a small JSON dataset. Its root attribute is `files`, which is an array of objects. Now we have to define this data for our application:

```
var MediaFile = new Ext.data.Record.create([{
  name: 'Name',
  mapping: 'name'
},{
```

```
    name: 'FilePath',
    mapping: 'path'
  },{
    name: 'FileSize',
    mapping: 'size',
    type: 'float'
  },{
    name: 'LastModified',
    mapping: 'lastmod',
    type: 'date',
    dateFormat: 'Y/m/d'
  }]);
```

We've applied a `name` that each field will be referenced by within our application, mapping it to a variable within a `dataset` object. Many variables will automatically be typed, but you can force (cast) the 'type' of a variable for greater definition and easier manipulation.

The various variable types are:

- `auto` (the default, which implies no conversion)
- `string`
- `int`
- `float`
- `boolean`
- `Date`

We've also applied special string formatting to our `Date` object, to have our output the way we want.

> Dates are typically passed as `string` objects, which usually have to be converted into `Date` objects for proper manipulation. By specifying a `Date` format, Ext JS will handle the conversion using the `dateFormat` we define. The Ext JS documentation for the `Date` object provides an extensive format list, which we can use to define the hundreds of `Date` string permutations we may come across in our code. As of Ext JS 3.0, custom `Date` formats may also be defined.

## More on mapping our data

In the previous example, we covered the definition of a simple JSON object. The same technique is used for XML objects, with the only difference being how to map a record field to a specific node. That's where the `mapping` config option comes in. This option can take a DOM path to the node within the XML. Take the following example:

```
<band>
  <members>4</members>
  <member>
    <firstname>Jimmy</firstname>
    <lastname>Page</lastname>
  </member>
  <member>
    <firstname>Robert</firstname>
    <lastname>Plant</lastname>
  </member>
  ...
```

To create a mapping of the `first_name` node you would have the config look like this:

```
{name: 'First Name',
mapping:'member > first_name,',
type: 'string'}
```

In creating our `mapping`, we utilize an Element Selector that states 'all direct children of `member` that have `first_name`'. To get a good handle on selector syntax, review the Ext JS API documentation on the `Ext.DomQuery` class.

JavaScript arrays are easier, as they don't require mapping, other than defining each field in the same order it would be seen in the array:

```
var PinkFloyd = [
  ['1','David','Gilmour'],
  ['2','Roger','Waters'],
  ['3','Richard','Wright'],
  ['4','Nick','Mason']
]
```

Note here that we won't `create()` a record constructor, but just use the `fields` config option of the `Store`.

```
fields:[
  {name:'id'},
  {name:'first_name'},
  {name:'last_name'}
]
```

# Pulling data into the Store

It is almost as easy to retrieve data from the server as it was to populate the `Panel` object earlier, and we can do so using a very similar syntax.

**Example 3**: `scripts\chapter15_03.js`

```
var ourStore = new Ext.data.Store({
  url:'Chapter15Example.cfc',
  baseParams:{
    method: 'getFileInfoByPath',
    returnFormat: 'JSON',
    queryFormat: 'column',
    startPath: '/images/'
  },
  reader: new Ext.data.CFQueryReader({
    id:'name'
  },[
    {name:'file_name',mapping:'name'},
    {name:'file_size',mapping:'size',type:'int'},
    'type',
    {name:'lastmod',mapping:'datelastmodified',type:'date'},
    {name:'file_attributes',mapping:'attributes'},
    'mode',
    'directory'
  ]),
  listeners:{
    beforeload:{
      fn: function(store, options){
        if (options.startPath && (options.startPath.length > 0)){
          store.baseParams.startPath = options.startPath;
        }
      },
      scope:this
    },
    load: {
      fn: function(store,records,options){
        console.log(records);
      }
    },
    scope:this
  }
});
ourStore.load();
```

This ties all of our pieces together to create our data `Store` object. First, we use the `url` config option to define the location from where we will get our data. Then, we set the initial set of parameters to pass on the load request. Finally, it may be that we want to conditionally pass different parameter values for each request. For this, we can define a special 'listener' to pass new information. In this case, whenever the `load()` method is called, if the `startPath` property is passed into the method as an argument, before the `Store` retrieves the data it will change the `startPath` base parameter to match the value passed in.

> **Where's the screenshot?**
>
> Ok, that's a valid question. A data `Store`, by itself, has no visible output in the browser display. This is why tools like Firefox with the Firebug plugin, or the Aptana development IDE can be so important when doing JavaScript development. These tools can allow you to direct processing output to special windows, to monitor what's going on within your application.

# Using a DataReader to map data

In our previous code example we used a custom `DataReader` to "read" the data being returned from the server-side call. Some applications can natively return data in XML, or even JSON, but it might not always be in the format Ext JS is expecting. As an example, the `JsonStore`, with its built-in `JsonReader`, expects an incoming dataset in the following format:

```
{
  'rootAttribute': [
    {
      'attr1': 'First record',
      'attr2': '0'
    },{
      'attr1': 'Second record',
      'attr2': '3.5'
    }
  ]
}
```

This (JSON) object has a `rootAttribute` property, which is the name of the *root* of the dataset, containing an array of objects. Each of these objects has the same attributes. The attribute names are in quotes. Values are typically in quotes, with the exception of numbers, which may or may not be in quotes.

So, if a server-side call returns data in this expected format, then the base `JsonReader` included within the `JsonStore` will automatically parse the received datasets to populate the `Store` object. We'll emulate this in our next example, by using an example JSON set from earlier in this chapter, and feeding it into a `JsonStore` object through its `data` attribute:

**Example 4**: `scripts\chapter15_04.js`

```
var dataSet = {
  files: [
    {name: 'beatles.jpg', path:'/images/', size:46.5,
lastmod:'2001-12-21 00:00:00'},
    {name: 'led_zeppelin.jpg', path:'/images/', size:43.2,lastmod:
'2001-12-21 00:00:00'},
    {name: 'the_doors.jpg', path: '/images/', size:24.6,
lastmod:'2001-12-21 00:00:00'},
    {name: 'jimi_hendrix.jpg', path: '/images/', size:64.3,lastmod:
'2001-12-21 00:00:00'}
  ]
};
var newSt = new Ext.data.JsonStore({
  data: dataSet,
  root: 'files',
  idProperty: 'name',
  fields:[
    'name',
    {name:'FilePath',mapping:'path'},
    {name:'FileSize',mapping:'size',type:'float'},
    {name:'LastModified',mapping:'lastmod',type:'date'}
  ],
  listeners:{
    load: {
      fn: function(store,records,options){
        console.log(records);
      },
      scope:this
    }
  }
});
```

A call to a server-side application that returns JSON in the standard format would behave the same way. But what happens if the server-side application uses a slightly different format? As an example, the Adobe ColdFusion server (starting from version 8) can automatically return JSON datasets for remote requests, translating any of ColdFusion's native data types into JSON data. But ColdFusion's JSON formatting is typically different, especially when dealing with query data (which is what a dataset would usually be created from). Here's an example of a JSON dataset being returned from a ColdFusion query object:

```
{
  "COLUMNS":["NAME","SIZE","TYPE","DATELASTMODIFIED","ATTRIBUTES",
                                              "MODE","DIRECTORY"],
  "DATA":[
    ["IMG1.jpg",582360,"File","June, 13 2003
     23:50:08","","","H:\\wwwroot\\ExtBook\\images"],
    ["IMG2.JPG",1108490,"File","June, 13 2003
     23:50:52","","","H:\\wwwroot\\ExtBook\\images"],
    ["IMG3.JPG",1136108,"File","June, 13 2003
     23:51:02","","","H:\\wwwroot\\ExtBook\\images"],
    ["IMG4.JPG",1538506,"File","June, 13 2003
     23:51:12","","","H:\\wwwroot\\ExtBook\\images"]
  ]
}
```

All of the data we need is here, but the format can't be properly parsed by the base `JsonReader`. So what do we do now?

# Using a custom DataReader

Ext JS's built-in classes provide outstanding ease of use 'out-of-the-box', but (as we can see) sometimes we need something a little special, possibly due to a different implementation for a specific application server (such as ColdFusion), or possibly due to an external application API (Flickr for example). We could probably implement something on the server-side to put our data in the necessary format, but this creates unnecessary overhead on our server-side platform. Why not just use the client to handle these minor transformations? This helps distribute the load in our applications, and makes more effective use of all of the resources that we have on hand. Ultimately, though, the true point is that we don't always have control of our remote data sources, and that we can adapt our Ext JS applications to accept data from most any source.

Ext JS provides us with the facilities for creating custom DataReaders for mapping our data, as well as simple means (the `reader` config option) for defining these readers in our `Store`.

In our current exercise, we're lucky in that we don't have to write our own DataReader. As the Adobe ColdFusion server platform is so widely used, the Ext JS community has already produced a custom reader just for this task. A simple search of the Ext JS forums (`http://extjs.com/forum/`) will help you find many custom readers for data in a variety of formats. Just take the time to verify (read) the code prior to use, and thoroughly test, because it is being provided by a third party. By using the `CFQueryReader`, with a few minor modifications to our script we can easily read the JSON data format being returned by ColdFusion.

Include a `<script>` tag in your calling template to include the `CFQueryReader.js` file, prior to the `<script>` tag for your custom script. Then we'll define our custom reader by specifying some details about our data; the field to use as a record ID, and the field definitions:

```
new Ext.data.CFQueryReader({
  idProperty:'name'
},[
  {name:'file_name',mapping:'name'},
  {name:'file_size',mapping:'size',type:'int'},
  'type',
  {name:'lastmod',mapping:'datelastmodified',type:'date'},
  {name:'file_attributes',mapping:'attributes'},
  'mode',
  'directory'
]);
```

Next, we'll change our data `Store` from being a `JsonStore` to being the base `Store` object type, and apply our custom reader to the `reader` config attribute:

```
var ourStore = new Ext.data.Store({
  ...
  reader: new Ext.data.CFQueryReader({
  ...
```

We also remove the `fields`, `id`, and `root` properties from the `Store` definition, as these are now all handled from within the reader's definition, or by the custom reader itself.

The last thing we'll do is apply another custom listener to our script, so that we can verify whether the dataset is properly loaded. Let's modify our `listeners` config option, so that we can attach a function to the `Store` object's `load` event listener:

```
listeners:{
  load:{
    fn: function(store, records, options){
      console.log(records);
```

```
        },
        scope: this
      }
    }
```

If you're using Internet Explorer for development, then this line of code will break, as the `console` object isn't natively supported in that environment (you can include additional scripts to use the `console.log()` method in IE, like the one found at `http://www.moxleystratton.com/article/ie-console`). Firefox, with the Firebug plugin, will now give you some output once the data has been retrieved, parsed, and loaded into the data `Store`, so that we can see that the data is now in our `Store`.

> A word about events:
>
> Many Ext JS objects have events that are fired when certain actions are taken upon them, or when they reach a certain state. An event-driven application, unlike a procedural programming model, can listen for changes in the application, such as the receipt of data or the change of a Record's value. Ext JS provides an extensive API, giving us the ability to apply custom event listeners to key actions within the application. For more information, review the object information within the Ext JS API at `http://extjs.com/deploy/dev/docs/`.

Our final script might now look like this:

```
var ourStore = new Ext.data.Store({
  url:'Chapter13Example.cfc',
  baseParams:{
    method: 'getFileInfoByPath',
    returnFormat: 'JSON',
    queryFormat: 'column',
    startPath: '/images/'
  },
  reader: new Ext.data.CFQueryReader({
    id:'name'
  },[
    {name:'file_name',mapping:'name'},
    {name:'file_size',mapping:'size',type:'int'},
    'type',
    {name:'lastmod',mapping:'datelastmodified',type:'date'},
    {name:'file_attributes',mapping:'attributes'},
    'mode',
    'directory'
  ]),
  listeners:{
    load: {
```

```
        fn: function(store,records,options){
          console.log(records);
        }
      },
      scope:this
    }
  });
  ourStore.load();
```

We've setup the `load` listener to notify us (in Firebug) when the records are received into our data `Store`. The `load()` method makes the remote data call, using the defined parameters, but the data isn't available until it's been returned from the server and properly parsed by our custom DataReader. The load event is then fired, and our `load` listener will respond accordingly.

This now wraps up our code pieces, defining what our data will look like, configuring our custom reader, and setting up our data `Store` to pull in our JSON data. The `load` listener will display (within the Console tab of Firebug) the records retrieved from the server that are now in our `Store`.

# Writing a custom DataReader

Sometimes we can't find a prebuilt custom reader in the Ext JS forums. In that case, we will have to write our own. Ext JS provides several readers already: the `ArrayReader`, `JsonReader`, and `XmlReader` classes. When defining our own custom DataReader, we will extend one of these classes. Our first step is to identify which class is best suited for us to extend. Going off our previous examples, let's take another look at the data returned for a ColdFusion query:

```
{
  "COLUMNS":["NAME","SIZE","TYPE","DATELASTMODIFIED","ATTRIBUTES",
                                                  "MODE","DIRECTORY"],
  "DATA":[
    ["IMG1.jpg",582360,"File","June, 13 2003
     23:50:08","","","H:\\wwwroot\\ExtBook\\images"],
    ["IMG2.JPG",1108490,"File","June, 13 2003
     23:50:52","","","H:\\wwwroot\\ExtBook\\images"],
    ["IMG3.JPG",1136108,"File","June, 13 2003
     23:51:02","","","H:\\wwwroot\\ExtBook\\images"],
    ["IMG4.JPG",1538506,"File","June, 13 2003
     23:51:12","","","H:\\wwwroot\\ExtBook\\images"]
  ]
}
```

Analyzing this data packet, the first thing that comes to mind might be "this is JSON." Well, it is. But, if we look very closely, our data is actually an array, with each record being an array. Knowing this, the `ArrayReader` class seems be our best choice for our base reader class. Now we have to figure out how to extend that base class, so that our data will be properly read into our data `Store`.

> We covered extending Ext JS components in *Chapter 13, Code for Reuse: Extending Ext JS.*

We start that process by analyzing the `ArrayReader` class itself. No, not the API (though that may help), but the actual code itself. Within the Ext JS code, that we downloaded at the beginning of this book, you will see a `pkgs` directory under the root directory. Within this directory we will find a `data-json-debug.js` file. Open this file, and find the `Ext.data.ArrayReader` class.

The first thing that we will notice is that the debug files contain a fair amount of comment documentation. Reading the initial comments for the `ArrayReader`, we can see that it extends the `Ext.data.JsonReader`. This means we might have to really research both classes, as figuring out how to extend the reader may require us to review the code for its base class as well. (This is suggested, as many functions called, within the methods of the `ArrayReader`, are defined within the `JsonReader` itself.) If we thoroughly review the code, we gain a better understanding of how each class currently performs its tasks, and gives us a blueprint for how to progress.

After a thorough review of the code we find that the core of any data reader is the `readRecords()` method. This is the method that consumes the raw JSON output, interprets it, and places the records into the `Store`. Typical usage of the `ArrayReader` requires us to write our field definitions in the column order that data will come in. ColdFusion may return query columns in any order, so that method wouldn't be helpful. Luckily, the `COLUMNS` element of the base JSON element defines the order of data in each array element. After discovering this, it also becomes apparent that the `ArrayReader` is not the best choice for our base class, but rather an extension of the `JsonReader`.

Because of this, the author of the `CFQueryReader` chose to override the `readRecords()` method of the base `JsonReader`, writing a solution for parsing the unique data formatting returned by ColdFusion. By studying the `ArrayReader`, the `JsonReader`, and the base `DataReader` (in the `data-foundation-debug.js` file), the author of `CFQueryReader` was able to figure out how to create proper data accessor methods so that a `Store` configured with the `CFQueryReader` would function just as any of the base `Store` objects would.

Here is what the final Custom Reader would look like (with comments):

```
Ext.data.CFQueryReader = Ext.extend(Ext.data.JsonReader, {
    readRecords : function(o){
        this.jsonData = o;
        var s = this.meta,
            Record = this.recordType,
            f = Record.prototype.fields,
            fi = f.items,
            fl = f.length,
            reset = false;
        // For backwards compatability with Ext 2.x
        if(typeof this.getJsonAccessor != "function"){
            this.getJsonAccessor = this.createAccessor;
        }
        /*
         * Creating 'property' accessors, based on the availability
         * (or lack of) of certain meta properties
         */
        if (!this.ef || !this.getQueryRoot) {
            if(s.successProperty) {
                this.getSuccess = this.getJsonAccessor(s.
successProperty);
            }
            /*
            * Providing built in support for CF query objects within
            * structure objects, as is the case when a developer
            * uses the ConvertQueryForGrid() function of CF
            */
            if(s.root){
                this.getRoot = this.getJsonAccessor(s.root + '.DATA');
                this.getQueryRoot = this.getJsonAccessor(s.root);
            } else {
                this.getRoot = (o.QUERY) ? this.
getJsonAccessor('QUERY.DATA') : this.getJsonAccessor('DATA');
                this.getQueryRoot = function(){
                    return (o.QUERY) ? o.QUERY : o;
                };
            }
            if(s.totalProperty) {
                this.getTotal = this.getJsonAccessor(s.totalProperty);
            } else if(o.TOTALROWCOUNT) {
                this.getTotal = this.getJsonAccessor('TOTALROWCOUNT');
            }
        }
```

```
        var root = this.getRoot(o),
            c = root.length,
            totalRecords = c,
            success = true,
            cols = this.getQueryRoot(o).COLUMNS;
        /*
         * ColdFusion typically uppercases column names in it's
return,
         * but certain ColdFusion frameworks maintain casing. To
account
         * for this, and standardize returns and processing, we will
         * internally ensure that the column names are uppercased
         * for consistency
         */
        for (var i = 0;i < cols.length;i++){
            cols[i] = cols[i].toUpperCase();
        }
        // Update the totalRecords if a total was passed in the base
JSON object
        if(s.totalProperty || o.TOTALROWCOUNT){
            var v = parseInt(this.getTotal(o), 10);
            if(!isNaN(v)){
                totalRecords = v;
            }
        }
        // Update the success if a success was passed the in the base
JSON object
        if(s.successProperty){
            var v = this.getSuccess(o);
            if(v === false || v === 'false'){
                success = false;
            }
        }
        // Create a array location mappings according to the COLUMNS
output
        for(b=0;b < fl; b++){
            var fMap = (fi[b].mapping !== undefined && fi[b].mapping
!== null) ? fi[b].mapping : fi[b].name;
            fi[b].mapArrLoc = cols.indexOf(fMap.toUpperCase());
        }
        // Now we create data accessor functions
        if (!this.ef || reset === true) {
           // Create methods for getting a record's ID value
           if (s.id || s.idProperty) {
                 var g = this.getJsonAccessor(s.id || s.idProperty);
```

```
                this.getId = function(rec){
                    var r = g(rec);
                    return (r === undefined || r === "") ? null : r;
                };
            } else {
                this.getId = function(){return null;};
            }
            // Create extractor functions by field
            this.ef = [];
            for(var i = 0; i < fl; i++){
                f = fi[i];
                var map = (f.mapping !== undefined && f.mapping !==
null) ? f.mapping : f.name;
                this.ef[i] = function(rec){
                var r = rec[map];
                return (r === undefined || r === "") ? null : r;
                };
            }
        }
        var records = [];
        // Create individual records and put in the records array
        for(var i = 0; i < c; i++){ // loop all rows of data
            var n = root[i]; // n is a 'row' of data
            var values = {};
            for(var j = 0, jlen = fl; j < jlen; j++){
                f = fi[j]; // field reference
                var k = f.mapArrLoc !== undefined && f.mapArrLoc !==
null ? f.mapArrLoc : j; // get the array position within the row for
the field ref
                var v = n[k] !== undefined ? n[k] : f.defaultValue; //
value is that array position within current row
                v = f.convert(v, n); // convert the value if necessary
(as in type casting to date and stuff)
                values[f.name] = v; // build a values object by
applying the current value to a key of the current 'field'
            }
            var rec = new this.recordType(values, this.getId(values));
// create Ext Record object of values object, assigning the id
            rec.json = values; // put raw values object in the 'json'
attribute of the Record object
            records[i] = rec; // Build the complete array of Records
to populate the Store
        }
        return {
            success: success,
```

```
                records : records,
                totalRecords : totalRecords
            };
        }
    });
```

Custom Data Readers often get updated as the Ext JS library matures. The Ext Team is constantly improving on the handling of data from remote sources. They try very hard to maintain backwards compatibility as much as possible, but custom readers aren't generally written by the Ext Team. This means that, should the Ext Team make changes to the core `Ext.data` package classes, a custom DataReader may need to be updated to function correctly. Just remember that we should test our application's data readers any time the core library is updated. The above DataReader is maintained in a repository on RIAForge (`http://cfqueryreader.riaforge.org`).

# Getting what you want: finding data

Now that we have data (or so Firebug tells us, once it's received from the server), we'll typically need to manipulate it. Once we've loaded our data `Store` with records, the entire dataset remains resident in the browser cache, ready for manipulation or replacement. This data is persistent until we move away from the page or destroy the dataset or the data `Store`.

Ext JS provides many different options for dealing with our data, all of which are documented within the API. Here, we'll explore some of the most common things to do.

# Finding data by field value

The first thing we might want to do is find a specific record. Let's say we needed to know which record from our previous examples contains the picture of Jimi Hendrix:

```
var jimiPicIndex = ourStore.find('NAME','Jimi',0,false,false);
```

This method would return the index of the first record that had `Jimi` as part of the value of the `NAME` field. It would start its search from the first record (0), as it is in JavaScript array notation, look for the string from the beginning of the field's value (using `true` here will search for the string in any location of the `NAME` field within any record), and perform a case-insensitive search.

## Finding data by record index

Having the index is nice; at least we know which record it is now. But we also need to retrieve the record:

```
var ourImg = ourStore.getAt(jimiPicIndex);
```

The `getAt()` method of the `Store` object will get a record at a specific index position within the `Store`.

## Finding data by record ID

The best way to look for a unique record is by `ID`. This is the best way because your record `ID` is unique to the record as well. If you already know the `ID` of your record, this process just becomes easier. We used the `NAME` field as our `ID`, so let's find the record for the same:

```
var ourImg = ourStore.getById('jimi_hendrix.jpg');
```

So, now we can find a record by partial value within a field, get a record by its specific index, or retrieve a record by its `ID` value.

# Getting what you want: filtering data

Sometimes, you only need a specific subset of data from your `Store`. Your `Store` contains a complete dataset (for caching and easy retrieval), but you need it filtered to a specific set of records. As an example, the `cfdirectory` tag we used in our ColdFusion server-side call can return an entire directory listing, including all subdirectories. After retrieving the data, it may be that we only need the names of the files within the `startPath` that we posted. For this, we can filter our client-side cached dataset to get only the Records of type, `File`:

```
ourStore.filter('TYPE','File',false,false);
```

This filters our dataset using the `TYPE` field. The dataset will now only contain records that have a `TYPE` field, with a value of `File` (matched from the beginning, and case-insensitive).

After working with our filtered dataset, there will come a time when we want our original dataset back. Setting a filter on a `Store` persists on that object until we turn it off. When we filtered the dataset, the other records didn't go away. They're still sitting in cache, to the side, waiting to be recalled. Rather than query the server again, we can simply clear our filter:

```
ourStore.clearFilter();
```

# Remote filtering: the why and the how

Client-side filtering is great, reducing our trips to the server. Sometimes, however, our record set is just too large to pull in at once. A great example of this is a paging grid. Many times, for performance reasons, we'll only be pulling in 25 Records at a time. The client-side filtering methods are fine if we only want to filter the resident dataset, but most of the time we'll want a filter applied to all of our data at the time we request it from the server.

Sorting data on remote calls is pretty easy, as we can set the `Store` object's `remoteSort` property to `true`. So, if our `Store` was attached to a grid object, clicking on a column heading to sort the display would automatically reload the data, passing the value in its AJAX request.

Filtering data on remote requests is a bit harder. Basically, we need to pass parameters through the `Store` object's `load` event, and act on those arguments in our server-side method.

So, the first thing we'll need is some server-side code for handling our filtering and sorting. We'll return to our ColdFusion component to add a new method:

**Example 3**: `Chapter_15\Chapter15Example.cfc`

```
 <!---
/  METHOD: getDirectoryContents
/
/  @param  startPath:string
/  @param  recurse:boolean (optional)
/  @param  fileFilter:string (optional)
/  @param  dirFilter:string (optional - File|Dir)
/  @param  sortField:string (optional -
  NAME|SIZE|TYPE|DATELASTMODIFIED|ATTRIBUTES|MODE|DIRECTORY)
/  @param  sortDirection:string (option - ASC|DESC
                                 [defaults to ASC])
/  @return  retQ:query
 --->
<cffunction name="getDirectoryContents" access="remote"
                      output="false" returntype="query">
 <cfargument name="startPath" required="true" type="string" />
 <cfargument name="recurse" required="false" type="boolean"
                                         default="false" />
 <cfargument name="sortDirection" required="false" type="string"
                                           default="ASC" />
 <!--- Set some function local variables --->
 <cfset var q = "" />
```

```
    <cfset var retQ = "" />
    <cfset var attrArgs = {} />
    <cfset var ourDir = ExpandPath(ARGUMENTS.startPath) />
    <!--- Create some lists of valid arguments --->
    <cfset var filterList = "File,Dir" />
    <cfset var sortDirList = "ASC,DESC" />
    <cfset var columnList =
    "NAME,SIZE,TYPE,DATELASTMODIFIED,ATTRIBUTES,MODE,DIRECTORY" />
    <cftry>
      <cfset attrArgs.recurse = ARGUMENTS.recurse />
      <!--- Verify the directory exists before continuing --->
      <cfif DirectoryExists(ourDir)>
        <cfset attrArgs.directory = ourDir />
      <cfelse>
        <cfthrow type="Custom" errorcode="Our_Custom_Error" message="The
  directory you are trying to reach does not exist." />
      </cfif>
      <!--- Conditionally apply some optional filtering and sorting
       --->
      <cfif IsDefined("ARGUMENTS.fileFilter")>
        <cfset attrArgs.filter = ARGUMENTS.fileFilter />
      </cfif>
      <cfif IsDefined("ARGUMENTS.sortField")>
        <cfif ListFindNoCase(columnList,ARGUMENTS.sortField)>
          <cfset attrArgs.sort = ARGUMENTS.sortField & " " &
            ARGUMENTS.sortDirection />
        <cfelse>
          <cfthrow type="custom" errorcode="Our_Custom_Error"
           message="You have chosen an invalid sort field.
           Please use one of the following: " & columnList />
        </cfif>
      </cfif>
      <cfdirectory action="list" name="q"
        attributeCollection="#attrArgs#" />
      <!--- If there are files and/or folders,
       and you want to sort by TYPE --->
      <cfif q.recordcount and IsDefined("ARGUMENTS.dirFilter")>
        <cfif ListFindNoCase(filterList,ARGUMENTS.dirFilter)>
          <cfquery name="retQ" dbtype="query">
          SELECT  #columnList#
            FROM  q
            WHERE  TYPE = <cfqueryparam cfsqltype=" cf_sql_varchar"
                   value="#ARGUMENTS.dirFilter#" maxlength="4" />
          </cfquery>
```

```
        <cfelse>
          <cfthrow type="Custom" errorcode="Our_Custom_Error"
            message="You have passed an invalid dirFilter.
            The only accepted values are File and Dir." />
        </cfif>
      <cfelse>
        <cfset retQ = q />
        </cfif>
      <cfcatch type="any">
        <!--- Place Error Handler Here --->
      </cfcatch>
    </cftry>
    <cfreturn retQ />
  </cffunction>
```

This might look complicated, but it really isn't! Again, our mission here isn't to learn ColdFusion, but it is important to have some understanding of what your server-side process is doing. What we have here is a method that takes some optional parameters related to sorting and filtering via an HTTP POST statement. We use the same `cfdirectory` tag to query the file system for a list of files and folders. The difference here is that we now conditionally apply some additional attributes to the tag, so that we can filter on a specific file extension, or sort by a particular column of the query. We also have a Query-of-Query statement to query our returned `recordset` if we want to filter further by the record TYPE, which is a filtering mechanism not built into the `cfdirectory` tag. Lastly, there's also some custom error handling to ensure that valid arguments are being passed into the method.

We'll make a few modifications to our previous `Store` script as well. First, we'll need a few methods that can be called to remotely filter our `recordset`:

```
filterStoreByType = function (type){
  ourStore.load({dirFilter:type});
}
filterStoreByFileType = function (fileType){
  ourStore.load({fileFilter:fileType});
}
clearFilters = function (){
  ourStore.baseParams = new cloneConfig(initialBaseParams);
  ourStore.load();
}
```

We have methods here for filtering our `Store` by `TYPE`, for filtering by file extension, and for clearing the filters. The values passed into these methods are mapped to the proper remote method argument names. The `beforeload` listener of the `Store` automatically applies these arguments to the `baseParams` prior to making the AJAX call back to the server. The important thing to remember here is that each added parameter stays in `baseParams`, until the filters are cleared.

It's also important to note that the `load()` method can take an options argument made up of four attributes:

- `params`
- `callback` (a method to perform on load)
- `scope` (the scope with which to call the callback)
- `add` (pass true to add the load to the already-existing dataset)

```
ourStore.load({params:{dirFilter:type},callback:someMethodToCall,scope
:this,add:false});
```

The `clearFilter()` method does not work with remote filtering, so we need to have a way to recall our initial `baseParams` when we need to clear our filters, and get our original dataset back. For this, we first abstract our `baseParams` configuration:

```
var initialBaseParams = {
   method: 'getDirectoryContents',
   returnFormat: 'JSON',
   queryFormat: 'column',
   startPath: '/testdocs/'
};
```

We then need a way to clone the config in our actual `Store` configuration. If we passed the `initialBaseParams` into the `baseParams` config option directly, and then filtered our dataset, the filter would be added to the `initialBaseParams` variable, as the variable gets passed by reference. As we want to be able to recall our actual beginning `baseParams`, we'll need to clone the `initialBaseParams` object. The clone gets set as the `baseParams` config option. Filters don't touch our original object, and we can recall them whenever we need to `clearFilter()`.

For this, we'll need a simple method of cloning a JavaScript object:

```
cloneConfig = function (config) {
    for (i in config) {
        if (typeof config[i] == 'object') {
            this[i] = new cloneConfig(config[i]);
        }
        else
```

```
            this[i] = config[i];
        }
    }
```

We can then change our `baseParams` attribute in our `Store` configuration:

```
baseParams: new cloneConfig(initialBaseParams),
```

We used the same function within our `clearFilters()` method, to reset our `baseParams` to their initial configuration. Here is what our entire script looks like now:

**Example 4**: `scripts\chapter15_04.js`

```
cloneConfig = function (config) {
    for (i in config) {
        if (typeof config[i] == 'object') {
            this[i] = new cloneConfig(config[i]);
        }
        else
            this[i] = config[i];
    }
}
Ext.onReady(function(){
    var recordModel = [
        {name:'file_name',mapping:'name'},
        {name:'file_size',mapping:'size',type:'int'},
        'type',
        {name:'lastmod',mapping:'datelastmodified',type:'date'},
        {name:'file_attributes',mapping:'attributes'},
        'mode',
        'directory'
    ];
    var ourReader = new Ext.data.CFQueryReader({idProperty:'name'},
                                                        recordModel);
    var initialBaseParams = {
        method: 'getDirectoryContents',
        returnFormat: 'JSON',
        queryFormat: 'column',
        startPath: '/testdocs/'
    };
    var ourStore = new Ext.data.Store({
        url:'Chapter12Example.cfc',
        baseParams: new cloneConfig(initialBaseParams),
        reader: ourReader,
        fields: recordModel,
        listeners:{
```

```
            beforeload:{
              fn: function(store, options){
                for(var i in options){
                  if(options[i].length > 0){
                    store.baseParams[i] = options[i];
                  }
                }
              },
              scope:this
            },
            load: {
              fn: function(store,records,options){
                console.log(records);
              }
            },
            scope:this
          }
      });
      ourStore.load({params:{recurse:true}});
      filterStoreByType = function (type){
          ourStore.load({params:{dirFilter:type}});
      }
      filterStoreByFileType = function (fileType){
          ourStore.load({params:{fileFilter:fileType}});
      }
      clearFilters = function (){
          ourStore.baseParams = new cloneConfig(initialBaseParams);
          ourStore.load({params:{recurse:true}});
      }
  });
```

To test our changes, we can put some links on our HTML page to call the methods that we've created for filtering data, which we can then monitor in Firebug.

**Example 4**: `Chapter_15\ch13ex5.html`

```
<div id="chap15_ex05">
  <a onclick="filterStoreByType('File')"
   href="javascript:void(0)">Filter by 'File's</a><br />
  <a onclick="filterStoreByFileType('*.doc')"
   href="javascript:void(0)">Filter by '.doc File's</a><br />
  <a onclick="clearFilters()" href="javascript:void(0)">
                                     Clear Filters</a><br />
</div>
```

After the page has loaded, we see the console logging the initial recordset being loaded into the `Store`. Clicking our first link will remove all of the directory records through filtering. Clicking our second link takes it a step further, and filters out any files other than those ending in `.doc`. The last link resets the filters to the original `baseParams` and reloads the initial recordset.

# Dealing with Recordset changes

One of great things about Ext JS data `Store` objects is change management. Our applications might attack changing records in a variety of ways, from editable data `Grids` to simple `Forms`, but changing that data on the client won't update the remote data `Store` at the server.

One of the easiest things to do this is to apply an `update` event listener to our `Store` object. We applied the `load` listener before. Now, let's apply an update listener to our script.

```
listeners:{
  load: {
    fn: function(store, records, options){
      console.log(records);
    },
    scope: this
  },
  update: {
    fn: function(store, record, operation){
      switch (operation){
      case Ext.record.EDIT:
          // Do something with the edited record
          break;
      case Ext.record.REJECT:
          // Do something with the rejected record
          break;
      case Ext.record.COMMIT:
          // Do something with the committed record
          break;
      }
    },
    scope:this
  }
}
```

When a record is updated, the `update` event fires in the `Store`, passing several objects into the event. The first is the `Store` itself, which is good for reference. The second is the record that's been updated. The last object is the `state` of the record that was updated. Here, we have laid out a quick `switch`/`case` statement to trigger different actions according to the state of the record. We can add code into the action block for the `Ext.record.EDIT` state to automatically send every edit to the server for immediate record revision.

One other option that we can address is the `Ext.record.COMMIT` state. It is sometimes better to let the user affect many different changes, to many different records, and then send all the updates at once.

```
ourStore.commitChanges();
```

This will collect all of the edited records, flag them by using `Ext.record.COMMIT`, and then the `update` event would fire and affect each record. Our last operation `state` is perfect for processing this situation, for which we can add additional client-side validation, or AJAX validation, or whatever our process might call for.

The `Ext.record.REJECT` state is generally set directly by the data `Store`, whereby the `Store` rejects any changes made to the record, and will revert the record's field values back to their original (or last committed) state. This might occur if a value of the wrong data type is passed into a field.

# Taking changes further: the DataWriter

Ext JS 3.0 introduced many new packages and classes for working with data. Ext JS has always supplied DataReaders, but now we may also take advantage of DataWriters. In fact, we can create APIs around our data access, providing simple CRUD (Create, Read, Update, Delete) access directly from within our configurations.

Much of the interaction that we were previously required to script out, we may now handle via simple configuration. Our data `Store` objects know, automatically, when records have changed, and we can now handle these events without adding in a ton of additional code.

Let's go back and look at the code from Example 2. Here we had pulled a single record from a database by passing in an author ID. Let's expand upon this by pulling all of the current records and putting them into a small editor grid.

**Example 5:** `Chapter_15\ch15ex6st1.html`

```
Ext.onReady(function(){
  var recDefinition = [
    {name:'authorID',type:'int'},
```

```
    'firstName',
    'lastName',
    'bio'
  ];
  var ourReader = new Ext.data.CFQueryReader({idProperty:'authorID',ro
ot:'query'},recDefinition);
  var ourStore = new Ext.data.Store({
    url:'Chapter13Example.cfc',
    baseParams:{
      method: 'GetAuthors',
      returnFormat: 'JSON',
      queryFormat: 'column'
    },
    reader: ourReader,
    listeners:{
      load: {
        fn: function(store,records,options){
          console.log(records);
        }
      },
      scope:this
    }
  });
  var fm = Ext.form;
  var ourGrid = new Ext.grid.EditorGridPanel({
    store: ourStore,
    cm: new Ext.grid.ColumnModel({
      columns:[{
        id: 'authorID',
        dataIndex: 'authorID',
        width: 40
      },{
        id: 'firstName',
        dataIndex: 'firstName',
        header: 'First Name',
        width: 150,
        editor: new fm.TextField({
          allowBlank: false
        })
      },{
        id: 'lastName',
        dataIndex: 'lastName',
        header: 'Last Name',
        width: 150,
```

```
          editor: new fm.TextField({
            allowBlank: false
          })
        },{
          id: 'bio',
          dataIndex: 'bio',
          header: 'Bio',
          width: 350,
          editor: new fm.TextField()
        }]
      }),
      renderTo: 'chap13_ex06',
      width: 750,
      height: 600,
      title: 'Authors',
      frame: true,
      clicksToEdit: 1
    });
    ourStore.load();
  });
```

**Example 5**: `GetAuthors` **method**

```
<cffunction name="GetAuthors" access="remote" output="false"
returntype="struct">
  <cfset var retVal = StructNew() />
  <cfset var q = "" />
  <cfset retVal['success'] = true />
  <cftry>
    <cfquery name="q" datasource="cfbookclub">
      SELECT authorID,
          firstName,
          lastName,
          bio
      FROM Authors
    </cfquery>
    <cfif q.recordcount>
      <cfset retVal['query'] = q />
    </cfif>
    <cfcatch type="any">
      <!--- Error Handling Here --->
      <cfset retVal['success'] = false />
      <cfset retVal['errorMsg'] = "There was an error retrieving
records." />
    </cfcatch>
```

```
    </cftry>
    <cfreturn retVal />
  </cffunction>
```

This populates all records of the `Author` table to an `EditorGridPanel`. This is only the first step. Right now we can edit the grid, changing the records in the local data `Store`, but that isn't changing the data back at the server. For this, we really need our DataWriter.

DataWriters allow us to configure a proxy object for handling all of our basic CRUD operations. Let's configure a standard `HttpProxy` object by defining an API for our basic CRUD operations. First we'll write the API strictly to do exactly what our previous example does, creating our proxy and adjusting our `Store` configuration.

**Example 5:** `scripts\chapter15_06_02.js`

```
var ourProxy = new Ext.data.HttpProxy({
  api:{
    read: 'Chapter13Example.cfc?method=GetAuthors&returnFormat=JSON'
  }
})
var ourStore = new Ext.data.Store({
  proxy: ourProxy,
  reader: ourReader,
  listeners:{
    load: {
      fn: function(store,records,options){
        console.log(records);
      }
    },
    scope:this
  }
});
```

We've placed our ColdFusion specific params directly in the `url` attribute of the API call, though we could use a restful `url` to specify our calling methods, should we have a controller to handle them. Let's further extend our API to handle updated records.

First we'll need to add the `DataWriter` to our script. We can choose between a `JsonWriter` or an `XmlWriter`. Since ColdFusion can easily handle JSON, we'll use the `JsonWriter`:

```
var ourWriter = new Ext.data.JsonWriter();
```

We can then add an update item to our API proxy:

```
var ourProxy = new Ext.data.HttpProxy({
  api:{
    read: 'Chapter13Example.cfc?method=GetAuthors&returnFormat=JSON',
    update: 'Chapter13Example.cfc?method=UpdateAuthors&returnFormat=J
SON'
  }
});
```

In this default configuration each cell change of the Editor grid will change a value, and with each change a db call would be made to the update API method, passing a query object with the ID of the record (the `authorID`) , and the field/value pair. This has advantages, but it makes sense to call the server with a complete record, or even a batch of records. This is done by setting the `autoSave` attribute of the `Store` to `false`, then calling save only when ready.

```
var ourStore = new Ext.data.Store({
  proxy: ourProxy,
  writer: ourWriter,
  reader: ourReader,
  autoSave: false
});
```

We'll also want to change our `DataWriter` as well. We can use the `listful` attribute, to make the records returned to the server an array, for one record or a hundred. This will make it easier to write generic server processes. We'll also use the `writeAllFields` attribute so that we send all of the fields of a record, not just those that changed. This is a little more data back and forth, but it helps us to write better process.

```
var ourWriter = new Ext.data.JsonWriter({listful: true,writeAllFields:
true});
```

The last thing we'll do is add a `Store` listener to the `save` event, so we can clear those 'dirty' flags from the grid once our updates are made.

```
var ourStore = new Ext.data.Store({
  proxy: ourProxy,
  writer: ourWriter,
  reader: ourReader,
  autoSave: false,
  listeners:{
    save:{
      fn: function(store, batch, data){
        store.commitChanges();
```

```
        },
        scope: this
      }
    }
  });
```

We can now update multiple records at one time, by making the changes in our `EditorGridPanel` and clicking the "Save Changes" button.

**Example 5**: `scripts\chapter15_06_03.js`

```
Ext.onReady(function(){
  var recDefinition = [
    {name:'authorID',type:'int'},
    'firstName',
    'lastName',
    'bio'
  ];
  var ourReader = new Ext.data.CFQueryReader({idProperty:'authorID',ro
ot:'query'},recDefinition);
  var ourWriter = new Ext.data.JsonWriter({listful:true,writeAllField
s:true});
  var ourProxy = new Ext.data.HttpProxy({
    api:{
      read: 'Chapter13Example.cfc?method=GetAuthors&returnFormat=JS
ON',
      update: 'Chapter13Example.cfc?method=UpdateAuthors&returnFormat
=JSON'
    }
  });
  var ourStore = new Ext.data.Store({
    proxy: ourProxy,
    writer: ourWriter,
    reader: ourReader,
    autoSave: false,
    listeners:{
      save:{
        fn: function(store, batch, data){
          store.commitChanges();
        },
        scope: this
      }
    }
  });
  var fm = Ext.form;
```

```
var ourGrid = new Ext.grid.EditorGridPanel({
  store: ourStore,
  cm: new Ext.grid.ColumnModel({
    columns:[{
      id: 'authorID',
      dataIndex: 'authorID',
      width: 40
    },{
      id: 'firstName',
      dataIndex: 'firstName',
      header: 'First Name',
      width: 150,
      editor: new fm.TextField({
        allowBlank: false
      })
    },{
      id: 'lastName',
      dataIndex: 'lastName',
      header: 'Last Name',
      width: 150,
      editor: new fm.TextField({
        allowBlank: false
      })
    },{
      id: 'bio',
      dataIndex: 'bio',
      header: 'Bio',
      width: 350,
      editor: new fm.TextField()
    }]
  }),
  renderTo: 'chap15_ex06',
  width: 750,
  height: 600,
  title: 'Authors',
  frame: true,
  clicksToEdit: 1,
  bbar:[{
    text: 'Save Changes',
    handler: function(){
      ourStore.save();
    }
  }]
});
```

```
    ourStore.load();
});
```

`Chapter15Example.cfc` `UpdateAuthors` method:

```
<cffunction name="UpdateAuthors" access="remote" output="false"
returntype="boolean">
  <cfargument name="query" required="true" type="string" />
  <cfset var retVal = StructNew() />
  <cfset var q = "" />
  <cfset var i = 0 />
  <cfset ARGUMENTS.query = '{"data":' & ARGUMENTS.query & '}' />
  <cfset pairs = DeserializeJson(ARGUMENTS.query) />
  <cfset retVal["success"] = true />
  <cfloop array="#pairs.data#" index="i">
    <cftry>
      <cfquery name="q" datasource="cfbookclub">
        UPDATE Authors
        SET firstName = '#i.firstName#',
            lastName = '#i.lastName#',
            bio = '#i.bio#'
        WHERE authorID = #Val(i.authorID)#
      </cfquery>
      <cfcatch type="any">
        <!--- Error Handling Here --->
        <cfset retVal['errorMsg'] = "There was an error" />
        <cfset retVal['success'] = false />
       </cfcatch>
    </cftry>
  </cfloop>
  <cfreturn retVal["success"] />
</cffunction>
```

Although we won't cover it here, it's just as easy to add the 'create' and 'destroy' methods to your API. The 'destroy' would remove the record from the datasource by `authorID`, while the 'create' would write a new record to the datasource, returning the `authorID` that was created.

# Many objects use a Store

The beauty of the `Store` object is in its many uses. So many objects, within the Ext JS library, can consume a `Store` as part of their configuration, automatically mapping data in many cases.

## Store in a ComboBox

For example, the `ComboBox` object can take a `Store`, or any of its subclasses, as a data provider for its values:

```
var combo = new Ext.form.ComboBox({
    store: states,
    displayField: 'state',
    valueField: 'abbreviation',
    typeAhead: true,
    mode: 'remote',
    triggerAction: 'all',
    emptyText: 'Select a state...',
    selectOnFocus: true,
    applyTo: 'stateCombo'
});
```

This `ComboBox` takes a `Store` object called `states`, and maps its **state** field to the display, while mapping the **abbreviation** field to its underlying selected value.

## Store in a DataView

The `DataView` object is one of the most powerful objects within Ext. This object can take a `Store` object, let us apply a Template or `XTemplate` to each Record (which the `DataView` refers to as a `Node`), and have each item render within the `DataView`, contiguously, wrapping items as they run out of space. The `DataView` opens up some very interesting ways to visually produce contact lists, image galleries, and file system explorers, and opens up our applications to be able to exchange data among a variety of objects through custom drag-and-drop functionality.

## Stores in grids

We've seen examples of applying a data `Store` to grid in *Chapter 5* of this book. There are several different types of grids (Editor, Grouping, Property, and Basic Grids), but all of them take `Store` objects as input, and the applicable `ColumnModel`, to coordinate their data display.

The `Grid` objects and the `ComboBox` are probably the most prevalent uses of `Store` objects, with the `Grid` and the `DataView` being the two primary means of displaying multiple records of data. The `Tree` object takes a special data source called a `TreeLoader`. The `TreeLoader` is actually part of the `Tree` package of classes, and does not extend the base `Store` object, although it operates in much the same way. Rather than `Record` objects, the `TreeLoader` takes an array of objects, which it then converts into `Node` instances. The structure to its incoming data is something like this:

```
var dataset = [{
  id: 1,
  text: 'Node 1',
  leaf:: false
},{
  id: 2,
  text: 'Node 2',
  leaf: true
}];
```

When a leaf is `true`, then it is an expandable item, which will query the server for further data when passing the node data. A `leaf:false` statement says that the `Node` has no children.

# Summary

In this chapter, we've learned how to pull dynamic, server-side data into our applications. Ext JS's `Store` objects, with their versatility and mappable syntax, are easily-configured as data sources for a lot of Ext JS objects. In this chapter, we've bound simple external data to a `Panel` object, gone over the various data formats that Ext JS can consume, and seen a basic overview of the data `Store` object and some of its more important subclasses.

Getting into the meat of things, we learned how to define our data using the record object, after which we learned how to populate our `Store` with records from a remote data source. We also learned about the purpose behind `DataReader` instances, the different ones available to you, and how to create a custom `DataReader`.

We got busy learning `Store` manipulation techniques such as finding records by field values, indexes, or IDs. We also touched on filtering our `Store` objects to get a working subset of data records. We also talked about dealing with local data changes via the `update` event listener. Then we started sending data back, registering local data `Store` changes back to the server with `DataWriter` definitions.

Finally, we covered some of the other Ext JS objects that use the `Store`, opening the doors to external data within multiple facets of our applications.

# 16
# Marshalling Data Services with Ext.Direct

When the Ext team set out to update Ext JS, for their 3.0 release, they began by looking at code from hundreds of developers, trying to see what holes needed to be filled; what needs weren't being met by the library that developers re-wrote over and over again. Overwhelmingly, they kept coming back to how developers accessed and updated data with the server. Developers would write thousands of lines of repetitive code to handle data transfer, in and out. From this discovery spawned `Ext.Direct`, a specification and supporting classes that allowed developers to define all of their server data interaction points from one consolidated location.

In this chapter, we'll discuss:

- How a developer goes about tapping into the power of `Ext.Direct`
- Writing our own server-side stack
- Choosing a configuration that works for our environment
- Building out our API
- Setting up our own Programmatic Router to 'direct' our requests where we need them to go
- Finally, we'll put all of the pieces together

## What is Direct?

Part of the power of any client-side library is its ability to tap nearly any server-side technology (as we demonstrated in *Chapter 15, It's All About the Data*). That said, with so many server-side options available there were many different implementations being written for accessing the data.

`Direct` is a means of marshalling those server-side connections, creating a 'one-stop-shop' for handling your basic Create, Read, Update, and Delete actions against that remote data. Through some basic configuration, we can now easily create entire server-side API's that we may programmatically expose to our Ext JS applications. In the process, we end up with one set of consistent, predefined methods for managing that data access.

# Building server-side stacks

There are several examples of server-side stacks already available for Ext JS, directly from their site's `Direct` information. These are *examples*, showing you how you might use `Direct` with a particular server-side technology, but Ext provides us with a specification so that we might write our own. Current stack examples are available for:

- PHP
- .NET
- Java
- ColdFusion
- Ruby
- Perl

These are **examples** written directly by the Ext team, as **guides**, as to what we can do. Each of us writes applications differently, so it may be that our application requires a different way of handling things at the server level. The `Direct` specification, along with the examples, gives us the guideposts we need for writing our own stacks when necessary. We will deconstruct one such example here to help illustrate this point.

Each server-side stack is made up of three basic components:

- Configuration—denoting which components/classes are available to Ext JS
- API—client-side descriptors of our configuration
- Router—a means to 'route' our requests to their proper API counterparts

> To illustrate each of these pieces of the server-side stack we will deconstruct one of the example stacks provided by the Ext JS team. I have chosen the ColdFusion stack because:
>
> - It is a good example of using a metadata configuration
> - It works well with our examples from *Chapter 15, It's All About the Data*
> - DirectCFM (the ColdFusion stack example) was written by Aaron Conran, who is the Senior Software Architect and Ext Services Team Leader for Ext, LLC
>
> As we've stated before, the purpose of this book isn't to teach you a server-side programming language. Each of the following sections will contain a "Stack Deconstruction" section to illustrate each of the concepts. These are to show you how these concepts might be written in a server-side language, but you are welcome to move on if you feel you have a good grasp of the material.

## Configuration

Ultimately the configuration must define the classes/objects being accessed, the functions of those objects that can be called, and the length (number) of arguments that the method is expecting. Different servers will allow us to define our configuration in different ways. The method we choose will sometimes depend upon the capabilities or deficiencies of the platform we're coding to. Some platforms provide the ability to introspect components/classes at runtime to build configurations, while others require a far more manual approach. You can also include an optional `formHandler` attribute to your method definitions, if the method can take form submissions directly. There are four basic ways to write a configuration.

## Programmatic

A programmatic configuration may be achieved by creating a simple API object of key/value pairs in the native language. A key/value pair object is known by many different names, depending upon the platform to which we're writing for: HashMap, Structure, Object, Dictionary, or an Associative Array. For example, in PHP you might write something like this:

```
$API = array(
  'Authors'=>array(
    'methods'=>array(
      'GetAll'=>array(
        'len'=>0
      ),
```

```
            'add'=>array(
              'len'=>1
            ),
            'update'=>array(
              'len'=>1
            )
          )
        )
      );
```

Look familiar? It should, in some way, as it's very similar to a JavaScript object. The same basic structure is true for our next two methods of configuration as well.

# JSON and XML

This may look far more familiar, after all we've been through this book. When we've written Ext code so far, we've often passed in configuration objects to our various Ext components. The same is true for this configuration, as we can pass in a basic JSON configuration of our API:

```
{
  Authors:{
    methods:{
      GetAll:{
        len:0
      },
      add:{
        len:1
      },
      update:{
        len:1
      }
    }
  }
}
```

Or we could return an XML configuration object:

```
<Authors>
  <methods>
    <method name="GetAll" len="0" />
    <method name="add" len="1" />
    <method name="update" len="1" />
  </methods>
</Authors>
```

All of these forms have given us the same basic outcome, by providing a basic definition of server-side classes/objects to be exposed for use with our Ext applications. But, each of these methods require us to build these configurations basically by hand. Some server-side options make it a little easier.

## Metadata

There are a few server-side technologies that allow us to add additional metadata to classes and function definitions, using which we can then introspect objects at runtime to create our configurations. The following example demonstrates this by adding additional metadata to a **ColdFusion component** (CFC):

```
<cfcomponent name="Authors" ExtDirect="true">
  <cffunction name="GetAll" ExtDirect="true">
    <cfreturn true />
  </cffunction>
  <cffunction name="add" ExtDirect="true">
    <cfargument name="author" />
    <cfreturn true />
  </cffunction>
  <cffunction name="update" ExtDirect="true">
    <cfargument name="author" />
    <cfreturn true />
  </cffunction>
</cfcomponent>
```

This is a very powerful method for creating our configuration, as it means adding a single name/value attribute (`ExtDirect="true"`) to any object and function we want to make available to our Ext application. The ColdFusion server is able to introspect this metadata at runtime, passing the configuration object back to our Ext application for use.

## Stack deconstruction—configuration

The example ColdFusion Component provided with the DirectCFM stack is pretty basic, so we'll write one slightly more detailed to illustrate the configuration. ColdFusion has a facility for attaching additional metadata to classes and methods, so we'll use the fourth configuration method for this example, Metadata.

We'll start off with creating the `Authors.cfc` class:

```
<cfcomponent name="Authors" ExtDirect="true">
</cfcomponent>
```

Next we'll create our `GetAll` method for returning all the authors in the database:

```
<cffunction name="GetAll" ExtDirect="true">
  <cfset var q = "" />
  <cfquery name="q" datasource="cfbookclub">
    SELECT AuthorID,
           FirstName,
           LastName
    FROM Authors
    ORDER BY LastName
  </cfquery>
  <cfreturn q />
</cffunction>
```

We're leaving out basic error handling and stuff, but these are the basics behind it. The classes and methods we want to make available will all contain the additional metadata.

# Building your API

So now that we've explored how to create a configuration at the server, we need to take the next step by passing that configuration to our Ext application. We do this by writing a server-side template that will output our JavaScript configuration. Yes, we'll actually dynamically produce a JavaScript include, calling the server-side template directly from within our `<script>` tag:

```
<script src="Api.cfm"></script>
```

How we write our server-side file really depends on the platform, but ultimately we just want it to return a block of JavaScript (just like calling a `.js` file) containing our API configuration description. The configuration will appear as part of the `actions` attribute, but we must also pass the `url` of our Router, the `type` of connection, and our `namespace`. That API return might look something like this:

```
Ext.ns("com.cc");
com.cc.APIDesc = {
  "url": "\/remote\/Router.cfm",
  "type": "remoting"
  "namespace": "com.cc",
  "actions": {
    "Authors": [{
      "name": "GetAll",
      "len": 0
    },{
      "name": "add",
```

```
            "len": 1
        },{
            "name": "update",
            "len": 1
        }]
    }
};
```

This now exposes our server-side configuration to our Ext application.

## Stack deconstruction—API

The purpose here is to create a JavaScript document, dynamically, of your configuration. Earlier we defined configuration via metadata. The DirectCFM API now has to convert that metadata into JavaScript. The first step is including the `Api.cfm` in a `<script>` tag on the page, but we need to know what's going on "under the hood."

```
Api.cfm:
<!--- Configure API Namespace and Description variable names --->
<cfset args = StructNew() />
<cfset args['ns'] = "com.cc" />
<cfset args['desc'] = "APIDesc" />
<cfinvoke component="Direct" method="getAPIScript"
argumentcollection="#args#" returnVariable="apiScript" />
<cfcontent reset="true" />
<cfoutput>#apiScript#</cfoutput>
```

Here we set a few variables, that will then be used in a method call. The `getAPIScript` method, of the `Direct.cfc` class, will construct our API from metadata.

`Direct.cfc getAPIScript()` method:

```
<cffunction name="getAPIScript">
  <cfargument name="ns" />
  <cfargument name="desc" />
  <cfset var totalCFCs = '' />
  <cfset var cfcName = '' />
  <cfset var CFCApi = '' />
  <cfset var fnLen = '' />
  <cfset var Fn = '' />
  <cfset var currFn = '' />
  <cfset var newCfComponentMeta = '' />
  <cfset var script = '' />
  <cfset var jsonPacket = StructNew() />
  <cfset jsonPacket['url'] = variables.routerUrl />
  <cfset jsonPacket['type'] = variables.remotingType />
```

```
    <cfset jsonPacket['namespace'] = ARGUMENTS.ns />
    <cfset jsonPacket['actions'] = StructNew() />
    <cfdirectory action="list" directory="#expandPath('.')#"
  name="totalCFCs" filter="*.cfc" recurse="false" />
    <cfloop query="totalCFCs">
      <cfset cfcName = ListFirst(totalCFCs.name, '.') />
      <cfset newCfComponentMeta = GetComponentMetaData(cfcName) />
      <cfif StructKeyExists(newCfComponentMeta, "ExtDirect")>
        <cfset CFCApi = ArrayNew(1) />
        <cfset fnLen = ArrayLen(newCFComponentMeta.Functions) />
        <cfloop from="1" to="#fnLen#" index="i">
          <cfset currFn = newCfComponentMeta.Functions[i] />
          <cfif StructKeyExists(currFn, "ExtDirect")>
            <cfset Fn = StructNew() />
            <cfset Fn['name'] = currFn.Name/>
            <cfset Fn['len'] = ArrayLen(currFn.Parameters) />
            <cfif StructKeyExists(currFn, "ExtFormHandler")>
              <cfset Fn['formHandler'] = true />
            </cfif>
            <cfset ArrayAppend(CFCApi, Fn) />
          </cfif>
        </cfloop>
        <cfset jsonPacket['actions'][cfcName] = CFCApi />
      </cfif>
    </cfloop>
    <cfoutput><cfsavecontent variable="script">Ext.ns('#arguments.
  ns#');#arguments.ns#.#desc# = #SerializeJson(jsonPacket)#;</
  cfsavecontent></cfoutput>
    <cfreturn script />
  </cffunction>
```

The `getAPIScript` method sets a few variables (including the `'actions'` array), pulls a listing of all ColdFusion Components from the directory, loops over that listing, and finds any components containing `"ExtDirect"` in their root meta. With every component that does contain that meta, it then loops over each method, finds methods with `"ExtDirect"` in the function meta, and creates a structure with the function name and number of arguments, which is then added to an array of methods. When all methods have been introspected, the array of methods is added to the `'actions'` array. Once all ColdFusion Components have been introspected, the entire packet is serialized into JSON, and returned to `API.cfm` for output.

One item to note is that the script, when introspecting method metadata, also looks for a `"ExtFormHandler"` attribute. If it finds the attribute, it will include that in the method struct prior to placing the struct in the `'actions'` array.

# Routing requests

By looking at our previous example of the API output, we notice that the `url` attribute is pointing to a server-side file. This is the final piece of the `Direct` stack, a file that will 'route' requests to the proper server-side class and method for processing.

# What is a Router

A **Router** is a server-side template that takes in all requests from our Ext JS application, and passes those requests off to the respective object and method for action. Ultimately, a Router is fairly agnostic; it will take any request, maybe apply some basic logic to the incoming variables, and then pass the request along according to data in the transaction.

## Transactions

When we send data to our Router, we're creating a `transaction`. Data coming from our Ext JS application will come in one of the two ways: form post (like when we upload files), or a raw HTTP post of a JSON packet. The parameters of each type are slightly different.

A standard JSON post will look like this:

```
{"action":"Authors","method":"GetAll","data":[],"type":"rpc","tid":27}
```

It's important to notice that `Direct` passed along information that came directly from our configuration, such as the `action` and `method` we're trying to access. Each of these transactions would contain the following:

- `action`—the class/ object/component we're attempting to access.
- `method`—the method/function we're trying to invoke.
- `data`—the arguments being sent to the method, in the form of an array.
- `type`—we'll use `"rpc"` for all remote calls.
- `tid`—our own transaction ID. This helps us identify responses from the server, connecting them to whichever transaction was initiated. This is especially beneficial whenever you batch process multiple requests, as it helps to tell us what was requested, for which, by what, and place our return results where they are needed.

## Stack deconstruction—HTTP post transaction

DirectCFM's Router will first create an instance of it's `Direct.cfc` class, then pull in the request and deserialize it , casting it into a native ColdFusion variable.

```
<cfset direct = CreateObject('component', 'Direct') />
<cfset postBody = direct.getPostBody() />
<cfset requests = DeserializeJSON(postBody) />
```

If the variable isn't an array, it will copy it into a temp variable, create an array, and place the temp object as the first element of the array. This is to maintain consistent process.

```
<cfif NOT IsArray(requests)>
  <cfset tmp = requests />
  <cfset requests = ArrayNew(1) />
  <cfset requests[1] = tmp />
</cfif>
```

We now need to loop over the requests that came from our Ext JS application. For each element of the array, we call the method that was requested.

```
<cfset result = direct.invokeCall(curReq) />
```

`invokeCall()` is a method of the `Direct.cfc` class, which is used to dynamically call a method. It's very generic by nature. The `curReq` variable, being passed in as an object, is an element of our requests array.

`Direct.cfc` `invokeCall()` method:

```
<cffunction name="invokeCall">
  <cfargument name="request" />
  <cfset var idx = 1 />
  <cfset var mthIdx = 1 />
  <cfset var result = '' />
  <cfset var args = StructNew() />
  <!--- find the methods index in the metadata --->
  <cfset newCfComponentMeta = GetComponentMetaData(request.action) />
  <cfloop from="1" to="#arrayLen(newCfComponentMeta.Functions)#"
index="idx">
    <cfif newCfComponentMeta.Functions[idx]['name'] eq request.method>
      <cfset mthIdx = idx />
      <cfbreak />
    </cfif>
  </cfloop>
  <cfif NOT IsArray(request.data)>
    <cfset maxParams = 0 />
```

```
  <cfelseif ArrayLen(request.data) lt ArrayLen(newCfComponentMeta.
Functions[mthIdx].parameters)>
    <cfset maxParams = ArrayLen(request.data) />
  <cfelse>
    <cfset maxParams = ArrayLen(newCfComponentMeta.Functions[mthIdx].
parameters) />
  </cfif>
  <!--- marry the parameters in the metadata to params passed in the
request. --->
  <cfloop from="0" to="#maxParams - 1#" index="idx">
    <cfset args[newCfComponentMeta['Functions'][mthIdx].
parameters[idx+1].name] = request.data[idx+1] />
  </cfloop>
  <cfinvoke component="#request.Action#" method="#request.method#"
argumentcollection="#args#" returnvariable="result">
  <cfreturn result />
</cffunction>
```

Here we find the `action` class, then the `method`, and then verify that the `method` was passed with enough parameters in the request. After an arguments object is created we finally dynamically invoke the class related to the `action`, calling the `method` requested. The result is sent back to the Router.

## Form transactions

Form posts send a slightly different data set, forming their attributes in such a way as to easily differentiate a form post from a standard HTTP post:

- `extAction`—The class/object/component to use
- `extMethod`—The method that will process our form post
- `extTID`—The transaction ID of the request (form posts cannot batch requests)
- `extUpload`—An optional argument for a file field used for file upload
- Any other fields needed for our method

Our Router should take in the request, call the correct class/object/component, and invoke the appropriate method. We know the object to call, from our `action`/`extAction` parameters, as well as the method, from our `method` parameter. This makes it simple to write dynamic statements for invoking the proper server-side architecture for our requests.

## Stack deconstruction—form transactions

DirectCFM handles form post transactions in nearly the same manner that it handled the JSON requests. First, we see if it is a form post. In ColdFusion, this is done by looking for values in the `form` scope.

```
<cfif NOT StructIsEmpty(form)>
</cfif>
```

If it is, we'll set up our initial object to hold our JSON return.

```
<cfset jsonPacket = StructNew() />
<cfset jsonPacket['tid'] = form.extTID />
<cfset jsonPacket['action'] = form.extAction />
<cfset jsonPacket['method'] = form.extMethod />
<cfset jsonPacket['type'] = 'rpc' />
```

We can then dynamically invoke the `action` (class) and `method` requested during the form post.

```
<cfinvoke component="#form.extAction#" method="#form.extMethod#"
argumentcollection="#form#" returnVariable="result" />
```

Now all we have to do is return the results of our method calls.

## Response

The final piece of the puzzle is to take the return from our dynamically invoked methods and formulate a proper response object to pass back to our Ext JS applications. The response should be a JSON encoded array of each transaction. The response of each transaction should contain the following:

- `type`—`"rpc"`
- `tid`—the transaction ID
- `action`—the class/object/component that was called
- `method`—the method we invoked
- `result`—the result of the method call

This would give us a response similar to:

```
[{
  "type":"rpc",
  "tid":14,
  "action":"Authors",
  "method":"GetAll",
  "result":{
```

```
        "COLUMNS":"ID,FIRSTNAME,LASTNAME",
        "DATA":[
          [1,"Stephen","King"],
          [2,"Robert","Ludlum"]
        ]
      }
    },{
      "type":"rpc",
      "tid":15,
      "action":"Authors",
      "method":"add",
      "result":{
        "success":true,
        "ID":3
      }
    }]
```

## Stack deconstruction—JSON HTTP response

The Router builds out the rest of the response object, carefully to remove the `"DATA"` used to make the request.

`Router.cfm`:

```
<cfif IsStruct(result) AND StructKeyExists(result, 'name') AND
StructKeyExists(result, 'result')>
  <cfset curReq['name'] = result.name />
  <cfset curReq['result'] = result.result />
<cfelse>
  <cfset curReq['result'] = result />
</cfif>
<cfset StructDelete(curReq, 'data') />
```

The last thing to be done is to return the data as JSON output:

```
<cfcontent reset="true" /><cfoutput>#SerializeJson(requests)#</
cfoutput>
```

Form post responses are only slightly different. A standard post method will return the result in the same manner, except the JSON response is not part of an array. In the case of a file upload, the JSON should be wrapped inside a `<textarea>` element within a valid HTML document:

```
<html>
  <body>
    <textarea>{"type":"rpc","tid":15,"action":"Authors","method":"uplo
adPhoto","result":{"success":true,"ID":3}}</textarea>
  </body>
</html>
```

Notice there's only one response here. Remember that form posts cannot handle batch requests, so we can only do one at a time.

## Stack deconstruction—form post response

We can serialize the JSON result of the method, and output the response back to the browser, conditionalizing the response for those requests that were file uploads.

```
<cfset jsonPacket['result'] = result />
  <cfset json = SerializeJson(jsonPacket) />
  <cfif form.extUpload eq "true">
    <cfoutput>
    <cfsavecontent variable="output"><html><body><textarea>#json#</
textarea></body></html></cfsavecontent>
    </cfoutput>
  <cfelse>
    <cfset output = json />
  </cfif>
  <cfcontent reset="true" />
<cfoutput>#output#</cfoutput>
```

## Exception responses

Ok, we all make mistakes. Because of this, we have to be able to write in exception handling. An exception response is a basic JSON packet, containing the following info:

- `type`—`'exception'`
- `message`—an informative message about the error that occurred
- `where`—tells us where the error occurred on the server

Exception responses are only handled when the Router is configured in debugging mode, and it is suggested that you do not return these responses in a production environment, as it could expose vital information about your server's file system that would pose a security risk.

## Stack deconstruction—exceptions

ColdFusion allows us to use standard try/catch error handling for capturing errors for graceful error handling. If an error were to occur in our method handling, we could 'catch' that error and form our Exception Response:

```
<cfcatch type="any">
  <cfset jsonPacket = StructNew() />
  <cfset jsonPacket['type'] = 'exception' />
  <cfset jsonPacket['tid'] = curReq['tId'] />
  <cfset jsonPacket['message'] = cfcatch.Message />
```

```
    <cfset jsonPacket['where'] = cfcatch.TagContext.Line/>
    <cfcontent reset="true" />
    <cfoutput>#SerializeJson(jsonPacket)#</cfoutput><cfabort/>
</cfcatch>
```

This creates a new `jsonPacket` structure, to which we apply the necessary key/value pairs required for an exception object. We then output the JSON response, and abort further processing of the method.

# Putting the pieces together

Now that we have a basic understanding of how we can create a stack, it's time to tie all of the pieces together to use it with our Ext JS applications.

# Make your API available

The first thing we need to do, in order to be able to access our configuration, is include the API within our application. This was touched on briefly in our review of the API. All it requires us to do is include a `<script>` tag within our application, calling the server-side script that renders the API configuration:

```
<script src="Api.cfm"></script>
```

We need to include this after our Ext base script files, but prior to our own application files. Next, we need to attach that API as a Provider for `Ext.Direct`, within our JavaScript application file:

```
Ext.Direct.addProvider(com.cc.APIDesc);
```

This now gives us access to any actions and methods provided through our configuration.

# Making API calls

Now that our actions and methods are available to our application, it comes down to making actual requests. Say, for instance, that you wanted to create a data store object to fill in a grid. You could do this by creating a `DirectStore` object, calling one of the exposed methods to populate the store:

```
var dirStore = new Ext.data.DirectStore({
    storeId: 'Authors',
    api: {
        read: com.cc.Authors.GetAll,
        create: com.cc.Authors.add,
```

```
            update: com.cc.Authors.update,
            delete: com.cc.Authors.delete
        },
        paramsAsHash: false,
        autoSave: false,
        reader: new Ext.data.CFQueryReader({
        idProperty: 'AuthorId'
        },[
            {name:'AuthorID',type:'int'},
            'FirstName',
            'LastName'
        ]),
        writer: new Ext.data.JsonWriter({
            encode: false,
            writeAllFields: true
        })
    });
```

We begin with our `DirectStore` configuration. The `DirectStore` is a new object of the `Ext.data` package, specifically designed to call data from an `Ext.Direct` source. The `api` attribute is now used to define actions and basic CRUD methods against our store, but notice that the majority of the configuration is just like any other data store. We did use the `CFQueryReader` custom reader object that we discussed in *Chapter 15, It's All About The Data,* to parse out the query object returned by the ColdFusion application server, as well as the `JsonWriter` configuration to handle changes to our remote source.

Next, we'll apply this store to a basic data `EditorGridPanel`:

```
// shorthand alias
var fm = Ext.form;
var dirGrid = new Ext.grid.EditorGridPanel ({
  width: 400,
  height: 500,
  title: 'Ext.DirectStore Example',
  store: dirStore,
  loadMask: true,
  clicksToEdit: 1,
  columns: [{
    header: 'AuthorID',
    dataIndex: 'AuthorID',
    width: 60
  },{
    header: 'First Name',
    dataIndex: 'FirstName',
```

```
        width: 150,
        editor: new fm.TextField({
          allowBlank: false
        })
      },{
        header: 'Last Name',
        dataIndex: 'LastName',
        width: 150,
        editor: new fm.TextField({
          allowBlank: false
        })
      }],
      viewConfig: {
        forceFit: true
      },
      tbar:[{
        text: 'New Author',
        handler: function(){
          var author = dirGrid.getStore().recordType;
          var a = new author({
            AuthorID: 0,
          });
          dirGrid.stopEditing();
          dirStore.insert(0,a);
          dirGrid.startEditing(0,1);
        }
      }],
      bbar:[{
        text: 'Save Changes',
        handler: function(){
          console.log(dirStore.save());
        }
      }]
    });
    dirGrid.render('chap16');
    dirStore.load();
```

There's nothing new here. We apply our `store` to our editor grid configuration just as we would apply one to any other `store` object. Once we render the grid, we then `load` the `store` from our `Direct` exposed configuration, just as we would `load` any other `store`.

Going back to our class object, we have an `add` and an `update` method, both taking an author as an argument. The `add` method should return a valid `AuthorID` in its response, which we might want to apply to a new record in our `store`. We've added a button to the TopToolbar to add records to the grid for editing:

```
tbar:[{
  text: 'New Author',
  handler: function(){
    var author = dirGrid.getStore().recordType;
    var a = new author({
      AuthorID: 0,
    });
    dirGrid.stopEditing();
    dirStore.insert(0,a);
    dirGrid.startEditing(0,1);
  }
}],
```

Once a new record has been added, or an existing record has been edited, we need to save those changes to our remote server. Here we've added a button to the bottom Toolbar that will save any new and changed records to the server, by invoking the appropriate method to take upon the record:

```
bbar:[{
  text: 'Save Changes',
  handler: function(){
    dirStore.save();
  }
}]
```

New records will go to the `add` method of the `Author` action. Changed records will go to the `update` method of the `Author` action. Since this is a JSON request, we can batch-process our changes.

# Summary

In this chapter, we've discussed how a developer can write his/her own Ext.Direct server-side stacks for marshalling data services under a single configuration. We've discussed each of the individual pieces:

- Configuration
- API
- Router

We've talked about the four different ways of writing a configuration:

- Programmatic
- JSON
- XML
- Metadata

We've also deconstructed one example stack provided by the Ext JS development team, illustrating how the server-side code might generate our APIs, and route our requests. Finally, we talked about how we implement Direct within our own Ext applications. In our final chapter we'll show you a few hidden gems of the Ext JS framework, and talk about some community resources for further information.

# 17
# The Power of Ext JS: What Else Can You Do?

Throughout this book, we've gone over some of the core components of Ext JS: Windows and Dialogs, Grids, Trees, Data Stores, and more. This is some of the flashiest, coolest, and most consistent stuff on the Web today, for taking a drab old HTML display and giving it the sizzle and pop such a dynamic development platform deserves. But we've still only scratched the surface of what's available within the complete Ext JS library. Here we'll look at some of the deeper bits of the framework, while pointing you to additional learning resources that you can explore and use to grow your knowledge of Ext JS.

In this chapter, we cover:

- Form widgets
- Data formatting
- Application managers
- Working with the DOM and styles
- Ext JS on the desktop
- Community extensions
- Community resources

# So much to work with

The Ext JS site (`http://www.extjs.com`) provides a wealth of information for those learning to develop with Ext JS. A quick view of the **Samples and Demos** area of this site will show us quite a bit of what we've covered in this book, but a thorough examination of the source code will show us some things that we may not immediately have known were available. These are the pieces that aren't necessarily apparent, such as a panel or a grid, but these little things ultimately hold it all together and truly allow us to create robust applications.

# Form widgets

What's a widget? Well, a widget is a tiny piece or component of a graphical user interface, say (for instance) a slider or a progress bar. Most applications are made up of forms, so it's no accident that Ext JS includes some form widgets that we can't get with straight HTML. `TextFields` and checkboxes and radio buttons are standard fare, but Ext JS sweetens the pot by going to the next level, providing us with components that we're used to seeing in most desktop applications.

## DateField

The **DateField** is a perfect example. Handling dates within most HTML forms can be a chore, but Ext JS provides a very basic component for handling dates:

**Example 1**: `chapter17_01.js`

```
Ext.onReady(function(){
  var formPanel = new Ext.form.FormPanel({
    title:'DateField Example',
    applyTo:'chap14_ex01',
    layout:'form',
    labelAlign:'top',
    width:210,
    autoHeight:true,
    frame:true,
    items:[{
    xtype:'datefield',
      fieldLabel:'Date of Birth',
      name:'dob',
      width:190,
      allowBlank:false
    }]
  });
});
```

What we have here is a basic `FormPanel` layout that puts our `DateField` into proper context and allows for certain necessary attributes (like putting our label above the field). Within the layout we have a single `DateField` component. On initial load, it looks like a basic `TextField`, with the exception of the **trigger** to the right. Clicking the trigger shows the beauty of Ext JS's consistent component "look-and-feel", displaying an attractive calendar layout for the selection of a date. You can select a day, move from month-to-month, or even click on the month itself to choose a different month and year.

Apart from its rich display, the **DateField** also provides a rich set of attributes for specialized customization, including the ability to determine different accepted date formats, and the ability to disable entire blocks of days. The component will also automatically validate manually-entered data.

# TimeField

Dealing with time can be more difficult than dealing with dates, but Ext JS also provides a component to assist us. The **TimeField** is a basic `ComboBox` that will automatically show a set of time, in increments that we want, for quick selection:

**Example 2**: `chapter17_02.js`

```
Ext.onReady(function(){
  var formPanel = new Ext.form.FormPanel({
    title:'DateField Example',
    applyTo:'chap14_ex02',
    layout:'form',
    labelAlign:'top',
```

```
    width:210,
    autoHeight:true,
    frame:true,
    items:[{
      xtype:'timefield',
      fieldLabel:'Time',
      minValue: '9:00 AM',
        maxValue: '6:00 PM',
        increment: 30
    }]
  });
});
```

As in our last example, this simple `FormLayout` contains one item, in this case the `TimeField`. Click on the **trigger**, and we get our options, defined by our code as times between 9 A.M. and 6 P.M. in increments of 30 minutes. Other configuration options allow you to define multiple accepted time formats, and also implement custom validation. Basic validation is provided by default.

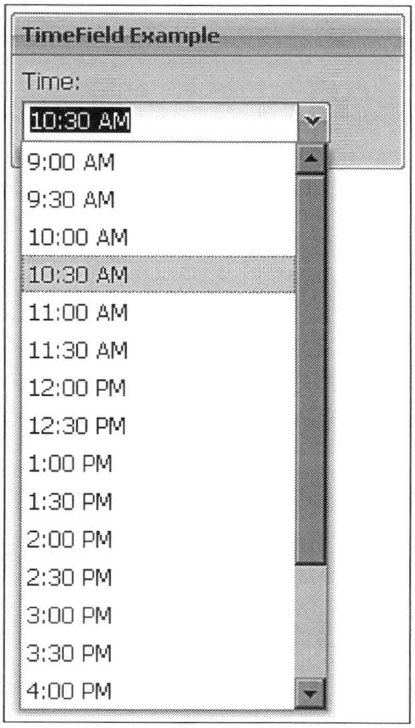

# NumberField

The **NumberField** doesn't *look* very special—it's just a basic 'text' field. What makes it special is how it allows us to 'dummy-proof' our Ext JS applications. Client-side data validation is essential for ensuring data integrity prior to sending values to the server, allowing us to prevent errors from our remote procedure calls. Components such as this one simplify that process for us. The `NumberField` provides automatic keystroke filtering and validation to allow the entry of only numeric data, allowing us to specify whether it can take negative numbers or float values, and even specify how many decimal places are accepted.

# CheckboxGroups and RadioGroups

Ext JS 2.2 brought two new form controls: the `CheckboxGroup` and the `RadioGroup`. These controls allow us to 'group' sets of checkbox or radio buttons, providing them with custom formatting and special, group-level validation capabilities. For example, say we have a form with two checkboxes for the users to select their gender. By placing these within a `CheckboxGroup`, we can apply our validation to the *group* so that at least one option is selected when the form is submitted. We can apply many more complex validation rules as well, depending upon the scenario. See the *Ext JS API* for more details.

# HtmlEditor

Ext JS includes a nice, limited, WYSIWYG `HtmlEditor`, to drop right into your forms:

**Example 3**: `chapter17_03.js`

```
Ext.onReady(function(){
  var formPanel = new Ext.form.FormPanel({
    title:'HtmlEditor Example',
    applyTo:'chap14_ex03',
    layout:'form',
    labelAlign:'top',
    width:600,
    autoHeight:true,
    frame:true,
    items:[{
      xtype:'htmleditor',
      id:'bio',
      fieldLabel:'Blog Entry',
      height:200,
      anchor:'98%'
    }]
  });
});
```

Here, we dropped the `HtmlEditor` into our `FormLayout` for a quick demonstration. The `HtmlEditor` is applied to a basic text area, in much the same way as other WYSIWYG editors, say FCKEditor or TinyMCE. We have the ability to enable or disable the various menu buttons related to formatting, as well as call various methods (like those to get or set the text of the editor, its position, and so on), or apply event listeners, just like the other components of Ext JS.

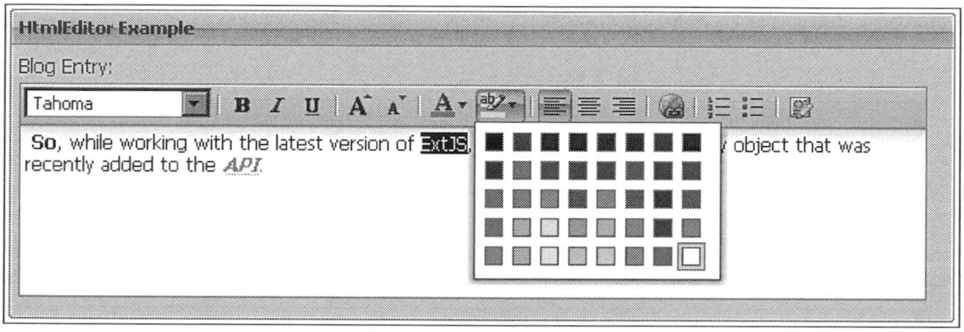


We get the same, consistent Ext JS look and feel, while giving our users the ability to format their own content directly from within our applications. In this image, note that the `HtmlEditor` uses Ext JS's built-in **ColorPalette** component for selecting colors.

# Data formatting

We all know that we don't always receive data in the format in which we want it to be displayed. Ext JS provides many different components specifically for addressing such issues. First among these is the `Format` object in the `Ext.util` package, which gives us a wide variety of functions for everything from creating the U.S. currency format for a number to methods for stripping scripts and HTML from strings. The Ext JS library also extends several native JavaScript objects and provides us with additional methods for manipulating them. Specifically, the `String`, `Number`, and `Date` objects have all been extended. You can now strip off unnecessary whitespace, constrain numbers to a minimum and maximum value, and even create `Date` objects from a variety of format options.

# Basic string formatting

The `String` object has been extended to provide several formatting options, including the `format()` method. This simple method allows you to return a formatted string of text, with the first parameter being the string to return, and all other parameters (as many as you like) being *bound* to pieces of the string, using a basic form of binding expression, whereby curly braces surround a variable reference. Typical binding expressions, used by Ext JS, would contain a dot-notated variable reference surrounded by curly braces (that is, `{this.firstName}`), but this instance will bind values to the arguments that will follow using their array order:

**Example 4**: `chapter17_04.js`

```
Ext.onReady(function(){
  var cls = "Band";
  var member = {
    firstName: 'Eric',
    lastName: 'Clapton',
    position: 'Lead Guitarist'
  };

  var pnl = new Ext.Panel({
    applyTo: 'chap14_ex04',
    width: 200,
    height: 100,
    bodyStyle: 'padding:5px',
    title: 'Band Member',
    html: String.format('<div class=\'{0}\'>{2}, {1}: {3}</div>',
            cls, member.firstName, member.lastName, member.position)
  });
});
```

This small block of code displays a simple `Panel` element, which calls the formatting function to build the HTML of the `Panel`. The arguments of the `format()` method are applied to different parts of the string that we are building.

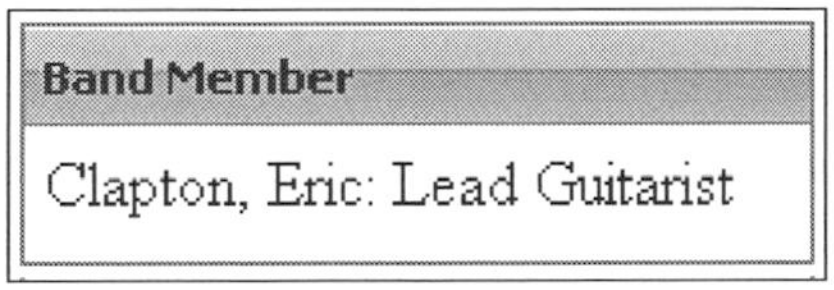

# Formatting dates

The `Date` object has also been extended to provide additional formatting and parsing capabilities. The API provides a complete listing of the date part identifiers that can be used when parsing a string into a `Date` object, or when outputting a `Date` object in the desired format:

**Example 5**: `chapter17_05.js`

```
Ext.onReady(function(){
  var cls = "Band";
  var member = {
    firstName: 'Eric',
    lastName: 'Clapton',
    position: 'Lead Guitarist',
    birthDate: new Date('03/30/1945')
  };

  var pnl = new Ext.Panel({
    applyTo: 'chap14_ex05',
    width: 200,
    height: 100,
    bodyStyle: 'padding:5px',
    title: 'Band Member',
    html: String.format('<div class=\'{0}\'>{2}, {1}: {3}<br />DOB:
{4}</div>', cls, member.firstName, member.lastName, member.position,
member.birthDate.format('F j, Y'))
  });
});
```

We've extended our previous example to add Eric's birthday. We've created a new `Date` object, as part of the `Member` object, and then used the `format()` method of the `Date` object to format our date for display.

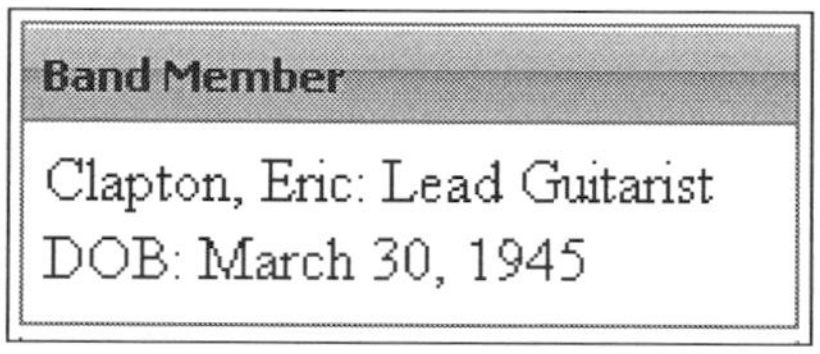


# Other formatting

The `Ext.util` package provides many different classes and methods for formatting various types of data, including many for working with `strings`, `dates`, and `numbers`. A good example is the `usMoney()` method:

```
var annualSalary = 123456.345;
Ext.util.Format.usMoney(annualSalary);
```

This will return a pre-formatted US currency string of `$123,456.35`. This can come in very handy when working with e-commerce applications.

> **Author's note**:
>
> The `usMoney()` method in the `Format` class is currently the only method for formatting a currency type. But with Ext JS's extensible architecture, it would be possible to create methods for formatting other foreign currencies. A quick search of the Ext JS forums will pull up several posts on creating formatting methods for other currency types.

Another common need is the ability to strip HTML from a `string`. Say we have a simple comment form on our page, and want to ensure that the user doesn't include any HTML in the input, so that our data isn't polluted before going to the server. Ext JS includes a simple method for stripping out HTML from any string:

```
var firstName = '<b>jimi</b>';
var adj = Ext.util.Format.stripTags(firstName);
```

We may also want to make sure that a particular input, say a name, is capitalized before we pass it back to the server:

```
var adj2 = Ext.util.Format.capitalize(adj);
```

We may also want to apply a default value to a variable in case one does not exist already:

```
var adj3 = Ext.util.Format.defaultValue(favoriteBlog,
                                        'Cutter\'s Crossing');
```

A thorough review of the API will provide you with a full understanding of all of the various formatting options that are available.

# Managing application state

At the core of any application (especially an event-driven application) is maintaining and controlling the application state. This can encompass many different things, from keeping user preferences on grid sorting, to managing multiple windows or layout areas on the screen, and even being able to use the **Back** button in the browser and have it change your application without reloading the wrong page. Luckily, Ext JS provides several `Manager` objects for handling many of these scenarios.

# Basic state management

The `Ext.state.Manager` class is automatically checked, and utilized, by every state-aware component within Ext JS. With one simple line of code we can set this manager in place, and with little or no additional work our application's view state is automatically registered.

To put this in perspective, suppose that we have a rather large application, spanning many different HTML documents. Ext JS plays a part in the application, because we've implemented a data grid for displaying users. While we work on our grid, it may be necessary to change the sort order from the default **LastName** column to another column, for example, the **UserName** column. Now let's say we had to go into an inventory editor for a moment. If we use the `Manager`, when we return to the user editor our grid will automatically come up sorted again by **Username**, as that was the last state change that we made:

```
Ext.state.Manager.setProvider(new Ext.state.CookieProvider());
```

This line creates our `state Manager`, setting the provider to a `CookieProvider`. What this means is that the application state is saved to a value within a cookie on the client machine, which in turn is read to re-enable the state upon returning to a state-aware component.

> **Side Note:**
>
> The `CookieProvider` also provides a simple API for the general management of client-side cookies for our sites, and can be used as a standalone class for referencing and manipulating cookie objects.

# How do I get that window?

Many Ext JS applications will be confined to a single HTML page, and might commonly come down to a collection of Ext JS `Window` objects on the screen. But what happens if a user is in one window, and we want to show them another window that is already open, without closing the one they've been working on? By default, all Ext JS windows are created, and registered, within the global `WindowGroup`. We can easily control the visibility and z-index of these windows by using the `WindowMgr` class. This manager class allows us to grab any window of a `WindowGroup`, and bring it to the front, send it to the back, or even hide all of the windows in the group.

# Using the back button in Ext JS applications

One common problem among **Rich Internet Applications** is handling the **Back** button of the browser. Say we have a large Ext JS-based application with tabs, grids, and accordions. A user navigating our application by using these components might hit his/her **Back** button to go back to their last action, screen, or panel. This is an expected behavior in most Internet applications, because most Internet applications go from one HTML page to another.

But most Rich Internet Applications, like those built with Ext JS, are usually a collection of different states within the same HTML page, and the **Back** button would typically take a user out of our application and back to the last viewed HTML page. Thankfully, Ext JS introduced the `History` class, giving us the ability to control how the browser history is used, and how the browser's **Back** button would be handled within our applications.

> **Manage this**:
>
> There are several other manager classes within Ext JS. The `StoreMgr` provides easy access to our various data store objects. The `ComponentMgr` allows us to quickly retrieve specific components to act upon. The `EventMgr` allows us to control events within Ext JS objects. A good review of the Ext JS API will give us more information on these manager objects and their many uses.

# Accessing the DOM

Custom library adapters allow for the use of Ext JS with other libraries, say jQuery or Prototype. But Ext JS provides its own internal libraries for DOM manipulation as well.

# Finding DOM elements

The first task when manipulating the **DOM (Document Object Model)** is to find what we're looking for. The `DomQuery` class provides us with several methods for this purpose, including returning entire groups of DOM nodes that meet specific criteria, or selecting a single node by its selector. We can even start the search from a specific node in the page. There are several different selector types that can be used when searching for a specific element:

- `base Element` selectors
- `Attribute` selectors
- `Pseudo` classes
- `CSS Value` selectors

What's more, we can chain together a series of selectors to find the exact element we're searching for:

```
var myEl = Ext.DomQuery.selectNode
            ('a.iconLnk[@href*="cutterscrossing"]:first');
```

This will return the first anchor element with a class name of `iconLnk` that contains **cutterscrossing** within its `href` attribute:

- `a`—is an anchor element
- `.selectNode`—has a class of `selectNode`
- `[@href *= "cutterscrossing"]`—has an `href` attribute containing 'cutterscrossing' somewhere within its value
- `:first`—is only the first element matching the criteria

# Manipulating the DOM

The `DomHelper` class allows us to manipulate the DOM of the rendered page on-the-fly. Whether we want to add a new element below a collection of others, remove a specific element, or even overwrite the body content of an element, the `DomHelper` class contains the methods that can accomplish the task: For example:

```
Ext.DomHelper.insertAfter(ourGrid, newForm);
```

This line will place the `newForm` object directly after `ourGrid` in the current page's DOM. You could just as easily use `insertBefore()` to place the form before the grid. You could even use `insertHtml()` to insert a block of HTML into the DOM with a particular relation to a specific DOM element. A thorough review of the API will give you a complete view of the power of the `DomHelper` class.

# Working with styles

The `DomHelper` class also provides a simple method for setting the style of an individual element, through the use of the `applyStyles()` method. But sometimes we may need to change the stylesheet of our entire document. For this, Ext JS has the `Ext.util.CSS` class, which allows us to create a new stylesheet that will automatically be appended to the `Head` of our document, remove entire stylesheets, or swap one stylesheet for another. We can even act upon their entire set of rules:

```
Ext.util.CSS.swapStyleSheet('defaultDisplay','print.css');
```

This little script will swap out the current stylesheet, which is identified by the link tag's `id` attribute, and replace it with the `print.css` stylesheet.

# Ext JS for the desktop: Adobe AIR

One of the great things about being a Web application developer is that we have the opportunity to write truly cross-platform applications. The traditional model for this has always been writing browser-based applications that work primarily under a client/server paradigm, with the browser as the client and a Web application server as the server.

But desktop applications have a lot of their own benefits, including access to their own local file systems (something you cannot do with Web-based applications, because of security concerns). The biggest issue with building desktop applications is writing them all for Windows, Unix/Linux, and the Mac. None of these systems share common display libraries or file access systems, so writing a cross-platform application would require writing separate versions of the code to accommodate each system. There are languages that provide cross-platform virtual machines, which give this kind of access to the system resources, but they require learning languages that may be outside of the average Web developer's toolbox.

Adobe came up with an interesting idea. How could they let people develop cross-platform applications using Web-based technologies such as HTML, JavaScript, AJAX, and Flash?

With their purchase of Macromedia, Adobe gained the rights to the Flash player and the Flash application platform. The Flash player is distributed on 97 percent of the user desktops as a plug-in for every major browser. They also gained access to a new technology called **Flex**, which is a framework and compiler that allows developers (rather than designers) to script Flash-based applications.

But, part of what they truly gained was an understanding of how to create a cross-platform application delivery engine. So, they built upon their newfound knowledge, and set out to create the **Adobe Integrated Runtime**, better known as **AIR**. AIR is a desktop engine for rendering content written in HTML, JavaScript, and/or Flash (and more), which allows local access to the client system's resources, regardless of the operating system. Built upon the open source **WebKit** platform, which is the same platform used by **Apple** in their **Safari** Web browser, AIR has access to the local file system and storage, while maintaining Internet awareness, thereby creating a bridge between offline process and online content. AIR even provides access to local databases created with SQLLite. SQLLite is a server-less library for delivering databases with its own transactional SQL database engine that can be directly embedded into an application.

Adobe and Ext JS already have a great relationship, because Adobe contracted Ext JS so that it could use the Ext JS component library as the foundation of the AJAX-based components generated by ColdFusion Markup Language, which is processed on Adobe's popular ColdFusion application server. Considering the cross-platform nature of AIR, it was befitting that some of the first HTML/JavaScript sample applications were written in another cross-platform library, Ext JS. The **tasks** sample application is included with the Ext JS download, and is an excellent primer on how to write HTML and JavaScript applications for AIR.

Ext JS 2.1 was released on the same day that Adobe AIR was officially released, and included an entire package of components dedicated to developing Ext JS-based AIR applications. The classes of the `Ext.air` package interact with AIR's own classes for interacting with the runtime and the desktop. Aptana, a popular JavaScript editor and Eclipse plugin, added support for creating AIR applications directly as projects from within its IDE (Aptana already supported Ext JS development), with simple wizards to help get you started, as well as for packaging completed AIR applications.

The `Ext.air` package includes special packages for managing application state, including the `NativeWindowGroup` and `FileProvider` classes (AIR's answer to the `WindowGroup` and `CookieProvider` classes). There are even classes for controlling sound and system menus.

**More information:**

For more information on developing Adobe AIR applications, visit the AIR and AJAX Developer Center (`http://www.adobe.com/devnet/air/ajax/`). For details look at AIR/Ext JS integration, and study the 'tasks' sample application, included in the `Ext.air` Pack download. There's also the `Ext.air` *for Adobe AIR* topic within the Ext JS Forums.

# Ext JS community extensions

*Chapter 13* of this book discussed how developers can write their own custom extensions to Ext JS. Being an open source project, the Ext JS community is very active in contributing new components to extend existing functionality, and sometimes these components even go on to become a part of the framework.

Many custom extensions are found directly in the forums area of the Ext JS website, as posts from members who have come up with solutions to a problem they had identified. There is, however, a section of the **Learning Center** area of the site that is dedicated to showcasing custom extensions. Let's look at a few fan favorites.

# DatePickerPlus

Building on the `DateField` class, the **DatePickerPlus** provides multi-calendar displays, allowing a user to select a range of dates. There are multiple configuration options available, and the level of control available to the developer is very comprehensive.

# PowerWizard

The `PowerWizard` class allows us to create powerful, multi-step 'wizard-like' processes, with field (and multi-field) validation and decision trees, as well as data persistence between frames.

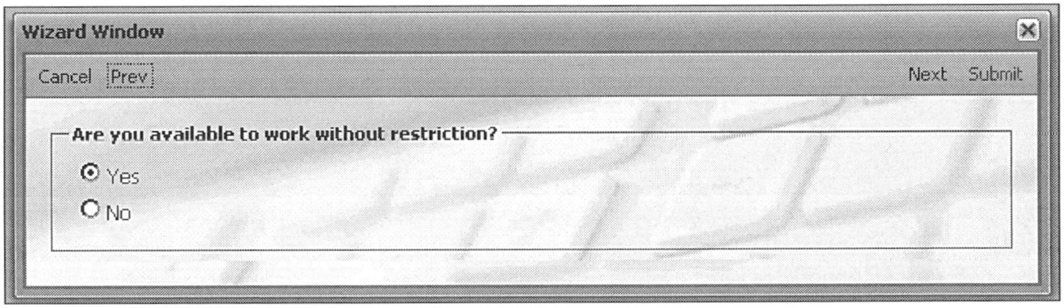

# TinyMCE

Yes, for those times when the `HtmlEditor` just isn't enough, someone wrote a custom extension to wrap the TinyMCE WYSIWYG editor into the Ext JS applications.

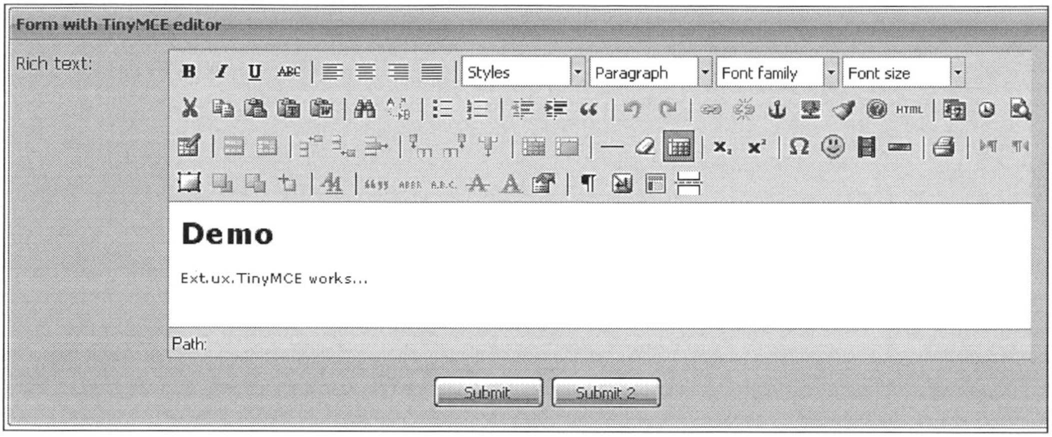


# SwfUploadPanel

How many times would it have been nice to be able to upload more than one file at a time through our Web application interface? Someone converted the popular **SwfUpload** project into a custom Ext JS component, allowing multi-file uploads from within our application.

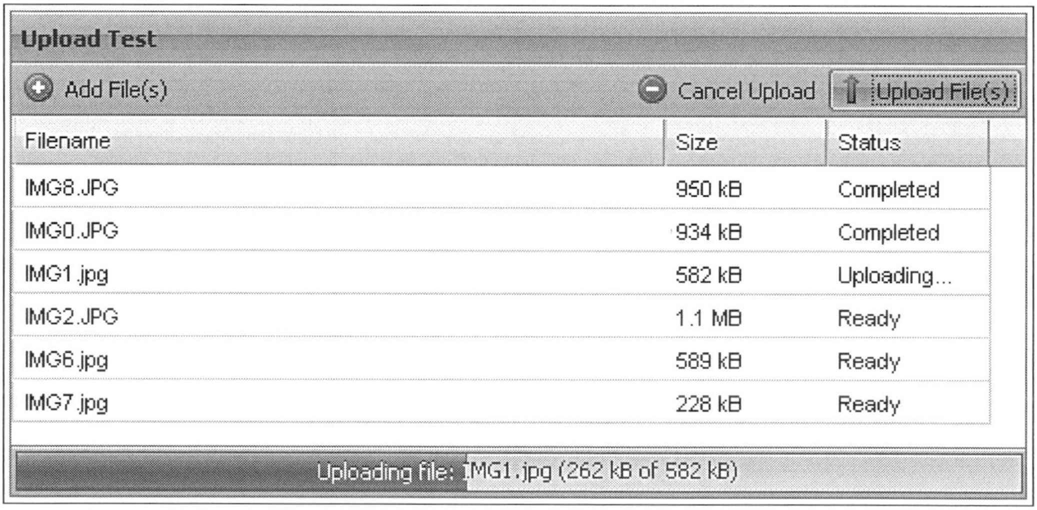

# ColorPicker

The built-in `ColorPalette` component can seem rather limiting, only showing a few of the colors available for web display. For this reason, there is the `ColorPicker` giving the user the option of selecting any color they wish.

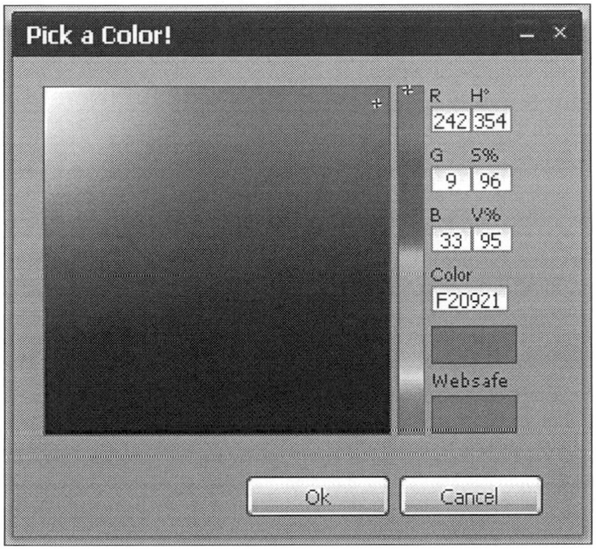


These are just a few of the outstanding community contributions to the library. There are many more available through the **Community Extensions** section of the **Learning Center** area of the Ext JS website, as well as throughout the **Forums**. (Check out the *Ext: User Extensions and Plugins* topic for more.)

# Additional resources

Knowing where to find good information is the biggest trick to learning anything new. Although this book is a good resource, there is a wealth of information available on the Internet, especially on the Ext JS site (`http://www.extjs.com`).

## Samples and Demos

The **Samples and Demos** area of the Ext JS site (`http://extjs.com/deploy/dev/examples/samples.html`) will likely be the first real exposure that anyone has to the power of the Ext JS library. These small samples are broken down into various categories, providing us with solid examples of how to use many of the components of Ext JS. With easily-accessible source code, we can see exactly what it takes to write this type of functionality for our own applications.

# Ext JS API

The Ext JS interactive API (`http://extjs.com/deploy/dev/docs/`) is an outstanding resource, giving us access to the underlying properties, methods, and events that are available within each class of Ext JS. The API documentation is written in Ext JS itself, and it's menu is a tree style navigation with expanding members, allowing us to expand each package to see information on their specific classes. Peppered throughout are additional code samples to illustrate their use. The Ext JS team even provides a desktop AIR version of this API browser, so that we can have it available offline.

> **Side note:**
>
> The Ext JS team also supports the older 1.1 framework, which is what runs the underlying AJAX components of the older **Adobe ColdFusion 8** server. The samples and demos for the 1.1 framework are actually included in the 1.1 API browser (`http://extjs.com/deploy/ext-1.1.1/docs/`), which is available through the **Learning Center** area of the website (`http://extjs.com/learn/`).

# Ext JS forums

The forums for Ext JS (`http://extjs.com/forum/`) show what an active community there is, developing the Ext JS library. With over 40,000 threads and more than 200,000 posts, this is the place to ask questions. Topics range from the very easy to the ultra-advanced, and members of the core Ext JS development team are frequent contributors.

# Step-by-step tutorials

**Step-by-step tutorials** (`http://extjs.com/learn/Tutorials`) can be found within the **Learning Center**, with content ranging from simple component usage to advanced project development. Some of these tutorials come directly from the Ext JS development team, but many are contributed by members of the Ext JS community.

# Community Manual

One can also find the **Ext JS Community Manual** within the **Learning Center**. This wiki-style development manual is maintained by the Ext JS community itself, and contains topics relating to most of the aspects of Ext JS development.

## Spket IDE

We can find resources for Ext JS all over the Internet. One good example is from Spket Studios (`http://www.spket.com/`), makers of the Spket IDE. This free IDE comes as a plug-in for the **Eclipse** development platform. With a few simple steps, Spket can provide complete code introspection for our Ext JS classes and extensions, as well as in-depth code assistance. It even has a built-in theme builder to automatically create new skins for your components.

## Aptana Studio

**Aptana Studio** is quickly becoming a major contender in the web-based IDE market. Even the free version provides code introspection and assistance with multiple JavaScript libraries, built-in wizards for creating Adobe AIR applications, built-in debugging tools, and much more.

## Google

Yes, Google (or any other search engine) is a fantastic resource, because there are thousands of articles, tutorials, and blog posts available. A quick search on "Ext JS" brings up over a million possible matches, and that's growing every day.

# Where do we go from here?

It is our hope that, with this brief introduction to the Ext JS JavaScript component library and framework, we've given our readers a good foundation upon which some truly amazing things can be built. Ext JS provides such an immense wealth of user interactivity within Web applications, possibly to a degree never achieved before. With its deep, consistent, and rich component set, its full-featured and intuitive API, and its constant development and growth, Ext JS has the potential to truly springboard Web (and even desktop) applications beyond the traditional paradigms, by providing users with an experience well beyond the Web applications of the past.

> *Our imagination is the only limit to what we can hope to have in the future.*
>
> **Charles F. Kettering**
>
> *US electrical engineer and inventor (1876-1958)*

# Summary

In this chapter we've discussed some of the lesser known pieces of the Ext JS library. We briefly covered some of the form components not found in traditional HTML, such as the `DateField` and the `HtmlEditor`. We also learned about the various classes available for formatting data for the desired output, as well as those classes needed for managing application state and manipulating the DOM.

Finally, we also talked about the various resources that are out there for continuing to learn about Ext JS development. We talked about the community extensions, the brilliant samples, and API browser, as well as the forums, tutorials, and the community manual. We even touched on some IDE's for doing Ext JS development.

# Index

## Symbols



## A



## B

## C

## D

# E

## F

## N



## O



## P

## Q



## R



## S

# T

## U



## V



## W

[PACKT] open source
PUBLISHING
community experience distilled

## Ext JS 3.0 Cookbook

ISBN: 978-1-847198-70-9 Paperback: 376 pages

Liferay Portal 5.2 Systems Development

1. Master the Ext JS widgets and learn to create custom components to suit your needs

2. Build striking native and custom layouts, forms, grids, listviews, treeviews, charts, tab panels, menus, toolbars and much more for your real-world user interfaces

3. Packed with easy-to-follow examples to exercise all of the features of the Ext JS library

---

## jQuery UI 1.7: The User Interface Library for jQuery

ISBN: 978-1-847199-72-0 Paperback: 392 pages

Build highly interactive web applications with ready-to-use widgets from the jQuery User Interface library

1. Organize your interfaces with reusable widgets: accordions, date pickers, dialogs, sliders, tabs, and more

2. Enhance the interactivity of your pages by making elements drag-and-droppable, sortable, selectable, and resizable

Please check **www.PacktPub.com** for information on our titles

9847428R0

Made in the USA
Lexington, KY
02 June 2011